INTRODUCTION TO EARLY CHILDHOOD EDUCATION

A Developmental Perspective

MARIAN MARION
Governors State University

Merrill

Upper Saddle River, New Jersey
Columbus, Ohio

Library of Congress Cataloging-in-Publication Data

Marion, Marian
  Introduction to early childhood education : a developmental perspective /
Marian Marion. -- 1st ed.
    p. cm.
  ISBN 978-0-13-113932-9
1. Early childhood education--Textbooks. I. Title.
  LB1139.23.M37 2010
  372.21--dc22

                        2008043372

Vice President and Editor in Chief: Jeffery W. Johnston
Acquisitions Editor: Julie Peters
Development Editor: Bryce Bell
Permissions Coordinator: Rebecca Savage
Editorial Assistant: Tiffany Bitzel
Senior Managing Editor: Pamela D. Bennett
Senior Project Manager: Linda Hillis Bayma
Project Coordination: Susan McNally, Nesbitt Graphics, Inc.
Senior Art Director: Diane C. Lorenzo
Cover Image: Jupiterimages

Text and Cover Design: Candace Rowley
Photo Coordinator: Shea Davis
Media Producer: Autumn Benson
Media Project Manager: Rebecca Norsic
Senior Operations Supervisor: Matthew Ottenweller
Operations Specialist: Susan Hannahs
Vice President, Director of Sales & Marketing: Quinn Perkson
Marketing Manager: Erica DeLuca
Marketing Coordinator: Brian Mounts

This book was set in Minion by Nesbitt Graphics, Inc. It was printed and bound by C. J. Krehbiel. The cover was printed by Phoenix Color Corp.

Photo credits appear on page 355, which constitutes a continuation of this copyright page.

Pearson® is a registered trademark of Pearson plc
Merrill® is a registered trademark of Pearson Education, Inc.

Pearson Education, Ltd., London
Pearson Education Singapore, Pte. Ltd.
Pearson Education Canada, Inc.
Pearson Education–Japan
Pearson Education Australia PTY, Limited

Pearson Education North Asia, Ltd., Hong Kong
Pearson Educación de Mexico, S.A. de C.V.
Pearson Education Malaysia, Pte. Ltd.
Pearson Education Upper Saddle River, New Jersey

Merrill
is an imprint of

www.pearsonhighered.com

10 9 8 7 6 5 4 3 2 1

ISBN-13: 978-0-13-113932-9
ISBN-10:   0-13-113932-0

To the memory of President Lyndon B. Johnson and his remarks in the White House Rose Garden on May 18, 1965, when he announced the creation of Head Start:

> *. . . We set out to make certain that poverty's children*
> *would not be forevermore poverty's captives. . . .*
> *We called our program Project Head Start. . . .*
> *The bread that is cast upon these waters*
> *will surely return many thousandfold. . . .*

ABOUT THE AUTHOR

MARIAN MARION, a professor of early childhood education at Governors State University in Illinois, has been a teacher educator for many years. She was a Head Start, preschool, and kindergarten teacher as well as a director of a university child development center. She has written many articles about child guidance and has written two other textbooks for Pearson/Merrill: *Guidance of Young Children* and *Using Observation in Early Childhood Education.* She reviews manuscripts for *Young Children* and presents regularly at the NAEYC and state conventions.

PREFACE

In the Spring of 1965, I was reading a newspaper article about President Johnson's speech announcing the creation of Head Start, a new approach to learning for young children. Instantly intrigued, I read other items that described what children would gain from participating in this program. There was a lot of excitement generated by this project. So, I applied for and was awarded a teacher's aide position with Head Start in my hometown. At the time, I was an elementary education major fully intending to teach fifth grade. Looking back, I remember the teacher's aide job as a defining event in my life.

When I was hired, I still was not sure about what Head Start would look like but quickly learned that it involved a play-based approach to learning. I observed preschool children eagerly reading books, building vocabulary, and working with other children in the block corner and at the water table. I had never seen anything so amazing. The lead teacher, a first-grade teacher during the school year, told me that preschool children ". . . are not the same as the first graders" and that I needed to teach "in ways that are beneficial for 4 year olds." I changed my schedule that next semester to include courses in early childhood curriculum and have been studying, writing about, and teaching it ever since. I never got around to teaching fifth grade.

A TRULY DEVELOPMENTAL APPROACH TO EARLY CHILDHOOD EDUCATION

What startled me in my Head Start summer was the emphasis on children and their development as the starting point for everything that we did. In my early childhood education courses we used child development in our planning and were challenged to explain how our plans would foster children's development and learning. This, then, was *the developmental approach*. This approach encourages teachers not only to construct a working knowledge of child development but also to use their knowledge to create environments in which children develop and learn. For example, research tells us that young children construct knowledge through physical activity and hands-on learning. Therefore, we provide a variety of play-based activities so that they can explore by moving, using their bodies, hands, minds, and all their senses. The developmental approach also helps teachers understand how to interact (speak, listen, and otherwise communicate) with children in developmentally appropriate ways.

With this book I hope to convey some of the wonder and joy that I discovered when I first worked with young children. I would also like to pass along some of my major beliefs about early childhood education. These beliefs have been formed from my understanding of *theory and research* and how I've *applied* that understanding to my work with children and with future teachers. Theory and application: One is dependent upon the other and they cannot be separated.

- **I believe that we have a choice about how we think about and work with children.** As humans we can always make choices. Students need to know that they can choose how they approach teaching. Yes, we are accountable for meeting standards, but we also get to choose the strategies that we use in our teaching to meet those standards. We can choose to use developmentally appropriate strategies. We can choose to keep children's development and learning as the most important part of our practice. We can choose to have an open mind and to try to understand cultures that are different from the ones that are most familiar to us.

- **I believe that effective teachers use child development as the base for planning and teaching.** They deliberately learn about child development and about families and then use that knowledge when working with children. They focus on the whole child, while understanding theory and research in the different developmental domains.

- **I believe that *all* children can learn and that children have different strengths when it comes to learning.** "All children" means *each and every* child—those who develop typically and those who face challenges. "All children" means children who are learning English, children who speak English fluently, and children who are fluent in more than one language. "All children" includes the gifted, the homeless, and those of affluent or of less economically advantaged backgrounds. "All children" includes children with emotional problems. We have to discover each child's learning strengths.

- **I believe that children construct knowledge and understanding of their world.** They are not sponges, but they are curious, active, question-asking people. They take in information and make sense of it, actively building concepts and understanding. Our classrooms and our activities need to reflect this reality.

- **I believe that children need to play and to be active learners.** Children construct different types of knowledge by working with real objects. As teachers, I believe that we have a responsibility to provide an environment conducive to active and play-based learning even as we strive to meet state standards.

- **I believe that children need to collaborate with other children and with teachers.** Learning is social and one of the best ways to help children learn is to encourage collaboration and cooperation with other children. As teachers we need to take the lead in helping children understand a variety of ideas that they can learn only as they work with others who are more knowledgeable than they are such as teachers and other children.

- **I believe that we need to build partnerships with families.** Teachers and parents are important members of the systems influencing children's development and learning. We help children most effectively when we build active partnerships with families and respect diversity.

PURPOSE AND SCOPE OF THIS BOOK

My purpose in writing this book is to give students a solid grounding in theory and research so that they will quickly grasp the major tenets of the profession of early childhood education. It is designed for courses such as Introduction to Early Childhood Education or Foundations of Early Childhood Education.

- After reading this text students will understand a developmental approach and will be able to apply it as they work with children. Working with elementary and secondary students is quite different from working with children in the early childhood years, when development is especially crucial. My intent is for students to understand this thoroughly.
- The content of this text will encourage students to learn to reflect on their practices, an essential goal and disposition of effective teachers.
- This text is organized around the standards for initial licensure from the National Association for the Education of Young Children (NAEYC) and has many features that will help students to learn, remember, and then feel confident enough to use the principles and concepts presented. Each chapter's structure and Guiding Questions are based on NAEYC's standards.

GUIDING QUESTIONS:

- What are the various paths and career opportunities in working with young children?
- How are early childhood education teachers considered to be professionals?
- Why are the basic principles of child development important to a teacher's educational approach?

FEATURES OF THE BOOK

Several features in this book will help students understand and remember what they are reading. Some features will help them to apply their knowledge.

VIGNETTES: Each chapter begins with several short vignettes. Each vignette focuses on infants and toddlers, preschoolers, kindergartners, or children in the primary grades. They give readers a good picture of what a concept looks like in the real world with real children. The reader then focuses on each vignette at specific points in each chapter. For example, these are the vignettes opening Chapter 5.

INFANT/TODDLER
Continuity of Care

Nick, now 2 years old, first entered Mr. Bjornrud's class as a 10 month old. Nick's father chose this caregiving arrangement because of the school's policy of continuity of care for the children. "This means," Nick's father said to a friend, "that Nick will be with the same caregiver until he is 3 years old and I'm glad about that because he shouldn't be shifted from one person to another."

PRESCHOOL
Pronouncing Names Correctly

Pedro was new to Mrs. Chang's class. He had arrived from Mexico 3 weeks before with his parents. Pedro's home language is Spanish, and he is now learning English—he is an English language learner. The teacher asked his parents and Pedro to pronounce his name and then she repeated it until she saw a smile light up Pedro's face, indicating that she had pronounced it correctly. Then, she told each of his classmates how to pronounce his name. As she does with all children new to her class, she assigned a partner to Pedro to show him what he needs to do, for example, when working at the play dough table.

KINDERGARTEN
A Conflict

Juanita and Joseph, finished with a cooperative collage, were framing their art.

"NO!" shouted Juanita, "put the frame the other way."

"The frame goes *this* way," said Joseph, who looked annoyed. Mr. Hernandez watched this conflict unfold, and then put the classroom's conflict resolution plan into action.

Later in the chapter, after learning about steps in resolving conflicts, readers are encouraged to say how they would help these 5 year olds resolve their conflict.

Three teachers, Mr. Bjornrud (infant and toddler), Mrs. Chang (preschool), and Mr. Hernandez (K to 2 multiage, looping classroom), appear throughout the book in these vignettes. They demonstrate how teachers put the developmental approach to work in early childhood classrooms.

EXAMPLES: There are many examples within chapters. All examples relate directly to a concept under discussion, connecting the discussion to a classroom.

Andy, a preschooler, observes the teachers in his school as they interact. He watches Mrs. Chang and the parent volunteers as they work together every day. Mrs. Chang is friendly and respectful with each parent, patiently explaining the parent's duties for the day.

TEACH INTENTIONALLY: Early childhood teachers must be *deliberate* and *intentional* in their teaching. Readers will see examples of this throughout this text, in the Teach Intentionally boxes. Each shows how teachers intentionally use what they know about child development to build classroom practices. Here is an example from Chapter 1.

TEACH INTENTIONALLY

The Post Office

What the teacher did: Mrs. Chang developed a post office in the dramatic play center after the children had visited the local post office. She encouraged children to think about things that they could use as props, and they worked together in the post office to sell stamps, weigh packages, and sort mail. She and the children made a sign, "Post Office."

How the teacher was intentional: Mrs. Chang used her knowledge of how young children develop. She believes that children learn through play and social interactions, and she deliberately designed the environment to encourage the children to play. She based this play opportunity on a topic that was very real and meaningful to the children because they had visited the post office and had taken a photo of the sign, "post office" which they duplicated back in their classroom. She also encouraged children to gather a few of the props, which required them to think and plan.

CHECK YOUR UNDERSTANDING: There are two or three Check Your Understanding exercises in most chapters. They appear at the end of specific sections. Completing these brief exercises gives readers a chance to make sure that they understand what they have just read before going on to the rest of the chapter. This example comes from Chapter 7.

CHECK YOUR UNDERSTANDING
A Child's Brain Controls Movement

Explain two things about the brain's development that allows a 4 year old to pick up and hold a paintbrush. Explain why he could not perform this fine motor skill when he was an infant.

KEY TERMS: Learning the terms and definitions for each topic should be easier with the Key Terms feature, which appears in two different formats. First, every key term appears in bold within the chapter and the definition appears in the margin. Second, a list of key terms appears at the end of the chapter, allowing readers to do a review and self-assessment, as shown below.

KEY TERMS

Adaptation, 68
Characteristics of families, 60
Child with a disability, 65
Conferences, 81
Culturally competent, 78
Developmental delay, 67
Differentiated instruction, 68

Diverse population of children and families, 60
Early intervention services, 65
IDEA, 66
IEP, 67
IFSP, 67
Overlapping spheres of influence, 60

Parent involvement, 81
Partnership with parents, 60
Poverty level, 63
Reciprocal relationship, 73
Resources for families, 76
Respectful relationship, 73
Toxic stress, 63

myeducationlab VIDEO AND RESOURCE INTEGRATION: This feature is an online resource, and references to it are included in every chapter. Readers will see an apple logo and a small photo in the margin. This directs them to a video or classroom artifact directly related to what they are reading. For example, when reading about children's work samples, readers can watch a video on children's work samples from a second-grade classroom and answer online questions associated with the video in "Activities and Applications." In addition, the "Building Teaching Skills and Dispositions" module on this site has elaborated learning experiences in which students have the opportunity to practice developing teaching and reflection skills by viewing video and getting used to applying their new knowledge by answering questions about development, play, observation and assessment, curriculum, and so forth.

Go to MyEducationLab and select the topic "Child Development." Under Activities and Applications, watch the video *Emotional Development: Infancy,* which gives a good picture of changes in how children understand emotions from infancy to middle childhood.

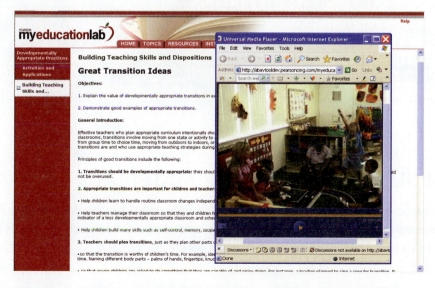

The Resources tab contains numerous resources, including

- Lesson Plan Builder—online template to create, update, and share a lesson plan
- Portfolio Builder—online template to create, update, and share a teaching portfolio

- Preparing a Portfolio—guidelines for creating a teaching portfolio
- Licensure and Standards—provide state licensure standards and national standards
- Beginning Your Career—extensive information on writing a resume and preparing for job interviews, handling issues around your first year of teaching (classroom set-up, organizing for teaching and assessment, guiding children), NCLB directives, requirements of IDEA, and more.

QUESTIONS FOR REFLECTION: Reflection is an active and intentional problem-solving process and a constructive way for a teacher to recognize that she or he is continually learning new ideas. One feature at the end of every chapter, Questions for Reflection, gives readers an opportunity to reflect on what they think about some aspect of a chapter that they have just read.

QUESTIONS FOR REFLECTION

1. Reflect on a time when one of your teachers used scaffolding to help you learn something new. Use the information on scaffolding from the Vygotsky theory section to jog your memory.

2. In your view, why did President Lyndon Johnson focus on preschool education for children of the poor as one way to lift people from poverty?

APPLY YOUR KNOWLEDGE: WHAT SHOULD THIS TEACHER DO? Readers have a chance to apply what they have learned in chapters with this feature. This allows them to use their knowledge to solve typical problems that most teachers face, as in this example from Chapter 10.

APPLY YOUR KNOWLEDGE

What Should This Teacher Do?

1. The "yeah, but . . ." Recall that Mr. Hernandez's class worked with circles divided into sections, including a pie divider. A parent observed his child working with the divider and asked the teacher, "Yeah, looks like fun, but what are they learning?" How should the teacher respond?

2. In a conference, a parent of one of the first-grade children asked Mr. Hernandez, "The children really seem to like talking to other children as they work. But doesn't the talking get in the way of academics?" How should the teacher respond?

ANCILLARY INSTRUCTOR MATERIALS

All instructor ancillary products are available online and can be downloaded from www.pearsonhighered.com in the Educators section by professors and instructors who adopt this text. The following ancillary materials are available:

- *Online Instructor's Manual.* The manual contains elements intended to support and enhance a student's reading from the text. For every chapter, it includes a statement of what the chapter emphasizes and an outline of essential content. It also contains suggested teaching strategies, in-class activities, suggestions for using MyEducationLab, and additional resources.

- *Online Test Bank and TestGen.* The *test bank* that accompanies this text contains different types of questions: multiple-choice, true/false, and essay. The multiple-choice questions contain lower-level items intended to evaluate whether a student understands principles, concepts, and definitions. Others are higher-order questions requiring a student to apply knowledge to a situation in a classroom. In addition to the Online Test Bank is test-generator software called TestGen that instructors can use to create and make customized exams.
- *Course Management.* Assessment items from the Online Test Bank are also available in both WebCT and Blackboard formats. In addition, the *Online PowerPoint Slides* can be placed on a course management site.
- *Online PowerPoint Slides.* One set of slides is provided per chapter. These summaries of content will help students understand key concepts from the chapters.

ACKNOWLEDGMENTS

I think that this book is beautiful, and it has been an honor to work with so many dedicated professionals in producing it. My Pearson/Merrill editor, Julie Peters, who truly understands early childhood education, has been unfailingly responsive, positive, and helpful throughout this process. Bryce Bell, development editor, has given helpful and specific writing suggestions. I have appreciated his excellent directions for the MyEducationLab materials. I credit the design of the book to Julie Peters and the design team, including Diane Lorenzo and Candace Rowley. Photo coordinator Shea Davis chose the pictures that so nicely illustrate concepts in the chapters. Susan McNally of Nesbitt Graphics led the production process, turning my manuscript into a book. Tiffany Bitzel, editorial assistant, has capably assisted the editor in the review process and with many other details.

I thank the following reviewers for their insight and constructive feedback that have enriched the content and structure of *Introduction to Early Childhood Education: A Developmental Perspective*: Rachel Adeodu, Northeastern Illinois University; Ann Aull, Ivy Tech Community College; Angela Baum, University of South Carolina; Diane Cerreto, Eastern Connecticut University; Mary Cordell, Navarro College; Leslie Craigo, Borough of Manhattan Community College; Dede Dunst, Mitchell Community College; Fran Favretto, University of Maryland; Benita Flores, Del Mar College; Annapurna Ganesh, Arizona State University; Priscilla Garcia, Laredo Community College; Elizabeth Geyer, University of Missouri-Columbia; Erin Glenn, College of the Canyons; Vivian Harper, San Joaquin Delta College; Kathryn Ingrum, Grossmont College; Michelle LaRocque, Florida Atlantic University; Paulette E. Mills, Washington State University; Deborah A. Moberly, University of Memphis; Kaitzer P. Puglia, Pasadena City College; Ruslan Slutsky, The University of Toledo; Susan Stover, Central Piedmont Community College; Efleda Tolentino, University of Vermont; Sandra J. Wanner, University of Mary Hardin-Baylor; and Nillofur Zobairi, Southern Illinois University at Carbondale.

My early childhood education colleagues at Governors State University—Jeannine Klomes, John Powers, Evie Plofsky, and Ty Jiles—are focused on helping students become effective teachers of young children. I enjoy being a part of this group.

I acknowledge the many kindnesses of the staff of the Valparaiso, Indiana, Panera Bread restaurant while I worked on several chapters of this book. I can now tell them that, "Yes, I did finish that book."

Once again, I thank my husband, Bill, for his continuing support. I also acknowledge the purrs and woofs of affection from my feline companions Nami Fiona, Leo Allesandro, and Casper Mateo and my canine companions Lucy Ann and Zoe-Gracie. Please feel free to email me with comments and suggestions about this book.

Marian Marion
email: m-marion@govst.edu

BRIEF CONTENTS

CONTENTS

PART II   UNDERSTANDING DEVELOPMENT

Chapter 12 Early Childhood Teachers: Lifelong Learners   288

Note: Every effort has been made to provide accurate and current Internet information in this book. However, the Internet and information on it are constantly changing, so it is inevitable that some of the Internet addresses listed in this textbook will change.

INTRODUCTION TO EARLY CHILDHOOD EDUCATION

CHAPTER 1

Early Childhood Professionals

Committed to the Whole Child

- What are the various paths and career opportunities in working with young children?
- How are early childhood education teachers considered to be professionals?
- Why are the basic principles of child development important to a teacher's educational approach?

ALICIA

Alicia, who has worked in her church's preschool since high school, has a goal of earning a teaching license. To achieve this goal, she first earned a Child Development Associate (CDA) credential while continuing to work at the church and now plans to enroll in an Associate of Arts (AA) degree program at the community college in her town.

THOMAS

Thomas, who teaches second grade in a private school, has a degree in psychology. After volunteering as an athletic coach when his son was young, he decided to become a licensed teacher. He enrolled as a graduate student in a child development master's degree program. He took the required coursework in early childhood education, passed the required state teaching exams, completed his student teaching, and earned his teaching license.

EMY

After high school graduation, Emy enrolled in the early childhood education program at a university. After earning her degree and a teaching license, she taught kindergarten for 6 years. During those years, she earned a master's degree in child development. Three years later, she had earned a doctoral degree in child development and early childhood education and is now teaching in a university where she directs the program for infants and toddlers.

Alicia, Thomas, and Emy are among the 2.1 million members of the profession of early childhood education (ECE) in America (NAEYC, 2005). It is a proud profession because of its unwavering focus on helping children to develop and learn. These teachers perform different roles, work with children of different ages, and work in different settings. Even though each has taken a different career path, they take pleasure in teaching young children and working with families. They share a similar knowledge base, are committed to using evidence-based practices, and are all lifelong learners (Table 1.1). In this chapter,

TABLE 1.1 Number of Early Childhood Educators, 2004	
Employed Early Childhood Educators	2,163,057
Center-based* teachers	352,447 (16%)
Center-based administrators	74,325 (3%)
Other center-based staff	493,723 (23%)
Home-based educators	735,710 (34%)
School-based ECE staff except teachers	112,723 (5%)
School-based prekindergarten and kindergarten teachers	240,957 (11%)
ECE staff in other** industries	153,172 (7%)

*Other center-based staff include professionals who deal with children (e.g., teachers, assistant teachers, and teacher's aides).

**Center-based institutions include private and public, for-profit and not-for-profit child-care centers, Head Start centers, and stand-alone nursery schools and preschools. School-based refers to early childhood occupations employed by elementary schools. Home based refers to family and group child-care homes and private household child-care workers.

Sources: Herzenberg, S., Price, M., & Bradley, D. (2005). *Losing ground in early childhood education: Declining workforce qualifications in an expanding industry, 1979–2004.* Retrieved on September 11, 2008, from http://www.epi.org/studies/ece/losing_ground-full_text.pdf and NAEYC (no date). Critical facts about the early childhood workforce. Retrieved on September 11, 2008, from http://www.naeyc.org/ece/critical/facts3.asp.

we look at early childhood education as a profession, its specific knowledge base, code of ethics, professional organizations, and system of licensure and certification.

You will get a snapshot of child development by looking at children of different ages: infants and toddlers, preschool and kindergarten, and primary grade children. Teachers who genuinely like working with young children appreciate the growth in all intertwined domains of development, including physical, emotional, social, cognitive (including language), and aesthetic development. Their focus is on the *whole child*, or all of the domains put together. During early childhood, children's ability to make friends blossoms and they find pleasure in words, poetry, reading, music, and dance. They gleefully investigate the natural world as they splash in puddles or use a magnifying glass to look closely at sand and snowflakes. We see their beginning sense of compassion, self-control, and sense of humor. Their memory improves tremendously, and they learn to understand and express their emotions responsibly. The appearance of their body changes as they gain in height and weight and as they develop motor skills. They move with more grace and agility as they get older. The brain's neural circuits become better coordinated and information can then make its way through the brain more easily. Why is it important to understand how children develop? Very simply, because children are growing and learning so quickly that supporting their development is how teachers teach them.

EARLY CHILDHOOD EDUCATION IS A PROFESSION

Early childhood education Profession devoted to the care and education of children and to work with families during the early childhood stage.

Profession A group of people called to a vocation or mission.

Early childhood education is a **profession**, which is a group of people called to a vocation or mission. All early childhood professionals should have the following attributes in common:

- specific knowledge base
- code of ethics
- professional organization

- system of licensure and certification. In early childhood education, there are many different credentials, highlighting the many paths to learning about children, teaching, and working with families

The primary focus in early childhood education is young children and their families. A society forms a social contract or agreement with different professions, defining its duties and rights and permitting it to provide important services needed within that society. Early childhood education's duties and rights center on the vital service of caring for and educating young children and working with families.

Specific Knowledge Base of the Early Childhood Profession

Any professional has to master the complex body of knowledge and skills specific to a profession (Cruess, Johnston, & Cruess, 2004). What do early childhood teachers need to know to do their work effectively, that is, what complex body of knowledge do they need to learn? What are the skills that they must develop?

Early childhood education knowledge and skills reflect five **core standards** that guide programs preparing early childhood professionals. Standards describe knowledge, skills, and dispositions that all well-prepared early childhood teachers should have (NAEYC, 2001). The core standards are listed, and then described briefly here.

Core standards Statements describing the knowledge, skills, and dispositions that all well-prepared ECE teachers should have.

- **Promoting Child Development and Learning.** Candidates learn about children's development and factors influencing development. They learn how to prepare environments conducive to children's healthy development.
- **Building Family and Community Relationships.** Future teachers learn about children's families and communities and use this knowledge to build respectful and reciprocal relationships with families.
- **Observing, Documenting, and Assessing to Support Young Children and Families.** Candidates learn about the use of assessment and how it can help children and families.
- **Teaching and Learning.** Future teachers learn how to design and carry out situations that will enhance all children's development. They use their knowledge about good relationships with children and families and about developmentally appropriate teaching strategies to organize learning activities.
- **Becoming a Professional.** Candidates learn about the early childhood education profession and the attributes of professional teachers. They learn to value ethics in decision making; advocacy for children, families, and the profession; and to value lifelong learning and reflection on their own practices.

The standards as stated by the National Association for the Education of Young Children (NAEYC), early childhood education's major professional organization, are in the Appendix (NAEYC, 2001).

Core standards exist for three different program levels. At the *associate* level, a student usually obtains an associate's degree from a 2-year junior or community college or technical school. In the *initial licensure* level, a candidate usually obtains a bachelor's degree and licensure as a teacher after meeting program and state requirements. At the *advanced* level, the candidate usually obtains a graduate degree, a master's or a doctoral degree, and might obtain a teaching license.

The five core standards are identical for all three levels because NAEYC believes that it is valuable for all early childhood education professionals, whether they have an associate's degree, a bachelor's degree, or an advanced degree, to share a similar set of outcomes. What distinguishes the three levels from one another is the depth of understanding and performance required of each.

Let's look now at a more in-depth explanation of each of the five core standards.

Promoting Child Development and Learning

We name and describe briefly the phases of development during early childhood and the domains or areas in child development. We get a closer look at development during infancy and toddlerhood, preschool, kindergarten, and the primary grades later in this chapter.

The human life consists of several stages: prenatal development, early childhood, middle childhood, adolescence, and adulthood (early, middle, and late adulthood). **Early childhood**, the second of the stages, accounts for about 11% of the human life span (Broderick, Blewitt, & Weaver, 2002); and consists of different phases.

Early childhood Period of human development from birth through age 8.

Phases of Development During Early Childhood.

The early childhood stage, extending from birth through age 8, consists of three briefer periods nested within the overall stage. This is a useful way to think about the early childhood stage because young children have different care and education needs during each of the three phases (Bredekamp & Copple, 1997). One of the most deep-seated beliefs in our profession is that we value children's lives for what they are at the moment.

- *Infancy and toddlerhood.* Occupying the first 3 years, this phase includes *young infants* from birth to 9 months, *mobile infants* from 8 to 18 months, and *toddlers*, from 16 to 36 months.
- *Preschool and kindergarten.* Children are between 3 and 6 years old.
- *Primary grades.* Children are in first, second, or third grade and are typically between 6 and 9 years old.

Domains of Child Development.

Teachers who understand child development know how to meet children's needs. For example, to help children learn how to show respect for one another and for animals, a teacher needs to know about when they are first capable of showing compassion and

Phases of Early Childhood

Infants and toddlers
(Birth–36 months)

Preschool and kindergarten
(3–6 years)

Primary grade children
(6–9 years)

factors affecting this trait. Teachers can acquire this knowledge in several ways, such as through reading, studying, observing children, discussing findings, and reflecting.

There are different aspects or parts of a child's overall development. These are the **domains of child development** (Berger, 2003) and include

- social;
- emotional;
- physical and motor;
- cognitive, including language; and
- aesthetic.

Domains of child development Aspects of a child's development, including social, emotional, physical, cognitive, including language, and aesthetic.

Teachers strive to help children develop in all of the ways possible. They want to help them develop their cognitive and intellectual powers and to use language effectively. At the same time, they help children become emotionally healthy and develop good relationships and social skills. They also want to help children develop healthy bodies, capable of using gross and fine muscles effectively. Teachers help children learn to see, appreciate, and create beauty in their world.

The domain of *social development* involves changes in children's ability to get along with others in interactions, in relationships, and in groups and to changes in social skills. Some children are more competent socially than are others. For example, a socially competent child might demonstrate respect for another child by listening as the other speaks during large group time.

The domain of *emotional development* involves changes in how children feel, express, and understand feelings. They move from action and body-oriented expression of feelings during infancy and the toddler years to using symbols such as words during preschool through the primary grades, ages 4 through 8. Contrast the arm waving, scrunched up face, and crying of a frustrated young infant with an angry 4-year-old's statement, "You can't come to *my* birthday party." An older child, a first-grade boy, shows further development in this domain when he cradles his puppy and croons, "I love you, Max." A second grader's face might register a feeling of disgust when he tastes burned toast, but his emotional response consists solely of that facial expression. He can now hide emotions or moderate his response much better than when he was a toddler or a preschooler.

The domain of *physical development* describes, for example, changes in height, weight, body proportions, and brain development. *Motor development* refers to changes in a child's ability to move the body effectively, including gross, or large, and fine motor skills. Some examples are an infant who gains six pounds; a 3 year old who fits a peg into the pegboard; a mother who marks her 6-year-old child's height on the wall, noting that this mark is one inch higher than the mark from last year; and a third grader expertly catching a baseball.

The domain of *cognitive development* refers to changes in children's ability to think and to the delight that they take in constructing knowledge. For example, three preschool children observe that gelatin changes from liquid to a shivery red mass. Other examples are two kindergartners, in the dramatic play center, who each take a different role, and a second-grade girl who solves a math problem by using blocks.

The domain of *language development* involves acquiring the rules of one's culture for communicating thoughts and feelings. Speech refers to talking and how the child learns to express language. Language rules can also be expressed with gestures, signs, and writing. Milestones for language development are guides to what is considered normal development, and they help professionals determine whether a child might need assistance with this domain (National Institute on Deafness and Other Communicative Disorders, 2001).

Go to MyEducationLab, at www.myeducationlab.com and select the topic "Teaching Strategies." Under Activities and Applications, read the strategy *Attention Span* for a closer look at changes in children's attention spans as they develop.

The domain of *aesthetic development* involves a child's emerging appreciation of beauty and the arts, such as music, dance, painting, and drawing. A preschooler might, for example, swirl finger paint onto smooth paper. A kindergarten child who observes a masterpiece in a museum later picks out the same painting from a series of art postcards, and a third grader writes two haiku poems, later illustrating one with a dance.

Teachers play a crucial role in children's development and learning. They must be able to *use* their knowledge of child development to create respectful and challenging environments in which all children can learn. They are most effective when they use teaching and care practices based on high-quality research.

For example, ample research evidence has demonstrated that high-quality, social interactive pretend play helps children to development in every domain (Kalliala, 2006; Seifert, 2004) and contributes to the development of a child's brain (Frost, 1998). Understanding that children learn through activity, play, and social interaction with other children is the first step. The next logical step is to act on the belief that play is not a luxury but a real need for young children (Elkind, 2006) by arranging the classroom and daily schedule to encourage play. Throughout this text, Teach Intentionally boxes highlight examples of teachers' deliberate, intentional classroom practices that are built on their knowledge of child development. Teachers who teach intentionally know the reason for doing what they do.

Building Family and Community Relationships

Culture The set of rules and traditions that a group expresses through values, beliefs, and goals.

Effective teachers understand that different systems, family, community, and **culture** affect children. A child's family, whatever its structure, has a major influence on different aspects of development such as self-esteem (Kernis, Brown, & Brody, 2000) and their levels of kindness and generosity (Oliner & Oliner, 1988).

Early childhood teachers need to understand the characteristics of children's families and then use their knowledge to build trusting, reciprocal relationships with all families. Teachers must also know how to form a partnership with families, and they

TEACH INTENTIONALLY

The Post Office

What the teacher did: Mrs. Chang developed a post office in the dramatic play center after the children had visited the local post office. She encouraged children to think about things that they could use as props, and they worked together in the post office to sell stamps, weigh packages, and sort mail. She and the children made a sign, "Post Office."

How the teacher was intentional: Mrs. Chang used her knowledge of how young children develop. She believes that children learn through play and social interactions, and she deliberately designed the environment to encourage the children to play. She based this play opportunity on a topic that was very real and meaningful to the children because they had visited the post office and had taken a photo of the sign, "Post Office," which they duplicated back in their classroom. She also encouraged children to gather a few of the props, which required them to think and plan.

must understand the characteristics of the community and culture in which children exist (Bredekamp, 1997). For example, some children grow up in large cities divided into smaller neighborhoods, others in small rural towns and villages, and others in suburban neighborhoods. Some children live in one place throughout childhood while others move several times. Teachers also must understand the effect that culture has on children because they will teach children from different cultures. The United States is increasingly diverse, and teachers work with multicultural, multilingual children and their families.

Observing, Documenting, and Assessing to Support Young Children and Families

Effective teachers rely on observing, assessing, and documenting in chair work with young children and their families. Effective early childhood teachers understand the difference between authentic, performance, and play-based assessment and standardized testing. They realize that authentic assessment, assessment done in the classroom as the child is learning, is important in giving a good picture of the whole child. They also understand how authentic assessment benefits children, parents, and teachers, and they develop specific skills in observing, assessing, and documenting children's development and progress, as the following example reveals:

> Mr. Hernandez has learned about and regularly uses anecdotal records (brief written notes) about different aspects of a child's development and progress, such as when Theresa said, "Look, a 'T,' just like my name!" He uses his notes in making teaching and learning plans and in constructing curriculum.

Teachers also need to understand the idea of assessment partnerships with parents or other professionals. Parents or other family members or legal guardians who are the primary caregiver for the child, having insight about their child, can work with teachers as a team. Teachers need to work with other professionals such as special educators who work with specific children or assist regular education teachers to meet a child's needs in an inclusive classroom. *Inclusive classrooms* are those that include *all* children in the regular classroom, those who are developing in a typical manner and those who have unique educational or developmental needs. Most important is the ultimate goal of assessment—using information gleaned from assessment to meet children's needs.

Teaching and Learning

Teachers of young children must understand the central concepts in the **content areas** in early childhood education. The content areas include literacy and language arts, mathematics, science, social sciences, the arts (music, dance, and visual arts), child development (social and emotional), cognition, and physical development and health. For example, early childhood teachers often plan learning activities that help children understand emotions and getting along with others. This is child development content in action, specifically emotional and social development.

Early childhood teachers then have to learn how to use effective teaching strategies to introduce children to the world of knowledge in the different content areas. They often focus on more than one content area at a time, an integrated curriculum approach. When playing a circle game, for example, a teacher might focus on social skill development while the children also learn math as they count children in the circle.

Content areas In early childhood education, these include child development, mathematics, science, social sciences, literacy and language arts, the arts and physical development and health.

Becoming a Professional

What does it take for a person to become an excellent, effective, early childhood professional? Effective teachers blend their professional knowledge and skills with personal attributes.

Dispositions Habits of mind or tendencies to act in a particular way.

Dispositions.   These attributes, also known as **dispositions**, are habits of mind or tendencies to act in a particular way, such as listening carefully before speaking. They tell us how a teacher meets responsibilities, their views of what children need, their appreciation of childhood itself, and their commitment to the benefit of the children they teach. Excellent early childhood teachers possess many admirable personal attributes (Nieto, 2005; Rike & Sharp, 2006; Vallence, 2000). These are categorized in four main groups.

1. *They love the job of teaching.* Effective early childhood teachers:
   - Have real enthusiasm for teaching as a profession.
   - View teaching as a privilege and are grateful for the opportunity to spend time with children and to work with families.
   - Have genuine, nonpossessive love and affection for the children in their classes.
   - See themselves as a part of something larger than themselves, a profession dedicated to the care and education of the very young.
   - Have a forgiving attitude and a healthy sense of humor.
   - Demonstrate honesty and integrity.
   - Act ethically.

2. *They are competent and humble.* Others view them as excellent teachers, which often surprises them, because they view themselves as doing what a teacher is supposed to do. They:
   - Are motivated to *do good* and to serve others.
   - Admit that they have good organizational skills, are prepared for teaching, and that they meet deadlines.
   - Recognize their limitations.
   - Readily acknowledge the gifts and abilities that other teachers possess.
   - Believe strongly that they are learners who benefit from the knowledge of others, including colleagues, parents, and children.

3. *They are committed to the whole child.* They believe that teachers should concentrate on directly meeting children's needs. They:
   - Believe in and are committed to all areas of children's development.
   - Show concern for children who face challenges, such as learning English, who have disabilities, or who are homeless.
   - Are committed to making sure that all young children have opportunities to achieve to the best of their potential.
   - Keep in mind what a young child might be feeling and thinking in school.

4. *They are personally committed to the benefit of the children whom they teach.* To maintain this characteristic is very challenging because there are many demands placed on teachers. Excellent teachers, however:
   - Seem to transcend or rise above the demands because of their commitment to children. They keep their "eye on the prize," which they see as helping children develop and learn.
   - Are energized and emotionally and intellectually nourished by their teaching, especially when they work directly with children.
   - Are committed to building on what they already know and to lifelong learning.

Go to MyEducationLab and select the topic "Professionalism/Ethics/ Standards." Under Activities and Applications, watch the video *Teaching First Grade*, in which a teacher describes her feelings about teaching.

CHECK YOUR UNDERSTANDING
Your Favorite Teacher

Think of a favorite teacher from your early childhood (or from any grade level). What do you remember most about this teacher? What are some of your teacher's personal attributes that stand out when you think of him or her?

Reflection. **Reflection** is an active and intentional problem-solving process and a constructive way for a teacher to recognize that she is continually learning new ideas. A teacher who reflects well does several things. He logically and systematically connects ideas and understands that his beliefs heavily influence what he thinks about any *pedagogical* issue, any issue related to teaching. Reflective teachers acknowledge that strong feelings about any issue undoubtedly affect thinking about and resolving problems. For example, if you strongly believe that using workbook pages to help children learn mathematics is an *in*appropriate teaching strategy, then you will carry your feelings into any discussion or reflection on the topic.

A teacher who reflects well also knows that the process is bumpy, that issues are complex, and that they are not resolved quickly or easily. He accepts the idea that he will very likely have many qualms or misgivings as he reflects. He accepts the uncertainties as a natural and normal part of reflection (Dewey, 1933). Many people think, therefore, that pedagogical reflection goes far beyond analysis of practices. These people view reflection as a virtue (Birmingham, 2004).

> For example, Mr. Hernandez critically analyzed the possibility of using math workbook pages with his kindergarten children. One page, for instance, required children to draw a circle around a shape when the teacher said the name of that shape. He rejected this teaching strategy for a variety of reasons.

Mr. Hernandez made his decision by first reflecting on his own strong distrust of workbook pages. He reread information on how young children learn through social interaction and activity and by reviewing recent research on how children actually learn mathematical concepts (Geist, 2008; Ginsburg, 2005). He then read the joint position statement from the NAEYC and the National Council for Teachers of Mathematics (NAEYC & NCATE, 2002), which contains suggestions for teaching early childhood mathematics. Wanting children to experience mathematics in meaningful ways, he decided to emphasize active learning, problem solving, reasoning, and communicating ideas.

> Instead of requiring children to draw lines around different shapes on paper, for example, Mr. Hernandez worked with a small group in a center and encouraged children to make pictures of a person by *using* paper shapes and small blocks (NAEYC & NCATE, 2006). This approach, he reasoned, was active, encouraged collaboration between children, built on what children already knew, focused on problem solving, and resulted in children communicating their results.

Using Resources of the Profession. **Research** is a powerful professional resource that supports teachers in performing their role. Teachers enhance children's development and learning by using **evidence-based practices**, which are practices informed by research (Dunst, Trivett, & Cutspec, 2002).

Research is organized study with the researchers systematically investigating some issue. Good research builds on previously published research. **Theory**, a set of ideas

Reflection An active and intentional problem-solving process.

Research Organized study in which an issue is systematically investigated.

Evidence-based practices Actions that teachers can document with well-done, ethical, useful research.

Theory A set of ideas based on study of observable facts and an analysis of that data.

based on study of observable facts and an analysis of that data, drives research. We will examine theories of early childhood education in Chapter 2. The researcher uses methods that are appropriate to the question investigated. The researcher gives information about the methods used so that others can replicate the study and check the results. The researcher's peers review the research and decide whether it is worthy of publication. If it is, then the research is published for the early childhood education community to read and use.

Any research conducted with children must protect them from any possible harm. Families have the right to know about the nature of the proposed research so that they can give what is known as **informed consent**. When children participate in a research project, the researcher must explain things so that the child understands. Families and children should also have the right to refuse to participate in research or to withdraw at any point in the project.

Good research, conducted ethically and using accepted methods, answers questions and increases the early childhood knowledge base. Well-done research helps teachers make decisions about their practices; it is the foundation for evidence-based practices. Teachers can document their actions with research. Teachers who use evidence-based practices are better equipped to enhance children's development.

The Technical Assistance Center on Social Emotional Intervention for Young Children conducts and reviews research dealing with challenging behavior. The center assists practitioners in adopting evidence-based practices when confronted with challenging behaviors. For example, the center describes a method for preventing challenging behavior, a method that it bases on several well-done research studies. The research studies help build a case for three evidence-based practices to prevent challenging behaviors: constructing a developmentally appropriate physical classroom environment, developing a good schedule, and developing helpful routines and rituals (TACSEI, www.challengingbehavior.com).

Teachers can conduct research on their own, and their research is usually designed to answer some question arising from their teaching and children's development and learning or about supporting families. For example, one teacher had questions about the social development and relationships of two toddlers in her class. Her research method was to document the social interaction of these children and to accompany a photo essay with anecdotal observations (Henderson, Meier, & Perry, 2004).

Another, a second-grade teacher, had questions about a method for helping her children practice spelling in a more developmentally appropriate way. She conducted action research, developing several activity-based spelling practice strategies, including using magnetic letters, writing in shaving cream, and bending fuzzy wire into the practice words. She gave children the option of continuing to use the workbook-based spelling practice or the activity-based strategies. She interviewed the children about their preferences and documented their choices (DeNeve, 2006).

Code of Ethics

All professions have a **code of ethics**, the set of standards of conduct, that defines honorable behavior of its members. A significant marker of early childhood education as a profession is its Code of Ethical Conduct (Baptiste & Reyes, 2008; NAEYC, 2005), a document published by the NAEYC (see the Appendix). Teachers have many different questions as they work with children, families, and colleagues. Some questions revolve around issues of morality, what a person believes is good and right and what he believes his obligation to be. The field of **ethics** is the study of obligations, right, and wrong. Teachers are involved in ethics when they have to think about what is right or wrong or when they have to choose between different moral courses of action, the choices often conflicting with one another.

Informed consent
Agreement to participate in research based on accurate and honest information about the nature of the research.

Code of ethics The set of standards of conduct that defines honorable behavior of members of a profession.

Ethics Study of obligations, right, and wrong.

The early childhood Code of Ethical Conduct provides common ground for educators facing decisions involving morality and ethics. It provides a moral compass as educators face the daily questions, ethical responsibilities, and dilemmas involved in working with children and families. It clearly outlines our **ethical responsibilities** to children, families, and colleagues and to community and society. The code also helps teachers deal with **ethical dilemmas**, the not-so-clear-cut issues that teachers also face.

The Code of Ethical Conduct contains a *statement of commitment*. While not a part of the code, the statement of commitment signifies that an early childhood teacher accepts the values of early childhood education. These core values that form the base for the Code of Ethical Conduct and the first part of the statement of commitment are shown in Figure 1.1.

Ethical responsibilities A behavior in which a professional must or must not engage.

Ethical dilemmas A moral conflict; the clash of moral responsibilities.

FIGURE 1.1   Core Values and Statement of Commitment in Early Childhood Education

- Appreciate childhood as a unique and valuable stage of the human life cycle.
- Base our work on knowledge of how children develop and learn.
- Appreciate and support the bond between child and family.
- Recognize that children are best understood and supported in the context of family, culture, community, and society.
- Respect the dignity, worth, and uniqueness of each individual (child, family member, and colleague).
- Respect diversity in children, families, and colleagues.
- Recognize that children and adults achieve their full potential in the context of relationships that are based on trust and respect.

Statement of Commitment*

As an individual who works with young children, I commit myself to furthering the values of early childhood education as they are reflected in the ideals and principles of the NAEYC Code of Ethical Conduct. To the best of my ability I will:

- Never harm children.
- Ensure that programs for young children are based on current knowledge and research of child development and early childhood education.
- Respect and support families in their task of nurturing children.
- Respect colleagues in early childhood care and education and support them in maintaining the NAEYC Code of Ethical Conduct.
- Serve as an advocate for children, their families, and their teachers in community and society.
- Stay informed of and maintain high standards of professional conduct.
- Engage in an ongoing process of self-reflection, realizing that personal characteristics, biases, and beliefs have an impact on children and families.
- Be open to new ideas and be willing to learn from the suggestions of others.
- Continue to learn, grow, and contribute as a professional.
- Honor the ideals and principles of the NAEYC Code of Ethical Conduct.

*This Statement of Commitment is not part of the Code but is a personal acknowledgment of the individual's willingness to embrace the distinctive values and moral obligations of the field of early childhood care and education. It is recognition of the moral obligations that lead to an individual becoming part of the profession.

Source: National Association for the Education of Young Children. 2005. *Position Statement: Code of Ethical Conduct and Statement of Commitment.* Washington, DC: Author. Online: http://www.naeyc.org/about/positions/pdf/pseth05.pdf. Reprinted with permission from the National Association for the Education of Young Children.

How Teachers Can Use the Code of Ethical Conduct

Teachers can use the Code of Ethical Conduct as a guide for resolving problems that arise in their work with children, families, and other professionals. Here is a typical problem for which the Code offers valuable help. After the example is an explanation for resolving this problem by using the Code.

> A kindergarten teacher is speaking with the father of 5-year-old Scott, a child in his class. Scott's father is divorced from the child's mother and shares custody with her, but they seem to argue quite a bit about their child. He asks the teacher, "Scott stayed with his mother last night. Could you tell if he had eaten breakfast this morning?"

With this problem, the teacher faces an ethical responsibility, a behavior in which a professional must or must not engage. Ethical responsibilities are definite, specific, and listed in the Code of Ethical Conduct (Baptiste & Reyes, 2008; NAEYC, 2005). For example, Principle 2.14 of the Code is

> In cases where family members are in conflict with one another, we shall work openly, sharing our observations of the child, to help all parties involved make informed decisions. We shall refrain from becoming an advocate for one party.

This principle gives teachers clear directions in how to act and spells out a professional's responsibility, in this case to the family. The responsibility is to recognize that these parents are in conflict and that a teacher must work openly and must share observations so that the parents can make informed decisions. Most of all, the teacher is obligated, ethically, *not* to take sides with either parent.

CHECK YOUR UNDERSTANDING
Using the Code of Ethical Conduct

Use Principle 2.14 as your guide. Choose one of the following statements in response to Scott's father. Choose a statement that most clearly lines up with Principle 2.14 of the Code of Ethical Conduct. Explain your choice.

1. "That's really none of my concern."
2. "I'll ask his mother and get back to you."
3. "Scott seems to be happy and healthy. I know that you will speak with his mother about any concerns that you have."

Other problems are not as clear-cut and fall into a murkier category, as the next example shows.

> A teacher observes one of the other kindergarten teachers speaking to a child in a way that most reasonable people would consider disrespectful. What should this teacher do?

Use the Code of Ethical Conduct to make a decision. The Code tells us about ethical responsibilities, in this case, to two people—the other teacher and the child. This issue, however, is not as clear-cut as the issue with Scott's father. This is an ethical dilemma, a moral conflict. The teacher has views of morality, what he thinks is right and proper, and he has views about his obligations.

Teachers face an ethical dilemma when they perceive conflicting professional responsibilities. In this case, the teacher has an ethical responsibility to his colleague, the teacher, which is spelled out in the Code. In addition, and this is what makes the issue an ethical dilemma, he also has an ethical responsibility to the child in the incident, which is also spelled out in the Code.

Using the Code of Ethical Conduct would help in resolving this ethical dilemma. The Code can help teachers think differently about such an issue. They would reflect on and possibly discuss the issue before acting. They would decide what a good early childhood teacher would do in such a situation by using the Code's core values of the profession in making a decision (Figure 1.2) (Baptiste & Reyes, 2008; Freeman & Feeney, 2004). They could use a five-step process for resolving ethical dilemmas (Baptiste & Reyes, 2008):

1. Make sure that they are dealing with an ethical dilemma (and not an ethical responsibility). Here, there are two conflicting ethical responsibilities (to the colleague and to the child).
2. Use the Code of Ethical Conduct as a guide. Figure out a way to resolve the conflicting responsibilities.
3. Exercise and act on their ethical judgment.
4. Reflect on the ethical judgment.
5. Make the professional change.

In the ethical dilemma presented here, one part of the Code, Principle 1.1, will be the most important guide, whatever the teacher's responsibility to his colleague who has used inappropriate guidance. Principle 1.1 is

> Above all, we shall not harm children. We shall not participate in practices that are emotionally damaging, physically harmful, disrespectful, degrading, dangerous, exploitative, or intimidating to children. This principle has precedence over all others in this Code.

Our main ethical responsibility, above all others, therefore, is for children's welfare. An early childhood teacher's responsibility is to protect children. In this case, the teacher's main ethical responsibility is to protect the child as he also fulfills his ethical responsibility to the other teacher. One way to do this is to speak privately with the teacher. The purpose would not be to accuse but rather to state his observations in a self-responsible, friendly, and objective way. For example, "You were talking with Jada in the hallway this morning and I heard you say, 'Stop crying now, Jada. You need to stop being such a big baby.' " Then I heard Jada cry even more loudly and you said, 'I-said-stop-it.' Jada looked afraid."

Professional Organizations

Every profession represents its members, practicing professionals, and, in some cases, students studying for the profession, through a **professional organization**. A professional organization is national in scope but typically has regional and local branches. Professional organizations work on issues important to the profession. Members of the organization elect a governing board, which then governs the professional organization. Governing an organization includes functions such as establishing standards for knowledge in that field and the profession's code of ethics.

Professional organization
Group representing members of a profession.

Early childhood teachers have professional organizations such as the National Association for the Education of Young Children (NAEYC), which serves as the example here. This major professional organization for early childhood educators has approximately 100,000 members. Regional, state, and local affiliates give members opportunities to work with other members living in the same vicinity. Membership is open to anyone who is interested in working for excellence in early childhood care and education. The Governing Board consists of 17 elected persons.

Professional organizations provide services to those belonging to the group. They sponsor web sites and usually publish journals as shown in Figure 1.2. They publish books or other items focusing on the knowledge base of the profession. Thus, the profession enlarges its knowledge base and circulates information about (Copple & Bredekamp, 2008) the profession. The organizations promote continuing education and professional development to members through regularly scheduled meetings and conferences.

FIGURE 1.2 Two Early Childhood Education Journal Covers

Source: Reprinted with permission from the National Association for the Education of Young Children.

The NAEYC provides a core of services to members. It works with the National Council on the Accreditation of Teacher Education in establishing standards for what all early childhood teachers should know and be able to do. It has also developed the profession's Code of Ethical Conduct and its statement of commitment.

NAEYC promotes excellence in early childhood education through an accreditation process. It focuses on helping programs for young children, such as preschools and child-care centers, meet standards for accreditation. This professional group also participates in the accreditation process for college and university programs, awarding associate, bachelor's, and graduate degrees. The web site address for NAEYC is at the end of this chapter.

Professional groups also publish journals, books, videos, DVDs, and other resources such as position statements. These resources provide members with evidence-based information on all aspects of early childhood education. The professional group's annual national conference and the regional and state affiliate conferences offer members the opportunity for professional development and networking with other early childhood professionals. Research and other professional development activities, therefore, are available through the Internet, conferences, and through its journals and books.

Other professional organizations of interest to early childhood educators are the Association for Childhood Education International (ACEI), which acts on behalf of

FIGURE 1.3   Ways to Serve as an Advocate for Children and the Early Childhood Education Profession

Leader: provides vision. The leader keeps an advocacy effort headed in the right direction.

Advisor: is willing to share expertise on an advocacy topic with decision makers and lawmakers. For example, an expert testifies about child abuse and neglect before state lawmakers considering a change in the child abuse laws or statutes.

Researcher: collects and summarizes data about an issue. This advocate might write the report used by an advisor in testimony on child abuse.

Contributor: performs a specific task necessary in any advocacy effort. For example, a teacher might be willing to write letters in support of changing legislation on child abuse. Another early childhood education professional might be willing to print signs for a march.

children from birth to adolescence and has an international focus. The Council for Exceptional Children (CEC) is dedicated to improving education for children with disabilities and for gifted children. Especially useful for early childhood teachers is this group's early childhood section, Division of Early Childhood (DEC), which contains information on special education. The web site addresses for both organizations are listed at the end of this chapter.

Advocacy

Advocacy is a process that actively support and promote best practices in early childhood education. They protect children and families, and they advance the profession's goals by joining with others in actively advocating for public policies that support children and families. Teachers serve as advocates not only for children and families but also for improved quality of programs and services for children and for professional status or improved working conditions for early childhood education professionals.

Professional organizations help teachers carry out their responsibility to serve as advocates for the profession and for children. For instance, the *NAEYC Advocacy Toolkit* gives specific and practical information about how to advocate effectively at different levels (NAEYC, 2004). There are many ways to serve as an advocate. Each requires that teachers manage time and resources so that their efforts are effective. Figure 1.3 lists different ways to serve as an advocate.

Advocacy Professional responsibility of teachers in which they support and promote best practices in early childhood education.

System of Licensure and Certification

A final indicator of early childhood education as a profession is its system of **licensure** and **certification**. This system acknowledges the continuum of preparation for work in this field (Hyson, 2003). Teachers and caregivers of young children work in a wide range of settings with children from birth through age 8 as well as with diverse families, children with disabilities, children who are learning English, and with adults. Figure 1.4 describes the scope, context, and roles within early childhood education.

Licensure Granting of a license to practice a profession.

Certification Documentation of having met all state requirements for licensure.

Certificates and Licensure

There is no single way to become an early childhood education teacher. Instead, there are multiple entry points and many different career paths, all tied to a common knowledge

FIGURE 1.4 **Early Childhood Education: Scope, Context, and Roles**

Scope of Early Childhood Education

- Birth through age 8 years
- Need knowledge about this entire age range
- Might also work with adults who are learning about young children or working with parents

Context of Early Childhood Education

ECE professionals work in many different settings (contexts):

- Private schools
- Public schools
- Infant–toddler classrooms
- Preschools
- Kindergartens
- Primary grades
- Center- or home-based child-care settings
- Before- and after-school programs
- Resource and referral programs
- Head Start
- Home visiting programs
- Colleges or universities

Roles

An early childhood education professional's role relates to specific major functions that the person performs:

- Resource and referral: works with a team that delivers information about community resources for families to parents
- Assistant teacher: supports and works closely with the lead teacher in designing and carrying out functions related to teaching children and working with families
- Lead teacher (leader of a teaching team): works closely with assistant teachers and administrators; responsible for planning curriculum, building relationships with families, and observing and assessing young children's development and progress
- Director or principal: performs administrative functions; responsible for smooth functioning of a center or school program; deals with policies such as finances, hiring, performance reviews, and professional development
- Teacher educator: prepares early childhood professionals in CDA programs, community colleges, or in colleges or universities
- Training roles: consulting; familiar with state regulatory agencies and professional regulatory agencies such as the National Council on the Accreditation of Teacher Education (http://www.ncate.org)

base and set of skills. The same vision and values about children and families guide professional preparation, whatever the path taken. However, teachers with specific coursework and fieldwork in child development and in early childhood education structure more appropriate classrooms and curriculum than teachers with no education in child development or early childhood education (Tout, Zaslow, & Berry, 2005).

FIGURE 1.5   Paths to Working with Children and Families

Early Childhood Education Certificates

Many career paths lead to certificates or credentials that recognize knowledge and skills in specific areas of early childhood education:

- Child Development Associate (CDA) credential: This credential is earned by persons working with children and families in center-based programs, family child care, and home visitor programs. There are 200,000 CDAs in the United States, and approximately 15,000 people apply for the CDA each year.

- Certificate for a specific age group in early childhood education: This type of certificate provides students with basic entry-level knowledge and skills for working with children and families in a support role. Students usually earn this type of credential in 1 year or less. It requires fewer credits or courses than would the associate's degree.

- After-School Care: Certificate earned after taking four to five courses related to after school care.

- Child-Care Center Director: This type of certificate usually meets a state's requirements for becoming a center director. For example, a minimum number of clock hours of education in child care and duties of a center director are required.

- Parent Education: This certificate is earned, quite often, on the graduate level. It is a certificate of completion earned after taking coursework on parenting education.

Early Childhood Education Degrees

Some career paths require a 2-year, a 4-year, or a graduate degree in child development and/or early childhood education:

- Associate's Degree: Earned in two years from a community college and requiring study in general education and a significant number of early childhood education courses.

- Bachelor's Degree: Earned from a 4-year college or university and allows candidates to apply for licensure as a teacher.

- Advanced Degree: These are master's or doctoral degrees, usually in child development or early childhood education. Some professionals earn licensure as a teacher at this graduate school level.

Teachers acquire the knowledge and skills needed for different roles in a variety of settings. Many career paths lead to one of many types of credentials. A **credential** is a document. It confirms that a person has met specific requirements and has demonstrated knowledge and skills required at the level for which the credential is granted. Credentials include different types of certificates as well as licensure for teaching.

Many states assist teachers with information about the credentials available to them. For example, the state of Illinois' Gateway to Opportunity is a statewide support network offering a coordinated approach to the variety of credentials available to those completing different levels of education and fieldwork (Illinois Early Care and Education Professional Development Network, 2007). Figure 1.5 lists and explains certificates and degrees available to early childhood education professionals. A few examples of often-traveled paths are included.

Credential Document confirming that a person has met specific requirements and has demonstrated knowledge and skills required at the level for which the credential is granted.

FIGURE 1.6   Martha Muñoz's Professional Journey in Early Childhood Education

Martha Muñoz, a second-generation Mexican-American, was an eager participant in the first Phoenix Head Start class. Years later, golden memories from that experience led her into early childhood education. Earning her CDA was the starting point for Martha to go on to receive her associate, bachelor's, and master's degrees. Now, she has received her doctorate in higher education administration from the University of Texas at Austin.

None of this happened overnight. Martha volunteered at the local YMCA preschool program when her 3-year-old daughter was enrolled and discovered her true connection with young children. This inspired her to seek her CDA, and during that process, Martha met Cheryl Foster, director of CDA training at Central Arizona College, who mentored her. The CDA credential opened doors for Martha and gave her the confidence to move forward in her education, with Martha then earning her associate degree in child-care administration.

Martha went on to graduate with honors from Arizona State University and eventually received her master's degree. She supervised the child-care center at the community college, worked at Central Arizona College, and later served as dean of teacher education. Martha continues to give back to the community of early childhood educators by being active in NAEYC and other professional boards. She presently serves as an advisor to many who are continuing their education, and she is in demand as an NAEYC presenter and motivational speaker. Recently, Martha has played an active role in the establishment of a national accrediting system for associate degree programs in child care and education.

Having just earned her doctorate in higher education administration, Martha discovered that having a mentor means to *become* a mentor to someone else. This is what Martha has done, providing a hand up to many others who are seeking to pursue careers in early childhood education.

Source: Adapted and used with permission from the Council for Professional Recognition. Retrieved on February 15, 2008, from http://www.cdacouncil.org/newsletter/ab_new_07_4.html.

Child Development Associate Credential. Martha Muñoz, whose story is told in Figure 1.6, started her career in early childhood education by earning a CDA. Child-care regulations in 49 of 50 states accept this credential. Anyone earning the CDA has demonstrated knowledge of child care through formal study and has 480 hours of experience working with children in child-care settings (Council for Professional Recognition, 2008) (Figure 1.6). The Head Start for School Readiness Act of 2007 (legislation proposed by Senators Kennedy, Enzi, Dodd, and Alexander) established goals for Head Start's workforce. This bill called for all assistant teachers in Head Start to have a CDA within 5 years, thus recognizing the value of this credential.

Some states require not only the CDA for child-care settings but also help students use that credential to advance in their careers. The state of California, for instance, accepts the CDA for coursework at different levels and toward some of the work for a formal degree.

- The California Child Development Permit is a six-level child development permit required for all early childhood teachers in the California system [Education Code, Title 5; State subsidized care].

- At the second level, 12 credits of Early Childhood Education courses are required for Associate Teachers. *The CDA is acceptable as an alternative qualification to the traditional coursework for this level.*
- Level 3, requiring 24 units of Early Childhood Education coursework, plus 16 units of experiential work is required to be qualified as a Teacher. *An existing CDA counts towards nine of the 24 units.*
- All California community colleges accept the CDA as nine credits towards an Associate of Arts or an Associate of Science degree (Fite, Spencer, Toomey, & Tran, 2003, p. 24).

Associate of Arts Degree. The Associate of Arts degree is earned at a community or junior college. Students seeking the AA degree in child development or early childhood take general education and early childhood education courses, including fieldwork with children and families. NAEYC standards for associate degree programs guiding preparation at this level are the same standards applied to 4-year programs. The Head Start for School Readiness Act of 2007 also recognized the role of an AA degree in strengthening the Head Start workforce. It proposed that all teachers in this program hold an associate's degree within 5 years.

Students earning an associate's degree have several good options. Many, for example, start to work with children and families immediately upon graduation. Others transfer to a 4-year institution, right away or after working for a time with children, to seek licensure as a teacher. This calls for a public policy that removes barriers when a student transfers credits in early childhood education from a 2- to a 4-year institution. Several states have indeed been working on this issue of *articulation* (Hyson, 2003). The state of Maryland's associate of arts degree in teaching is viewed as cost effective, and New Mexico's 2- and 4-year colleges have decided to base coursework on common competencies (Child Care Bureau, 2006). About 20% of teachers who eventually attain a teaching license started their careers by earning an associate's degree (NAEYC, 2006).

Licensure. Licensure is the granting of a license to practice a profession. Each state has the power to grant a teaching license for practicing the profession of early childhood education (as well as other areas in education). States grant a teaching license to persons who have met the state's requirements. Students very often meet their state's requirements in programs granting a bachelor's degree. NAEYC calls this the *initial licensure* level. Licensure involves official recognition that an early childhood education candidate meets several requirements. Anyone earning a teaching license for early childhood education may apply for teaching positions requiring an early childhood education license, such as in public schools.

Candidates for licensure demonstrate knowledge, skills, and dispositions required of *all* education majors as well as for early childhood education (Hyson, 2003; National Council on the Accreditation of Teacher Education, 2007). They must pass state-required teaching examinations, such as the Praxis™ tests. Bachelor degree programs in early childhood education or child development usually require these, or similar, teacher examinations during a student's program.

There are different Praxis tests. The Praxis *I*® Pre-Professional Skills Tests measure basic skills in mathematics, writing, and reading. The Praxis *II*® Tests measure subject matter and teaching skills in specific areas, such as early childhood.[1] Candidates in teacher

---

[1]Go to www.ets.org for information on the Praxis™ tests.

education programs are certified teachers when they complete their programs and when they meet all requirements for licensure.

The most important focus for all early childhood professionals is children and their development and learning. Focusing on children's total development keeps professionals centered on the *whole child*, a topic to which we now turn.

PRINCIPLES OF DEVELOPMENT

Principles of development Universal patterns in children's development that explain the orderly changes during a child's early years.

Effective teachers believe that *all* children are competent and that each phase reveals more sophisticated or new abilities. They realize that **principles of development,** the universal patterns that we see in children's development, explain the orderly changes during a child's early years. Thus, the focus in this part of the chapter is on the principles of child development, which help teachers see that child development is orderly and predictable (Ruffin, 2001).

Development Proceeds in Two Directions

First, children develop from the head downward, which is the cephalocaudal direction, which means from head to tail. This principle is especially evident in motor development. The portraits of development show that infants, for example, control their heads and shoulders before they can use their legs efficiently. They also develop from the midline or center of the body outward, the proximodistal direction, which means from near to far. Children, for example, gain control of their arms and hands well before acquiring control of their fingers.

This child gained control of her arms and hands before controlling her fingers.

Development Involves Predictable Sequences of Skill Building

Skills developed later are based on those acquired earlier. You will see this sequencing in the different domains as you read the upcoming portraits and the chapters on each domain. For example, older preschool, kindergarten, and primary grade children build skills in managing emotions based on skills in identifying emotions that they acquire during toddlerhood and the early preschool years.

Development Proceeds from Simple and Concrete to Complex and More Abstract

This principle is evident in every domain as shown in the portraits. For example, infants are just beginning to be able to use their bodies effectively and spend the first year developing very basic motor skills. At age 3, we see more complex motor skills develop and by age 8, a child uses motor skills and a stronger, bigger body to perform complex movements. Children's learning also shows this progression. They learn through sensory experiences where they experiment with concrete materials and later extend this learning to a pictorial representation and finally, a more complex, abstract form of learning

As another example, very young children describe people in concrete terms: "My mommy is pretty. She smells good!" Older children, with greater cognitive and linguistic skills and more life experience, are able to describe people in more psychological terms, such as "John is kind and helpful."

Children Have Individual Rates of Development

While there are sequences and patterns to development, there are also variations in each child's timing of development. For example, in physical development, there is a range of ages for motor skills, such as walking. Some children walk as early as 9 months and others walk independently at 15 months. All would be developing normally if they start to walk within a certain age range.

Development Depends on Learning and Maturation

The portraits of development describe the interaction between maturation or increasing maturity, and growth of the brain and body and learning throughout early childhood. Preschool children are capable, for example, of somewhat better self-control than when they were toddlers, and this depends partly on their brain's development, especially in the prefrontal cortex. However, children must also *learn* about self-control from parents and teachers.

The principles of development are evident in the following portraits of children's development.

THE WHOLE CHILD: PORTRAITS OF CHILD DEVELOPMENT

Teachers need an overall picture of children's development in the different phases of early childhood. They should be able to describe, for example, a preschooler's or a primary grade child's general developmental abilities. They can then use this knowledge in preparing a learning environment appropriate for a given phase. The learning experience will then be interesting, motivating, and appropriately challenging for the child.

We focus here on describing the whole child during the major phases of early childhood: infants and toddlers, preschool and kindergarten, and the primary grades. In addition, and even though it is technically beyond the early childhood years, information on development of 9 year olds, or fourth graders, is described here because some states include fourth grade in their early childhood or primary grades certification.

The portraits show what child development experts expect a child to attain during a specific period. Keep in mind, however, that individual children have different rates of development (American Academy of Pediatrics, 2007; Bredekamp & Copple, 1997; Centers for Disease Control and Prevention, 2005; James, 2005; PBS Parents, 2002).

Infants and Toddlers

Infants and toddlers are competent, curious, and active. They like to be with their favorite people and spend their time taking in the wonders of their world and building their knowledge.

One Year Old

The cephalocaudal or top-to-bottom principle is evident when we see that infants gain control of their body in the head region first and then gradually in shoulders, arms, and legs. For example, an infant gets to a sitting position without help, creeps on knees and hands, crawls on her tummy, gets from sitting to crawling, goes from sitting to lying on her tummy, pulls herself up to stand, walks holding on to things such as furniture, stands without support, and finally walks without support for a few steps.

We also see the proximodistal or near-to-far principle in the baby's progression from opening and shutting his hands, swinging arms at objects over the crib, and raking at items (instead of picking them up) in the first 3 months to somewhat better control of his arms and hands. An infant, by about 12 months of age, uses a pincer grasp, which is using his thumb and fingers to pick up objects. He also uses an index finger to poke at things, attempts to imitate scribbling, places objects in containers, and takes objects out of containers.

Infants are in the sensorimotor stage of cognitive development, meaning that they act on and understand the world through direct actions related to their senses. They feel and manipulate things, put things into their mouth, look at things, objects, and people alike. They communicate very well even though they have limited language skills. Their cries, cooing, and other vocalizations serve them well if their parents and caregivers are responsive and listen to the message.

Social development starts in infancy with the baby's attachment, the bond, or feeling of closeness with his primary caregiver. Some babies have a very secure attachment, but others do not. A securely attached infant has a much easier time with emotional development as he moves into toddlerhood. By about 2 months, an infant gets excited when another baby is nearby and he tries to engage the other infant in mutual gaze, that is, the two babies look at each other. At around 6 to 9 months, he smiles, vocalizes, and directs looks at others. Finally, between 9 and 12 months, he watches others even more and imitates a partner or points at things.

An infant has social skills, although most adults might not recognize them as such. His repertoire includes smiles and frowns and gestures, such as reaching out. He uses these skills by directing them at a potential play partner. He shows interest by watching another baby and he responds to a partner's behaviors. If another infant or an adult shows interest in playing with him, he will reach out to that person. Building relationships with others is extremely important to infant social development.

An infant is able to differentiate his father and mother's emotions. This should not be mistaken for understanding those emotions, however, because this would require cognitive skills that the infant does not have. Infants feel and express basic emotions. For example, between birth and 6 weeks, he can feel *contentment* and *distress*. Between 6 weeks and 14 months, he adds *anger*, *fear*, and *joy* to his list of basic emotions. However, infants cannot understand emotions. Consequently, they cannot control their emotions.

Emotional development is connected to other aspects of development. For example, the amygdala in the brain is almost fully formed in newborns and this is the part connected with warning about danger. However, the part of the brain used for thinking and regulating emotions is not yet fully developed; therefore, a young infant cannot think about or control his emotions.

Two Year Old

Toddlers seem to delight in practicing their improving motor skills. By about 24 months, a toddler's large motor skills include walking up and down stairs while holding on to a person or railing, climbing onto and off furniture without help, standing on tiptoe, kicking a ball, running, carrying large toys while walking, and pulling a toy while walking. They also enjoy newfound small muscle abilities such as scribbling, emptying containers, building towers of four or more blocks, and beginning to use one hand more often than the other.

The toddler continues to enjoy being with others, children and adults alike. His interactions, however, can now last longer and are more complex because he can move around much more easily and can now use words to communicate with others. He uses these abilities to try to engage a partner in activity if the partner shows signs of stopping.

Cognitive or thinking powers are changing, with toddlers able to represent their experiences in many ways. He can use words, for example, to tell about playing in snow. He can also remember something that he has seen in the past and imitate it, such as building a snowman. In fact, imitation is a major new skill. He can represent his experience through drawing and painting, although his representations differ from those of older children.

His new cognitive and linguistic skills allow him to engage in themes or simple games and a simple type of imitation, which is the foundation for later pretend play. He can now engage in the beginnings of turn-taking in which he observes and responds to another child and then observes a bit more and waits. He is now aware when somebody imitates him and he, for the first time, helps others and shares.

Toddlers continue to feel all the basic emotions but now add a new type—complex or self-conscious emotions. He can now feel anxiety, disgust, embarrassment, guilt, overconfidence, jealousy, pride, sadness, and shame. These emotions are only now possible because he has a developing sense of self and is conscious of his self for the first time. For example, he can feel shame if somebody does something to humiliate him.

Anybody who has worked with toddlers knows about how quickly their mood can change. One second a teacher observes a very happy toddler playing in the sand and a nanosecond later, she is observing a melt-down, a very upset 2 year old. They have no difficulty feeling and expressing the complex emotions at around 2 years. They are limited greatly, however, in the words that they can use to express feelings. For example, 50% to 83% of 18 month olds understand "happy" and "mad," but only 7% use the words.

What happens is this: They *feel* an emotion and they *express* the emotion, but they still do not understand emotions and cannot manage their feelings. During this time older infants and toddlers begin to notice how their specific culture tells people how they may express emotions. Some cultures, for instance, tell children that boys are not supposed to cry. A toddler growing up in that culture undoubtedly learns this rule for expressing feelings.

Preschool and Kindergarten (Ages 5–6)

Young preschoolers, 3 year olds, enjoy moving. Their developing brain and improving coordination now allow them to improve their large motor skills. They can now walk and run effortlessly. They climb very well and use this skill in climbing and descending stairs with one foot per stair step. A 3 year old can pedal a tricycle. He can also bend over easily without falling, demonstrating his improving balance. His increasingly good fine motor control allows him to do things like turn the pages of a book. His ability to hold a pencil also improves. He can now turn handles and use markers and crayons to draw lines and circles. His improved hand-eye coordination is evident in the ability to build a tower of six or more blocks.

Older preschoolers, 4 year olds, are more agile and enjoy activities in which they can use their new large and fine motor skills. They can now hop and stand on one foot for about 5 seconds, showing a developing sense of balance. They can climb and descend stairs with no support. A child can now catch a ball that is bounced to him most of the time and can throw a ball overhand. Fine motor skill improvement shows up in how well he uses scissors and eats with a spoon and fork. A big accomplishment for a child

Go to MyEducationLab and select the topic "Child Development." Under Activities and Applications, view the artifact *Basic Scribble (Preschool)* to observe the product of a fine motor activity.

is the ability to use the bathroom alone with only occasional help from adults. The child can also dress and undress.

Five year olds, usually in kindergarten, need opportunities in which they can use their rapidly increasing motor skills. Improved balance and coordination and even better small muscle development enable them to play new games and engage in even more creative activities. They can ride a bike with training wheels. Added to their running and walking skills is the new ability to change direction even more smoothly. Moreover, they can change the speed with which they move and they use drawing and writing instruments more effectively.

The changes in social interaction during preschool and kindergarten are remarkable and wonderful to observe. Children can now have longer, more frequent, and more complex interactions with other children. They engage in all forms of interaction: unoccupied, onlooking, solitary, parallel, and cooperative activities. Children continue to play next to other children throughout these years, and solitary, sensorimotor play decreases. However, constructive play in which a child works alone to build something increases. We see sociodramatic play now, which is a complex form of group interaction in which a child takes a role and interacts with other children taking roles.

Five year olds, however, are still not able to take another person's perspective and this plays a role in their social development. The tendency to focus primarily on their own perspective affects how they act when working and playing with other children. For example, a child might want to work in the dramatic play center with other children but still might have difficulty understanding that one of the other children might want to take the same role that he wants.

Children begin to rate themselves as athletic or nonathletic, based on how they view their skill in conventional sports or activities.

Positive interactions increase as children get older. Aggression does increase with age, but positive interactions predominate. Children with better language skills have an advantage when working and playing with others because they now direct more speech to other children. Older preschoolers are better skilled in making requests because they have had experience, someone has taught them, and they have better language skills.

The brain's prefrontal cortex shows growth and makes it possible for a preschool child to show more self-control—not as sophisticated as an older child, but the beginnings of an important part of development. The self-conscious emotions continue to develop with a major change evident. A preschool child now begins to use more of the emotion words that he understands but not all. One important change is that he gets better at decoding the emotions in another person's face. He can identify happy facial expressions accurately. In addition, some 5 to 6 year olds realize that people can have more than one emotion at a time. This ability, like so many in children's development, improves as children get older.

Primary Grades (Ages 6–9)

We begin to see that a 6- to 8-year-old child's level of physical activity affects motor skills. More active children develop better motor skills than children who are less active because they have more opportunities to play games, try new sports, and practice basic skills such as catching and throwing. At the beginning of the primary grades, first graders or 6 year olds are still excited about movement and work enthusiastically at new games and activities. Their balance improves even more, and they are still gaining skill in kicking, throwing, and catching. They enjoy art projects, which calls on their ever-developing fine motor skills. By 8 years, children begin to rate themselves as athletic or nonathletic. They base their evaluation on their perceived skill and success in motor skills and conventional sports or activities such as soccer, dance classes, or baseball.

Nine year olds are at the beginning of middle childhood and begin to gain body strength, hand dexterity, better reaction time, and coordination. All of this allows them to compete in sports if they are interested and if opportunities are present. Fine motor skills get even better, with handwriting improving and children now able to build models, for example, and to complete art projects.

Many 6 to 9 year olds are in a new stage of cognitive development without the limitations of thinking in 3 to 5 year olds. They now understand that things can remain the same in spite of surface changes, their memory improves tremendously, and their perceptual skills improve. The prefrontal cortex continues to develop, now allowing them even better self-control. Their language skills, including vocabulary, continue to improve. They become readers and writers and can use these skills to show what they know and can do. For example, not only can a child write but he can use writing to tell a story or to record data about a science experiment.

Social interactions take on a new tone with generosity, helpfulness, and cooperation increasing. This makes it possible for children to work with classmates on projects, other cooperative learning activities, and games or sports. Children's aggression also takes on a new form with a change from physical to verbal aggression now possible. Hostile, person-oriented aggression is also possible now. Children enjoy playing games and especially enjoy games with rules.

We see great changes in how children deal with emotions as they get older. They get better at regulating emotions, especially if someone has helped them learn how to do this. For example, they can now purposely make a facial expression that differs from how they really feel. This means that they can now conceal their real feelings when they need to do so. They can now decide how long an emotion will last, that "I don't want to keep feeling upset," for example. They are also much better at managing how strong their emotions are: again, if someone has helped them with this. A child might be jealous of another child, for instance, but can now think, "OK, he won the spelling bee but I spelled a lot of words right, too."

A 6 to 9 year old moves slowly and steadily toward better emotional regulation. He uses more of the emotion words that he understands. For example, over 60% of 6 year olds understand *embarrassed* and *jealous* and over 50% actually use the words. He gets better at decoding emotions in another person's face, which gives him information about how others are feeling. He can identify typically happy expressions most accurately.

He also continues to use his culture's guidelines for how to express emotions. He also gets better at understanding what another person needs but still cannot feel what the other person feels. This is perspective taking, an ability that will develop only with advances in his cognitive development much later in childhood. He can change a reaction to a stirred up emotion, such as acting very calm when he is really feeling irritated. He can also amplify feelings if he needs to get someone's attention. For example, he might moan and groan at breakfast, pretending to be sick, if he wants to get his father's attention. All of this makes it possible for the child to begin to regulate emotions but still not as well as he will when he is older.

Nine year olds begin to see parents, teachers, coaches, or any adult with authority as people for the first time. They can now pick out faults that adults might have and some children are willing to point out such weaknesses or quirks. This is unnerving for some adults who are not accustomed to children thinking this way. Children now tend to use made-up languages, secret codes, rules, and rituals with other children, and we notice that they really enjoy being members of clubs or teams.

To summarize, these portraits describe children in development for the first 9 years of life. They reveal the increasing complexity and predictability of development.

SUMMARY

Early childhood education is a proud profession focused on teaching children and working with families. Members of the early childhood education profession master a specific knowledge base reflecting five core standards.

1. They understand child development and learning and then know how to use their knowledge to prepare environments that help children develop and learn.
2. They know how to build family and community relationships.
3. They learn how to observe and assess child development and progress and use assessment to support children and families.
4. They learn how to design and carry out experiences that will enhance all children's learning.
5. They understand what it means to be a professional and to value ethics in decision making.

The profession of early childhood education also has a Code of Ethical Conduct, which serves as a guide to teachers in their work with children, colleagues, parents, other professionals, and the community. The profession has professional organizations, which represent the interest and needs of teachers. It also has a system of licensure and certification.

A teacher's knowledge about child development is based on an understanding of the principles of development.

- Development proceeds in two directions, from the top of the body to the bottom, the cephalocaudal direction, and from the midline of the body to the outer parts of the body, the proximodistal direction.
- Development involves predictable sequences of skills. Later, more sophisticated skills depend on the development of basic skills.
- Development proceeds from simple and concrete to complex and more abstract.

- Children have individual rates of development. Even though sequences in all areas of development are predictable, children progress through the sequences at their own rate.
- Development depends on maturation and learning. For example, all children are capable of kindness and compassion, but they need to have the cognitive and emotional skills underlying these characteristics. They also need adults to help them learn how to be compassionate.

Early childhood education teachers focus on helping children develop and learn. They focus on the whole child, always keeping in mind the many ways in which children develop—cognitive and language, physical and motor, social and emotional, and aesthetic.

- They realize that a child develops in all of these domains, not one at a time, but all together.
- They understand that each domain affects all the others and is influenced by the others.
- They acknowledge children's need for active learning and involvement from infancy through the primary grades.
- They acknowledge a child's need for warm, positive relationships in every phase of early childhood.
- They understand that they have a crucial role in children's development and learning. For example, they know that children learn to manage emotions responsibly because of developing cognitive and linguistic skills. They also understand that healthy management of emotions comes about because parents and teachers help them learn this skill.

QUESTIONS FOR REFLECTION

1. Teachers often tell young children "Use your words instead of hitting" when the child has hit another child. How might this guidance strategy help the child grow in the emotional and social domains of development?

2. Suppose that a child does not *know* the words to use. How might the teacher help her learn the words?

APPLY YOUR KNOWLEDGE

What Should This Teacher Do?

Dealing with an ethical dilemma: You observe one of the other teachers changing diapers and *not* washing her hands afterward. What should you do?

1. Consult the NAEYC Code of Ethical Conduct in the Appendix. Identify the sections that apply to your ethical responsibilities to your *colleague* in this case.

2. Identify the sections applying to your ethical responsibility to *children* in this case.

3. After finding the appropriate sections, say how you might meet your most important ethical responsibility, which is to children, *while you also* meet your responsibility to your colleague.

KEY TERMS

Advocacy, 17
Certification, 17
Code of ethics, 12
Content areas, 9
Core standards, 5
Credential, 19
Culture, 8
Dispositions, 10

Domains of child development, 7
Early childhood, 6
Early childhood education, 4
Ethics, 12
Ethical dilemmas, 13
Ethical responsibilities, 13
Evidence-based practices, 11
Informed consent, 12

Licensure, 17
Principles of development, 22
Profession, 4
Professional organization, 15
Reflection, 11
Research, 11
Theory, 11

WEB SITES

Advocacy for Children
http://www.stand.org
Home page for the Stand for Children organization. The group works on advocacy issues affecting children.

Association for Childhood Education International
http://www.acei.org
This professional organization focuses on development and education of children from birth through early adolescence.

Childcare and Early Research Connections
http://www.researchconnections.org/servlet/
DiscoverResourceController?displayPage=
understanding.jsp
Main page for the Child Care and Early Education Research Connections. Contains links to a variety of issues dealing with research.

Child Development Associate (CDA)
http://www.cdacouncil.org/cda_what.htm
Information about the Child Development Associate credential.

Council on Exceptional Children (CEC)
http://www.cec.sped.org
CEC's main page; good information on children with special needs.

National Association for the Education of Young Children
http://www.naeyc.org
Main page for the National Association for the Education of Young Children. Many links to standards, using research, and information about child development and teaching.

Questions and Answers about Teacher Licensure
http://www.alleducationschools.com/faqs/certification
.php
Common questions, with answers, about teacher licensure. You can follow the links provided to get to your state's rules on teacher licensing for early childhood educators.

Technical Assistance Center on Social Emotional Intervention on Young Children
http://www.challengingbehavior.org/index.htm
One of the best resources for information on challenging behavior, with many resources.

CHAPTER 2

Foundations and Programs

GUIDING QUESTIONS:

- What are the historical forces that have shaped the field of early childhood education in America in the 20th century?

- Why is research a good foundation for early childhood educational practices?

- What do the major influential theorists in early childhood education believe about how young children learn?

- What are some of the current program models in early childhood education?

KINDERGARTEN
"Does a Circle Have Corners?"

It was September and Mr. Hernandez worked with a small group of kindergarten children. He showed a square pillow and the children counted the sides. Then, they made a big square with chalk, having to recall first how many sides in a square and then where to place each line for the square. Then they walked along all the sides, counting as they went. They also counted the corners.

Next, they tackled the circle. Before walking around the circle, however, Mr. Hernandez picked up a cylinder block, turned in so that the children could see the end, the circular shape, and encouraged each child to run a finger around the edge. This time he said, "H-m-m, how many sides does the circle have?" "Only one because it just keeps on going around,"

replied Lily. "OK . . . now tell me if this circle has corners." Robert took the cylinder, nodded a yes, pointed to the circle, and started to count, "One, two, three . . . ."

The next day, Mr. Hernandez worked with the same group. This time, when they walked the square, they made hard stops at each corner: walk along a side, stop, turn, walk along the next side, stop, turn . . . until all came to the end of the shape. For the circle, Mr. Hernandez stood at the center of the circle and held onto a string. He handed the other end of the string to a child who slowly walked along the circle with the teacher slowly turning at the center. Then, he asked if the child had made any stops and turns as they had done on the square.*

This teacher has actively involved the 5 year olds in thinking about mathematics. He was surprised by Robert's assertion that a circle had corners and realized that he needed to help him understand exactly what a circle was and the nature of a corner—it required a hard stop and a turn. He decided to help them build their mathematical understanding

*Linda Proudfiet, Governors State University, contributed to this example.

through activity and conversation and not all in one sitting but gradually over time. As you will see in this chapter, Mr. Hernandez based his teaching strategies on theories of and research in early childhood education.

In this chapter, we examine three foundational elements of early childhood education: history, research, and theory. Our field has a long and rich history, and we will look at past decisions about providing care and education for young children. Research provides us with evidence upon which to base our practices. Theories of early childhood education are backed up by observations, facts, and research and explain the facts or data and organize knowledge about children and how they learn. We will examine the thinking of major theorists affecting early childhood education. Finally, we will highlight current program models. We will look at how each views a child's development and learning and how beliefs are translated into classroom practices. We also examine research related to each approach. You will quickly see that all the programs have some striking similarities.

HISTORICAL FOUNDATIONS OF EARLY CHILDHOOD EDUCATION IN AMERICA

Our profession has a long and proud history. What can 21st century educators learn from those of the 20th century that will help us to provide developmentally appropriate settings? Many factors affect children's development, including schools, other children, and families. Other factors, such as the values that the society holds about children, set the tone for a society.

As educators, we can certainly learn from our profession's progress by getting a global view of the factors that drove programming for young children in the recent past. For example, what was the effect of the Great Depression of the 1930s on the economy? How did this affect families and children, and what was the government's response to this crisis? How did the Great Depression affect early childhood education? Looking at forces influencing our field in the past yields clues about potential effects of events on early childhood education in the present.

An example of macrosystems or forces affecting or setting the tone for early childhood education in the last century is the values of our culture such as the desire to reduce poverty. Additional forces include social trends such as mothers entering the workforce or the acceptance of research as a way of finding out about children and significant events such as a war.

The Child Study Movement: Early 20th Century

Child Study Movement
Late 19th and early 20th centuries, a time devoted to the scientific study of children and their development.

The **Child Study Movement** arose in the last part of the 19th century and the early part of the 20th century because society began to see that children were different from adults and because of interest in how children develop. Researchers such as G. Stanley Hall of Clark University (Brooks-Gunn & Johnson, 2006) and Arnold Gesell of Yale University studied and documented children's growth patterns and development.

This era of scientific child study spurred the development of laboratory schools, like the Bank Street school described later in this chapter, for studying child development and educational methods for young children. Lab nursery schools opened in universities and colleges such as Vassar College, Ohio State University, Cornell, and many others during the 1920s and 1930s. They continued the research tradition, applied scientific findings to programs for young children, and very often served as training sites for future early childhood teachers. Many of the laboratory schools still exist.

All of this coincided with the nursery school and kindergarten movements in general in the United States. The major early influence in kindergarten education was Friedrich Froebel from Germany who started the first kindergarten. Patty Smith Hill, for example, at Teachers College, Columbia University, advanced knowledge about kindergarten education in the United States. Hill based her work on John Dewey's theory (explained later in this chapter) and emphasized activity and creativity in children's learning (Swanson, 2007).

The Child Study Movement's emphasis on research with young children continues. For example, the Bing Nursery School at Stanford University opened in 1966 as a model preschool program and research laboratory for the Psychology Department (Lepper, 2002). One of the most famous studies in child development and psychology was undertaken at Bing, Albert Bandura's groundbreaking *Bobo doll experiments*, through which he demonstrated that children learn aggression by observing it (Bandura, Ross, & Ross, 1961, 1963).

In summary, the force driving the Child Study Movement was the desire to gather scientific knowledge about children's development and learning. Educators started early childhood education schools to provide a place for researchers to carry out their work as well as to provide a place for teacher education students to gain practical experience in working with children.

The Great Depression of the 1930s

The stock market crash in 1929 was a catastrophic economic event, which led to the Great Depression of the 1930s. After the crash, banks failed and people with money in those banks lost it all. People lost their homes. Manufacturing plummeted. Unemployment soared in this worst economic disaster in our history with up to 15 million or one-third of nonfarm workers out of work (Eleanor Roosevelt Papers, 2003).

President Franklin D. Roosevelt, the 33rd president of the United States, was elected on his promise of a *New Deal* for the American people. This was legislation and a domestic program aimed at neutralizing the effects of the depression. One of the president's many programs was the effort to give millions of unemployed adults jobs such as maintaining roads, planting trees, constructing buildings, painting murals, mending library books, or working in child care. This program was operated by the Works Progress Administration (WPA, later the Works Projects Administration) and was federally funded (National Archives, no date).

One WPA program was the *Nursery Project,* intended to employ persons as preschool and nursery school teachers. This was primarily an employment project, not one to do research on what children needed. Training of the adults employed as teachers was not rigorous, and the preschools were closed when the WPA was eliminated.

World War II

During the Second World War (1939–1945), there was a great sense of having to work together for the war effort. Women entered the workforce to perform jobs that, up until the war, had been off-limits to them. These jobs included essential war work such as building warships. Of course, the families of these women needed child care and the government, realizing the need for women's labor in industry, provided the funding to build and staff nursery schools. Once again, early childhood schools were publicly funded, not primarily out of concern for children's education and development or for research but because women were needed as workers for the war effort.

The Kaiser shipyards in Vanport City, Oregon, operated two nursery schools, with Mr. Kaiser writing the costs of running the centers into the contracts that he had with the federal government. The public paid, therefore, for the cost of the schools. Lois Meek Stolz and James Hymes, early childhood educators, advised the shipyard owner about the school and directed the centers. The schools, located at the entrance to the shipyards, served 1125 children whose mothers worked on one of three around-the-clock shifts. Therefore, during this wartime emergency, we had a model of publicly funded, center-based, early childhood education to support working mothers (Tuttle, 2004).

Values of Our Culture: Great Society Programs

When elected, presidents usually have an agenda they wish to accomplish. President Lyndon B. Johnson, 39th president of the United States, named his plan the *Great Society*, one goal of which was to attack some of the root causes of poverty (The White House, no date). One of the many significant parts of the **war on poverty**, as the anti-poverty program was known, was the creation of a preschool program, Project Head Start, for children of the poor (Project Head Start, 2000).

Head Start, an 8-week summer program in 1965, still exists. It has served over 25 million children in its 45-year history. Head Start now has an array of programs designed to serve children, including infants and toddlers, and families. However, it is not fully funded to serve all eligible children. It has always included parents in programming and administration, which is one of its strengths. Head Start awards grants to local agencies to offer preschool programs focusing on development of the whole child so that she build's the strengths and skills that will help her be successful right now as well as in school (Office of Head Start, 2008). It provides comprehensive services, including education, nutrition, and health care to low-income families and children. See the Head Start web site listed at the end of the chapter for information on the different parts of this program as it now exists.

Here again we have a federally funded early childhood program, but the reasons for starting it were based on very different ideas than those during the Great Depression or during World War II. The reasons reflected fundamentally and profoundly different values about society's role in children's healthy development. President Johnson was concerned about children who lived in poverty. His primary motivation was to help children, not merely to take care of children so that mothers could work, and not simply to provide jobs.

Research, as we will now see, has an important role in early childhood education.

RESEARCH FOUNDATIONS OF EARLY CHILDHOOD EDUCATION

Best practices in working with children and families build on a solid foundation. The base of research should reflect relevant theory, be scientifically conducted and objective, and give enough information so that the study can be replicated to verify results (NAEYC, no date). Early childhood education practices draw strength from research in a number of different disciplines, including the natural sciences, psychology, child development, and early childhood education.

Research in the sciences, such as neuroanatomy, provides scientific knowledge on which teachers can base their work with children. For example, researchers studying brain activity in young children and in adults when the subjects were using working memory found that the same region of the brain was activated in both children and

War on poverty Anti-poverty program in the administration of President Lyndon Johnson; Head Start was a part of this program.

Go to MyEducationLab and select the topic "Curriculum/Program Models." Under Activities and Applications, watch the video *Head Start* to see an overview of this model.

adults, demonstrating that 5- to 6-year-old children's brains allow them to use their working memory (Tsujimoto, Yamamoto, Kawaguchi, Koizumi, & Sawaguchi, 2004). A teacher could use this information in choosing learning activities that call for her kindergarten children to use working memory, as Mr. Hernandez did with his first graders.

> The class sat before the large sheet of paper. Mr. Hernandez asked the children to think about the fire drill from the day before and then to list the things that they have to do during a fire drill.

Research in child development and psychology has yielded an enormous amount of information on a variety of topics, including aggression. We know that some children come from families in which children become aggressive. Parents in an aggression-teaching family are often, but not always, insensitive to and nonsupportive of their children, a style of caregiving that sets the stage for increased aggression (Dubow, Heusmann, & Boxer, 2003).

Early childhood researchers have recognized for decades the need for well-designed research. For example, in the 1970s, researchers were concerned that Head Start might intervene in children's development a bit too late. The Abecedarian Project, therefore, examined the effects of working with children from birth through age 5 on the children's cognitive and social development. Each child was prescribed a set of educational activities and was monitored to the age of 21. Results showed, for example, that children who participated in the early intervention program had higher cognitive test scores from the toddler years to age 21 and that their academic achievement in both reading and math was higher from the primary grades through young adulthood (The Carolina Abecedarian Project, 1974, 2008).

In addition to research on specific program models, explained later in this chapter, research in different aspects of early childhood education can help teachers make evidence-based decisions about many issues. Suppose, for example, that you are a preschool teacher and you want the children in your class to adjust well to kindergarten. You could get some good information from research done on this topic. Researchers found that many preschool teachers use *transition practices* such as discussing the curriculum or specific children with a kindergarten teacher. Kindergarten teachers judged children as having greater social competence and fewer behavior problems if the child's preschool teacher had used transition practices (LoCasale-Crouch, Mashburn, Downer, & Pianta, 2008).

The early childhood commitment to the idea of the whole child has grown and continues to grow from research in the various domains of child development. The chapters on emotional, social, physical, and cognitive development will give you a good picture of some of the research done in each domain. Such research has helped us form an accurate picture of the whole child (see Chapter 1).

We move, now, to the theoretical foundations of early childhood education, how influential theorists have explained how young children develop and learn.

THEORETICAL FOUNDATIONS OF EARLY CHILDHOOD EDUCATION

Effective early childhood teachers rely on **theory** to make decisions about guiding children, curriculum, teaching strategies, and working with families. This theoretical foundation is based on observations, facts, and research directly related to child development as well as to how families function. For example, the theory presented here explains its belief that children learn through activity.

Theory *Not* a hunch or a guess; an explanation about something in the natural world, substantiated by observations, facts, and research.

Dewey's ideas about active learning and creating a community of learners have influenced early childhood education.

John Dewey

John Dewey (1859–1952) was born in Vermont and attended school and college there. After graduating from college, he taught school for 2 years and then, after earning his doctoral degree, started his long career as a philosopher, educational thinker, and social commentator. Dewey was committed to democracy and the development of thinking that would help it flourish. His influence on education and educational reform has been far-reaching and profound. He formulated many ideas in the field of early childhood education.

Primary Interests of the Child

Dewey explained that children have four primary interests. They have a great desire to investigate and discover things with inquiry: How does water get to the faucet? or How does a bird stay in the air? Children also are inclined to communicate. They have conversations, ask questions, and tell teachers what they think and what they have done. Third, children find great joy in making and constructing things. Children, for example, work industriously at the workbench or during a project when they might construct a cardboard model of a truck that they have observed. Finally, they enjoy expressing themselves through visual arts, music, dance, and poetry.

Education Begins with the Curiosity of the Learner

Education begins with a child's questions and awe about the world. This curiosity is the telltale sign of a child's intellectual power and ever-increasing knowledge base. This inquisitiveness can tell a teacher much about a child's level of development, and carefully observing children's interests gives teachers clues about the strategies that will enhance development and learning. This is an idea from Dewey's Pedagogical Creed (Dewey, 1897).

> For example, a teacher observes as a child walks the perimeter of a large square and then as she walks around a large circle drawn on a sidewalk. "Look!" she said about the circle, "What happened to the corners?"

An observant teacher would notice this child's question and figure out a strategy to further help her understand a geometric concept. The teacher would help her reflect on the nature of the circle. Helping children become reflective thinkers enhances their skill as problem solvers. Reflection helps us connect what we know and what we still have to learn (Dewey, 1933).

Curriculum Based on Children's Interests and Involvement

Dewey's philosophical perspective known as pragmatism put forth the idea that knowledge develops as humans adapt actively to their environment (Dewey, 1902). The human mind, in this view, does not act like a sponge, passively absorbing information. Instead, a person confronts a problem or issue and then actively works to solve the problem. Humans dynamically seek and construct knowledge. Early childhood educators can use this idea in constructing a curriculum and in choosing teaching strategies.

From Dewey, we have learned that children should see curriculum as engaging and relevant, something in which they are interested (Dewey, 1913). Children's natural enthusiasm for learning calls for a curriculum worthy of children's time, and they should be actively involved in appropriate challenging and meaningful experiences (Dewey,

1902). Suppose, for example, that a teacher observes the children in her class run to the fence to observe the garbage truck dump the contents of large trash containers into the truck. Are the children interested in this event? Yes. Would this be a good starting point for learning? Again, yes, if you follow Dewey's advice.

The children's interest in this commonplace event is actually a good base for investigating things such as how machines work (science) or finding out about people's jobs (social studies). This example shows how a teacher can *integrate* the curriculum by combining areas such as science and social studies. Teachers should not teach science, math, social studies, and language arts as isolated subjects. Instead, children learn most effectively by working with other children and investigating real events in social situations where they communicate freely.

Many teachers currently use projects, in-depth examinations of topics in which children are interested, as one way to organize a part of the curriculum (Katz & Chard, 2000; Project Approach web site listed at end of chapter). This practice, based on Dewey's theory, clearly builds on children's interests. In the garbage truck project, the teacher would find out what children already knew about trash collection. She would also probe for what they do not know by eliciting their questions about the process. From such a web of questions, the teacher would develop learning experiences through which the children could answer their questions.

Create a Classroom Community

Dewey envisioned schools as a place in which children would develop the critical thinking skills and attitudes for life in a democratic system (Dewey, 1938; Hlebowitsh, 2006). Classrooms in which democratic values flourish call for respectful treatment of every member of the class. Everyone is included in decision making. Communication is open, direct, and courteous. Teachers help children learn about resolving problems by acknowledging the issues and then using effective problem-solving strategies. Children begin to see that they are important as individuals and that their individual actions affect other individuals, and the whole class. They learn that they are linked to others.

CHECK YOUR UNDERSTANDING
Would John Dewey agree with this?

True or False: John Dewey would agree with the current practice in many public school kindergartens of having children sit at tables and work on workbook pages for a good part of every day. Explain your choice by referring to the section that you just read about Dewey.

Jean Piaget

Jean Piaget (1896–1980) was born and educated in Switzerland. He studied the natural sciences and published many papers in this area before concentrating on how children think. **Constructivism** was Piaget's perspective on how children's knowledge develops, how they build or construct knowledge. Piaget believed in stages of development, specifically that children's thinking is qualitatively different at each of four stages (Figure 2.1) (Piaget, 1983). Some of Piaget's most basic ideas influencing

Constructivism/Constructivist The perspective that children build their own knowledge.

FIGURE 2.1   Piaget's Stages of Cognitive Development

Sensorimotor Stage (from Birth to About 2 Years)

- Babies center on their own bodies for the first 7 to 9 months.
- They gain information about the world mainly through motor activity and coordinating movements as well as through the senses.
- The ability to use *symbols* emerges at the end of this stage.

Preoperational Stage (from 2 Years to About 7 Years)

- Children can now use symbols to represent their experience and mental images: words, paintings, drawings, movements, deferred imitation (observing some action and imitating it later).
- They do not think as logically as they will in later stages.
- They are captured by how something *appears* and ignore other relevant information. For example, the same amount of water is poured into two glasses, one short and wide and the other tall and thin. The child will say that the tall, thin glass has more water because it appears that way to him. He cannot seem to take into account the idea that he watched you pour the same amount of water into each glass. This is called conservation.
- They cannot reverse things. They would not think about just pouring the water from our two different glasses into the original identical containers.

Concrete Operations Stage (from About 7 Years to About 11 Years)

- Children are no longer captured by the appearance in the conservation experiment.
- They can now reverse operations. They would say, "All you have to do is to pour that water from the tall glass and the short glass back into the first glasses. Then, you'd see that it's the same."
- They now think more logically but are limited to thinking about concrete objects.

Formal Operations Stage (from About 11 Years Through the Rest of One's Life)

- The child or adolescent can now apply logic to abstract ideas.
- They can now think through problems more efficiently.
- They can think about many possible reasons for an existing problem and many ways to solve problems.

early childhood education deal with how children learn and with stages of cognitive development.

Piaget used his own three children as subjects, observing them closely to see how they actively engaged in their own development. His clinical method was instrumental in obtaining important information as he asked questions and then refined teaching strategies to address children's mode of thinking.

Children Need to Interact with Objects and People

Piaget did *not* believe that children were blank slates. Instead, he theorized that children were very curious and actively involved in their learning by working with objects and discovering their properties. For example, they find out that blocks stacked too high topple, Ping-Pong balls float, and rocks sink. They build or construct their own knowledge. Thus, children actively participate in their own development; they are not passive in the process (Piaget, 1952).

Children interact with people as well as with objects. Here, too, they discover that other people have viewpoints, perspectives, different from their own. For example, when voting on a name for the class pet, Jason discovered that the name he favored did not get the most votes. Other children did not share his view.

Assimilation and Accommodation Help Children Adapt to Their Environment

Piaget described processes involved when children construct knowledge—**assimilation** and **accommodation**. They take in or assimilate new information from their activity into existing cognitive structures or schemes. For example, a preschooler who has frequently tossed balls through a hole in a target might identify quickly a small beanbag as something he can also toss into the target's opening. He has assimilated the beanbag into his this-is-something-that-I-can-toss-through-the-target scheme.

Often, children observe or hear something that does not fit easily into anything that they already understand; it does not fit well into any concept or scheme that they already have (McDevitt & Ormrod, 2004). A preschooler, for example, was puzzled when he observed archery practice on television. The arrow was something that he could not toss through *his* target. His father explained that arrows were not toys and could be dangerous. This child was confronted with a brand new idea, something that did not fit his existing scheme or idea. He had to change his idea of things that he may aim at a target. He has accommodated to this new information and has formed a scheme of a type of target practice with potentially dangerous items.

These two processes, the taking in or assimilation and changing or accommodation move children toward greater understanding of ideas, things, and people in their world. They continue to do this throughout their lives, taking in information, fitting it to an existing idea, or creating a new scheme in which to fit the new idea.

When children face a problem, question, or new information their cognitive balance is upset. This is not necessarily a bad thing because the imbalance encourages them to do something to restore balance, a process known as equilibrium. Their sense of **equilibrium**, or balance, rights itself after they assimilate information and have accommodated to it.

Jerome Bruner

Jerome Bruner is an American psychologist with deep and abiding interests in many areas of development and learning. His work in cognitive psychology with interests in memory and problem solving led him to examine children's cognitive development. He was especially intrigued by how children represented thought or showed what they were thinking. He, like others, believed in a constructivist approach in which children build knowledge through mental activity and acting on the environment. Born in 1915, Bruner remains on the faculty of New York University.

Bruner's work, like the writings of other theorists illustrated in this chapter, has had a lasting impact on our thinking about how young children learn. Early childhood educators using the developmental approach base their work on ideas from Bruner's theory.

Assimilation Piagetian concept referring to the taking in of new information.

Accommodation Piagetian term referring to how children fit new information to an old idea or develop a whole new concept into which the new information can fit.

Equilibrium The sense of cognitive balance that a child feels after he or she assimilates information and has accommodated it.

Knowing Is a Process

Knowing something is not a product; instead, it is a process (Bruner, 1977). Moreover, it is an active process. Take mathematics as an example. Bruner studied how children come to understand mathematics in an instructional setting but did not merely focus on right and wrong answers to math problems. Instead, he zeroed in on the processes through which children learn mathematics (Ginsburg, Klein, & Starkey, 1998). Bruner believed that teachers should not teach math so that children merely memorize rules about math but so that children learn to think like a mathematician. The process of getting knowledge is important—not the product (Bruner, 1966).

The Process of Learning Is Like a Spiral

Children are capable of using what they already know to build even greater understanding. They might have a question about an original idea, make guesses, look for new information, make decisions, and revise the original idea. Revising ideas is a lively, dynamic process. Children's idea building does not lurch from one place to another in a disconnected way but spirals gracefully, connecting new ideas to original, supporting ideas for more and more sophisticated understanding. Children do not lose old ideas but instead incorporate them into the spiral of understanding and increasing complexity.

Bruner described different ways of representing knowledge. The *enactive* mode is based on actions such as spatial awareness or manipulating objects. The *iconic* represents ideas visually with images such as drawings or photos. The *symbolic* mode represents knowledge in a more abstract way, for example, with words or mathematical symbols.

Teachers Help Children Learn

Bruner believes that teachers and children should talk about what children are learning, with the teacher helping children think about an idea, as the teacher did in the chapter opener vignette, "He asked if the child had made any stops and turns as they had done on the square." Teachers need to know when to assist children and when to stand back as children begin to understand an idea or to demonstrate a skill (Wood, Bruner, & Ross, 1976). A teacher, therefore, should provide help to children when they need help. Both Bruner's and Piaget's ideas have been used by current researchers, such as Kamii (Chapter 6).

Lev Vygotsky

Lev Vygotsky, a Russian psychologist, was born in 1896, the same year in which Piaget was born. Vygotsky graduated from Moscow University in 1917, just as the Russian Revolution started, and died at the age of 37. Early childhood educators have used the major ideas in Vygotsky's theory to develop curriculum and instructional practice (Berk & Winsler, 1995). These ideas include the role of play and social interaction in cognitive development and children's learning and the role of language in children's development and learning.

Social Interaction Is Important in Children's Learning

Vygotsky stressed the important role of social interaction in children's learning. Learning, he believed, occurred first between people and later within a person (Vygotsky, 1978). Children's learning takes place, in this theory, because the give-and-take between a more knowledgeable other (MKO) and a child makes learning possible. Teachers, for example, act as an MKO from the larger culture. The person with more knowledge would ask questions and provide other assistance to help children learn. Vygotsky believed that children's learning is better when they work with other people, either other children or adults.

FIGURE 2.2 Zone of Proximal Development (ZPD)

This end of the ZPD is what Tim can learn or accomplish with his teacher's help. He can learn how to express his emotions more responsibly.

This is Tim's current ability, what he understands about managing emotions on his own, without adult help.

Learning Occurs in the Zone of Proximal Development

Suppose you are worried about a child who often strikes out at others when he gets angry and you want to help him learn to manage his emotions more responsibly. If you use Vygotsky's framework, then you would have to know about his idea of the **zone of proximal development (ZPD)**, where learning and development take place (Figure 2.2).

At one end of the ZPD is a child's current ability, what he understands about some topic and what he can do on his own without adult help. Teachers usually try to figure out what a child already knows about a problem. What does this child know about managing emotions? Does he use words to express anger? Does he generate or use the word *angry*, *mad*, or *furious* on his own? Can he identify facial expressions of anger, sadness, and other emotions? Does he even know that he can use words instead of his fists to express emotion?

Now, suppose that you have discovered that the child can look at an *angry* face and label it as *mad* but that he does not spontaneously use the word when he feels angry. You have discovered his current ability, what he can do on his own. You also know what he cannot do: He cannot use words to express anger. That leads you to the other end of the ZPD—what the child can learn or accomplish with the help of a more knowledgeable other from the culture (Bodrova & Leong, 1996).

Teachers Scaffold Children's Learning in the Zone of Proximal Development

Scaffolding is a strategy that adults use to help a child learn something. Scaffolding is a teacher's changing support as a child constructs new knowledge or skills. Children are the main construction workers, constructing or building their own knowledge, skills and competencies, and ideas about kindness, morality, and gender. A child, therefore, is like a building under construction. Buildings under construction usually have a series of scaffolds, platforms that support construction workers. Adults help children in their construction by serving as guides, by scaffolding or supporting the child's learning and investigations.

Zone of proximal development (ZPD) Space where learning takes place; the difference between what a child can do *unassisted* and what the child can do with help from a more knowledgeable other.

Scaffolding Strategy in which an adult supports a child's learning; implies changing levels of support as the child gains knowledge or skills.

Teachers usually give more help when a task is new or a child is having difficulty. They should listen, ask questions, offer suggestions, and model a skill when children are building knowledge or skills. Teachers can ask children to engage in problem solving or ask questions that prompt children to come up with solutions. They can give children examples of strategies or model a skill. As a child gains skill in constructing knowledge, the adult can gradually step back, providing progressively less help.

For our child working on learning better emotional regulation, you can model using words and then coach him in practice sessions. With your help, for example, he can learn to say, "I'm mad that you took my place!" rather than pushing the child who jumped ahead of him. This is something that he is not likely to have learned on his own, but he would learn it interacting with you.

Play Has a Role in Children's Development and Learning

Vygotsky (1933) believed that play is important and beneficial in children's development. Children learn self-control when they have to pay attention to rules in any play episode, such as having to wait their turn while playing with others. Children can also gratify their own wishes or needs when they play. For example, the desire to drive a racing car is not an option for a young child in real life but she can certainly pretend to drive a racing car while playing (Bedrova & Leong, 1996). Therefore, play provides a scaffold or source of support for children as they learn about the world.

Talking Is Important in Children's Learning

Good scaffolding relies heavily on dialogues or conversations between adults and children. A teacher, the MKO, uses language when conveying information, asking questions, or giving suggestions. The talking, that is, using language, conveys meaning to children and helps them build on their existing ideas. The talk is at first on the outside, external, between two people. Gradually, a child internalizes the words and then uses private, self-directed, inner speech in working out problems.

TEACH INTENTIONALLY

How to Walk Quietly

What the teacher did: Mr. Hernandez talked with his first graders about walking to the lunchroom. "I'd like you to think of an idea that would help you to remember to walk really quietly past all the other rooms when we go to the lunchroom." Children offered ideas: ". . . tiptoe? Put a finger on your mouth? Say, s-h-h, before we start out?" The class chose one idea to try.

How the teacher was intentional: Mr. Hernadez used Vygotsky's theory. He supported the children in learning how to solve a problem. He first identified a problem and then deliberately supported children in coming up with a solution. He did not provide the solution. The children did, which is a part of good problem solving. He scaffolded their understanding by asking questions.

Erik Erikson

Erik Erikson (1902–1994), born in Germany, attained citizenship after moving to the United States in 1933. In his career as a professor and a therapist, he developed a theory of psychological development describing human psychological growth from birth through death, which is a life-span perspective. Erikson proposed eight stages of psychological development, each presenting humans with a psychosocial crisis. The person's interactions with the social environment affect whether he resolves the challenge of each stage in a positive or negative way.

Parents and teachers influence young children's resolution of the childhood challenges by using their knowledge about child development. For example, a toddler has new motor and language abilities and wants to establish himself as an independent person. We can *use* this information when working with toddlers by encouraging their independence within limits. Erikson's theory guides our relationship building with children at all of their different stages. Forming good relationships with young children is one of an early childhood professional's main responsibilities and the base for all of our developmentally appropriate practices. His theory is also helpful as we strive to develop good relationships with parents and other professionals, each of whom is going through one of Erikson's stages.

In the following list, each of Erikson's stages is briefly described. The first word indicates a positive resolution of the crisis and the second word indicates a less healthy, negative resolution.

1. *Trust* versus *Mistrust*: Infancy, birth to 18 months. Children develop the positive trait of trust when their needs are met consistently.
2. *Autonomy* versus *Shame* or *Doubt*: Toddlers, 18 months to 3 years. Here the positive trait of autonomy develops when adults encourage toddlers to do things by and for themselves when such independence is possible and safe.
3. *Initiative* versus *Guilt*: Preschool and kindergarten, 3 to 5 years. The positive trait of initiative develops more easily when adults encourage children's burgeoning desire to explore and make sense of their world. Recall that Dewey also views children as active, curious information seekers, as do most of the other early childhood theorists.
4. *Industry* versus *Inferiority*: Primary grades and part of elementary school, 6 to 12 years. Here, a child operates quite often in systems, such as school and clubs, beyond his family. He can develop the positive trait of industry if those systems support his new abilities to learn and take on challenges of which he is now capable.
5. *Identity* versus *Role Confusion*: Adolescence. This is a time of rapid development in all domains and a time when an adolescent must deal with the world outside his family on his own. This is a time of coming to grips with the many demands from one's adolescent peer group and a time in which the young person can develop a stable identity.
6. *Intimacy* versus *Isolation*: Young adulthood.
7. *Generativity* versus *Stagnation* or *Self-Absorption*: Middle adulthood.
8. *Integrity* versus *Despair*: Late adulthood.

In the the last three stages we establish lasting relationships and the trait of intimacy when we engage in meaningful and fulfilling work and creative endeavors and develop the positive trait of generativity. During the last stage, we can develop the wisdom that comes from a productive, well-lived life and we can develop a sense that our contributions have made a difference in the world. We face death with a sense of integrity.

Psychosocial crises In Erikson's theory, the challenges that humans face at each of the eight stages of psychological development.

Howard Gardner

Multiple intelligences
Theory that humans possess a *set* of intelligences and not just one form of intelligence; eight different intelligences have been proposed.

Gardner, a professor at the Harvard Graduate School of Education, proposed his views on **multiple intelligences** (MI) in the early 1980s (Gardner, 1983). He believed that humans did not just possess one form of intelligence but that they have many different forms of intelligence. He said that all humans possess the entire set of intelligences and that each person's tends to see and operate in the world better when using his own predominant grouping of the intelligences (Gardner, 1983). He originally proposed seven different intelligences but has added an eighth.

1. *Linguistic Intelligence*: While every child possesses this, some have a higher level ability to use language for a variety of purposes—to learn, remember things, communicate, and create things such as poetry. A child with high linguistic intelligence might easily produce a poem, give a speech, or tell a story
2. *Logical-Mathematical Intelligence*: This is the type of intelligence linked with mathematical thinking. It involves the abilities to see patterns, to reason well, and to think logically. Children with high logical-mathematical intelligence would probably enjoy solving mysteries and math problems and would be able to detect patterns well.
3. *Musical Intelligence*: This is the ability to perform, compose, or appreciate patterns in music. Children with high musical intelligence would gravitate to many musical activities and would easily learn and find pleasure in singing and listening or even writing music.
4. *Bodily-Kinesthetic Intelligence*: Involves using the body and its parts to tackle problems. A child high in this intelligence might prefer to demonstrate that he can make a V, not with a marker but by lifting his arms in a V. To measure how long the play tunnel on the playground is, he might lie inside it, mark the spot, and move forward, continuing to measure with his body.
5. *Spatial Intelligence*: Involves thinking in pictures, being aware of space and one's body in space. Children high in this intelligence do puzzles and mazes well. They would probably enjoy drawing and activities like map reading or drawing simple maps.
6. *Interpersonal Intelligence*: This involves very good ability to understand what other people intend, want, and need. A child with high interpersonal intelligence plays and works well with other children.
7. *Intrapersonal Intelligence*: Involves understanding and knowing oneself. A child high in this intelligence would understand, for instance, that she really likes chess but is afraid of competing publically. She knows her strengths but also understands her fears.
8. *Naturalist Intelligence*: Involves the ability to recognize and categorize elements of the natural world and the environment created by humans. A child high in this intelligence would be interested in how things are put in groups. For example, he chooses a poster for his room that shows how dogs are categorized by breeds. He might be very good at summer camp in classifying different types of leaves and trees.

Educators have found the theory of multiple intelligences helpful in meeting children's different learning needs (Campbell, 2007). That is, they *use* the theory and integrate it into classrooms and the school to help children learn effectively. When they are deciding, for example, how best to help children detect and use patterns, they might decide that some children would benefit from painting patterns, others from singing or producing patterns with a musical instrument, and others by using a computer to produce patterns.

The theories that we have examined help us to understand children and how they learn. Other theories can help us understand how a child's family functions and how other systems affect children's development.

Urie Bronfenbrenner

Urie Bronfenbrenner (1915–2005) was born in Moscow and came to the United States as a young child. He was a professor of Human Development and Family Studies (*Guide to Urie Bronfenbrenner Papers*, 2004) at Cornell in New York for most of his career. His theories help us understand how many levels of systems affect children's development. One of Bronfenbrenner's many gifts was his ability to articulate and use his ideas to spur the development of beneficial policies and programs. For example, he was a cofounder of Head Start in the mid-1960s. (See page 34 for a description of Head Start.)

Bronfenbrenner urged us to consider that children's families, home, school, and society wrap around them to affect development. He recognized how economic, political, sociological, and family systems, work together, to influence children's development not only during childhood, but throughout an entire lifespan (Bronfenbrenner, 1994). Until he did this, researchers had studied the systems separately. Bronfenbrenner then described and explained the **ecology of human development**, the idea that children exist in several environments nested within each other (Figure 2.3).

Ecology of human development Human development explained as affected by several different nested systems.

At the center of development is a child who is nested within a series of systems, each progressively broader. The *microsystem* includes the child, a child's family and extended family, school, peer group, child-care center, and neighborhood. Relationships between family members and the quality of a child's school as well as resources within a neighborhood all work together to affect development. Roberto's parents, for example, both work full time. Microsystem members grandmother and Aunt Celia take care of him while his parents are at work.

The *mesosystem* is the connected network formed by the microsystems. Good relationships between two systems can enhance development. For example, good family-school partnerships result in higher reading and math scores for children and in higher state achievement test scores (Henderson & Mapp, 2002).

The *exosystem* consists of groups not having much direct contact with the child but that, nevertheless, affect his development. These might include a parent's workplace, recreational facilities such as health clubs or parks, and organizations such as social services. In Roberto's neighborhood, for example, families have access to parks with picnic facilities, walking trails, and boat rentals. His family frequently uses the park system, which contributes to Roberto's appreciation of the outdoors and to his love of exercise.

The exosystem nests within a larger *macrosystem*. The macrosystem includes elements such as the values of a culture, type of government, social trends, and significant events, a war, for instance, the effects of which reverberate through every other system, ultimately affecting, indirectly, the child at the center. Macrosystems are like guiding documents for a society in that they embody the opportunities and dangers to which children are exposed. For example, one society views children's health as an important macrosystem cultural value. Governmental policies reflect this in legislation funding children's preventive health programs. Communities use money from federal and state grants to provide children with preventive health care.

The *chronosystem* refers to the degree of change or consistency of various systems over time. These changes affect a person's developmental path. The society that values

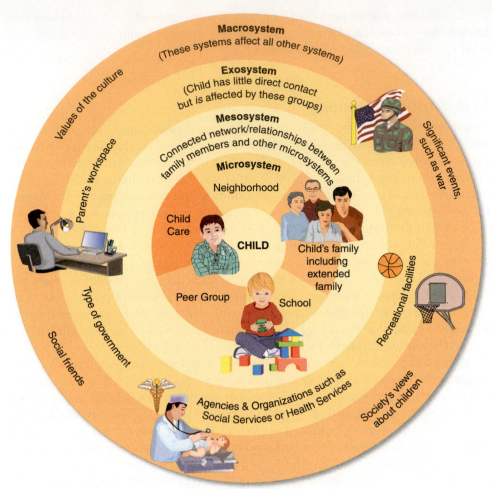

FIGURE 2.3 Children exist in several *systems*, nested within each other. All of these systems affect a child's development. Systems closest to the child, such as family, schools, and the child's neighborhood, have a more direct effect. Systems on the outer rings have a somewhat more indirect effect. For example, the society's views about children affect laws that are enacted, which, in turn, affect the child.

parks and recreation for its citizens might have to cut back on services if the economy goes into recession.

Family Systems Theory

Effective teachers develop partnerships with families. One good way to start is to build our understanding of families in addition to our understanding of children and their development. To do this, we step into a theory different from the developmental theories of Bruner and Piaget and others to understand **family systems theory**, which focuses on family rather than individual behavior or communication patterns. Family systems theory helps professionals understand that families have developed a set way of interacting and communicating with one another, and that they repeat the patterns in different circumstances.

Family systems theory explains that a family is a group of interconnected people, each affected by and affecting others in the group in very predictable ways. Children develop

Family systems theory
Focuses on family behavior and family communication patterns.

patterns of behaving within their families and bring those patterns to their classroom. Understanding how a family system operates and affects children helps teachers work more effectively with children from all families. Family systems have many characteristics, some of which are relevant to early childhood education teachers, including boundaries, roles, and rules (Christian, 2006).

Boundaries refer to a family's ideas about togetherness and separateness. Some families favor independence and a sense of each individual's autonomy, but others favor a greater sense of togetherness and what might appear to be greater control over each member of the system. Teachers see the concept of boundaries in action when, for example, one entire family participates in a family night while only a father from another family attends. Effective teachers do not make judgments about which family is better. They use the concept of boundaries to understand how each family makes decisions.

Roles refer to the responsibilities or jobs taken on by different members of families. Family systems theory explains that family members take different roles, for example, peacemaker, helper, scapegoat (taking blame for things), and savior. Families tend to assign a role to children, and children with a specific part to play in a family bring that role to school, playing it out in the classrooms. A teacher needs to be aware that children's behavior often reflects a role that they have in their family system. For example, you might find that one child is a peacemaker, acting as a go-between in any conflict. While this is an admirable trait, children need also to experience other roles.

Rules are standards or traditions telling family members how to interact with each other and with others outside the family. For example, one family rule might be that children address all adults in a formal fashion by using titles such as Mr., Mrs., Aunt, or Uncle before saying the person's name. Another family rule, very different, allows children to call any adult by the first name. Rules pervade family life and are often embedded in a family's culture such as whether boys may hold dolls, whether girls may play sports, how children dress, or whether boys and girls have different types of work. Teachers who observe carefully will see family rules in action as a boy, for example, refuses to wash the table when it is his job because, "Boys don't wash up! Only girls do that."

Creators of current program models in early childhood education have relied on the historical and research foundations of the field. The theories explaining how children develop and learn, including their learning of family, roles, rules, and boundaries, are evident in current influential program models in early childhood education, which we now examine.

PROGRAM MODELS IN EARLY CHILDHOOD EDUCATION

There are many ways to organize schools and learning experiences for young children. Here, we examine five current approaches to early childhood education exemplifying appropriate practices for young children: Bank Street, High/Scope, Montessori, Reggio Emilia, and Responsive Classroom. While they might look different in name, location, or even some specifics of daily classroom life, there are distinctive threads of similarity running through all five model programs are premised on the need for:

- an active approach to learning,
- children collaborating with others,
- children working with real objects, and
- children talking with adults skilled in mediating learning.

Bank Street: Developmental Interactive

The Bank Street School for Children is a part of the Bank Street College of Education and is located in New York City. Currently, the School for Children serves over 400 children ages 3 through 13. The Infant and Parent Center in the College, like the School for Children, focuses on research and teacher education.

The Bank Street School for Children, whose goal is to improve education for all children, grew from the effort of a group of researchers starting in 1916. Two years later, the researchers decided to open a nursery school so that they could study how children think and learn. During the 1930s, the school added elementary grades to the school and opened a teacher education college, the Bank Street College of Education. In the 1960s, the Bank Street College of Education took part in the creation of Head Start and it continued to do research such as a study of the psychological impact of two different types of schools on the development of young children (Minuchin, Biber, Shapiro, & Zimiles, 1969).

How This Model Views Children's Development and Learning

Bank Street identifies with the *developmental-interaction approach*. A central concept in this approach is attention to each child's individual development. This model emphasizes fostering growth in all domains of development, physical, emotional, social, and intellectual. It is based on the idea that domains of development are intertwined, developing together (Biber, 1973; updated 2005).

They also emphasize the type of environment that would foster a child's development (Nager & Shapiro, 2000). For example, children learn most effectively, according to this model, through activity and interacting with the people and things in their environment, including children's families and community locales. For example, Mr. Hernandez's class visited a flower shop where one of the fathers works as a flower arranger. Children interpret their experiences and can then extract understanding and knowledge from their experiences. From the flower shop investigation, they would likely learn about the role of specific workers in their community.

How This Model Puts Its Beliefs into Practice

All classrooms at Bank Street, regardless of the age of the children, encourage active learning, creativity, and social interaction. Children interact with things, other children, and teachers in small group learning centers as well as in large groups. Concrete experiences take center stage, with cooking, block building, painting and other art experiences, dramatic play, woodworking, working with manipulatives, reading, music, physical activities, and field trips, the child's major vehicle for learning and making meaning of experiences (Bank Street, no date).

The Bank Street model focuses on play as a young child's main source for learning and development. The curriculum at Bank Street incorporates all content areas, such as science, mathematics, music, and physical activity but always presents content in an integrated, developmentally appropriate way for young children, with play and active exploration, not textbooks or workbook pages, the chosen approach.

Research Relating to This Model

Preprimary programs can have long-term effects on children's cognitive and emotional development. The programs can be especially helpful to children in economically challenged families. However, benefits from preprimary education are greatest when programs, such as Bank Street, are high in quality and focus on both intellectual and emotional/social development (Barnett, 2002). Empirical research supports the Bank

Street type of model, with its emphasis on play and children trying to extract meaning from experiences, and a child-centered approach combined with an active role for the teacher in developing curriculum (Golbeck, 2002).

High/Scope: Active Participatory Approach

The High/Scope Educational Research Foundation, founded in 1970, is a nonprofit organization located in Ypsilanti, Michigan. The Foundation trains teachers for preschool, kindergarten, primary, and upper elementary school grades in workshops and seminars of varying lengths and formats. It also publishes books and materials for teachers, develops curriculum, operates conferences, and conducts research and outreach to schools (Epstein, 2003).

How This Model Views Children's Development and Learning

High/Scope identifies with the *active participatory learning* approach and Piaget's constructivist theory. A central belief in this approach is **active learning**, in which children participate actively with materials, other children, and their teachers (Epstein, 2003, 2007). Another key belief is that children should become independent and secure learners, able to make wise choices. A third belief is that children should gain knowledge and skills in accepted content areas, such as mathematics and science. A fourth High/Scope belief is that children need to learn how to plan and reflect on their learning (Epstein, 2003).

How This Model Puts Its Beliefs into Practice

High/Scope classrooms encourage active learning through their room arrangement, the daily schedule, and materials provided. Teachers arrange classrooms into learning centers, which helps children to see all centers and to move with ease to any center. Materials are appropriate for the age of the child using them and are stored easily so that children may retrieve and return materials independently.

High/Scope calls its classroom schedules the *daily routine.* The daily routine includes several specific segments: the *plan, do, and review time,* large group time, small group activities, outdoor, transition, and eating and resting times. This schedule, and the room's arrangement, was developed intentionally to encourage children to make choices and to learn through play and activity. The *plan, do, and review time,* for instance, gives children time to plan on what they will do during the morning. Then, they have a 45 to 60 minute period to *do* what they planned, followed by a review period (Epstein, 2003).

Teachers are active partners with children in the teaching and learning process at High/Scope. They are educated in child development, observe children carefully, and identify children's gifts and areas for growth. Teachers provide materials upon which children act. There are several interaction strategies in the High/Scope model (High/Scope web site, no date).

- Adults offer children comfort and contact. Adults are a calming and comforting presence in the classroom, offering support and nurturing contact.
- Adults participate in children's play. They do not dominate a child's play but follow a child's lead. Adults might offer suggestions but, even here, stay in the child's theme.
- Adults converse as partners with children. Again, they take the child's lead, speaking in a natural, give-and-take fashion. They do ask questions, but the queries are respectful and related to the child's ongoing activity.
- Adults encourage problem solving. They encourage children to solve their own problems with adult support when needed.

Go to MyEducationLab and select the topic "Curriculum/Program Models." Under Activities and Applications, watch the video *High/Scope* to see how one classroom uses this model.

Active learning Children participate dynamically with other children, objects, and adults.

High/Scope classrooms, like other programs based on developmentally appropriate practices, are set up intentionally to encourage children to make choices and to learn through play and activity.

Parents, as their child's first teacher, are also an important part of the High/Scope approach. Parents participate in the assessment part of the program. This involves learning how to use the program's major assessment instrument, described next, and to plan learning activities for their child (Fox, 2004).

Teachers assess 2 ½- to 6-year-old children in this model with the *Preschool Child Observation Record* (Preschool COR). This assessment instrument is a checklist and enables teachers to look at 32 dimensions of learning in six different categories related to school success:

- Initiative
- Social relations
- Creative representation
- Movement and music
- Language and literacy
- Mathematics and science

The assessment is done as a part of the ongoing activities of a classroom and yields information on each child's development but does not assess or screen for disabilities (High/Scope, 2003).

Research Relating to This Model

High/Scope has an extensive record of research on its curriculum and model. The Perry Preschool Study has now been in place since the 1960s when the children in the study were in preschool. The latest part of the study is called the *Perry Preschool Study through Age 40*, making this a longitudinal study in which the same children have been followed into early middle age (Schweinhart, Montie, Xiang, Barnett, Belfield, & Nores, 2005; Schweinhart, 2006). A group of 123 3- and 4-year-old children thought to be at risk for poor performance in school was included in the study. Children were randomly assigned to either a high-quality preschool (High/Scope) or to no preschool. Information was gathered yearly until the children were 11, and then again, when they were 14, 15, 19, 27, and 40.

The results of this study, which produced many monographs over the years of the study, demonstrated that the high-quality program was effective in several ways. When they became adults, children who had attended the preschool program were much more likely to hold a job, earn more money, were more likely to have graduated from high school, and had committed far fewer crimes. The group who had attended the high-quality preschool performed better on language and intellectual tests during early childhood. They also did better on achievement tests from ages 9 to 14 and on literacy tests at ages 19 and 27.

Go to MyEducationLab and select the topic "Curriculum/ Program Models." Under Activities and Applications, watch the video *Montessori* for a look at this model in action.

Montessori

The Montessori model started in Rome, Italy, under the leadership of Dr. Maria Montessori (1857–1952). Born and educated in Italy, she was the first woman to practice medicine in that country. A scientist and keen observer of young children, she became interested in how children develop and learn and she started her work as an early childhood educator. She opened her first school in 1907 in one of the poorest sections of Rome, Italy. Montessori programs today serve early childhood and elementary school age children throughout the world. There are a few Montessori high schools.

How This Model Views Children's Development and Learning

Montessori believed that children have an innate passion for learning and they have a tendency to want to work. She believed that children need to progress at their own rate and pace in learning. A fundamental principle of this method is the inborn ability to grow within oneself, and the method is frequently summarized as *auto education*. She also focused on the child's ability to develop self-discipline, to concentrate, and to function independently (*New York Times*, 1913).

Prepared environments
Montessori settings designed to help children develop to their fullest; filled with specifically prepared Montessori materials.

How This Model Translates Its Beliefs into Practice

Montessori classrooms are **prepared environments**, which are designed to help children develop to their fullest. Prepared environments are orderly, beautiful, and accessible to children. There is a balance of freedom with limits, with children able to choose their own learning activities from those set up by the teacher and work in large, uninterrupted blocks of time. Children are in mixed-age groups, for example, from 3 to 6 or from 6 to 9 years.

Children work with prepared materials through which they learn specific concepts. Dr. Montessori and her son developed a large array of Montessori materials. Materials are displayed attractively and, ideally, are kept scrupulously clean and in good repair. Montessori believed that children pass through *sensitive periods* or phases when they show interest in a particular concept and when they would benefit from working with materials related to the concept. Therefore, Montessori thought that children should use the materials when they are most receptive and when they are most likely to benefit from using a specific item.

This child is working with one example of Montessori materials.

Research Relating to This Model

A recent study found that children at a public inner-city school with a Montessori emphasis do better in several measures than children in a more typical school setting (Lillard & Else-Quest, 2006). For example, at the end of kindergarten, the Montessori children had better self-control, did better on standardized math and reading tests, got along better with other children, and understood social interactions better.

Reggio Emilia: Social Constructivism

During World War II in the 1940s, Italy had been controlled by a dictatorship. When the war ended, parents in the city of Reggio Emilia in northern Italy turned their attention to educating the young children of the region. They built schools that would help children develop the critical thinking skills needed to resist oppression and to be productive members of a democratic society (Gandini, 1997; New, 2000).

By 1963, this undertaking had resulted in the Municipal Infant-Toddler Centers and Preschools of Reggio Emilia, and a leader of this movement was Loris Malaguzzi (Gandini, 1994). Reggio leaders do not consider that their schools are a program model but that they are a philosophical approach. Preschools for children 3 to 6 years old opened first, and infant-toddler centers for children 3 months to 3 years opened later. This philosophy of early childhood education has been extraordinarily influential in Europe as well as in North America (North American Reggio Emilia Alliance, 2008) and other parts of the world (New, 2000).

How This Model Views Children's Development and Learning

The Reggio Emilia schools identify with the *social-constructivist approach* and one of their main beliefs is about the image of the child. Your image of a child has a big impact on how you make decisions about and how you relate to him or her (Donovan, 1997). Throughout history, different civilizations and societies have had differing views of children, some seeing children as powerless and incapable (Rinaldi, 1996) much like blank pages or empty containers waiting for ideas and knowledge to be poured in or written on them (Locke, 1690; abridged version 1994) by a teacher, a video game, or a worksheet. People with this picture of children would not think it important to listen to children to get an idea of their interests or questions. Instead, they might plan a curriculum for the entire year, even before they ever met their class.

Reggio beliefs about children are very different. In their eyes, *all* children are competent and capable (Solit, 2002). They believe that children are rich with potential and innate ability as investigators and researchers, capable, knowledgeable, powerful, and ready to learn from birth. They learn most effectively in a *social* setting with children and adults and by *building* ideas through collaboration and working with objects in the environments (Gandini, 1994, 1997; Rinaldi, 2006)—hence, the social-constructivist approach.

How This Model Puts Its Beliefs into Practice

Reggio schools reflect their belief in strong and competent children in several notable ways: through the environment, the commitment to collaboration, the **hundred languages of children**, the use of projects, and documentation, including using documentation in partnerships with parents.

When I take new teacher education students on a tour of our campus's Reggio-inspired preschool, I enjoy watching their reactions: wide eyes, slow head turning to take it all in, open-mouthed expression of wonder, and, after a while, questions flying. The students are surprised by the beauty of the school and classrooms.

Hundred languages of children Reggio term referring to the many ways in which children can represent experiences such as painting, building with blocks, and music.

A Reggio classroom is an amiable, friendly, welcoming space (Gandini, 1997) promoting interactions and relationships. Teachers put much thought into preparing the environment and about the effect that a space has on people. They create a beautiful, aesthetically pleasing, and peaceful setting. There are *no* cartoon-like creatures or commercially produced items anywhere. Many classrooms in North American schools are filled with such items (Tarr, 2001, 2004). Reggio schools are filled with natural light, pleasing and restful colors and furnishings, carefully arranged displays, and an abundance of items from the natural world.

Reggio schools have an *atelier* (pronounced ah-tall-YEY), an art studio, and classrooms have mini-ateliers with abundant art supplies, beautifully displayed. The Reggio approach values creativity, and it uses art as a major medium for representing what children are thinking about a project (Herzog, 2001).

Reggio environments are also personal in that they contain children's own work—paintings, drawings, and writings tell the tale of children industriously and creatively constructing knowledge. A Reggio classroom, therefore, is a teacher as it invites children to investigate, ask questions, work with objects, and to collaborate with other children and teachers and then provides them with the materials for their investigations.

Collaboration is central to the Reggio approach (Saltz, 1997). Every member of the system collaborates—teachers with teachers, teachers with children, teachers with parents, and parents with children. A belief in teamwork, relationships, and a cooperative spirit is obvious. Children work with teachers, for example, in small and large groups as well as individually and learn together and as teachers listen for indications of children's interests.

Children, capable of using symbols, can express their knowledge and observations in many different ways; thus, in the Reggio philosophy, they have a *hundred languages*. They use words, certainly, but they also, for example, draw, paint, dance, work with computers, build with blocks, and play music (Edwards, Gandini, & Forman, 1998). The Reggio schools in Italy developed a display, the Hundred Languages of Children, which has toured and has been replicated and which portrays children's many ways of representing their experience. The Reggio educators believe that children should have the chance to communicate all of their strength and potential through a variety of media (Reggio Children, 2008).

Projects, or long-term studies, a major part of Reggio children's learning experiences, acknowledge that children learn through activity. Projects evolve from children's interests or from teachers as they listen to children. Projects are not determined ahead of time (Gandini, 1997; Tarini, 1997). Time given to any project varies, but what never varies is the collaborative spirit as children and teachers talk, investigate, express understanding, very likely reinvestigate, and then express enhanced understanding.

Project An in-depth examination of topics in which children are interested.

Documentation is a process in which teachers observe, collect, organize, and interpret children's individual or group work (Stremmel, 2008). Teachers collaborate and reflect on the best ways to document children's investigations. Documentation can take many forms and often includes photographs, children's drawings or other productions, visual recordings, and interviews with children as they work. The Reggio approach has refocused the early childhood education profession on documenting children's search for knowledge. Reggio documentary displays, like the classrooms, are arranged beautifully and thoughtfully.

Documentation Process in which teacher observes, collects, organizes, and interprets children's individual or group work.

Schools can use documentation in their partnership with parents. Specifically, documentation can help teachers explain developmentally appropriate approaches

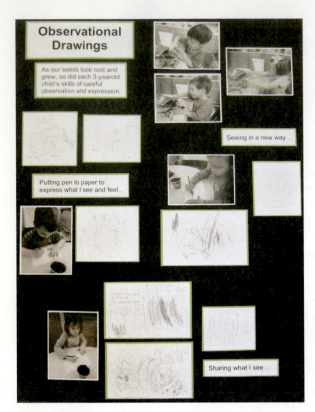

Documenting children's work with seeds.

to learning for young children (Gandini, 2008) as we see with Mrs. Chang, a preschool teacher.

> Mrs. Chang observed her class for several days and recorded examples of literacy in action: the class listening to a story, individual children reading books, children filling in the classroom pet's feeding chart, children dictating stories, children in the writing center, and children with clipboards recording observations of different plants in the yard. She created a display of the photographs along with children's comments about their activity, and printed a caption, "Literacy throughout the day."

She created a documentary display and used it when she and parents collaborated about literacy development. It seemed to help parents understand that literacy and language arts involved a variety of processes.

Research Relating to This Model

Reggio uses research methods that allow teachers to reflect on their practices and to improve the program for children (Edwards, 2002; Rinaldi, 2008). For example, documentation allows teachers to reflect on each child's understanding and to work with children in developing the next steps in the curriculum. Children's portfolios with samples of their work help parents understand their child's development and progress. Teachers in the infant and toddler rooms use memory books for the same purpose. Memory books trace a very young child's development while she is in the center.

Harvard University's Project Zero group has collaborated with the Reggio schools on a project called *Making Learning Visible*. This research focuses on helping professionals understand how documentation supports the power of individual and group learning for children (Project Zero and Reggio Children, 2001).

Responsive Classroom

The Northeast Foundation for Children in Turner Falls, Massachusetts, established the Responsive Classroom model of early education in 1981. This model evolved from a small demonstration school to working with teachers throughout the country. The foundation develops materials and books to support teachers in learning about and putting the Responsive Classroom model into action in their schools and classrooms. Teachers must be trained in this model through workshops and seminars. The foundation recommends that the whole school adopt this model so that there is consistency throughout the school. This model focuses on children and teachers in K to 8 classrooms.

How This Model Views Children's Development and Learning

This model's major belief is in the importance of social development in children, that social development is as important as intellectual or cognitive attainment typically espoused by schools. It advocates social interaction in the learning process and believes that children need a set of social skills such as self-control, responsibility, and cooperation for success in school. The Responsive Classroom model also focuses on teachers

Go to MyEducationLab and select the topic "Curriculum/Program Models." Under Activities and Applications, watch the video *Reggio Emilia* to observe a classroom using this approach.

knowing the developmental and cultural characteristics of the children in their classrooms (Wood, 2007). Finally, this model believes that teachers must understand the characteristics of the families with whom they interact and that we must treat parents and families as partners in the education of children.

How This Model Puts Its Beliefs into Practice

Teachers using the Responsive Classroom model learn about and use several classroom strategies that put their beliefs into practice (Figure 2.4). For example, the teachers use basic elements of developmentally appropriate child guidance strategies such as collaborative problem solving, positive teacher language, rule creation (Brady, Forton, Porter, & Wood, 2003), modeling, and logical consequences. Teachers organize classrooms so that children work with peers collaboratively and cooperatively and so that they make many choices (Clayton & Forton, 2001).

The Morning Meeting is one of the best known of the model's strategies. Each morning, children participate in a four-part morning meeting: the greeting, sharing, news, and an activity. The meeting is a time for children to learn social skills as well as mathematics or music in an active, low-key, low-stress setting in which all children are included (Kriete, 2002). This strategy puts the belief about social interaction into action. In the primary grades, children participate in academic choice in which teachers help children choose how they will learn content such as mathematics and social studies within choices structured by the teacher for their work time (Denton, 2005).

Morning meeting Teaching strategy; four parts, focusing on learning in a social setting.

Academic choice Teaching strategy from the Responsive Classroom model; teachers help children choose how they will learn content.

Research Relating to This Model

The Social and Academic Learning Study evaluated the effectiveness of the Responsive Classroom model (Rimm-Kaufman, 2006). This study examined the effect of the approach in six schools from 2001 to 2004. Teachers in three of the schools learned about and enacted teaching strategies from the Responsive Classroom model. Teachers at the other three schools did not receive training in this model and continued to teach as they had always taught.

Results of the research showed that the Responsive Classroom model is effective in fostering children's learning and in helping educators teach effectively. These results include

- Finding 1: Children in RC classrooms showed greater increases in reading and math scores. The gains were most pronounced in the third year of the program.
- Finding 2: Teachers in RC classrooms felt more positive about teaching.
- Finding 3: Children in RC classrooms had better prosocial skills, felt less fearful, and felt closer to teachers.
- Finding 4: Teachers in RC classrooms offered more high-quality instruction.
- Finding 5: Children in RC classrooms felt more positive about school, teachers, and peers.
- Finding 6: Teachers in RC classrooms placed a higher value on collaboration.

CHECK YOUR UNDERSTANDING
Active Learning in Early Childhood Program Models

Choose two programs described in this section. Explain how each puts its beliefs in an active approach to children's learning into practice.

Our field's history, research, and theory have helped us construct developmentally appropriate programs for young children. The field continues to meet the changing needs of families and children with programs such as preschool for all children in many states. What we do does matter, and President Lyndon B. Johnson seemed to understand this about early childhood education as evident in the brief excerpt (on the dedication page of this book) from his speech in the White House Rose Garden announcing Head Start's creation on May 18, 1965. He believed, as we still believe, in the benefits of educating young children and reducing poverty.

SUMMARY

Early childhood education's historical foundations can help teachers of the current era understand their origins. Theories can help us figure out how current events will affect our profession. Some of the main events and movements of the 20th century that affected the profession include

- The *child study movement* of the late 19th and early 20th centuries. This was a time of intense interest and research in child development. Educators of the time opened schools based on scientific knowledge of children. This era laid the foundation of knowledge upon which we now rely.
- The *Great Depression* of the 1930s. The Depression caused massive unemployment and hardship. It moved the federal government to fund schools for young children. The purpose was to provide employment to people. The concern was less focused on the needs of young children.
- *World War II*, which saw a similar phenomenon with federally funded child-care centers set up to serve the needs of women newly employed in war industries such as ship building. This was a good example of how the country could provide early childhood education to support working women and families.
- The *Great Society* program, which was on the agenda of President Lyndon B. Johnson in the early 1960s. There were several programs aimed at attacking the root causes of poverty and one of these was the Head Start program. Head Start still exists and has served over 45 million children in its 46-year history. It provides comprehensive services, including education, nutrition, and health services to low-income children and families. President Johnson's primary motivation for Head Start was the well-being of children.

Best practices in working with children and families build on a solid research foundation. Good research reflects relevant theory, is scientifically conducted, is objective, and can be replicated. Early childhood's foundation of research comes from areas such as the natural sciences, psychology, child development, and early childhood education.

Effective teachers rely on knowledge from theory in decision making about curriculum and teaching strategies. A theory is an explanation about something in the natural world supported by observations, facts, and research. A theory explains facts and organizes knowledge, for example, about learning through activity. Theories of John Dewey, Jean Piaget, Jerome Bruner, Lev Vygotsky, Erik Erikson, Howard Gardner, Urie Bronfenbrenner, and Family Systems have helped teachers build a solid foundation for their teaching. These theories

- explain the importance of activity in children's development and learning.
- explain how important it is for children to interact with other children and teachers in the learning process.
- show us that knowing is a process and not a product.
- explain the teacher's role in scaffolding children's learning and understanding.
- describe the psychological crisis faced by children at each phase in their development and explain the role of adults in helping children resolve the crisis in a positive way.
- explain the many ways in which children learn, their multiple intelligences.
- describe and explain the systems in which children exist and develop.
- explain how a family system operates and how it affects children's development. This helps teachers work more effectively with children from all families.

There are many ways to organize schools and learning experiences for young children. We have examined five current approaches to early childhood education exemplifying appropriate practices: Bank Street, High Scope, Montessori, Reggio Emilia, and Responsive Classroom. While they might look different in name, location, or even some specifics of daily classroom life, there are distinctive threads of similarity running through all five programs. All

- value an active approach to learning,
- focus on children's need to collaborate with others,
- urge that children work with real objects, and
- value children's need to talk with adults skilled in mediating learning.

QUESTIONS FOR REFLECTION

1. Reflect on a time when one of your teachers used scaffolding to help you learn something new. Use the information on scaffolding from the Vygotsky theory section to jog your memory.

2. In your view, why did President Lyndon Johnson focus on preschool education for children of the poor as one way to lift people from poverty?

APPLY YOUR KNOWLEDGE

What Should This Teacher Do?

1. Mr. Hernandez met with a parent who asked, "Why are the children in this class almost always working together?" How could the Responsive Classroom model's views be helpful when he responds to the parent?

2. The same parent said, "I really don't understand why these children always seem to be playing and building things and just plain moving around." How could the teacher respond briefly, with John Dewey's ideas in mind?

KEY TERMS

Academic choice, 55
Accommodation, 39
Active learning, 49
Assimilation, 39
Child Study Movement, 32
Constructivism/
   Constructivist, 37
Documentation, 53

Ecology of human development, 45
Equilibrium, 39
Family systems theory, 46
Hundred languages of children, 52
Morning meeting, 55
Multiple intelligences, 44
Prepared environments, 51

Project, 53
Psychosocial crises, 43
Scaffolding, 41
Theory, 35
War on poverty, 34
Zone of proximal development
   (ZPD), 41

WEB SITES

American Montessori Internationale
http://www.montessori-ami.org/
Organization founded by Maria Montessori to further Montessori's pedagogical principles. Many links to information about the Montessori method.

Bank Street
http://www.bankstreet.edu
Main page for this approach.

Children of the WPA
http://nutrias.org/exhibits/wpakids/nursery.htm
These are photographs of the nursery schools operated during the WPA in the 1930s.

Head Start
http://www.acf.hhs.gov/programs/ohs/
Office of Head Start official site; a rich source of information about all aspects of Head Start, including the numerous research studies on this program.

http://www.nhsa.org/about/index.htm
National Head Start Association's site.

High Scope Educational Research Foundation
http://www.High/Scope.org
Contains information on its approach, curriculum, and research. For example, http://www.High/Scope.org/videostreaming/wwawwd2006.wmv is a video explaining the High/Scope model.

The Project Approach
http://www.projectapproach.org
Describes and explains different aspects of the Project Approach. Good examples of projects for different phases within the early childhood period.

Reggio Emilia
http://www.reggioalliance.org
The North American Reggio Emilia Alliance's (NAREA) site; lists information about activities of Reggio educators who further the understanding of the Reggio approach.

http://zerosei.comune.re.it
The official web site of the municipal preschools of the city of Reggio Emilia, Italy.

Responsive Classroom
http://www.responsiveclassroom.org
Main page for this model.

CHAPTER 3
Working with Diverse Families

- What are the major characteristics of families that will affect my work with children?
- Are there some guidelines that I can follow in my work with parents and families?
- What are some practical and effective strategies for working with families?

TODDLER
Nick's Father Asks a Question

As one of the "Dad and Me!" playtime sessions ended, Nick's father asked Mr. Bjornrud a question. "Is it OK to let Nick get down from the table when he is finished eating? My mother-in-law says that we'll 'spoil him' if we let him get down from the table. I think that she's wrong. What do you think?"

PRESCHOOL
Parents Learn About Literacy

Mrs. Chang and the parents of the children in her class stood in front of a documentation panel showing the children engaged in a variety of literacy activities. Tonight, parents and children, including parents who spoke Spanish, were at school for "Pizza and reading night." Mrs. Chang had asked parents whether they preferred to read to their child in English or Spanish. A parent and child would read a book together, with some parents reading in English and other parents reading in Spanish. Then, they played *Letter Detective* (Soderman & Farrell, 2008), with directions in Spanish and English. (Spanish is used as the example here. However, a teacher would provide materials in the home language of the children in a class.)

KINDERGARTEN PRIMARY
A Story with Two Endings

Mr. Hernandez met with the parents of the children in his classroom after he had asked them what they wanted to learn about children. They had chosen *How to Help My Child Develop Self-Control*. Each parent read the same story of a child who felt very angry when another child excluded him from a group. [Rejection is a primary cause of anger in young children (Fabes & Eisenberg, 1992).] He then showed two endings to the story, one of which described teaching children how to express angry feelings in a responsible way, by using words to express anger. The other ending described ignoring the child who was angry, which results in a child remaining angry and then confused about being ignored. This child would *not* learn how to deal with anger effectively by being ignored. Parents discussed both endings and Mr. Hernandez gave information about why using words would help their children develop the self-control needed in school.

Partnership with parents
Collaboration between home and school to foster children's development and learning and to support families.

Effective teachers understand that children develop primarily in the context of their families and, therefore, forge a strong and supportive **partnership with parents**. Your teaching team includes parents who love and cherish their children, know their children's needs and talents, and want the best for them. They want children to love learning, build good friendships, and use all of their gifts. You will help children learn and develop most effectively by forming a supportive partnership with families. When we keep our eye on the prize of children's development and learning, children reap the rewards of our efforts to work with and support their families.

This chapter focuses on your professional role in working with families. A critical element in this part of your role is to develop and maintain a respectful working relationship with parents and families. We examine three issues in working with families. First, we examine some of the major **characteristics of families** that affect your practice as an early childhood teacher (Hyson, 2003; NAEYC, 2001). For instance, how is the population of early childhood children changing? How many families with young children live in poverty? How many young children have a disability? How will these and other family characteristics affect children's development and learning, and how will they affect your curriculum-planning role and your work with their families? Second, you will understand the major guiding principles forming the foundation of all work with early childhood families, whether the family has children who are infants, toddlers, or third graders (Hepburn, 2004). Third, you will understand some of the most effective strategies for helping families support their children's development and learning (Hyson, 2003).

Characteristics of families
Distinctive qualities, factors, in families affecting children's lives.

UNDERSTANDING CHARACTERISTICS OF FAMILIES

"Zoo siab txcies tos (Hmong). Soo Dhawaada (Somali). Bienvenidos (Spanish). Welcome (English)." These greetings are the first thing that you see on entering the Minneapolis, Minnesota, Public Schools web site.[1] There are 90 languages spoken in this urban Midwest school district. The Los Angeles Unified School District publishes a *Parent Student Handbook* in six languages: Armenian, Chinese, English, Russian, Spanish, and Vietnamese.[2] The New York City Department of Education's welcome message appears in Arabic, Bengali, Chinese, English, Haitian Creole, Korean, Russian, Spanish, and Urdu.[3]

Diverse population of children and families
Variety in family configuration, ethnic and racial groups, socioeconomic level, religious belief, and place of residence (Berger, 2008).

Overlapping spheres of influence Influence of family, school, and community on children's development and learning.

Schools today have a richly **diverse population of children and families**. Many acknowledge that children's success depends on recognizing the variety of families in which children grow up as well as different cultures and languages in a community. These schools understand that **overlapping spheres of influence**—families, the community, and a school—affect children's development and learning. The goal is to place children at the center and to develop a real partnership involving a child's family, her school, and her community (Figure 3.1) (Epstein, 1995; Epstein, Sanders, Simon, Salinas, Jansorn, & VanVoorhis, 2002). Some schools demonstrate commitment to working with the many different families. For example, schools can acknowledge the needs

[1]http://www.mpls.k12.mn.us
[2]http://notebook.lausd.net/portal/page?_pageid=33,161841&_dad=ptl&_schema=PTL_EP
[3]http://schools.nyc.gov/default.aspx

FIGURE 3.1   Overlapping Spheres of Influence.

Sources: Based on Epstein (1995); and Epstein, Sanders, Simon, Salinas, Jansorn, and VanVoorhis (2002).

of diverse families in many ways, including providing parents with written materials in their home language (Kaczmarek, 2006).

Several characteristics of today's families will have an impact on you as a teacher. In this section, you will first read some quick facts, or snapshots, of families today. Then, you will read what these characteristics of families mean for you as a teacher of young children.

Snapshot: A Diverse Population of Families

School populations are diverse with many configurations of families (Berger, 2008; Drucker, 1998; Reynolds, Wright, & Beale, 2003). Some children grow up in blended families, families headed by grandparents, multigenerational families, families in which both parents work, families headed by a single parent, or families headed by same-sex parents. Children also grow up in families from many different ethnic groups, of a variety of social and economic levels, and who adhere to different religious beliefs. Another factor contributing to the richness of diversity is location. Children grow up in rural, suburban, or urban environments. Teachers, therefore, work with many different types of families. In many cases, teachers work with families whose qualities and experiences differ from their own.

Here is some current information, quick facts, about today's diverse population of families (U.S. Census Bureau, 2007).

- Overall population = 300 million.
- There were 12.9 million one-parent families in 2006. Of these, single fathers headed 2.5 million families.
- Sixty-seven percent of the nation's children under 18 lived with two parents who were married (*Census Bureau News*, 2007).
- Many children live in families headed by gay or lesbian parents, almost 164,000 according to the 2000 Census. There is diversity within this group of parents (American Psychological Association, 2005).
- There are 44.3 million Hispanics and Latinos, 40.2 million African Americans, 14.9 million Asians, 4.5 million Native Americans and Native Alaskans, and 1 million Native Hawaiian and other Pacific Islanders in the United States.
- Hispanic/Latino groups are growing most rapidly, with one-third of the Hispanic/Latino group under the age of 18.
- Asians are the second fastest growing group.
- The African-American group shows a much slower rate of growth.
- Minority children under 5 years now constitute the majority of children in 12 states, and this will also happen in New Jersey soon (Roberts, 2008).

What Does This Mean for Teachers?

Expect that the children in your classes will be growing up in different types of families such as those described above. As noted in the opening to this section, some school districts, such as Los Angeles and Minneapolis, have an internationally diverse group of families. Teachers need to know about the groups represented in their centers or schools.

Teachers should understand that the very meaning of *minority* or *majority populations* is an ever-changing, shifting, and even controversial concept (Purnell, 2004). Even though the United States recognizes specific minority groups (Hispanic/Latino, African

Hispanic groups in the United States are growing most rapidly. One-third of the Hispanic/Latino group is under the age of 18.

American, Asian, Native American and Native Alaskan, and Native Hawaiian/ Pacific Islander), many people are asking, "Just what does it mean to be a *minority* group member?" (Friedman, 2006).

The Census of 2000 gave people the first chance ever to identify themselves, not as members of one of the recognized minority groups but as mixed race or mixed ethnicity. There are 7.3 million people in this category (Navarro, 2008). The number of mixed-race or mixed-ethnic children and youth is increasing in schools. School systems and teachers must examine how they talk and think about the race or ethnic backgrounds of the children in schools. Teachers need to acquire a broader view of groups within their schools, thus acknowledging that children might identify with more than one group (Lopez, 2003). Schools and teachers need to develop policies that include all families, whatever their ethnicity.

Teachers should also understand that there is variation within any family structure or ethnic or racial group. They need to understand some characteristics of single-parent families, for example. However, teachers also must understand that single parents are different in income level, educational level, and other characteristics. Likewise, Hispanics and Latinos, while sharing many characteristics, also show many of the same differences (Hernandez, 2008). They come from different economic and educational levels. Some parents in different ethnic or racial groups are young while others are older. Teachers work more effectively with parents by keeping the variations in mind.

Snapshot: Children Living in Poverty

- 15.6% to 17% of all families with children newborn to 18 years had incomes below the **poverty level**. A person with an income below a specific level is considered poor or living in poverty. The poverty level for two adults and two children in 1999 was $16,895 and in 2006, it was $20,444.
- Married couples with children comprise 6.6% of families with incomes below the poverty level.
- Families with female head of house comprise 37% to 47% of families with incomes below the poverty level.
- Non-Hispanic whites account for 44% of people living in poverty.[4]
- Of those reporting Asian as their only race, 11.8% were in poverty in 2003.
- People who reported black as their only race had a poverty rate of 24.4% in 2003.
- Hispanics and Latinos have a poverty rate of 22.5%.
- Some areas of the country have high percentages of children under age 18 years living below the poverty level: District of Columbia (32.2%), Mississippi (30.9%), Louisiana (28.4%), New Mexico (26%).
- Some areas of the country have lower percentages of children under age 18 years living below the poverty level, for example, Utah (10.9%) and New Hampshire (9.4%).

Poverty level An income level that does not allow a person or family to provide basic necessities. The exact figure is designated by the government.

What Does This Mean for Teachers?

Poverty winds itself around a child's family, enveloping the entire family in its grasp. A child living in poverty is at great risk for high levels of **toxic stress**. Toxic stress actually

Toxic stress Most threatening type of stress experience; persistent elevations of stress hormones; leads to altered levels of key brain chemicals; disrupts architecture and chemistry of the brain.

[4]Figures for poverty rates for different groups obtained from the U.S. Census Bureau (2004), http://www.census.gov/Press-Release/www/releases/archives/income_wealth/002484.html.

FIGURE 3.2   Poverty and Toxic Stress: Poison for a Child's Brain

Toxic stress levels are high for children living in poverty and are dangerous and damaging to a child's development.

Toxic Stress

- damages the *architecture* of the child's brain: disrupts its blood supply; disrupts connections between cells in the brain (synaptic connections)
- impairs a child's memory
- impairs a child's language development
- makes learning difficult
- disrupts a child's immune and metabolic regulatory systems
- sets children up for a lifetime of physical illnesses
- sets children up for mental illness

Sources: Cookson (2008); Farah et al. (2006); Fellmeth (2003); Harvard University's Center for the Developing Child (2007); Krugman (2008).

---

alters the child's brain, its structure and its chemistry (Harvard University's Center for the Developing Child, 2007). Figure 3.2 illustrates the clear and present danger of growing up in poverty.

Children living in poverty face great obstacles to their development and learning (Cookson, 2008; Farah et al., 2006; Fellmeth, 2003; Krugman, 2008). Poverty affects every aspect of a child's life. For example, poverty has an adverse effect on such things as children's nutrition, health, educational opportunities, vocabulary size, and ultimately, his or her life course.

Expect some of the children in your classes to come from families living below the poverty level. Teachers can expect that some members of all ethnic and racial groups live in poverty. However, should you be working with families or be hired as a teacher in a part of the country with a high rate of poverty, you will undoubtedly work with children living in poverty. Expect many of the children whom you teach to be exposed to continuously high levels of toxic stress.

Snapshot: Preschool Children

The number of preschool children in the population has increased. The quick facts (U.S. Census, 2007) are:

- Number of preschool children under 5 years = 20.4 million.
- Three states with the highest percentage of preschoolers in their population are Utah (9.7%), Texas (8.2%), and Arizona (7.8%).
- Three states with the lowest percentage of preschoolers in their population are Vermont (5.3%), Maine (5.3%), and New Hampshire (5.6%).
- Very young children living in poverty have smaller vocabularies than do children from families whose incomes are more adequate.
- Very young children living in poverty also add new words to their vocabulary at a much slower rate than children do from families with more adequate incomes (Hart & Risley, 2003).

What Does This Mean for Teachers?

Teachers need a clear view of the value of preschool education for a growing population of young children and their families. Preschool education is important for all children, but it is especially beneficial for children and families living in poverty. Developmentally appropriate preschool education can provide vital experiences for children living in poverty, experiences linked to school success. The No Child Left Behind Act advocates developing universal preschools throughout the United States. Although this directive has not been carried out in some states, there are such schools in other states. There is also an impetus to develop preschools within the public school systems as a way to meet children's needs. The state of Oklahoma, for example, has recognized the value of preschool and now publically funds preschool education. Seventy percent of 4-year-old children in the state of Oklahoma attend the publically financed preschool programs (Leonhardt, 2007).

Teachers have an excellent opportunity to establish relationships with families of children enrolled in preschool programs. Teachers, working with professional and state-level organizations, have an opportunity to develop policies that support all families with preschool children. Professional education organizations influence policy by telling legislators that spending money on preschool education pays for itself in reduced crime and increased worker productivity (Leonhardt, 2007).

Children with Disabilities

A **child with a disability** has one of the 13 disability categories defined in the **Individuals with Disabilities Education Act (IDEA)** (National Center for Learning Disabilities, 2007) and is, therefore, eligible to receive special educational services. The IDEA, first known as the Education for All Handicapped Children Act or Public Law (PL) 94-142 and revised periodically, mandates that all children get a free appropriate education whatever the nature of their disability. The most recent revision of IDEA was in 2004 with final regulations published in 2006. Figure 3.3 lists the 13 disability categories and explains each.

Families who have a child with a disability or a developmental delay must know how to get the help they need for their child, a topic to which we now turn (National Dissemination Center for Children with Disabilities, 2002).

Child with a disability A child who has one of the 13 disability categories defined in IDEA.

IDEA Individuals with Disabilities Education Act.

Infants and Toddlers

Infants and toddlers, birth to age 3, are eligible for **early intervention services** if they show evidence of a developmental delay, (Krapp & Wilson, 2006) such as

- cognitive,
- physical (including visual and auditory systems),
- social or emotional,
- communication, and
- adaptive development, which is taking care of oneself in daily living skills such as eating.

IDEA (Part C) provides for early intervention services to infants and toddlers and their families through the Early Intervention Program for Infants and Toddlers with Disabilities. Every state participates in this voluntary part of IDEA and receives federal grants to deliver services to families (Stahmer & Mandell, 2007). Early intervention

Early intervention services Assistance available to children birth to 3 years of age who show a significant developmental delay.

FIGURE 3.3   IDEA Disability Categories and Definitions

1. **Autism** is a developmental disability significantly affecting verbal and nonverbal communication and social interaction, generally evident before age 3, which adversely affects educational performance. Characteristics often associated with autism are engaging in repetitive activities and stereotyped movements, resistance to changes in daily routines or the environment, and unusual responses to sensory experiences. The term *autism* does not apply if the child's educational performance is adversely affected primarily because the child has emotional disturbance, as defined in #4 below.

   A child who shows the characteristics of autism after age 3 could be diagnosed as having autism if the criteria above are satisfied.

2. **Deaf-Blindness** is concomitant [simultaneous] hearing and visual impairments, the combination of which causes such severe communication and other developmental and educational needs that the child cannot be accommodated in special education programs solely for children with deafness or children with blindness.

3. **Deafness** is a hearing impairment so severe that a child is impaired in processing linguistic information through hearing, with or without amplification, that adversely affects a child's educational performance.

4. **Emotional Disturbance** is a condition in which the child exhibits one or more of the following characteristics over a long period of time and to a marked degree that adversely affects educational performance:

   (a) An inability to learn that cannot be explained by intellectual, sensory, or health factors.

   (b) An inability to build or maintain satisfactory interpersonal relationships with peers and teachers.

   (c) Inappropriate types of behavior or feelings under normal circumstances.

   (d) A general pervasive mood of unhappiness or depression.

   (e) A tendency to develop physical symptoms or fears associated with personal or school problems.
      The term includes schizophrenia. The term does not apply to children who are socially maladjusted, unless it is determined that they have an emotional disturbance.

5. **Hearing Impairment** is an inability to hear, whether permanent or fluctuating, that adversely affects a child's educational performance but is not included under the definition of "deafness."

6. **Mental Retardation** is significant subaverage general intellectual functioning, existing concurrently [at the same time] with deficits in adaptive behavior and manifested during the developmental period, that adversely affects a child's educational performance.

7. **Multiple Disabilities** are concomitant [simultaneous] impairments (such as mental retardation–blindness, mental retardation–orthopedic impairment, etc.), the combination of which causes such severe educational needs that they cannot be accommodated in a special education program solely for one of the impairments. The term does not include deaf-blindness.

8. **Orthopedic Impairment** is a severe orthopedic impairment that adversely affects a child's educational performance. The term includes impairments caused by a congenital anomaly (e.g., clubfoot, absence of a limb), impairments caused by disease (e.g., poliomyelitis, bone tuberculosis), and impairments from other causes (e.g., cerebral palsy, amputations, fractures or burns that cause contractures).

9. **Other Health Impairment** is having limited strength, vitality, or alertness, including a heightened alertness to environmental stimuli, that results in limited alertness with respect to the educational environment, that

   (a) is due to chronic or acute health problems such as asthma, attention deficit disorder or attention deficit hyperactivity disorder, diabetes, epilepsy, a heart condition, hemophilia, lead poisoning, leukemia, nephritis, rheumatic fever, and sickle cell anemia; and

   (b) adversely affects a child's educational performance.

10. **Specific Learning Disability** is a disorder in one or more of the basic psychological processes involved in understanding or in using language, spoken or written, that may manifest itself in an imperfect ability to listen, think, speak, read, write, spell, or to do mathematical calculations. The term includes such conditions as perceptual disabilities, brain injury, minimal brain dysfunction, dyslexia, and developmental aphasia. The term does not include learning problems that are primarily the result of visual, hearing, or motor disabilities; of mental retardation; of emotional disturbance; or of environmental, cultural, or economic disadvantage.

11. **Speech or Language Impairment** is a communication disorder such as stuttering, impaired articulation, a language impairment, or a voice impairment that adversely affects a child's educational performance.

12. **Traumatic Brain Injury** is an acquired injury to the brain caused by an external physical force, resulting in total or partial functional disability or psychosocial impairment or both, that adversely affects a child's educational performance. The term applies to open or closed head injuries resulting in impairments in one or more areas such as cognition; language; memory; attention; reasoning; abstract thinking; judgment; problem solving; sensory, perceptual, and motor abilities; psychosocial behavior; physical functions; information processing; and speech. The term does not include brain injuries that are congenital or degenerative or brain injuries induced by birth trauma.

13. **Visual Impairment Including Blindness** is an impairment in vision that, even with correction, adversely affects a child's educational performance. The term includes both partial sight and blindness.

Source: National Dissemination Center for Children with Disabilities (2002). Retrieved September 20, 2007, from http://www.nichcy.org/pubs/genresc/gr3.htm. This information is copyright free.

services include evaluating a very young child's needs, working with the family to identify their needs, and developing an **Individualized Family Service Program (IFSP)**.

Children Ages 3 through 9 (up to the Child's 10th Birthday)

States do not have to use one of the 13 disability categories with 3 through 9 year olds. States can instead use the term **developmental delay** for 3 through 9 year olds, just as they do with infants and toddlers. The categories of developmental delays are the same as with infants and toddlers. A child is still eligible for special services if the state uses the term *developmental delay* rather than one of the disability categories.

Each child over 3 years of age found to have a developmental delay or a disability has an **Individualized Education Program (IEP)**. This is a written plan required by IDEA,

IFSP Individualized Family Service Program; written plan serving families with infants and toddlers when the child has a developmental delay; to help the family meet the child's special needs.

Developmental delay Significant delay in any of several domains of development when compared with norms for a specific age.

IEP Individualized Education Program; the basis of a high-quality education for 3 to 21 year old children with disabilities; written document developed by a team of professionals and a child's parents; outlines child's needs and contains accommodations and supports to address those needs.

An IEP team includes a child's parents, teacher, and other members of the team. They write the IEP, which follows guidelines in IDEA.

and it is developed, reviewed, and revised following guidelines in IDEA. An IEP team develops the plan. IDEA designates specific members of an IEP team, which includes parents and teachers.

Children and Youth Ages 3 through 21

A 3 through 21 year old can receive special services for the 13 disability categories. To receive the special services, the disability must affect a child's educational performance.

What Does This Mean for Teachers?

By IDEA law, children with disabilities spend a good deal of time in an inclusive setting. Teachers in these settings meet regularly with other support personnel at school, assessing each child with an IEP. Then, teachers have a major responsibility to implement, track progress, and ensure that IEP objectives are being met in the classroom. This involves providing the **differentiated instruction** that children might need. This is accomplished through **adaptation**, the process of "...adjusting or modifying materials, environment, interactions, or teaching methods to enable the *individual child* to get the maximum benefit from the routines and activities of inclusive early childhood setting" (Cross & Dixon, 2004).

We now turn to examining the guiding principles that will help teachers work with families, all families.

GUIDING PRINCIPLES: WORKING WITH FAMILIES

Effective teachers use a set of guiding principles to assist them in their work with families. For each principle, you will read a *what we know statement*. Following this is an *apply this knowledge to working with families statement*. Here, you will learn to use your knowledge to make decisions about working with families. You will also read about some real

Differentiated instruction
A process for approaching teaching and learning for children who have different abilities in the same class; teachers meet children where they are and modify curriculum and strategies to help *every* child be successful (Hall, 2002).

Adaptation Process of adjusting or modifying materials, environment, interactions, or teaching methods to enable the *individual child* to get the maximum benefit from the routines and activities of inclusive early childhood setting.

world examples of the types of community resources that support families. The principles discussed in this section involve knowledge, relationships, resources, and culture.

- Knowledge: Use knowledge of child development
- Relationships: Build reciprocal, respectful relationships
- Resources: Link families with early childhood and community resources
- Culture: Use a cultural lens when working with families

Knowledge: Use Knowledge of Child Development

What We Know

Teachers taking a developmental approach understand child development and use that knowledge in working with children. They also think about parents as partners in education and, therefore, want parents to have information that will enable them to take this approach (Berger, 2008). Teachers are more effective in their role by helping parents increase their knowledge of children's development. Consider asking some basic questions to get started. For example, what might parents already know about development? Do they have accurate information? Do they have any misunderstandings? The answers to these questions will help you support parents in learning about child development.

Even though parents of young children do seem to understand how important they are to their child's development, they are eager to learn more about children. For example, parents have high aspirations for their children's school success. Parents want information about skills that will help their child achieve academic success. These skills include cognitive development, self-confidence, self-control, and language, communication, and literacy (Zero to Three, 2007). See Figure 3.4 for some practical suggestions. We also know that parents, like teachers, need accurate information about all the domains of child development (Hepburn, 2004; Zero to Three and Hart, 1997).

Parents need accurate information about all domains of child development.

FIGURE 3.4 Build on Parents' Strong Aspirations for Children's Success in School

Target your work with young parents to include the following. You will build on their strengths and will help them grow in their understanding of how they facilitate their child's language and literacy development.

Help parents understand language development. Help them understand *bilingual* language development if the language of school and home differ.

- All parents need accurate information on language development.
- Some parents need information on bilingual language development but often get confusing information.
- Make sure your information is accurate.

Help parents see that they are already doing literacy activities and that they can add to this existing teaching.

- This will help parents expand their perception of their role as parents to include the teaching part of the role.
- This builds on their desire to take good care of their children.

Encourage parents to speak to and read to their children.

- Speaking to and reading to children lays the foundation for successful reading and literacy.
- It is the speaking and reading that matters, not the language used.
- However, parents who speak a language different from that in their child's school need to feel confident that talking in and reading to their child in the home language will build school success skills.

Provide books and other literacy materials to parents.

- Teach all parents how to read to children.
- Teach about how reading to children, in any language, prepares children for school success.
- Choose reading materials that are appropriate for the community.

Sources: Colorin Colorado (see web sites for this chapter); Lopez et al. (2007); Soderman & Farrell (2008). Education (http://www.ncate.org).

Adults do understand quite a bit of accurate information about child development, but they also have some gaps in their knowledge. Any misunderstandings can have a significant impact on how they deal with children and ultimately on children's success in school. Specific subgroups have bigger gaps in what they know about children (Zero to Three, 2000). For example, fathers have less knowledge than mothers, and less well-educated and lower-income parents have less knowledge and more misunderstandings about development than more highly educated and higher-income parents. Similarly, people who are not yet parents but who plan to become parents seem to have greater misunderstandings about child development. Figure 3.5 offers tips on helping parents acquire accurate child development information.

Parents have somewhat more realistic expectations about children when they have access to evidence-based information about child development. Evidence-based information helps parents to understand why a child might do something. They are also less likely to ask a child to do something that she might not be able to do, and they make more reasonable and

FIGURE 3.5   Build on Parents' Knowledge: Help Them Understand Child Development

Parents might need to learn these things about very young children.

- about when children begin to take in and respond to the world
- when babies begin to sense moods of others
- that very young infants (about 4 months old) can be depressed
- that observing violence can have a long-lasting and negative effect on very young children

Help parents support children's intellectual development.

- Encourage parents who already read to and talk with children.
- Help them understand that their teaching will benefit their child's intellectual development.
- Help parents identify activities that are far *less* beneficial to their child's intellectual development—flash cards or playing alone at the computer.

Help parents understand the power of play.

- Parents might not know that play is important to *all* domains of child development.
- Parents might not realize how play builds intellectual skills.
- Parents might not realize the pretend play enhances their child's language development.
- Parents might not understand that play is as important for babies as it is for 3 to 6 year olds.

Help parents develop appropriate expectations of young children.

- Some parents do not understand that a young child is *not* capable of revenge.
- Others do not understand that a 3 year old needs to move and cannot sit still for very long.
- Some adults do not understand that a toddler cannot share.

Help parents learn about positive discipline.

- Some parents do not understand that some things are very appropriate for children at different ages, such as picking up a 3 month old when she cries, letting a 2 year old get down from the table when finished eating, or letting a 6 year old decide what to wear to school (within limits, of course).
- Parents need to know:
  - that physical discipline, such as hitting, leads to poor self-control.
  - that physical discipline, such as hitting, often leads to higher levels of aggression.
  - how to set limits appropriately.
  - about other appropriate guidance strategies.

Source: Marion (2007); Zero to Three (2000). Telephone survey of 3000 adults, 1066 of whom were parents of children newborn to age 6. See some of the survey questions and explanations at http://www.zerotothree.org/site/PageServer?pagename=ter_key_childdevt_surveydata&AddInterest=1153.

developmentally based suggestions and demands. For example, a parent who understands that infants typically walk at approximately 1 year would not expect a 4 month old to walk.

Another example comes from social and emotional development. Violence has been a major problem for some time and teachers and parents can work together to help children learn nonviolent, positive ways of interacting (American Psychological Association, 2003). Positive interaction skills are important in getting along with other children in school. To do this, parents need evidence-based information about the origins of anger and violence as Mr. Hernandez has done in the kindergarten and primary grade vignette at the beginning of the chapter.

Apply This Knowledge to Work with Families

Teachers can help parents to understand what children are like at different ages so that they have a good understanding of their child's capabilities. They can also help parents understand what the next stage will bring so that they can anticipate typical developmental changes. For example, parents of infants not only need to know about their baby's development right now but also benefit from learning about the growing sense of independence of toddlerhood. Teachers can gather articles and information on developmental stages for parents to read. This often helps parents to understand a teacher's curriculum. For example, information on how play fosters cognitive development would help parents understand why a kindergarten teacher provides many opportunities for play in his classroom.

Teachers play a critical role in teaching violence prevention. They often seek assistance from other professionals in school settings, such as a psychologist, social worker, or nurse. The professionals work together to help families understand that children develop the relationship skills that they need for adjustment to school and for getting along with others in a warm, supportive family environment (Kokko & Pulkkinen, 2000). Parents on your teaching team must learn that both violence and nonviolence are learned behaviors. Working with them helps them understand the things that usually trigger anger in young children and how children typically react to anger (Fabes & Eisenberg, 1992; Fabes, Eisenberg, Smith, & Murphy, 1996). Parents can learn to teach children to manage angry feelings responsibly (Marion, 1997).

Teachers can help parents to tune in to their child's individual strengths, how their child typically responds to things, learning style, and play. Parents can acquire good observation skills, and can be taught how to provide experiences for their child that foster the child's development and how to interact with their child? For example, some parents need to learn to let their child lead in a play session and need to learn how to follow their child's lead. Teachers help parents to understand the key skills needed for school success: language/literacy, self-confidence, self-control, and thinking skills.

CHECK YOUR UNDERSTANDING
Using Knowledge of Child Development

Before going on to the next principle, reflect on what you have learned about this principle. Read the toddler classroom and then the kindergarten and primary classroom vignette at the beginning of the chapter.

1. How could the toddler teacher use the information in Figure 3.5 to help Nick's father deal with his issue?
2. How has Mr. Hernandez, the kindergarten/primary teacher, used child development information to teach about self-control?

Relationships: Build Respectful, Reciprocal Relationships

What We Know

Healthy relationships are at the core of an effective teacher's work with children and families. When two people who know each other interact several times, they have developed a relationship. Teachers who have known a family or parent for some time have a long-term relationship but other relationships are newer (Rubin, Butkowski, & Parker, 1998) such as when a teacher first meets a family.

Supportive, effective teachers have a strength-based approach to working with families, just as they do with children. They believe that parents are strong, knowledgeable people, whatever their circumstances. The teacher approaches every interaction with parents from this perspective and strives to help parents build on their strengths. A teacher and a parent might have different educational backgrounds, for example, but they share the same goal: to help that parent's child develop and learn (Gonzalez-Mena, 2007).

Effective early childhood professionals establish **respectful relationships** with families (Ambry & Steinbrunner, 2007; NAEYC, 2006a) just as they do with children. Humans need to feel accepted and to feel safe and secure. Respectful teacher-family relationships meet satisfy these needs, sending the message that families belong and are welcome in their child's classroom. Parents know that the teacher likes them, they feel safe, and they appreciate the teacher's nonjudgmental attitude (Mitchell, 2003). The teacher's genuine liking of parents shines in courteous, polite, and civil interactions (Forni, 2002).

Effective teachers also establish **reciprocal relationships** (Hyson, 2003; NAEYC, 2001), which implies that there is give-and-take and shared responsibility in the relationship. There is a mutually beneficial exchange of ideas. The Teach Intentionally feature shows a reciprocal relationship in which the teacher and parent exchange

Go to MyEducationLab and select the topic "Families and Communities." Under Activities and Applications, read the case study *On the Front Lines: Connecting with Families* for information on how to establish good relationships with families.

Respectful relationship
All parties feel safe and secure, feel that they belong, are welcome, and are not judged.

Reciprocal relationship
Give-and-take and shared responsibility in the relationship.

TEACH INTENTIONALLY

Seeking Information from Parents

What the teacher did: Mrs. Chang, the preschool teacher, asked parents what their child liked to play with and about the child's preferences in books and made a record of what parents said. Then, she used the information to plan activities and to choose books for the classroom. She invited parents to come to the classroom (Gonzalez-Mena, 2007) to see the library. She asked the parents about the language that they preferred to use when reading to their children. She used this information about preferred language for reading to help parents find literacy resources. You saw Mrs. Chang's approach in action in the chapter opener preschool vignette.

How the teacher was intentional: This teacher was intentional in her work with parents by demonstrating respect for parent's observational skill. Parents could pinpoint their child's preferences in books. She demonstrated respect for parents by asking which language they would prefer to use for reading to their child. This teacher's interaction with the families on her teaching team was reciprocal because she intentionally encouraged an exchange of ideas and treated parents as partners in the planning and curriculum for the children (Mitchell, 2003). In the preschool vignette, she tuned in to parents' desire to help children with literacy, showing them excellent developmentally appropriate language arts learning activities.

information. The teacher uses the information to work effectively with children and to support the parents.

Apply This Knowledge to Working with Families

A teacher has the responsibility to establish respectful, reciprocal relationships with parents, and there are several ways to do this.

- Focus consciously on your beliefs about working with families.
- Consider the role of civility in your relationships.
- Acknowledge that it takes time to build a good relationship.
- Make time for honest, open noninterfering communication.
- Rely on the Code of Ethical Conduct.

As a starting point, *focus consciously on your beliefs about working with families* because beliefs drive many actions (Gonzalez-Mena, 2006). Do you, for example, really believe that parents are partners with you in educating their child? Do you believe that parents are their child's first and most important teachers? How do you view parents? Do you view them as strong, knowledgeable people who want the best for their children, whatever their resources and circumstances? Do you think that parents can or should help teachers make some decisions? If you answered "Yes" to most of these questions, then you will be much more likely to favor working closely with parents. For a true partnership to exist, there should be genuine mutual respect, communication, and making decisions together.

Then, *consider the role of civility in your relationships.* Civility embodies respectful behavior and involves good manners, valuing others, consideration, and politeness. Civility is the moral fiber in respectful relationships (Forni, 2002) with families. There is a connection between civility, the ethics of our profession, and our professional relationships. Teachers who have good professional relationships tend to have a higher-quality professional life. Good relational skills are the most basic element of good relationships. Taking the time and effort to build good relational skills and then good professional relationships yields lower levels of stress, better working conditions in a school, and a much friendlier place for parents and teachers (Forni, 2007). See Figure 3.6 for some suggestions for demonstrating respect for families.

Next, *acknowledge that it takes time to build a good relationship* and *take the time to build respectful relationships*—slowly and steadily. Consider asking parents how they would like to communicate with you. This might seem like extra work, but it is not. Parents are much more likely to stay in touch when you make communication easy for them and when you consider their preferences, a sign of respect that they appreciate. Many parents choose to keep in touch via email, while others might even prefer text messages. Some parents appreciate phone communication, and others prefer to speak with you in person at school. A few parents might prefer written messages. First, though, you have to ask and then you can plan your communications wisely.

Make Time for Honest, Open, Noninterfering Communication

For instance, block out time to make calls, to write email, text, or written messages. Most parents, whatever their preferred style, also enjoy speaking briefly with teachers at pick-up and drop-off times if they bring their children to school. You can ask, as a part of civil interaction, about the family's well-being. Suppose, for instance, that you greet Greta's father with "Good morning, Mr. Simmons. How are things going?" He replies, "Well, I think that Greta misses her mom." He then tells you that the mother, in the military, has had her tour of duty extended. You have been respectful, not intrusive, and

FIGURE 3.6   Demonstrate Respect When Working with Families

Effective teachers build respectful relationships with families. Some of the rules for considerate conduct in working with families are to

Acknowledge Parents.

- Learn and remember names and ask parents what they wish to be called.
- Greet parents.
- Compliment parents sincerely or thank them for something that they have done.

Listen to Parents.

- Listening is a difficult skill and must be learned and practiced.
- Pay attention. Observe well (see Chapter 8). Tune in and stay focused.
- Get rid of distractions. For example, turn off a cell phone, turn and face the parent; take your hands off your computer terminal, stop writing on the board.
- Look at the parent, if that is culturally acceptable, and maintain eye contact.
- Be conscious of listening. Say to yourself, "This is the time to listen."
- Stay focused on the parent as he speaks; do not shift attention to yourself.
- Show that you are listening: a nod, an "I see," or "Yes."

Speak Considerately to Parents.

- Figure out what type of contribution you need to make to the conversation: giving advice, support, information. Ask the parent what she needs if you are not sure.
- Get to the point, do not hurry, and avoid veering off topic.
- Use a restrained tone and volume.

Avoid Asking Personal Questions.

- Avoid asking idle, intrusive questions about private matters such as marital status, money, the cost of things, weight, religion, political views.
- Do not make comments or ask questions about a parent's accent.

Respect Parent's Time.

- Be punctual, always; make appointments with parents, specifying time for appointments.
- Return phone calls or email messages the same day.
- Do not take another call when talking with a parent on the phone.
- Stick to the topic for the meeting.

Deal With a Parent's Concerns With Civility and Respect.

- Acknowledge that parents will have concerns at some point or might even be agitated.
- Avoid jumping to conclusions and do not take things personally. Choose to show respect and act considerately.
- Have the courage to listen carefully to the concern. Then, be truthful while you also show concern for the parent as you negotiate the concern.

this parent has revealed information that would help you understand the child's current emotional state.

Finally, *rely on the Code of Ethical Conduct* (Baptiste & Reyes, 2008; NAEYC, 2005) of the early childhood profession as your guide when interacting with parents. It will help you grow in confidence in your work with families because it outlines a teacher's ethical responsibilities. The Code also assists teachers in dealing with ethical dilemmas that crop up in working with parents and families (see Chapter 1 for a description of ethical responsibilities and ethical dilemmas).

Resources: Link Families with Early Childhood Networks and Other Community Resources

What We Know

Parents and teachers share a vision of helping children develop and learn. Teachers take the lead in bringing the vision to life. One of a teacher's professional responsibilities is to work with and support a family's efforts in helping children develop and learn (Hyson, 2003; NAEYC, 2001). A good way to do this is to link parents with early childhood and community **resources for families**. These resources are the links within the early childhood community and the parent's community that support a family in meeting its own needs as well as its child's needs.

There are significant benefits when we help parents connect with resources such as other professionals in the school—the psychologist, social worker, or principal. Teachers can also familiarize themselves with local community agencies and resources such as the Parks and Recreation Department, the public library, the YMCA, or a mental health agency to which they can later refer parents. Teachers can provide written material such as articles or Internet resources to parents when they meet, either informally or in conferences. Find out if your community has a Family Resource Center, a place that provides outreach, support, and information to parents. These are locations, often in a public school, where parents can go for parenting classes, a connection to other community agencies, a place to feel welcome, and a place to meet other parents.

Consider, also, that teachers work with children who have special needs. Parents of a child with a disability would benefit by having resources that help them understand and deal well with their child's needs. Many developmental and behavioral challenges in children go undetected, and failing to provide proper services has a negative impact on the child's developmental path (Dworkin, Bogan, Carey, & Honigfeld, 2005).

Many communities do have appropriate services, but it is difficult for parents to know and get to these services on their own. Parents need access to a coordinated system of services (Dworkin et al., 2005). Teachers are a potentially strong part of the net of support to parents and need to know which systems are in place in their state and community. Teachers do not operate such systems, but they do need to know about them and should be able to tell parents about these valuable community resources. For example, Connecticut's 2-1-1 system is a three-digit telephone number linking people to a vast array of community resources. 2-1-1 provides an online database through which anybody, including parents, can connect with resources (United Way of Connecticut, 2007). A parent finds resources by calling 2-1-1 or through the Internet and explains his needs. Then, the Child Developmental Infoline connects the parent with the most helpful resources available.

Apply This Knowledge to Working with Families

Take a realistic, sensible, and practical approach because you will have to use your professional time efficiently. Parents need resources about child development and child guidance and about how to help their child do well in school. Some parents need additional specific information such as about certain disabilities. How can you link parents with good resources and what are some of the most valuable resources available? For teachers, good resources for families come from early childhood professional

Resources for families
Links within the early childhood community and the family's community that support them in meeting their needs and those of their child.

Go to MyEducationLab and select the topic "Special Needs/Inclusion." Under Activities and Applications, watch the video *Communication Disorder: George's Support* for an example of a family who makes good use of community resources.

organizations such as NAEYC (2006b), the Council on Exceptional Children, or pediatric groups and from community resources.

Learn about, record, and update a list of resources for parents. Teachers can make a simple written list or can record a list of resources in a computer file, which is very easy to consult, update, or send to parents who also use computers. For parents who do not have computers, print a list of the resources and periodically update the list. Work with school administrators to make a computer available for parents at school with bookmarked files on good resources. If your school has a newsletter, consider running a regular feature on resources. Figure 3.7 lists and briefly describes some of the most commonly available early childhood and community resources. You will very likely learn about other resources in your community and should add these to your list.

Culture: Use a Cultural Lens When Working with Families

Schools are embedded in a culture and some teachers share the culture of the children who they teach. Many other teachers do not come from the same culture as the children and families in their schools. The possibility exists that cultural mismatches can create discomfort for children and their families.

FIGURE 3.7   Where Can I Find Resources for Families?

Teachers can help parents and families find resources easily and from many sources. Two of the best places to find resources are within the early childhood network and within a family's community.

Early Childhood Network Resources: Examples

- Resources supporting teachers, strengthening families, from the NAEYC web site. An excellent list of a variety of resources. Contains links to all items. View at http://www.naeyc.org/ece/supporting/resources.asp.

- Facts for Families, from the American Academy of Child and Adolescent Psychiatry. These are brief fact sheets on timely topics about children. Available in English and Spanish. See these at http://www.aacap.org/page.ww?section=Facts+for+Families&name=Facts+for+Families.

- Parent's Corner, from the American Academy of Pediatrics. Superior resources on a variety of parenting concerns. A very good resource for child development information presented simply and well. See at http://www.aap.org/parents.html.

Community Resources: Examples

- Resource and referral agencies, such as the California Child Care Resource and Referral Network; at http://www.rrnetwork.org.

- Children's Trust Fund (CTF): Florida's CTF funds many projects for children and families, such as after school programs; at http://www.thechildrenstrust.org/Programs.asp.

- Parent education programs, such as Michigan's Parents as Partners in Education; at http://www.michigan.gov/mde/0,1607,7-140-5233_35207-00.html. Links to very good handouts and other items.

- School-based assistance: guidance counselors and school psychologists.

- Parks and recreation departments: provide a variety of programs for children and families.

- Public libraries and local bookstores: offer story and reading hours for children.

- Public health departments: health services for children.

What We Know

The reality is that there has been a decline in the number of diverse teachers in schools (Saluja, Early, & Clifford, 2002) at a time when cultural diversity of school populations has increased significantly. Families today send their children to schools in which the teachers are very likely to be from a different culture (Colombo, 2005).

Teachers need to be able to take the perspective of families. *Perspective taking* is a basic cognitive developmental skill (Selman, 1976), and perspective taking affects how teachers perceive events (Rand, 1998). Effective early childhood teachers operate at a high level of perspective taking: They are very good at controlling their own view of things when they consider the viewpoints of others. This also applies to working with families.

Effective early childhood teachers demonstrate good perspective taking when they adopt a strength-based approach to working with all families. They value each family's culture and language (U.S. Department of Education, no date) and view a family's culture or language as a strong starting point for positive respectful interactions. Effective teachers build on a family's characteristics and strengths, just as they build on children's strengths, regardless of the parents' circumstances. Their work with parents is appropriate for individual parents and families. Effective teachers recognize and acknowledge that all cultures have child care and rearing in common, however different the cultures appear to be.

Culturally competent
Open, accepting attitude about every family's customs and values and responsive to each family's needs; interacts effectively with families under many different circumstances.

Effective early childhood teachers are **culturally competent**, meaning that they have an open and accepting attitude about a family's customs and values. They interact more effectively with families under many different circumstances, and they are more accepting of and responsive to each family's needs than a less culturally competent teacher (Colombo, 2005). They understand that families from all cultures fulfill the functions of a family. For instance, all families provide food but the family's culture influences food chosen. Similarly, all families fulfill the function of educating their children but their culture shapes their views on educating children.

Effective teachers value each family's culture and language and see them as a starting point for positive, respectful interactions.

However, even teachers with good basic perspective-taking skills might still have difficulty taking the perspective of a parent whose culture is different. One's own cultural lens reflects the world to us from our cultural perspective. An effective way for teachers to move toward cultural competence is to have meaningful interactions with people from other cultures. Experiences with another culture challenge how we view the world but can be the starting point for helping us see things differently (Unten, 2003).

When you step into another culture, expect to feel a sense of disequilibrium, the sensation of being out of balance (Colombo, 2005; Sleeter, 1995). This is the feeling that children whose culture is different from a school's culture experience every day at school. All growth and development, however, including learning about another culture, comes from periods of disequilibrium or even feeling very confused and alone and then figuring things out and learning, and only then achieving a renewed sense of balance. A teacher has to put on the lens of a culture if she ever hopes to see things from that culture's perspective.

Apply This Knowledge to Working with Families

Teachers demonstrate respect for families in many ways and one of the most significant is to use a cultural lens when working with families. This allows a teacher to see that culture and language, in all their astonishing variations, are starting points, not obstacles, in relationships with families. Acknowledge cultural differences as your starting point (Colombo, 2005).

Focus, calmly and realistically, on the challenges that you and a family might face as you work as partners. Seek help from professional groups in dealing effectively and respectfully with challenges such as different languages. Maintain a clear focus on supporting all families in helping their children to develop school-success skills, such as literacy and language. Be sensitive to what parents really need and then support them appropriately. Figure 3.8 lists some of the things that teachers can do to become more culturally competent.

CHECK YOUR UNDERSTANDING
Parents and Teachers Working Together

In the chapter opener preschool vignette, how has Mrs. Chang demonstrated her willingness and ability to work in partnership with all of the families on her team? Explain how you think that she and the parents are working together to build school-success skills for the children in this class.

FIGURE 3.8   Becoming a Culturally Competent Teacher

Teachers can do many things to become more culturally competent. For example,

- Have the courage that it takes to confront and challenge any misconceptions that you have about different cultures.

- Acknowledge values and beliefs of another culture, for example, beliefs about discipline, food, personal space, or making eye contact. Acknowledge that there are differences between cultures, focusing on the strengths in the culture.

- Learn about other cultures through classes, seminars and conferences, or reading the literature of the culture, learning about art and music of the culture and through meaningful interaction in the cultures represented in a school.

- Focus on each family as a unique unit with specific needs; avoid thinking that families in a specific culture all think alike or have the same values.

- Speak the language of a culture; but, if that is not possible, then learn important and often-used phrases, asking parents for help.

- When using a translator, speak directly to parents or children, making eye contact if their culture accepts direct eye contact and appropriate facial expressions.

- Print classroom signs in the languages of the children in the class. Common locations for such signs are the family mailboxes, in writing centers, in washrooms, and on the door to the classroom. Teachers can also decorate the school and classrooms with paintings, photographs, fabrics, and other items from different cultures.

- Employ an antibias curriculum, using music, art, and books showing different ages, genders, countries, and disabilities.

Sources: Colombo (2005); Derman-Sparks & A.B.C. Task Force (1989); Gonzalez-Mena (2007); Soderman and Farrell (2008); Sutherby and Sauve (2003).

INVOLVING FAMILIES IN THEIR CHILDREN'S DEVELOPMENT AND LEARNING

A parent is a child's first teacher, and the setting or context for a child's earliest learning is in his family. All of a child's early learning and development begins with attachment to a parent. The parent then organizes the child's environment, provides stimulation, and provides nutrition and other basic care. Effective parents set the stage for learning and development but know when to step back and allow children to try things on their own (Hepburn, 2004).

Children learn so many things in a warm, supportive, and nurturing relationship with their parents. Just a few examples of what children learn in their families include things such as getting one's needs met, what and when to eat, and how to show or hide feelings. Parents also teach children how to think, how to control impulses, and how to show respect to animals. Parents teach specific skills such as in athletics, and they set the tone for learning. As teachers, we are interested in supporting parents in their teaching role because their teaching has such a profound impact on a child's development and learning.

Parental Behavior and Children's Development and Learning

Two types of parenting behaviors are especially influential in a very young child's development and later success in school (Lopez, Barrueco, Feinauer, & Miles, 2007). The first is a *parent's level of emotional responsiveness.* For example, do the parents tune in to their infant's emotional signals? Do they attempt to respond appropriately to the signals? Do they understand how important they are in their baby's emotional development?

The second powerful parenting behavior is *whether and then how frequently a parent engages in language and literacy activities* with very young children. Do they understand how important they are in their children's success with language? Do they talk to their baby? Does the family have books that they read to their child? Accumulating research shows that children develop better cognitive and motor skills when their parents respond appropriately to their emotional signals and when parents read to and talk to their infants, whatever language is spoken at home.

A family's influence continues as children enter school and effective teachers recognize the great potential of including families in the circle of teaching. Convincing evidence exists showing the powerful and positive effects that parental involvement has on children's development and school success, no matter what the parent's income or educational level. When schools reach out to families and when parents feel safe participating actively in their child's education, children do better in school. Children attend school regularly, adapt well to school, have better social skills, and earn higher grades. For example, good family-school partnerships result in higher reading and math scores for children and in higher state achievement test scores (Henderson & Mapp, 2002).

Partnerships with Parents: Building on Family Strengths

The early childhood profession focuses intentionally on finding practical and effective ways to create partnerships with parents because a family's influence and involvement is so important in a child's success in school. Probably one of the most effective ways to support all families is through a coordinated approach in which a school assesses each family's specific needs, plans **parent involvement**, and builds partnerships based on those needs (Kaczmarek, 2006).

There are six major types of parent involvement: parenting, communicating, volunteering, learning at home, decision making, and collaborating with the community (Epstein et al., 2002). Teachers and schools choose how to work with parents, and the specific method chosen depends on parents' identified needs, the teacher's knowledge and skills, and the support that a teacher has. The common thread in all effective family involvement is the clear focus on building family strength (Olson, 2006).

For example, families want their children to do well in school. This is a fundamental family strength. Schools should identify other strengths in families. For example, some families have a tradition of storytelling. When planning family literacy activities, a school could encourage these parents to teach others to tell stories. There is some evidence, however, showing that some young families tend to read to and share stories with toddlers and preschool children less than do other families. This can have an unintentionally negative effect on a child's literacy and language development. By kindergarten entrance, some children, for example, have less knowledge of the alphabet than do other children (Lopez, Barrueco, Feinauer, & Miles, 2007).

Teachers can help all young families understand how important they are in their child's success in literacy and language and can assist them in this teaching role. This is a strength-based approach that builds on a family's existing competence.

> Go to MyEducationLab and select the topic "Families and Communities." Under Activities and Applications, read the strategy *A Teacher's Experience in involving Parents in Their Children's Reading and Writing* and see how this teacher helps parents understand their role in literacy.

> **Parent involvement** Methods or strategies through which schools initiate or increase collaboration among parents, the school, and the community.

Effective Parent Involvement Strategies

There are many effective modes of involving parents and families in their young child's education. Parents of typically developing children and parents of children with disabilities can be invited to the circle of support for their child's development and learning. See Figure 3.9 for some practical strategies.

Communicating with Families in Conferences

Teachers have an ethical responsibility to inform parents and families about a child's progress, and they have a responsibility to do this in a way that enhances the family or parent's skill as a parent (Division for Early Childhood, 2002; Feeney & Freeman, 1999; Hemmeter, Maxwell, Ault, & Schuster, 2001). Communicating, a major component in working with families, involves establishing positive ways of getting information about children's progress between teacher and family.

Teachers communicate with families verbally, in writing, or with phones and computers. For example, a teacher might do a home visit or send home a newsletter or other handout.

Parents are important in your child's success in literacy.

The teacher might call parents or send homework information via a distribution list. A parent might write a note to the teacher, make a phone call, or fill out a questionnaire designed by the teacher (Epstein et al., 2002; Soderman & Farrell, 2008).

Parent **conferences** are an important form of communication. Knowing how to conduct a conference, a face-to-face meeting with a parent, or parent and child together (Young & Behounek, 2006) is a practical skill that all teachers need, including teachers working with children with special needs. There are several practical considerations in conducting an effective conference with a parent or family. The following list is adapted from Seplocha (2004):

> **Conference** Face-to-face meeting with a parent or parent and child.

FIGURE 3.9 Building Relationships and Communicating with Families: Selected Practical Strategies

- **Orientation for New Families:** welcomes parents who are new to school; gives helpful information; parents feel supported; a part of coordinated communication.
- **Family Handbook:** information about the curriculum and policies, how to contact teachers. Includes phone numbers, school email addresses, and information on times for talking. This can be in an electronic format as well as in hard copy.
- **Communication Notebook:** a notebook that goes between home and school. Parents and teachers write notes to each other.
- **Resource Library:** helps parents get information helpful to them and their families.
- **Mentor Families:** school offers to link new family with family familiar with the school.
- **Classroom Visits:** parents see classroom in action and have opportunity to talk to school personnel; parents see children in a setting different from home.
- **Newsletters:** gives parents information about events; can be used to deliver information on child development and other topics of interest to a specific group.
- **Phone Calls:** convenient, direct, interactive.
- **Email:** for parents with computers this can be a convenient and quick way to communicate with teachers.
- **Parent Meetings:** when planned well can support parents and help them learn about topics of interest to them as parents.
- **Routine Conferences:** see information within chapter.

Sources: Berger (2008); Gonzalez-Mena (2007); Kaczmarek (2006); Wright, Stegelin, and Hartle (2007).

- *Schedule the conference, and be flexible.* As much as possible, accommodate parents' busy schedules. Set some hours for morning, others for evening, and consider a Saturday meeting at a public library if that is the only time that a parent can meet. Allow sufficient time. You will need about 30 minutes for meeting with the parent and then a little time between conferences if you are having more than one. Use the minutes after the conference to organize your notes or to prepare for the next conference. In cases of two parents sharing custody, be sure to invite both parents to separate conferences.

- *Provide a welcoming setting and adopt a professional and welcoming manner.* Provide adult-sized furniture. Use a table if you plan to show items from a child's portfolio. Place chairs on the same side of the table so that you and the parent can look at portfolio items together, but place the chairs far enough apart to allow the parent his or her own personal space. Make sure that the area is clean and tidy and consider playing soft music in the background. Remember the purpose of the conference—to work together on behalf of a child. Be friendly but professional. Smile, face the parent, and look at them when speaking. Lean forward when appropriate. Stay tuned in to what a parent says. Listen carefully and respond appropriately.

- *Prepare and organize for the conference.* Send home a questionnaire before the conference for parents to complete and return to you, telling you their questions and concerns. You would then have the opportunity to prepare ahead of time for the conference with children's work samples, information, and assessments that might address concerns.

Think about and write down the purpose of the conference. Suppose, for example, that you want to show a child's work samples to her parents. You would also want to listen to parents' concerns and questions about their child's progress.

Choose the work samples, preferably with the child. Choose just a few so that you can finely focus the discussion. Plan what to say about each sample. If a child attends the conference, then help the child plan on how to show his or her work to the parent.

Use a interpreter. This will help you communicate accurately with parents and will convey your respect for the parent. A professional interpreter who speaks a parent's home language should be used to translate written materials or to translate during meetings and conferences. When talking about a child's progress or family issues, you must protect a child and family's privacy; therefore, interpreters should be held to rules of confidentiality. Teachers should avoid using children as interpreters. Interpreting for parents can cause anxiety for children and children do not have the vocabulary to interpret information conveyed by the teacher (Richardson, 2003).

- *Stay focused during the conference.* Focus on children's strengths. Acknowledge areas for growth. Maintain your teacher role, for which you would be certified, and avoid a counseling or therapist role, for which you most likely would not be certified. Stay focused on your purpose. For example, if you are presenting work samples, then state this goal at the start of the conference, "Welcome, Mr. Alvino. Paul (the son) wanted me to show you three things that show what he has learned in first grade."

  Adopt a positive attitude, even if you have to talk about something unpleasant. Start on a positive note and stay there. Consider showing a photo of the parent's child from the past week and describe the context of the photo. This will set a very positive tone for the conference. Show each work sample and briefly describe the learning involved. Note any problems that the child encountered, and emphasize how the child has overcome the problem or is currently working on the problem. Do not avoid talking about problems.

- *Be aware that parents have different attitudes to school.* Parents, understandably, might be anxious about a parent-teacher conference. Some parents have not had good school experiences themselves. Some parents are afraid to be in schools, and some parents are even hostile or angry. Your welcoming atmosphere, your professional manner, and your willingness to adjust to a parent's busy schedule should alert parents that you and they are really on the same team. Ask parents what they want to know about their child's progress or about your classroom and curriculum. Then, answer their questions briefly and honestly.

- *Learn from parents and give ideas about at-home activities.* A conference is a time to *share* information. It should never be one-sided. You can learn a lot from parents about a child, and this can help you plan for that child; however, you have to listen well to glean this information. Some parents have never been treated as a member of a teaching team and might be a little surprised when you ask them to describe their child's favorite type of television show or what their child does really well.

  Keep this simple. Parents do want to help their child be successful, but they are also very busy and you can help by giving them one or two very specific, practical, *inexpensive* things to do. Do they have questions about homework, for example? Then give one or two of your very best suggestions, something easy for the parents to carry through. Are they concerned about learning to read? Then, give them one or two simple-to-do activities and emphasize reading to children. Do not give long lists, and do not expect parents to buy expensive equipment.

Reflecting and Making Changes

Effective teachers plan well, but they also know that things do not always go smoothly. In addition to planning well, effective teachers reflect on their practices, noting what works and what does not work. Teacher reflection is especially important in working with families (Ginsburg & Hermann-Ginsburg, 2005).

Reflective teachers are interested in why things go well and why other things do not work out. They then think through a situation that does not go well and adjust plans. For example, suppose that you have carefully planned for a parent-teacher conference and have gathered three work samples to show to Pete's father. Pete's father, however, wants no part of looking at work samples. He wants to talk to you about the school's new homework policy. After the conference, you reflect and think about what you might do differently. You decide that you will ask parents ahead of time what they want to talk about but that you also want to show them what their child is learning at school. You decide to develop a short questionnaire to accompany the invitation to the conference.

SUMMARY

Effective teachers and schools understand that children develop primarily in the context of their families and, therefore, forge a strong and supportive partnership with parents.

- Schools today have a richly diverse population of children and families.
- Many schools acknowledge that children's success depends on recognizing the variety of families in which children grow up and different cultures and languages in a community.
- These schools understand that overlapping spheres of influence—families, the community, and a school—affect children's development and learning.
- The goal is to place children at the center and to develop a real partnership involving a child's family, her school, and her community.

Effective teachers also use a set of guiding principles in their work with families. They rely on their knowledge of child development and build respectful, reciprocal relationships with families. They link families with early childhood and community resources, and they strive to be culturally competent in their work with parents.

Early childhood education teachers understand that a parent is a child's first teacher and the setting or context for a child's earliest learning is in his family. Children learn so many things in a warm, supportive, and nurturing relationship with their parents such as getting one's needs met, what and when to eat, and how to show or hide feelings.

- Early childhood education teachers support parents in their teaching role because they have such a profound impact on a child's development and learning.
- We build on a family's strength and find practical and effective ways to create partnerships with parents. Some of the ideas for involving parents include orienting and supporting families new to a school, developing a family handbook, providing resources through a resource library, linking new families with a mentor family, communicating through phone calls, email, and newsletters, and routine conferences for discussing children's development and progress. Children are often included in the conference.

QUESTIONS FOR REFLECTION

1. Suppose that you speak only English and move to a country where the main language is Spanish. Many English-speaking children have also moved to this country. You notice that your child's school has printed all signs, web sites, handouts, and other materials in both Spanish and English. What message would this send to you as a parent?

2. Reflect on the suggestions in Figure 3.6, Demonstrate Respect When Working with Families. Choose one suggestion that you think is particularly important. Finish this sentence about the rule: "I think that _____ will help me develop a respectful relationship with families because _____."

APPLY YOUR KNOWLEDGE

What Should This Teacher Do?

1. It was November and Mr. Hernandez had developed a good relationship with each family, but he noticed that the mother of one of his first graders was clearly upset. She wanted to know why Mr. Hernandez was not using flashcards as part of the curriculum. Name one thing that this parent does not understand about child development. Refer to Figure 3.5 for assistance.

2. Use the same scenario. Work with another student to role-play how Mr. Hernandez would deal with the parent's concern in a respectful way. Consider reviewing Figure 3.6 and the section on civil, respectful interaction when planning your role-play.

KEY TERMS

Adaptation, 68
Characteristics of families, 60
Child with a disability, 65
Conference, 81
Culturally competent, 78
Developmental delay, 67
Differentiated instruction, 68

Diverse population of children and families, 60
Early intervention services, 65
IDEA, 66
IEP, 67
IFSP, 67
Overlapping spheres of influence, 60

Parent involvement, 81
Partnership with parents, 60
Poverty level, 63
Reciprocal relationship, 73
Resources for families, 76
Respectful relationship, 73
Toxic stress, 63

WEB SITES

Bilingual Web Site For School Success
In English:

http://www.colorincolorado.org
Colorín Colorado is a bilingual web site that provides information, activities, and advice on helping children learn to read and succeed at school. Developed by the **Reading Rockets** project (Reading Rockets 2002; 2007), Colorín Colorado features practical information for Spanish-speaking parents, beautiful illustrations from Caldecott Award–winning illustrator David Diaz, video clips of celebrities such as the late, beloved Celia Cruz, and skill-building activities that draw upon Spanish-language songs and rhymes.

In Spanish:

http://www.colorincolorado.org
Colorín Colorado es un sitio Web bilingüe que provee información, actividades y consejos sobre cómo ayudar a sus niños a que aprendan a leer y tengan éxito en la escuela. Desarrollado por el proyecto *Reading Rockets*, Colorín Colorado resalta información práctica para los padres de habla hispana, contiene hermosas ilustraciones de David Díaz, el ilustrador ganador del Premio Caldecott, además de videoclips de celebridades tales como la que

fuera nuestra querida Celia Cruz, y actividades que giran alrededor de canciones y rimas en el lenguaje español para desarrollar habilidades.

http://www.ldonline.org/article/6345
This site provides information on developing an Individualized Education Program (IEP). This article would be especially helpful to parents whose children require an IEP.

Learning About Tolerance
http://www.tolerance.org/index.jsp
Home page for the Teaching Tolerance web site, a project of the Southern Poverty Law Center. Good links for teachers and parents. Specific information on teaching about tolerance for children of different ages.

Linking Families with Community Resources
http://www.mchlibrary.info
Home page for the Maternal and Child Health web site from Georgetown University. Good site for information on linking families with community services.

National Center for Children in Poverty
http://www.nccp.org
Excellent source and presentation of tables and information about children in poverty.

CHAPTER 4

Supporting Children's Emotional Development

- What are the characteristics of emotionally healthy children, and what do children need for good emotional health?

- How do factors such as culture, brain development, or exposure to media violence affect children's emotional development?

- How can teachers foster children's emotional health?

INFANT-TODDLER
Babies Cry for Many Reasons

Four-month-old Gabe was crying as his father handed him to the teacher. The frustrated parent said, "I'd like it if he'd just listen to me when I tell him to stop crying." Holding Gabe gently against his chest and shoulder and stroking Gabe's back soothingly, Mr. Bjornrud, the teacher, said, "Babies do cry, don't they? Come on in for a few minutes, if you have a little time." They talked for a few minutes about why young infants cry.

PRESCHOOL
Different Reactions to Aviva's Distress

Aviva, an abrasion on her arm from having fallen on gravel, cried softly as Mrs. Chang examined the wound. While helping Aviva, Mrs. Chang observed that Aiko, Ian, and Beth, all playing nearby, responded in different ways to this clearly distressed child. First, Aiko hurried over and patted Aviva's hand. Ian looked intently at Aviva but then slowly turned and walked across the play yard visibly distressed himself. Finally, when the teacher turned away, Beth jumped from the climbing structure and instead of offering help, hissed, "Stop crying, you big baby!"

PRIMARY
Keep Your Face from Looking Mad

Seven-year-old Luis told Emma that his father punished him after he made a face when he saw his grandmother's gift of pajamas. Emma said that her mother told her to thank people who give you presents. Emma's mother had also told her that the gift giver would feel bad if your face looks mad. Luis said, "So even if I get pajamas, don't make a mad face?"

These vignettes reveal the puzzle-like nature of emotions, every emotion having three puzzle pieces—feeling, expressing, and understanding. All children can feel emotions as did infant Gabe, preschooler Aviva, and second grader Luis. All children can express feelings although they have much to learn about communicating them appropriately.

Young children, however, do not understand feelings and, therefore, have difficulty managing feelings on their own. The vignettes also reveal the developmental progression in feeling, expressing, and understanding emotions. Gabe's uncontrolled expression of distress gives way to 4-year-old Aviva's more reserved expression through whimpering. The 7 year olds demonstrate an older child's emerging ability to regulate feelings.

This chapter describes and explains children's movement from the action and body-oriented expression of feelings in very early childhood to the ability to express feelings symbolically, with words, pictures, and drawing from ages 4 through 8. We examine the characteristics of emotionally healthy children. We explore what children need to develop those characteristics so that they can begin to understand emotions as second graders, as Luis and Emma illustrate. We consider the crucial role of early childhood teachers in supporting children's emotional well-being. To help children, teachers must understand how entwined a child's emotional development is with other domains of development and with success in school. For example, children whose language skills are good find learning and using words for expressing feelings easier than children with poor language development. With all this in mind, we look at some practical strategies teachers use to support children's emotional well-being.

Effective teachers of young children need to

- know and understand young children's *emotional* characteristics and needs,
- know and understand the multiple influences on *emotional* development, and
- use knowledge about *emotional* development to create healthy, respectful, supportive, and challenging learning environments (NAEYC, 2001).

UNDERSTANDING CHILDREN'S EMOTIONAL CHARACTERISTICS AND NEEDS

Caring teachers, understanding the powerful, lasting, snowballing effects of positive or negative early emotional learning experiences, help children learn about emotions and become as strong and resilient as possible (Kovner, Kline, & Maerlender, 2003).

Characteristics of Emotionally Healthy Young Children

Optimal periods exist for different types of development and learning, and early childhood is a prime time for emotional development and for learning about feelings. Table 4.1 summarizes the sequence of emotional learning and development during the early childhood years.

Emotionally healthy children share four characteristics.

1. They have access to a full range of feelings and cope with emotions in age-appropriate ways.
2. They develop basic qualities of trust, autonomy, and initiative.
3. They are resilient.
4. They function well in school.

Full Range of Feelings and Emotions

Emotionally healthy children are aware of their own feelings and the feelings of others. This gives them a major advantage over children who lack awareness. Peers seem to like

---

TABLE 4.1   Developmental Sequence: Early Childhood Emotional Development

Birth to 12 Months

- Able to differentiate mother's and father's emotions, but this is not real empathy
- Feels and expresses basic emotions
- Amygdala, a part of the brain, almost fully formed in newborns
- Does not understand emotions, that is, cannot interpret or evaluate feelings
- Cannot regulate emotions

12 to 36 Months

- 50%–83% of 18 month olds understand "happy" and "mad"; only 7% use the words
- Feels and expresses self-conscious emotions (at about 2 years)
- Shows beginnings of empathy; does not have high-level empathy
- Begins to notice how culture says emotions should be displayed
- Does not understand emotions, cannot interpret or evaluate feelings
- Cannot regulate emotions
- At approximately 24 months of age, toddlers begin to use specific emotional displays to get support from their social environment

Preschool and Kindergarten

- 3–4 years, the brain's prefrontal cortex shows some growth; makes budding self-control and emotional regulation possible
- Self-conscious emotions continue to develop
- Now uses more of the emotion words that he or she understands: over 60% of 6 year olds understand "embarrassed" and "jealous," and over 50% actually use the words
- Gets better at decoding emotions in another person's face; identifies typically happy expressions most accurately
- Some 5 to 6 year olds realize that people can have more than one emotion at a time, but this knowledge is far less sophisticated than it will be at age 11 or 12
- Uses culture's scripts for how to express emotion
- Gets better at understanding what another person needs but still cannot feel the other person's feelings
- Changes a reaction to a stirred up emotion; can magnify feelings to get someone's attention
- Can put on a "pretend" facial expression, cannot say how this conceals real feelings

Primary Grades (after age 6)

- Gets better at regulating emotions
- Capable of putting on "pretend" facial expression, can say how it conceals the real emotion
- Capable of deciding how long an emotion will last
- Capable of better management of how strong their emotions are

---

children who are emotionally aware (Denham, McKinley, Couchoud, & Hold, 1990). Consequently, teachers who focus on emotional awareness also help children to gain acceptance and liking by others, one of their most fundamental needs.

Children seem to come equipped, from birth, with some emotions and then develop others as they grow and develop (Table 4.2). All children have a set of **basic emotions**, such as anger, contentment, or distress, at birth or within a few months after birth. **Self-conscious emotions** such as feeling proud of an accomplishment or feeling guilty about hurting an animal, emerge later, at about 24 months, during toddlerhood.

The label of self-conscious seems appropriate because a child is aware or conscious for the first time about three things. One, a very young child now has a *self* of which to be conscious. Two, at around 24 months, a toddler shows the emerging realization that he has some responsibilities in social relationships, and, three, toddlers show the beginnings of holding themselves accountable for meeting or not meeting the expectations.

As a toddler, Aiko had jumped into her teacher's lap just as another toddler had started to sit there. The teacher asked Aiko to look at Jessie, now crying, and said that Jessie was upset because Aiko had taken his spot. Without saying a word, Aiko slid over in the teacher's lap, allowing Jessie room to move in.

Basic emotions Emotions present at birth or shortly after birth; governed by the primitive parts of the brain; anger, contentment, distress.

Self-conscious emotions Emotions emerging during toddlerhood; tied to the developing brain and the child's sense of self; examples include guilt and pride.

TABLE 4.2 Basic and Self-Conscious Emotions		
Age at Which Children First Feel Emotions	**Basic Emotions**	**Complex, Self-Conscious Emotions**
Birth to 6 weeks	Contentment Distress	
6 weeks to 14 months	Anger Fear Joy	
2 years (24 months) and then continues to evolve through early childhood	Continues to feel all the above basic emotions and now acquires complex emotions	Anxiety Disgust Embarrassment Guilt Hubris (overconfidence or even arrogance) Jealousy Pride Sadness Shame

Source: Saarni, Mumme, and Campos (1998).

Decode emotions Observing changes in another's facial expressions and then making sense of the emotions.

Emotional regulation A child's ability to manage the way he or she reacts to emotions.

Emotionally healthy children are also aware of how others might feel. This ability depends on a child's ability to **decode emotions** in another person's face, the knack of observing changes in and then making sense of someone's facial expressions. There is a developmental progression in deciphering facial expressions. Infants can discriminate among mother's different emotions (Cohn, Campbell, Matias, & Hopkins, 1990; Termine & Izard, 1988). Three to 6 year olds, more accurate in detecting how another person feels, are especially proficient at spotting typically happy emotions (Gross & Ballif, 1991).

Some young children are aware that another person can feel more than one emotion at a time (Harter & Whitesell, 1989), but this usually does not happen until children are about 5 or 6 years old. Younger children would describe someone about whom they have two different feelings (Stein & Trabasso, 1989) by focusing on separate events. For example, Andy, 5 years old, said, "I'm mad because Dad took my bike away (event #1). My Dad took us to the water park and I was happy" (event #2). Older children can simultaneously put together two or more different emotions about the same person or animal. For instance, a 12 year old said, "I was happy to be with my friends but also nervous about the new teachers."

Emotionally healthy children are not only aware of emotions in themselves and others but can also express feelings without hurting themselves or others. **Emotional regulation** refers to children's ability to manage the way they react to emotions. Emotionally healthy children do no harm to

Children learn to decode emotions in another's face.

others when managing feelings. Children who manage emotions well tend to feel more connected to others and to have better relationships with other children than children who cannot control their emotions. They feel competent and capable, both components of positive self-esteem. They experience a general sense of balance in their emotions, and like anybody who manages emotions well, they have a sense of overall well-being (Skinner & Wellborn, 1994).

How would a young, emotionally healthy child act when managing the emotions that wash over him at school? He would use words to tell others how he felt, would know when to show or not show emotions, and stays relatively calm.

The child uses words to tell others how she feels. She does not hurt anybody when upset. When teachers say, "Use your words," they are helping children move from acting on feeling to expressing them symbolically, with words in this case. Early childhood is replete with examples of children using a symbol to stand for something else, to tell somebody else about their experience. They use symbols such as words, painting, drawing, dance, and drama to represent or stand for their experience. Teaching young children to use words when angry is a developmentally appropriate strategy based on Piaget's theory.

Recall that the third puzzle piece for emotions is *understanding the feeling*. Children have to be able to evaluate and interpret a feeling like anger before they can understand it. Talking about the feeling, using words, is an excellent way to begin to evaluate and interpret feelings (Brown & Dunn, 1996). Vygotsky's theory emphasizes that discussion between teacher and child helps children begin to understand their feelings.

Very young children seem to comprehend many more emotion words than they can easily use (Ridgeway, Waters, & Kuczaj, 1985). About 50% to 83% of toddlers understand emotion words *happy* and *mad*. However, only 7% actually use the words. In contrast, 60% of first graders know the emotion words *embarrassed* and *jealous*. Now, however, over 50% would actually use the words. Even so, some children are more proficient than others are in understanding and using word as labels for feelings (Dunn & Brown, 1994).

An emotionally healthy child also knows when it is acceptable to show that he is upset and when it is not suitable. He knows that it is sometimes better to mask an emotion. A child with this knowledge would make statements implying that he knows when it is acceptable to show emotions. He has learned to restrain emotions when somebody else's feelings might be hurt (Eisenberg, Fabes, Schuller, Carlo, & Miller, 1991) and can deliberately and appropriately change a reaction to a stirred up emotion. He might exaggerate, saying, "Oweee, oweee, OWEEE," minimize by asserting that, "It doesn't hurt at all," or even substitute emotions. For example, he might act angry when he feels fear (Brenner & Salovey 1997).

Managing emotional reactions begins when children are in preschool (Saarni, 1989). Buss and Kiel (2004), however, found that even 24-month-old toddlers displayed facial expressions of *sadness* and not anger or fear, when looking at their mothers, indicating that toddlers use specific displays of emotion to get support from their mothers. Before age 6, children can magnify their feelings to get someone's attention and can put one expression on their face even though they feel another emotion. However, they cannot say how this substituted facial expression conceals their real feeling. After age 6 a child can indeed explain that how someone's face looks might conceal a completely different emotion. See the photographs of children at different ages.

Finally, an emotionally healthy child can remain calm so that she can help someone else. This child does not get agitated. She uses emotional energy to consider the

Go to MyEducationLab and select the topic "Child Development." Under Activities and Applications, watch the video *Emotional Development: Infancy*, which gives a good picture of changes in how children understand emotions from infancy to middle childhood.

Infants cannot change their reaction to a stirred-up emotion.

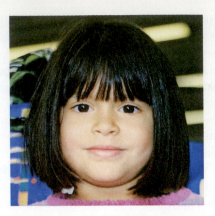

"This is my pretend face." Preschool children can put on a "pretend" facial expression. It is different from how they feel, but they can*not* say why.

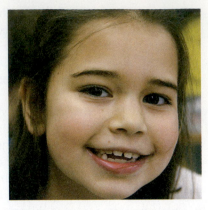

Children older than 6 can explain how the expression on someone's face might conceal another, different, emotion, for example, "I'm smiling for this picture, but I am really mad at Carlos."

other person's predicament and needs. Some children, however, do not help other children in distress even when they are empathic. Instead, another person's or animal's suffering distresses them to the point they avoid that person or animal, as Ian did in the preschool vignette at the beginning of the chapter. The other's anguish is *too much* to handle and our child becomes over aroused by emotions. A typical response to not being able to control one's emotional arousal is to escape from the situation.

Reluctance to help someone in distress grows out of not having one's own emotional needs acknowledged. A child might have had many experiences with adults who clamped down when the child himself felt anxious, angry, or distressed (Eisenberg et al., 1991), not giving the help needed. Consequently, the child is powerless to help others. This effect is even worse for children who have been abused. In one early study, very young children who had been abused showed no sympathy to another child who was distressed. Instead, they were even more frequently aggressive to other children and were likely to attack a distressed classmate as Beth does in the preschool vignette in the beginning of the chapter (Main & George, 1985).

Trust, Autonomy, Initiative, and Industry

Erik Erikson's theory describes eight stages in personality development (Chapter 1). Each of the stages presents a challenge to children with a positive or a negative outcome for each stage. Trust, autonomy, initiative, and industry are the positive outcomes of the first four stages, the stages of early childhood. Each positive quality developed allows a child to move more easily to the challenge of the next stage (Erikson, 1950).

Acquiring a sense of trust versus mistrust is the first stage and occurs during infancy. Parents and teachers who help a distressed baby get what he needs help him develop a **sense of trust.** The baby develops the sense that he can rely on important adults to try to read his signals and then to respond as appropriately as possible. Babies develop a **sense of mistrust** when parents or caregivers ignore their needs. Mistrust is the sense that important adults will not help him get what he needs. Maslow's theory suggests that a sense of safety and security is one of a human's most basic needs, and like Erikson's sense of trust, most easily develops in a reliable environment that meets an infant's needs in a loving way.

Mistrust, sense of Sense that important adults will not help a baby get what he needs.

Trust, sense of Develops when a baby senses that he can rely on important adults to read his signals and respond appropriately.

Achieving a sense of autonomy versus shame or doubt, the second stage, takes place during the toddler years. A toddler now has new skills like walking and talking and wants to make decisions. He wants to be independent (autonomous). Teachers help toddlers develop a **sense of autonomy** by encouraging toddler bids for independence. They also encourage toddlers to try again if they make errors. Toddlers who are not encouraged begin to doubt their abilities and develop a **sense of doubt** or might even feel shame for attempting independent actions.

Attaining a **sense of initiative** versus **guilt**, is the third stage. With all their new developmental abilities, preschool and kindergarten children now want to explore and investigate their world. Teachers and parents foster initiative in two main ways. First, we should support children as they try new and exciting roles and activities. Mr. Hernandez, for example, encouraged two of his second graders' initiative when they asked for permission to use fuzzy wire (pipe cleaners) to shape new spelling words. Then, teachers also need to help children understand that some things are not permitted and to learn reasonable limits. Two to 6 year olds are likely to feel guilty about wanting to try something new when someone ridicules or punishes them after they have taken initiative.

Attaining a **sense of industry** versus **inferiority** is the fourth stage, straddling early and middle childhood, from 6 to about 12 years. Children's development moves forward, allowing them to participate in increasingly advanced and complicated projects and activities. They can consolidate a healthy view of their competence, control, and worth, all elements of self-esteem. Children now move out from their families to participate in larger systems such as school, churches, and clubs. Adults who have contact with children during this stage, and for our purposes, their teachers, help children develop a sense of industry by encouraging their participation in activities that they like and want to do. We can help them accept challenges and learn how to deal with minor setbacks with grace.

Resiliency

Resilience is the ability to cope with difficulty rather than being defeated or overwhelmed by it or responding in a way that is destructive or self-destructive (Bardige, 2005). Resilient children are socially competent, can solve problems, can reflect critically on issues, are autonomous, and have a sense of purpose (Bernard, 1995). Resilient children can bounce back from upsets or bad moods, and they can tolerate stress reasonably well.

A resilient spirit is born when children believe that they are worthy of affection. Resilient children are connected, attached, to at least one significant person, often a teacher, who serves as a model of confidence and positive action. Children can learn to understand and manage potentially stressful feelings in caring, compassionate teacher-child relationships. Resilience-building teachers provide three **protective factors** that foster resilience: caring relationship, high expectations, and opportunities for participation.

Resilience-building teachers build caring relationships by acknowledging each child's existence, what that child does and creates, and how she feels. They have high but reasonable expectations that foster competence, control, and worth, the three building blocks of self-esteem. Teachers also understand children's need to function as a valued group member. A sensitive teacher observes children carefully to discover what they truly enjoy doing and then invents opportunities for participating.

Autonomy, sense of Sense of independence brought about by adult encouragement of new skills during toddlerhood.

Doubt, sense of Feeling unsure about new abilities brought on by lack of adult encouragement in toddlerhood.

Guilt, sense of Two- to 6-year-old child's sense of shame or blame for wanting to try new things.

Initiative, sense of Two- to 6-year-old child's joy and confidence in exploring new roles and activities.

Industry, sense of Six to 12 year olds engage in advanced projects and consolidate a view of their competence.

Resilience Ability to cope effectively with difficulty.

Protective factors Factors fostering resilience, include caring relationships, high expectations, and opportunities for participation.

Emotionally Healthy Children in School

They separate from their families with minimal stress, with very young children and developmentally delayed children likely to show more stress. Mentally healthy children can form an attachment with at least one adult at school. In school, emotionally healthy children settle down and concentrate on activities typically associated with a developmentally appropriate curriculum (Hoagwood, 1996). A 3 year old might concentrate on squishing play dough; a kindergartener could focus on a developmentally appropriate group time, while a second or third grader could attend to individual or group academic work. They can conform to school routines with ease. Even healthy 2 year olds, however, might likely balk and a healthy 4 year old occasionally tests limits during routines. Emotionally healthy children also adapt relatively easily to minor adjustments in the school environment, for example, when Mr. Hernandez's class had to check out library books in the hallway and not the library desk.

CHECK YOUR UNDERSTANDING
Analyzing Chapter-Opening Vignettes

Refer to the section that you just read, Characteristics of Emotionally Healthy Young Children, to answer these questions.

Infant: True or False? Infants are able to stop crying on command, as Gabe's father has ordered 4-month-old Gabe to do. Explain your response.

Preschool: Explain two ways in which Aiko demonstrates characteristics of an emotionally healthy child.

Primary grade: Explain what second grader Luis has learned about regulating emotions from Emma, also a second grader.

Teachers need to know about children's emotional health needs. We now look at some of these needs.

What Children Need for Good Emotional Health

Recognizing and meeting children's emotional needs allows emotional health to flourish. While a child's most fundamental emotional need is her family's unconditional love, teachers and schools can help children get what they need for good emotional health (National Mental Health Association, 2005). Three of a child's emotional health needs are:

1. Supportive nurturing teachers who create a safe, stable, developmentally appropriate school environment
2. Positive self-esteem and moral identity
3. Opportunities to play

Supportive Teachers and School Environment

Supportive, nurturing teachers show respect for all children in teacher-child interactions. Respectful teachers have a clear communication style, delivering messages simply, firmly, kindly, and consistently. They use persuasion, not force, to help children understand things. They use positive developmentally appropriate guidance strategies, which focus on teaching and not on punishment. Respectful teachers believe in giving simple, clear reasons and explanations in **discipline encounters**, interactions in which a teacher helps a child choose a more helpful course of action.

Supportive nurturing teachers set and maintain reasonable, fair limits and closely monitor and supervise children's activities. They are willing to cope with behavior that is clearly hurtful or inappropriate such as name-calling or physical aggression. They are firm yet kind and willing to take a stand even if doing so provokes a conflict. They are warm, and their actions tell children that they genuinely like each child. They also show a genuine concern for each child's welfare. Warm and nurturing teachers understand child development, which helps them have realistic expectations of children of different ages for emotional development (Ostrosky & Jung, 2003).

Psychologically and physically safe and secure classrooms and schools improve children's chances for good emotional health. Schools are safe places when children feel respected and never hurt, belittled, degraded, or humiliated. Safe schools understand the devastating effects of bullying and do everything possible to prevent this problem or intervene appropriately when bullying occurs (Royal College of Psychiatrists, 2004). Guidance practices are positive and reflect the same qualities expressed by supportive nurturing teachers. The school involves teachers, administrators, parents, and children in emotional learning programs that teach the skills necessary for making ethical and sensible decisions, such as whether or not to bully someone (Shriver & Weissberg, 2005). They might use **bibliotherapy** to help children who are dealing with stress and trauma, such as moving or the deployment of a parent in the military to a faraway place. Bibliotherapy is the use of books and literature to help children better understand and deal with stressful events and is a supportive resource for teachers.

In safe, stable school environments, teachers help children to become independent, learn to make sound choices and decisions, and to take initiative (Elkind, 2005). They do this by using a developmentally appropriate curriculum that emphasizes learning

Discipline encounters Interactions in which a teacher helps a child choose a more helpful course of action.

Bibliotherapy The use of books and literature to help children better understand and deal with stressful events.

This teacher uses books to help children understand stressful events.

Go to MyEducationLab and select the topic "Creative Arts." Under Activities and Applications, watch the video *Creative Arts* to see how art can foster healthy emotional development.

activities worthy of children's time and in which children are actively involved (DeVries, Zan, Hildebrandt, Edmiaston, & Sales, 2002; Rosberg, 2003; Work, 2002). Such an environment promotes play in the learning process (Elkind, 2006) that incorporates many concrete experiences (Helm & Katz, 2001) like stories, music, and center activities. Teachers in these environments use worksheets rarely, if ever (Burts, Hart, Charlesworth, Fleege, Mosley, & Thomasson, 1992).

Children build emotional strength when their interest and background knowledge are incorporated into center activities. In a true constructivist classroom, children select centers and direct their own activity while teachers act as observers and facilitators but do not take over a child's activity. Centers encourage social interaction and give children practice expressing their needs and thoughts and gaining confidence and skill in expressing emotions actively and responsibly. Many center activities give children a chance to express happiness, fear, sadness, or even anger and jealousy. Here are a few examples:

- Music and dance: listening, moving, and dancing to a variety of types of music, including that from different cultures; swirling scarves in time to music; playing musical instruments such as xylophones, drums, or tambourines.
- Art center/atelier: using many media such as finger paint or watercolors to represent ideas; pounding, pushing, and pummeling clay and play dough as a stress reliever.
- Water and sand table: relaxing with sand and water is therapeutic and helps to alleviate stress for young children.
- Dramatic play: working out concerns and feelings by taking on different roles (Community Empowerment, 2001).
- Books, puppets, and persona dolls: expressing emotion through the doll or puppet is often easier for children than expressing it by themselves. *Persona dolls* are nonsexist, authentically dressed, and culturally authentic (http://www.personal-doll-training.org, 2007).

Schools can be encouraging environments for *all* children, including those with any type of special needs, such as the gifted. While gifted children have the same emotional needs as all children, they especially need a good match between their specific high abilities and their school's environment. They need to be able to use their gifts without embarrassment and to collaborate with other gifted children. Another thing that contributes to a gifted child's emotional health is to learn to take risks and not to stick to only those things for which they experience automatic success (Neihart, 2002).

Mr. Hernandez, for example, encouraged Philip, gifted in mathematics, to take a risk with a writing project. Reluctantly, Philip accepted and, with a good deal of frustration combined with his teacher's encouragement, produced a story about his grandfather.

Water play is relaxing for young children.

TEACH INTENTIONALLY

Supporting English Language Learners

What the teacher did: Four-year-old Raul is learning English. His teacher showed him photographs of children making *angry and happy* facial expressions. Pointing to the *angry* face, he said, "This boy is *angry.*" The teacher then made an *angry* expression and pointed to Raul, indicating that he, too, should make the angry expression. The teacher did *not* force Raul to say the word *angry* (oral production).

How the teacher was intentional: This teacher believes that each and every child is competent and tries to figure out what each needs in order to learn. He is also concerned about how children feel about themselves and wants them to grow in confidence. He has observed that Raul is an eager learner but that he gets anxious when he has to use English words, so he did not force Raul to say the new words. Instead, he used a visual aid and gestures, both practices recommended when working with English language learners in the first stage of learning a new language, the silent, receptive stage (Reed & Railsback, 2003), Raul's current stage.

Effective teachers also consider the emotional needs of English language learners when they choose teaching strategies. Unpleasant emotions can interfere with many things, including learning a second language (Krashen & Terrell, 1983; Reed & Railsback, 2003). Learning a new language requires that children use the unfamiliar words in public, and this can arouse emotions such as anxiety or embarrassment. This, in turn, can block a child's learning of new words. Teachers who create a nonthreatening environment that validates a child's cultural heritage help children to take the risks of using new words.

Positive Self-Esteem and Moral Identity

Positive self-esteem—healthy, confidant, and balanced—provides a solid foundation for emotional development and resilience. Self-esteem is the judgment that children make about their competence, control, and worth. Teachers believing in a developmental approach and in Vygotsky's theory know that they cannot give children self-esteem. They understand that they can scaffold or support children in forming a healthy and balanced view of themselves. Children's initial judgment of their competence, control, and worth develops slowly in early childhood and tends to be stable (Verschueren, Marcoen, & Buyck, 1998).

Negative, unhealthy, unbalanced self-esteem is a shaky foundation for emotional development and resilience. Children with damaged self-esteem and bruised egos make a negative evaluation of their competence, control, and worth. The negative evaluation can stay with a child for decades, negatively affecting many aspects of her life. A damaging evaluation might well result in a lifelong struggle to meet these needs or to avoid situations where deficits would stand out.

Along with positive self-esteem, children need a strong, objective **moral identity,** a moral compass guiding behavior (Baumeister, 1996). Moral identity is a person's use of moral principles governing two things: the child's idea of the right thing to do and the reason for taking a specific course of action. Moral identity takes shape in later childhood, but younger children can construct ideas about the difference between right and

Self-esteem, positive
Healthy, confident, balanced evaluation of one's self.

Moral identity A child's use of moral principles governing the idea of the right thing to do and the reason for taking a specific course of action.

wrong, the first step to acting humanely and ethically. For example, Mr. Hernandez explained that cleaning the hamster's house is the right thing to do because the hamster needs a clean house.

Opportunities to Play

Play Powerful vehicle for children's learning; promotes healthy emotional development.

True **play** is not a luxury in schools but a child's most powerful vehicle for learning (Elkind, 2003, 2006). Play promotes mental health, and joyful, complex play is a sign of mental health. Play is one of the most important elements in children's healthy emotional development (Gensburg, 2007). Children who play, either alone or with others, can grapple with feelings in a nonthreatening way. A child who plays in the dramatic play corner's "doctor's office," for example, can deal with anxious feelings about going to the doctor. Playing outdoors also allows children to deal with the emotion of fear in safe situations. For example, climbing just a little higher, or running just a little faster, under safe conditions, can help children feel competent and confident in situations that were slightly scary to them.

We now turn to looking at some of the major factors influencing a child's emotional development.

MULTIPLE INFLUENCES ON EMOTIONAL DEVELOPMENT AND LEARNING

Observe any group of young children and you very quickly notice that some children can talk about feelings but others cannot. Some are aware of their emotions; others are not. Differences in children's emotional development and learning have several roots, including the child's

- brain development,
- relationships with adults,
- culture,
- individual developmental variations, and
- exposure to media violence (NAEYC, 2003).

Brain Development Affects Emotional Development

Different parts of the human brain affect how children gradually develop the ability to regulate emotions. A primitive part of the brain, centered around the amygdala, for example, governs basic emotions. Later, brain development progresses and the cortical part of the brain grows tremendously. Therefore, a toddler's developing brain allows for the development of more complex, self-conscious emotions. Table 4.3 explains the role of two parts of the brain, the amygdala and the prefrontal cortex, a part of the neocortex, in emotional development (Goleman, 1995).

Go to MyEducationLab and select the topic "Child Development." Under Activities and Applications, watch the video *Emotional Development in Toddlers,* an overview of how to help toddlers develop emotional health.

Relationships with Adults Influence Emotional Development

Children's brains are wired for emotions, but many things, including relationships with adults, influence their emotional development.

Positive Relationships Require Thinking and Effort

Teachers must develop good relationships with children, take an interest in their feelings, and take the time to help them understand their emotions. Such interest and

TABLE 4.3   Role of Amygdala and Prefrontal Cortex in Emotional Development

Part of Brain	Description, Location, When Developed	What This Part of the Brain Does	Examples	What This Means for Teachers
Amygdala	Part of the emotional center in brain Located at top of brain stem Almost fully formed at birth	Stores a memory of emotional quality of child's experiences, pleasant or unpleasant Monitors new experiences to spot dangers or joy Reminds children of previously stored memories of episodes of emotion Can seize brain and keep child from thinking	Four-year-old Beth's amygdala preserved her memory of the fear and anxiety during arguments between her parents and times when they hit her Beth observed an argument between two other preschoolers. Reminded Beth about her parent's arguments Upset, Beth ran from the center	Children who are abused are primed to interpret another person's behavior incorrectly. Normal classroom disagreements signal the amygdala that danger is imminent Moves child to action before she can think about things (teachers want children to learn to think before acting)
Prefrontal Cortex	Part of the rational part of the brain; connected to limbic system Located at front part of human brain Shows growth at age 3 or 4 By age 6 has developed further	Receives and processes signals from amygdala Helps humans choose how they respond by analyzing information Balances amygdala's purely emotional response Gives humans a chance to think about emotions sensibly	Mrs. Chang has helped Beth recognize signs of being upset and to "stop and think" At year's end, Beth did not automatically hit when angry Eight-year-old Tom looked at another child who had called him "dummy" and said, "I am not a dummy"	Expect infants and toddlers to express emotions quickly and not be able to regulate emotions (amygdala fully developed, prefrontal cortex is not) Expect preschool children to show emerging self-control and emotional regulation Expect primary grade children to show more self-control and emotional regulation

Source: Based on Goleman (1995); Marion, (2007).

teaching help children learn to communicate effectively about emotions and how to regulate them (Baumrind, 1996; Hardy, Power, & Jaedicke, 1993; Ostrosky & Jung, 2003; Saarni, Mumme, & Campos, 1998).

Teachers can do many things to foster positive teacher-child relationships (Ostrosky & Jung, 2003). All of the following suggestions are a part of a warm and caring environment in which a child feels safe and secure and where she can communicate and deal with feelings in a constructive way. Teachers have a responsibility to establish a classroom community in which every child feels valued and welcome.

- Interact with children one-on-one
- Get on the child's level for face-to-face interactions
- Use a pleasant, calm voice and simple language
- Provide appropriate physical contact, a hand lightly on the shoulder or back
- Acknowledge children's feelings
- Listen to children and encourage them to listen to others

Some Children Have Had Emotionally Damaging Relationships with Adults

Children's emotional development is threatened by one of two forms of aberrant parenting—physical abuse, in which parents do something harmful to a child, and neglect, in which parents leave something out of their interaction with their child. Consider the type of relationship that children have with abusive parents—unremitting aggression combined with sporadic and explosive episodes of anger and aggression. Abusive parents are often cold and aloof and model aggression for their children.

Physically abused children do not learn to recognize feelings in themselves or others. They tend to perceive anger even when no anger is expressed. They act aggressively when facing normal everyday conflicts at school (Pollack, Cicchetti, Hornung, & Reed, 2000). Severely abused children are likely to show symptoms of posttraumatic stress disorder (Harvard Medical School, 2004), which occurs after a child has experienced a traumatizing event.

Children who are neglected have few chances to interact with adults. Neglected children, therefore, do not have enough opportunities to learn about emotional signals. They have difficulty distinguishing among expressions of fear, sadness, or anger (Pollack et al., 2000). Like abused children, neglected children have difficulty recognizing and responding effectively to emotional signals from other children in a classroom. This makes a teacher's goal of helping children learn about and regulate feelings even more urgent and difficult, as Mrs. Chang has discovered with Beth.

Culture Influences Emotional Development

As noted in Chapter 2, Bronfenbrenner believed that children's development was influenced by a variety of systems. Children, their families, and communities are embedded in a culture which is defined ". . . as the customary beliefs and patterns of and for behavior, both explicit and implicit, that are passed on to future generations by the society they live in and/or by a social, religious, or ethnic group within it" (NAEYC, no date). Teachers can best understand children's emotional development and mental health by acknowledging how culture influences children's understanding of the world (NAEYC, no date; Parlakian, 2003). One culture might value nonviolence as a way to deal with conflict and express it in their opposition to violent movies and video games. Another culture might value a hard-hitting or harsh approach to dealing with conflict and express it by accepting violent movies.

Culture affects children's emotional development and mental health in two ways (Gordon, 1989). A child's family and community are embedded in a larger environment that is affected by physical or geographic and social or political circumstances. This is a child's larger emotional learning environment, the macrosystem. A culture like that in Sudan in Africa, particularly the region of Darfur (as of 2008), for example, is violent. Children spend their entire childhood fleeing or hiding from roving bands of killers, moving frantically from one place to another, and scavenging for food. Their culture of deprivation and terror shapes their emotional lives.

Second, older members of a culture model behavior patterns for children. For example, adult members of a child's culture identify what parents believe about rearing children. Adult members of a child's culture also identify the specific types of interactions acceptable to that culture. For example,

Mr. Hernandez uses a job chart to assign classroom jobs to his kindergarten, first, and second graders. At the beginning of the school year, he was surprised when one of his first-grade boys expressed disgust when he and a girl were both assigned to clean tables, "I'm not going to work with a girl!"

This child's culture clearly separates work by gender. Thus, one of Mr. Hernandez's classroom management practices—all children share in the work of taking care of the classroom—clashes with a cultural belief of one of the families, a belief expressed as an unwillingness for a boy to perform what his culture views as work assigned only to females.

Mr. Hernandez replied, "Do you remember in the first week of school how we all agreed to work together in our classroom? Everyone has the same opportunities to learn here and everybody shares in the work. We work together in our classroom—boys and girls." Mr. Hernandez responded calmly and in an instructive manner rather than sarcastically or otherwise inappropriately.

Additionally, modeling is one of the major cultural methods of influence. Through modeling, members of a culture demonstrate accepted ways of acknowledging another's feelings. Children observe other people's reactions to emotion (what the other person does) and learn from these models about their culturally accepted ways to interpret emotions themselves (Cassidy, Parke, Buttkovsky, & Braungart, 1992). Children learn from many different models, some giving lessons that work against a child's emotional development. Tim's father, for example, ignores other people's feelings, giving his son the lesson of indifference to the emotions of others (an unhelpful lesson).

Early childhood teachers who want to foster children's healthy emotional development and good mental health base their actions on culturally appropriate strategies, one part of Developmentally Appropriate Practices (DAP) (Bredekamp & Copple, 1997). Teachers must be culturally competent to engage in developmentally appropriate practices with children and their families (Parlakian, 2003). While this might seem to be a simple thing to do, in reality communicating effectively and building relationships with families from a variety of cultures can be very challenging. Figure 3.8 gives suggestions on growing in cultural competence.

Individual Developmental Variations Affect Emotional Development

Even though all children acquire the same basic and complex emotions, their paths of emotional development can differ greatly, the dissimilarities influenced by each child's distinct personality, family history, and culture. This section describes the effect of a child's behavioral style, the effect of different attachment histories, and the effect of developmental problems such as autism have on the trajectory of emotional development, the path of a child's ability to recognize, communicate about, and regulate emotions.

Effect of Behavioral Style and Attachment History on Emotional Development

A child's *behavioral style* accounts for some of the differences in emotional development. Her individual behavioral style affects how well she can regulate emotions. This effect is called level of emotionality (Saarni et al., 1998). Some children, with high levels of emotionality, have highly intense and often negative emotional reactions. For example,

When 4-year-old Carlos asked Beth to scoot over a little at group time for instance, Beth glared at Carlos, grabbed her carpet square (glaring and grabbing, the intense reaction), and slammed it down in the new spot (the negative emotional reaction).

Other 4- to 6-year-old children, with easier, milder behavioral style, are low in emotionality and use nonhostile words to let others know that they are upset (Eisenberg, Fabes, Nyman, Bernzweig, & Pinuelas, 1994). For example, Aiko said to Samir who had taken her markers without asking, "You're supposed to ask if you want to borrow things from somebody else."

Differences in children's attachment histories explain some of the differences in emotional development that teachers see in their classrooms. Infants develop an **attachment**, a bond or feeling of closeness, to their primary caregivers. Infant behaviors such as crying, cooing, looking at, and trying to make eye contact are attachment behaviors meant to draw adults to them to give them the care that they need in order to survive and to feel safe. It is in a child's earliest relationships that they develop early views of relationships (Ainsworth, Blehar, Waters, & Wall, 1978; Bowlby, 1982). Some children develop more secure attachments than others do.

Attachment Bond or feeling of closeness between child and primary caregiver.

Kochanska (2001) conducted a longitudinal study in which she observed children at 9 months of age and again at 14, 22, and 33 months. The researcher observed the children's fear, anger, or joy in a laboratory setting, assessed how secure each child was to his or her mother, and discovered that a child's attachment security had an effect on emotional development. Table 4.4 shows the findings of this study.

Effect of Disabilities on Emotional Development

Disability A physical or mental impairment that substantially limits one or more of the major life activities of an individual.

A variety of children's disabilities or exceptional needs affect different domains of development, including emotional development. A **disability** is a physical or mental impairment that limits, substantially, one or more of major life activities. A disability like autism, for example, can affect children's expression of emotion such as pride.

TABLE 4.4 Research Information: Effect of Different Attachment Histories on Emotional Development in Infants and Toddlers	
Security of Attachment	**Possible Effect on Child's Emotional Development: Joy, Fear, Anger**
Secure	Showed little distress in situations designed to elicit joy (14 months); became significantly less angry, showing less anger and fear in situations designed to elicit anger and fear (22 months, 33 months)
Insecure	Negative emotions increased (22 months, 33 months); more likely to develop anxiety disorders
Avoidant	Became more fearful (22 months, 33 months)
Resistant	Most fearful, least joyful, fear their strongest emotion; responded with stress in situations designed to obtain joy (14); became less joyful (22 months, 33 months)
Unclassifiable	Became more angry (22 months, 33 months)

Sources: Harvard Medical School (December, 2004); Kochanska (2001).

FIGURE 4.1   Children's Mental Health: Current Challenges

- One out of five children has a diagnosable mental, emotional, or behavioral disorder.

- Up to 1 in 10 children have a serious emotional disturbance (U.S. DHHS, 1999).

- 70% of children with a diagnosable disorder do not receive mental health services (Rand, 2001).

- 70%–80% of children who receive mental health services, get the services in school (Rones & Hoagwood, 2000).

- 32% of children living in poverty have diagnosable mental health problems (Buckner & Bassuk, 1997).

- 50% of children living in poverty are at risk for future problems but do not currently meet criteria for diagnosis.

- Children in minority populations are less likely to have access to mental health services and services they do have are often of poor quality.

- Hispanic children are the least likely of all minority groups to get needed mental health care (U.S. DHHS, 2001).

Source: Data from Olbrich (2002).

Kasari, Sigman, Baurngartner, and Stipek (1993) studied the expression of pride and mastery in children with autism, comparing how preschool children, with and without autism, expressed the emotion of pride. The preschool children in their study completed puzzles appropriate for children of this age. Some children were praised and some were not. Their results showed that children with autism smiled when they completed a puzzle; thus, children with autism experienced the emotion of pride and expressed their feeling with a typical response, smiling. However, they did not look up to communicate their pride to either their parents or to the researchers and they did not call attention to their success, not a typical response to the emotion of pride. Additionally, they failed to acknowledge praise, another uncommon response.

Children's Mental Health: Current Challenges

Figure 4.1 reminds us that many children are *not* emotionally healthy. Also disturbing is the difficulty that many children have in getting mental health care. The gap between those likely to get care and those unlikely to get care is even larger for specific groups of children.

While about 20% of children and adolescents show signs of a diagnosable mental illness in any year, only 5% of all children experience the most extreme impairment. Mental disturbance during childhood is not limited to any specific group. Children from any income level or ethnic background can develop an emotional disturbance.

An **anxiety disorder** is the most common type of emotional disturbance in childhood. Figure 4.2 describes behaviors that children with common anxiety disorders might display. Some anxiety is normal. For instance, emotionally healthy infants, toddlers, and preschool children might become distressed or anxious when they are separated from

Anxiety disorder The most common type of emotional disturbance in childhood.

FIGURE 4.2   The Most Common Anxiety Disorders in Children

Generalized Anxiety Disorder (GAD)

- Has great difficulty controlling fears and worries
- Restless, tense, tires easily, has trouble concentrating
- Seeks approval; needs constant reassurance, eager to please

Obsessive Compulsive Disorder (OCD)

- Seen in as many as 1 in 200 children and adolescents
- Has recurring thoughts or intrusive images; obsessions are not just normal worries, but often irrational
- Tries to eliminate the obsessive thoughts or images with specific, recurring, time-consuming behaviors or rituals; compulsions may be hand washing, keeping things in order, checking something over and over
- Is a brain disorder, tending to run in families
- One form of OCD develops or gets worse after a strep infection (antibodies intended to fight the strep infection mistakenly attack a region of the brain, setting off an inflammatory reaction)

Post Traumatic Stress Disorder (PTSD)

- Children are more easily traumatized than are adults
- Occurs after a child has experienced a traumatizing event, such as child abuse, an accident, animal attack, getting lost, natural disasters such as floods or fires, observing a murder
- Symptoms may include frequent memories of the traumatic event, terrifying dreams, physical symptoms such as stomach aches when remembering the event, agitation, sleep disturbances, problems with concentration
- Children who are traumatized repeatedly might dissociate, become numb to feelings so that they can block the trauma
- Symptoms last from several months to several years

Separation Anxiety Disorder

- Four percent of children and adolescents suffer from this emotional disturbance
- Some anxiety about separation from parents is normal for infants and toddlers
- Symptoms are intense worry and anxiety about separation from parents, excessive clinginess, excessive worry about parents' safety, fear of sleeping alone, nightmares
- The worry or anxiety interferes with the child's life, such as going to school or getting involved in play activities with children outside the family

Sources: AACAP (1997, 1999b, 2000); National Mental Health Association (2004); U.S. Department of Health and Human Services (1999).

primary caregivers, such as when they go to school for the first time or have a babysitter for the first time.

Anxiety, however, can become severe and begin to interfere with a child's life, such as overwhelming anxiety about attending school. Anxiety disorders affect up to 10% of children and adolescents (National Mental Health Association, retrieved December 13, 2004).

Media Violence Influences Emotional Development

Healthy emotional development includes the ability to make decisions about how to manage emotions. The media is a significant part of a child's emotional learning environment. Computers, television, movies, videotapes, DVDs, computer and game systems, and all other forms of media combine to form a significant socializing force in children's lives.

Any media to which children are exposed can convey either responsible or irresponsible emotional learning lessons; for example, Mr. Hernandez planned a responsible emotional lesson on apologies.

> His first graders watched a video about apologies and learned about the emotion of guilt after doing something that hurts another person or animal.

Children's emotional development and mental health are endangered by exposure to excessive media violence. Children in the United States live in a culture promoting violence-filled television programs, movies, and computer games. Modeling is an effective way for children to learn, and American children watch thousands of models of how to murder or commit violent acts by the time they leave elementary school. They, therefore, learn patterns of violence and aggression from violent screen time.

Children learn effectively when they actively participate in learning experiences in which they have high interest, a concept from Piaget's theory and constructivist theory in general. Active participation in violent computer games gives children plenty of practice in making decisions to use violence to solve problems. Such practice helps children construct ideas about dealing with feelings and solving problems with aggressive, violent means (AACAP, 1999a; Levin, 1998; NAEYC, 1994; Huston & Wright, 1996; NTVSC, 1997). Teachers can help children to have happy and healthy emotional lives, a topic to which we now turn.

USING KNOWLEDGE ABOUT EMOTIONAL DEVELOPMENT TO CREATE A HEALTHY, RESPECTFUL, SUPPORTIVE, AND CHALLENGING ENVIRONMENT

All children need support for their emotional development, but children who have not learned how to communicate effectively about or regulate emotions especially need encouragement. Children who have learned unhelpful ways for expressing how they feel need their teacher's help in writing better scripts.

Teachers foster children's emotional development when they

- create a supportive emotional learning climate,
- help children learn and use the vocabulary of emotions, and
- support children in understanding emotions.

Creating a Supportive Emotional Learning Climate

The **emotional climate in a classroom** is the verbal and nonverbal emotional communication that a child sees and hears. This includes statements such as, "I am so happy to see you today," as well as nonverbal signals such as sincere smiles, high-fives, thumbs-up.

Emotional climate in a classroom Verbal and nonverbal emotional communication seen and heard by a child.

We have known for almost 40 years that an emotional climate influences children (Briggs, 1970) and is key in teaching about a culture's approach to emotions (Davies & Cummings, 1994). Supportive emotional climates permit children to acknowledge all feelings and do not shame any emotion. Children do not have to hide feelings, and they are not criticized for having the feeling, even unpleasant feelings such as jealousy or disgust. They also learn that they may *not* hurt others or destroy things because of unpleasant feelings.

Healthy, supportive emotional classroom climates have clear, consistent, yet flexible boundaries about how to express emotions. Teachers who help children understand and manage emotions responsibly convey a simple, firm, consistent message about the child's right to have any feeling. They also help children express unpleasant emotions responsibly. For example, preschool teacher Mrs. Chang said,

"I can tell that you're upset because I see tears on your face.

"You sure are upset about getting pushed down. Let's figure out a way to *tell* Beth not to push you."

Developing a healthy emotional climate conveys important information about emotions. For example, "You have the right to feel sad or excited." However, it also tells children "I will help you talk about feelings, but I will not allow you to hurt or humiliate a person or animal because you are sad or angry or excited" (Baumrind, 1996).

Teachers in an emotionally stable classroom model how to manage angry feelings. Early childhood teachers realize that some of the children in their classes have watched hours of violent video games, television shows, or even background anger in their families and neighborhoods. Consequently, the children are constantly on alert and ready to argue. They tend to see anger-arousing situations as a signal that an attack is about to take place, putting them on high alert (El-Sheikh & Reiter, 1996).

Teachers relying on the developmental approach use Vygotsky's theory to guide their work. Recall from Chapter 2 that Vygotsky believed that children learn in the zone of proximal development (ZPD). Tim, for example, on his own does not have good skills for managing his feelings but can develop better ways with his teacher's help. This takes more time for some children than for others. Seven-year-old Tim, for example, is always on alert, has not had lessons on recognizing and expressing emotions, and frequently comes to school frustrated, angry, and itching for a fight. Vygotsky's theory advocates that teachers *scaffold* children's learning in the child's ZPD. This means that they support the child in learning, giving more support when a child is first learning and gradually offering less help as the child progresses. The teacher would identify what the child needs to learn to move to a higher skill level and would then offer help in logical and appropriate ways. Table 4.5 illustrates this teacher's approach to **scaffolding** Tim's understanding of how to manage emotions.

Scaffolding Strategy in which an adult supports a child's learning; implies changing levels of support as the child gains knowledge or skills.

This student is matching his facial expression to the emotion that his teacher has named.

Helping Children Learn and Use the Vocabulary of Emotions

Because children gradually acquire the ability to use words to express their feelings, teachers using the developmental approach make every effort to help children learn the words, the vocabulary, through which they can tell others that they are feeling, for example, happy, sad, proud, angry, or embarrassed.

Early childhood teachers have access to many developmentally appropriate methods to teach about emotion words. First, they assess a child's current abilities, as Mr. Hernandez does.

> Mr. Hernandez observed the words that his kindergarten, first, and second graders used to express emotions. He quickly saw that Tim, 7 years old, used no emotion words, in spite of Tim's frequent angry outbursts.

Second, they use the assessment information to develop appropriately challenging lessons that help children acquire and use emotion words. Mr. Hernandez, for example, used large group meetings to have children make faces showing emotions that he named, such as disgust, fear, happiness. He noticed that Tim enjoyed learning the words for feelings. A teacher chooses an instructional strategy that will best help a class or an individual child learn about emotion words. Examples are individual or group lessons, books focusing on emotion words, charts with emotion words as in Figure 4.3A, puppets who discuss emotion words, discussions about emotion words, and showing photos and naming emotions people in photos seem to show. In Tim's case, Mr. Hernandez worked individually with him in discussing emotion words as shown in Table 4.5.

TABLE 4.5   Scaffolding a Child's Understanding of Responsible Management of Emotions

Examples of Things That Tim Needed to Learn about Managing Emotions	How Mr. Hernandez *Scaffolded* (Supported) Tim's Learning	Comments
It is OK to have any feeling, but it is *not* OK to hurt somebody when you feel angry.	He stated this verbally and offered to help figure out a better way to tell someone that he was angry.	Tim had not learned this lesson. The teacher will need to repeat this when Tim is first learning.
You can use *words* to tell how you feel.	He stated this.	Another new idea for Tim. He will need to be reminded several times.
He needs to know which words to use.	He modeled some sentences that Tim could use. He even used puppets to demonstrate.	Modeling is an effective strategy for teaching this type of skill.
Tim needs to practice using words to express anger.	He and the child practice; the teacher saying the sentence first and Tim repeating. They used puppets as well.	Tim needs to practice a helpful approach. This is a good time because Tim is not upset now and can think.
Tim needs to try out his new skill with another child.	He observes Tim get upset and reminds him that he can use words with the other child just as they practiced. He *coaches* Tim, "Remember, use words to tell Jake that you are upset."	This is a big and scary step. Tim needs assurance that he knows what to do and that he can do it. Tim needs coaching as he takes this step. As he gains the skill, Mr. Hernandez can decrease the direct intervention. Progress will be slow, and there will be setbacks along with progress.

A preschool teacher, working with children younger than Tim, discover that most of the class knew the word label *happy*. The teacher decides that an appropriately challenging lesson would familiarize the children with new emotion words *joyful, glad,* and *cheerful* to expand their vocabulary for happy. She put the words in context, "I was really *glad* that the new library books arrived." As children get older, teachers can add more words to match children's ability to learn and interest in new words. A first- or second-grade teacher, might introduce words as Figure 4.3B illustrates.

Learning to Use Emotion Words

Early childhood teachers support children in using **emotion talk** in which they learn to use the emotion word labels that they know. Teachers do this through regularly planned lessons and activities or through interaction with children currently experiencing an emotion.

Emotion talk When children use emotion word labels that they know.

Suppose that a second-grade child calls another child a "dummy," something that elicits anger in most children (Fabes & Eisenberg, 1992). The teacher would first validate the insulted child's emotion, assuring him that it is reasonable to be upset when someone calls us a name. The teacher would then teach the child to use emotion words to express the feeling. For example,

> Mr. Hernandez reminded Tim to use "words" and then suggested specific words. "You can say, 'I am *mad* because you called me a name.'" He combined teacher-child talking with verbal encouragement when Tim used *words* to say how he felt.

Glad

Cheerful

Happy

FIGURE 4.3A Teaching new emotion words to preschool children.

Supporting Children's Understanding of Emotions

Children learn to communicate effectively about and to regulate emotions in healthy emotional learning environments with adults who model, teach, and encourage these skills. Teachers can help all children in a class gain even greater understanding about emotions, and they can help individual children. For example, a teacher might decide that a child needs help in understanding feelings, as Mr. Hernandez, did with 7-year-old Tim.

> "Did you notice, Tim, how upset Alida was when you called her 'four eyes'?" Tim sneered. ". . . she hid in the reading area. You insulted her. People get mad when they've been insulted."

The teacher knows that Tim sees his parents argue with each other every day and that his father seems to take pleasure in hurting others. Children in these circumstances have a model of hurtful and even malicious behavior. They come to school after having observed models of irresponsible emotional management for several years. Teachers like Mr. Hernandez, do not shirk their teaching role and do not excuse a child's behavior but are able to understand it. Mr. Hernandez ignored the sneer and simply plodded along, giving more positive and hopeful emotional lessons. This lesson in emotional understanding is one of the many that Tim has missed and that his teacher is helping him learn.

The teacher has slowly been helping Tim understand that other people have emotions, that there are clear signals of those emotions, for example, Alida hiding, and that his behavior brought on the other person's feeling. This does not mean that Tim will automatically apologize or that he will never be

Glad
—Delighted
—Pleased

Cheerful
—Jolly
—Jovial

Happy
—Contented
—Blissful
—Elated

Expanding the Range of Happy

FIGURE 4.3B Emotion words for primary grade children.

disrespectful again, but it does mean that he has now assimilated new information on the effect of his behavior, a concept from both Piaget's and Vygotsky's theories. Tim will undoubtedly take quite some time to accommodate to this information. He has a lot to learn and has to gain confidence in his ability to treat others well.

SUMMARY

Children grow in their ability to understand and manage their emotions, but this takes many years. Teachers want to help children become emotionally healthy, which means that a child:

- has access to a full range of feelings, pleasant and unpleasant, and copes with feelings in age-appropriate ways. Infants are born with or acquire soon after birth a set of basic emotions. They acquire a set of more complex, self-conscious emotions starting at age 2. Managing emotions begins when children are in preschool, but, again, this takes several years to develop fully.
- develops basic qualities of trust, autonomy, initiative, and industry, which are the qualities described by Erikson in his life-span approach to psychological development. Each of these qualities allows a child to move more easily to the challenges of the next stage.
- is resilient. An emotionally healthy child is able to cope with difficulty rather than being defeated or overwhelmed by it or responding in a destructive or self-destructive way. The child is socially competent, can solve problems, can reflect critically on issues, is autonomous, and has a sense of purpose.
- functions well in school. She separates from her family with minimal stress and forms an attachment with at least one adult at school. She settles down to concentrate on activities typically associated with a developmentally appropriate curriculum.

Recognizing and meeting children's emotional needs allows emotional health to flourish. While a child's most fundamental emotional need is her family's unconditional love, teachers and schools can help children get what they need for good emotional health. This includes supportive nurturing teachers who create a safe, stable, developmentally appropriate environment, positive self-esteem and moral identity, and opportunities to play.

- Psychologically and physically safe and secure classrooms and schools improve children's chances for good emotional health. These are safe places when children feel respected and never hurt, belittled, degraded, or humiliated. Safe schools understand the devastating effects of bullying and do everything possible to prevent this problem or intervene appropriately when bullying occurs.
- Children need positive and realistic self-esteem and a moral compass to help them make decisions about the right thing to do. They need to feel competent, confident, and worthy of others' time.
- Children need to play. Play promotes mental health, and joyful, complex play is a sign of good mental health.

There are many influences on children's emotional health, and it is difficult to separate the effect of factors that work together to affect a child. The factors work together to influence emotional well-being. The influences include:

- brain development. The prefrontal cortex develops gradually, providing the brain hardware necessary for self-control. Preschool and kindergarten children's better self-control is tied, in part, to their brain development.
- positive relationships with adults. Children feel safe and secure in warm and nurturing relationships with adults who teach self-control.
- culture. Older members of a culture model behavior patterns for children, such as how that culture expresses or deals with emotions.
- individual developmental variations, such as a child's basic temperament, attachment history, or disabilities.
- media violence. Many different forms of media exist, and they combine to form a significant socializing force in children's lives. Years of research demonstrate the harmful effects of watching media violence, and learning is particularly effective when children actively participate in violent games.

All children need support for their emotional development, but children who have not learned how to communicate effectively about or regulate emotions especially need encouragement. Children who have learned *unhelpful ways* for expressing how they feel need their teacher's help in developing better approaches. Teachers foster children's emotional development when they

- create a supportive emotional learning climate. Teachers set clear, consistent, yet flexible boundaries about how to express emotions. Teachers help children understand and manage emotions responsibly.
- help children learn and use the vocabulary of emotions. Teachers help children to learn the words with which they can label their feelings. They also work on helping children to expand their understanding of emotion words and to use emotion words.
- support children in understanding emotions. They help children understand that others have feelings, too, and that there are clear signals of how their emotions show in their face and actions.

QUESTIONS FOR REFLECTION

1. Describe a time when you have observed an adult dealing with one of a child's emotions listed in Figure 4.2. What seemed to elicit the child's emotion? How did the adult respond? What was the child's reaction to the adult's actions?

2. Please explain why it is an *inappropriate* practice to force very young English language learners to say new English words.

APPLY YOUR KNOWLEDGE

What Should This Teacher Do?

1. Mrs. Chang, the preschool teacher, was surprised to hear Serena say, "Icky" when she saw the fruit slices and yogurt dip that Larry and his father had prepared (the rest of the class liked the "fruit dippers"). Using Table 4.2, identify the emotion that Serena was expressing. Using Table 4.1 explain which of the skills Serena needs to learn.

2. When Mr. Hernandez's K to 2 class heard the announcement that school would close early because of a snow emergency, many of the children were overcome with the emotion of joy and were quickly losing control. Using the information from the section Brain Development Affects Emotional Development and from Table 4.3, explain why the children might be getting so excited and what the teacher can do to help them express their joy appropriately and to calm themselves.

KEY TERMS

WEB SITES

American Academy of Child and Adolescent Psychiatry (AACAP)
www.aacap.org
Home page of the major professional psychiatric association with links for the public. Find online versions of fact sheets for families useful for early childhood teachers.

Bibliotherapy
http://www.best-childrens-books.com/bibliotherapy.html
This is a list of books grouped by category. Each group lists several books about a topic such as death, divorce, bullying, and disabilities.

Humane Society of the United States
www.kindnews.org
Online magazine for children.

National Association for the Education of Young Children
www.naeyc.org
Read the position statement, *Media Violence in Children's Lives*.

National Association for Humane and Environmental Education
www.nahee.org
This site encourages kindness toward people, animals, and the earth. It ties in nicely with helping children develop empathy and communicate sympathy, one of the three skills necessary for communicating effectively about emotions.

National Mental Health Association
www.nmha.org
The Association has sponsored a program, Children's Mental Health Matters. Fact sheets on elements of good mental health and on children's mental health problems are posted.

CHAPTER 5

Supporting Children's Social Development

GUIDING QUESTIONS:

- What are some of the characteristics of socially competent children?
- What are some of the factors that influence children's social development and competence?
- What can teachers do to foster children's social development?

INFANT/TODDLER
Continuity of Care

Nick, now 2 years old, first entered Mr. Bjornrud's class as a 10 month old. Nick's father chose this caregiving arrangement because of the school's policy of continuity of care for the children. "This means," Nick's father said to a friend, "that Nick will be with the same caregiver until he is 3 years old and I'm glad about that because he shouldn't be shifted from one person to another."

PRESCHOOL
Pronouncing Names Correctly

Pedro was new to Mrs. Chang's class. He had arrived from Mexico 3 weeks before with his parents. Pedro's home language is Spanish, and he is now learning English—he is an English language learner. The teacher asked his parents and Pedro to pronounce his name and then she repeated it until she saw a smile light up Pedro's face, indicating that she had pronounced it correctly. Then, she told each of his classmates how to pronounce his name. As she does with all children new to her class, she assigned a partner to Pedro to show him what he needs to do, for example, when working at the play dough table.

KINDERGARTEN
A Conflict

Juanita and Joseph, finished with a cooperative collage, were framing their art.

"NO!" shouted Juanita, "put the frame the other way."

"The frame goes *this* way," said Joseph, who looked annoyed. Mr. Hernandez watched this conflict unfold, and then put the classroom's conflict resolution plan into action.

Children's social development and competence is important in its own right because this part of human development allows cooperation, empathy, compassion, and generosity to flower. However, at least two curious and notable factors highlight the need to focus on this domain. One is the high rate of *expulsions from early childhood programs*. In one state, 39% of preschool teachers reported expelling at least one child and this was

34 times higher than the expulsion rate for K to 12 grades (Gilliam & Sharhar, 2006). The main reason for the expulsions was problems with children's behavior. The expulsion rate has placed added importance to understand social development. The other factor is the current emphasis on children's preparedness for academic work. Children need effective social skills to do well academically (Fox & Smith, 2007; Zins, Bloodworth, Weissberg, & Walberg, 2004). A child's social and intellectual development, as well as success in school are linked (Bowman, Donovan, & Burns, 2000; Zins et al., 2004) as are antisocial behavior and failure in, or expulsion from, school (Zins et al., 2004).

The path of a child's social development can be changed, making a teacher's influence critical. If a child in a preschool, for example, has trouble getting along with other children, then his teacher can help him develop better self-esteem and learn the skills that he needs. He will then travel a path very different from the one he would have taken had the teacher not promoted good social skills. This chapter describes and explains children's social development. We will examine the characteristics of a socially competent child, explore what children need to develop those characteristics, and consider the crucial role of early childhood teachers in supporting children's social competence (Alliance for Childhood, 2004). Finally, we will look at some practical strategies teachers use to support children's social development and competence. Even though this chapter highlights social development, one should keep in mind that social and emotional domains are tied together very closely, as seen throughout this chapter. Children's relationships give them the chance to apply and use their emotional understanding. To foster children's social development effective teachers of young children must (Hyson, 2003; NAEYC, 2001):

- Know and understand young children's social characteristics and needs.
- Know and understand the multiple influences on social development.
- Use knowledge about social development to create healthy, respectful, supportive, and challenging learning environments.

UNDERSTANDING CHILDREN'S SOCIAL CHARACTERISTICS AND NEEDS

Recall from Chapter 2 that Howard Gardner described different types of intelligence. Two seem especially relevant to social development. *Interpersonal intelligence* involves very good ability to understand what other people intend, want, and need. A child with high interpersonal intelligence plays and works well with other children. *Intrapersonal intelligence* involves understanding and knowing oneself. A child high in this intelligence would understand, for instance, that she gets very upset when somebody embarrasses her. She knows her strengths but is also aware of her fears.

Some children are stronger in one or both of these intelligences but we can help all children develop enough intrapersonal and interpersonal intelligence to benefit their social and emotional development.

All children can develop social competence (Fox & Smith, 2007), which is a process and its foundation is laid in infancy and toddlerhood.

Becoming Socially Competent Is a Process: It Begins with Infants and Toddlers

A baby's first bond is her attachment with a parent whose love and care play a major part in the self that she develops (Bowlby, 1979). Parents and caregivers who meet their baby's physical needs and who play with, talk and read to, and introduce their infants and toddlers to other young children set them on a path of healthy social development. A secure attachment and consistent and loving care during infancy and toddlerhood helps children to develop a working model of how good relationships work, and this model influences their relationship style into adulthood (DiTomasso, Brannen-McNulty, Ross, & Burgess, 2003; Engin, Erdal, & Ramazan, 2005).

Some infants and toddlers face challenges as they start the process of developing socially competent behaviors. Many are cared for, for varying amounts of time, by persons other than parents, and the quality of care affects their development. For example, infants in one study were less likely to be securely attached when low maternal sensitivity and responsiveness was combined with poor-quality child care, more than minimal amounts of child care, or more than one care arrangement (NICHD Early Child Care Research Network, 1996).

Very young children clearly benefit from high-quality child care (little turnover of teachers, small teacher-child ratios, and well-educated staff) (Ceglowski & Bacigalupa, 2002). For example, children in high-quality child-care centers do better on measures of social skills and they have better social relationships in second grade (Peisner-Feinberg, Clifford, Yazejean, Culkin, Howes, & Kagan, 1998).

Continuity of care, having the same caregiver from the time an infant enters care to his third birthday, is crucial in an infant and toddler's life. Many centers, however, do not use continuity of care for infants and even fewer for toddlers. The decision to move an infant or a toddler to a different room, and, therefore, a new caregiver, is often made on whether the child has met a developmental milestone, such as walking, the child's age, or simply whether space is available in the other room (Cryer, Hurwitz, & Wolery, 2001).

Another study looked at the barriers to continuity-of-care practices and found something similar, that the biggest obstacle was a caregiver's unwillingness or inability to care for a child who had developed toddler abilities and directors' unwillingness to replace those caregivers with ones willing and able to care for children at different stages (Aguillard, Pierce, Benedict, & Burts, 2005). Thus, even though all children can develop social competence, some have a more difficult journey because of decisions made by persons in the systems providing infant and toddler care. This is an example of Bronfenbrenner's theory about the ecology of development (see Chapter 2). He believed that different systems, such as a child's family and child-care arrangements could affect a child's development.

In the chapter opening vignette on infants, we saw that Mr. Bjornrud's school believes in and practices continuity of care. It hires caregivers who understand development of both infants and toddlers. Each teacher has also learned about adjusting care practices to the changing abilities and needs of children as they become toddlers.

Teachers need to know what a socially competent child is like, a topic that we now examine.

Continuity of care (In infant and toddler child care) having the same caregiver from the time an infant enters child care to his third birthday.

The child in the striped shirt, now almost 3 years old, has had the same caregiver for the entire time that she has been in child care, since age 8 months.

Characteristics of Socially Competent Children

Socially competent children share several characteristics that they have developed over time in healthy relationships with important adults such as parents, grandparents, and other adults and siblings and by constructing ideas of how to get along with others. They have built, slowly but steadily, the relationship and social skills that they need.

Socially competent children relate well to other children. They also acknowledge and respond to others, are generally agreeable, and they have developed good social skills. Finally, socially competent children are very good at tuning in to important aspects of the social environment.

Socially Competent Children Relate Well to Other Children

Teachers are concerned about a child's level of **social competence in the peer group**, the ability to get along effectively at three different levels—the child's *interactions* with other children, his *relationships* with them, and how he functions *in groups of children*. A socially competent child has primarily positive interactions under many different conditions. He can initiate and sustain good relationships. Other children act in a friendly way toward him and invite him to play and work with them. He has positive group experiences.

> For example, 7-year-old Anna gets along well with every other child in her class. She has a couple of good friends, and the other children like to play and work with her.

Less socially competent children have difficulty getting along with peers at one or more of these levels (Rubin, Bukowski, & Parker, 1998).

Interaction refers to the social give and take in which each child in a pair responds to and draws out behavior from the other child. This is an important avenue for learning with children learning from peer interactions, serving as models for one another, and imitating each other's actions. Recent research demonstrates that children engage in a type of cooperative interaction very early in life, during their second year. One young child, sensing that the other is stopping the interaction, will deliberately try to reengage the other (Warkenen, Chen, & Tomasello, 2006).

Early childhood teachers see hundreds of interactions between children, the list seemingly endless. Instead of dealing with lists of peer interactions, we can categorize them into three major groups: moving *toward* others, in which a person greets, shows compassion, or helps; moving *away from* others, characterized by withdrawing from interaction or contact; and moving *against others*, such as, aggression in any form (Rubin et al., 1998).

As teachers, we need to be aware of children's rich and varied social interactions, their different abilities plainly visible. Some arrive in our classrooms unable to cope well, but others deal effectively with a wide range of social interactions. Figure 5.1 charts the developmental sequence of early childhood peer interaction.

Children who know each other and have a series of interactions are in a **relationship**. Different types of relationships exist: long-term or newer, more casual, and pleasant versus hostile. Two children, for example, sit together on the school bus every day (long-term, pleasant relationship). Some relationships exist between two individuals, a *friendship*, for example. Other relationships exist at a group level, such as *peer acceptance*. A **friendship** is a voluntary peer relationship recognized and acknowledged by a dyad or two children. It is characterized by shared "liking" or shared affection. Friendships are chosen; we cannot assign friends (Rubin et al., 1998).

Socially competent child Relates well to others, acknowledges others, generally agreeable, has good social skills, and tunes in to important aspects of the social environment.

Social competence in the peer group Child's ability to get along effectively in interactions, relationships, and in a group.

Interaction Social give and take resulting from an exchange of behavior of two individuals; each child responds to and draws out behavior from another person.

Relationship When children who know each other have a series of interactions.

Friendship Voluntary relationship characterized by shared liking or affection.

FIGURE 5.1   Developmental Sequence: Social Interaction During Early Childhood

Infants

- By 2 months: aroused by presence of peers, engages in mutual gaze
- 6 to 9 months: smiles, vocalizes, directs looks at others
- 9 to 12 months: watches others even more, imitates partner, points at things

Toddlers

- Interactions go on longer and are more complex
- Moves around easily and uses words to communicate in interactions
- Themes or simple games evident for the first time; give and take type of imitation, foundation for later pretense play
- Turn-taking behaviors evident
- Try to engage partner in activity when partner stops

Preschool: 2 to 5 years

- Frequency, length, and complexity of peer interaction increases
- All forms of interaction evident: unoccupied, onlooking, solitary, parallel, and group activities
- Frequency of parallel play remains constant from 3 to 5 years
- Solitary sensorimotor play (seemingly aimless repetitive actions) decreases
- Solitary constructive play increases (working alone to build something)
- Sociodramatic play evident: a complex form of group interaction
- Positive interactions more common with increasing age
- Aggression increases with age but positive behavior predominates
- Directs more speech to peers, linguistically competent children at a clear advantage
- Older preschoolers more socially skilled in making requests

Primary Grades

- Generosity, helpfulness, and cooperation increase
- Forms of aggression change from physical to verbal
- Hostile aggression now possible
- Pretend play declines in middle childhood
- Games with or without formal rules evident

Sources: Based on Rubin et al., (1998); Copple and Bredekamp (2005); Warkenen et al. (2006).

Consider how one aspect of development, **egocentricity** or the inability to focus on a different perspective from one's own, might affect how children look at friendship. For much of early childhood, children are more egocentric than they are during middle childhood and adolescence. A 5 year old, centered more on his own view of the world, thinks that a friend is simply the child who plays with him. At age 14 and far less egocentric, the same child has constructed the idea that friends understand and support each other, a major shift in thinking about a friendship-relationship.

Egocentricity The *inability* to focus on a different perspective from one's own.

Group Collection of children who influence each other.

Peer acceptance How well liked versus disliked a child is, on average, by members of a peer group.

A **group** is a collection of children who influence each other in some way. This is the third level at which competent children effectively interact with other children. As teachers, we are concerned about how each child functions in a classroom or school groups. Teachers want to help children feel comfortable in the group and accepted by peers. **Peer acceptance** is a type of relationship, different from a friendship between two children. It is defined at the *group* level and refers to how well liked versus disliked a child is, on average, by members of his or her peer group (Buhs & Ladd, 2001). Peer acceptance has consistently predicted children's academic readiness and classroom involvement (Ladd, Kochenderfer, & Coleman, 1997). Peer *rejection* has been linked with negative attitudes toward school, school avoidance, and underachievement (Ladd, Birch, & Buhs, 1999).

Socially Competent Children Agreeably Respond to Others

Socially competent children are usually pleasant, sociable, welcoming, and approachable. This is true even if another child is an acquaintance but not a friend (Mize, 1995) as Anna demonstrates.

> "Here's a seat," called Anna, 7 years old, as she pointed out the spot next to her to Willis, not Anna's friend but in her class.

Go to MyEducationLab and select the topic "Play." Under Activities and Applications, watch the video *Building Blocks: Small Group Activity* to see how a teacher fosters good group relationships.

Teachers can encourage children to be genuinely pleasant with everyone and work with a variety of children in the class while not forcing them to believe that they have to be everyone's friend. The morning meeting strategy (see Chapter 2), contains a *greeting* (Kriete, 2002). While there are scores of greetings, the essential element is that each child greets another child. They look at each other, might shake hands, and say, "Good morning, _____." Everyone is included, and it is a relaxing, enjoyable way to learn social skills and to help children interact in a friendly, welcoming way with every other person in the class.

Socially Competent Children Have Developed Good Social Skills

Children tend to develop better social skills when they have temperament qualities of persistence, flexibility, and a caring attitude and the good skills lead to being judged as socially competent (Prior, Sanson, Smart, & Oberklaid, 2000). Good social skills make it easier for children to have enjoyable peer interactions, relationships, and group experiences. **Social skills** are observable behaviors through which a child demonstrates that he can regulate thoughts and emotions. **Key social skills** include

Social skills Observable behaviors through which a child demonstrates the ability to regulate thoughts and emotions.

Key social skills Identifying emotions, regulating emotions, correctly interpret another's actions, turn-taking, following directions, coming up with good solutions to conflicts, carrying on conversation, and persisting at tasks.

- identifying emotions,
- regulating emotions,
- correctly interpreting another's actions,
- turn-taking,
- following directions,
- coming up with good solutions to conflicts,
- carrying on a conversation, and
- persisting at tasks.

The developmental sequence in social skills is shown in Figure 5.2.

Popular, socially competent children have good social skills as Andy demonstrates. Observing the teacher talking with another child, Andy stopped and stood next to Mr. Hernandez without speaking (Mr. Hernandez had taught this social skill to the class). Andy waited patiently, regulating his emotion of excitement.

FIGURE 5.2   Developmental Sequence: Social Skills

Birth to 12 Months

- Facial expressions (smiles or frowns) or gestures (reaching out a hand) directed to play partners
- Showing social interest by watching other babies
- Responding to a play partner's behaviors, for example, reaching out to a person who shows interest in playing with the infant

12 to 36 Months

- Child is aware that somebody is imitating her
- Can imitate another person's activity
- Turn-taking: observe peer, respond to peer, observe and wait
- Shows helping and sharing behaviors

Preschool, Kindergarten, and Primary Grades

- Able to share meaning in dramatic play and in rough and tumble play
- Indicates that they understand a listener's characteristics with forms of speech
- Spontaneous acts of kindness and compassion toward peers
- Appropriately expresses positive emotions
- Can control negative thoughts about social partner
- Knows how to start a conversation and keep one going in an interaction
- Able to "scope out" a setting and a partner in which an interaction might take place
- Can figure out what the consequences of her actions will be for her and for the person on the receiving end of the actions
- Speaks clearly and takes turns speaking when having a conversation; does not interrupt

Source: Based on Rubin, Bukowski, and Parker (1998).

Socially Competent Children Tune in to the Social Setting

Socially competent children are good observers. They watch other children at play and can figure out the others' interests. They scope out the other children's behavior. Thus, they learn some of the tools that they need to adapt (Mize, 1995). For example, if a socially competent child had tried to join an ongoing group and had been rejected, she would be more likely than a less skilled child to know how to integrate herself in their activity. She would not give up easily but would not be disruptive or aggressive. She would, however, know when to give up. As an example, Andy, a kindergarten child, wanted to play with the marbles and the marble machines, which were already being used in the sensory table.

> Kim, "We're using them, Andy." Andy observed and said, "OK, but it looks like you need more marbles." He gathered loose marbles saying, "I'm the marble maker and I'll make some more in my factory." Then, calling out "Marble delivery from the marble factory!" he delivered them to the other two children.

Socially skilled children, such as Andy, tend not to argue when rebuffed. Instead, they pick up on the ongoing play theme and extend it, allowing them to work themselves successfully into the activity. Socially competent children are not always successful, however, and had the other children still turned Andy down, he would likely have just found something else to do without getting upset.

Socially competent children do not arrive at school with a mature set of social skills, and they are not perfect in their skills. Acquiring the skills takes a long time, learning, practicing, making mistakes, and practicing again, often with help from adults. Social competence is a process.

CHECK YOUR UNDERSTANDING
Characteristics of Socially Competent Children

Choose one of the characteristics of socially competent children that you just read about. In your own words, explain why that ability is so important in social competence.

Teachers want to know how the children in their classes are doing in becoming socially competent. We now turn to examining how teachers can assess this part of children's development.

Assessing Children's Social Competence

Children who are socially competent stand a much better chance of succeeding in school than children who do not get along well with others (Denham, 2006). There are a number of different ways to assess social competence (Jalongo, 2006).

Interviewing a Child's Peers

One method relies on information from a child's peers. The interviewer shows small photographs of children in the class to a child and makes positive statements such as "I like to work with this person," or "This person is fun to play games with," or "I like to sit next to this person at lunch." What emerges is a picture of a child's peer acceptance, a snapshot of which children are nominated and how often each child is chosen. You would find that some children are nominated often, but others get very few or no nominations.

Anecdotal Notes

Another method involves teacher observation, using strategies described in Chapter 8. Some teachers, for example, write short notes about incidents revolving around social development, much like Mrs. Chang's notes about Ralph as he entered an ongoing group. This teacher prefers a printed form, while others use sticky notes that they then put right in a file folder in the order in which the notes were written.

> Ralph sat down at the play dough table . . . started patting and squishing his lump of dough . . . said, "This play dough is cold!" Jim said, "Feel my play dough, Ralph. It's *warm*.

Event Sampling

Event sampling A formal method of observation in which one sample of a specifically defined behavior is observed and recorded.

Event sampling is a formal method of observing children's behavior. Teachers use this method most effectively when they are interested in one specific aspect, in this case of

TABLE 5.1 Event Sampling Form		
Focus of the observation: the "event" that I am looking for is		
Date: day of week/date		
Time:		
A *Antecedent* event: What happened before the event?	**B** *Behavior.* Describe the event	**C** *Consequence*: What was the result of the event

social and emotional behavior. The observer identifies the specific category such as sharing, quarreling, cursing, biting, or hitting and then carefully defines the category. For example, a teacher defines *aggressive reaction to anger* as showing signs of anger and reacting in an aggressive way, such as hitting, name-calling, or yelling at another child. The teacher then observes the child's stream of behavior and records only instances illustrating the defined behavior. Event sampling is best used with behaviors that do not occur too frequently, such as an aggressive reaction to anger, quarreling, or tantrums. It gives teachers information about a child's developing abilities with social and emotional skills (Brassard & Boehm, 2007).

The teacher uses a preconstructed form to record a narrative in enough detail about the event to give an accurate portrayal (Bentzen, 2004; Zeren & Makosky, 2000). Table 5.1 shows that the A, B, C format of the form for recording antecedent are what is right before the event, the behavior, and the consequence or what happens as a result of the behavior. Event sampling is a useful method for teachers who want to help children whose emotional and social behaviors make being accepted by other children and enjoying school difficult for him or her. After gathering many examples over a reasonable period, the teacher will have a better view of this aspect of the child's social and emotional skills. Then, the teacher has vital information for planning how to help the child.

In addition to this description, a teacher might want to know how often the behavior occurs and would then use a frequency count in which she records a mark for every time the event occurs. This gives data about how frequently a behavior occurs and can reveal patterns.

Checklists

Teachers can also observe by using ready-made assessment tools. For instance, McClellen and Katz (2001) developed the *Social Attributes Checklist* for assessing young children's social development. The checklist (Figure 5.3) is based on research on elements of young children's social competence and on studies comparing behavior of well-liked children with that of children who are not as well liked (Ladd & Profilet, 1996; McClellan & Kinsey, 1999; McClellan & Katz, 2001).

This checklist does not compare one child with others. The authors caution that there is no "correct social behavior" but that teachers should use this checklist to "observe, understand, and support children as they grow in social skillfulness." For example, they emphasize that some children are simply shyer than others. Forcing a shy child into social relationships might well be quite uncomfortable and stressful for that child. A child does *not* have to get a specific number of checks. The items that *are* checked give

FIGURE 5.3 Social Attributes Checklist

Child's Name: _____

Date: _____

Observation # Circle one: 1   2   3   4

I. INDIVIDUAL ATTRIBUTES

The child:

____ Is *usually* in a positive mood

____ Is not *excessively* dependent on the teacher, assistant, or other adults

____ Usually comes to the program or setting willingly

____ Usually copes with rebuffs adequately

____ Shows the capacity to empathize

____ Has positive relationships with one or two peers; shows capacity to really care about them, miss them if they are absent

____ Displays the capacity for humor

____ Does not seem to be acutely lonely

II. SOCIAL SKILLS ATTRIBUTES

The child *usually:*

____ Approaches others positively

____ Expresses wishes and preferences clearly; gives reasons for actions and positions

____ Asserts own rights and needs appropriately

____ Is not easily intimidated by bullies

____ Expresses frustrations and anger effectively and without escalating disagreements or harming others

____ Gains access to ongoing groups at play and work

____ Enters ongoing discussion on the subject; makes relevant contributions to ongoing activities

____ Takes turns fairly easily

____ Shows interest in others; exchanges information with and requests information from others appropriately

____ Negotiates and compromises with others appropriately

____ Does not draw inappropriate attention to self

____ Accepts and enjoys peers and adults of ethnic groups other than his or her own

____ Interacts nonverbally with other children with smiles, waves, nods, etc.

III. PEER RELATIONSHIP ATTRIBUTES

The child:

____ Is usually accepted versus neglected or rejected by other children

____ Is sometimes invited by other children to join them in play, friendship, and work

____ Is named by other children as someone they are friends with or like to play and work with

Source: McClellan and Katz (2001).

valuable information as do items not checked. Suppose that a teacher observes a child for the third time and still has not checked *Shows the capacity to empathize*. This would alert the adult that the child probably needs assistance in empathizing, which is the ability to feel what another person or animal might be feeling or what her motives are.

The three parts to this checklist are individual, social skill, and peer relationship attributes. The characteristics in the checklist point to satisfactory social growth if a child *usually* displays them. Several factors, such as illness or high stress might cause slight variations in a child's social competence, but teachers look for an overall pattern of social skills. The checklist's developers advise teachers to observe each child several times using the instrument, and there is a place on the checklist to indicate if a teacher is observing a child for the first, second, third, or fourth time.

Technology Can Be Helpful in Observing

Advances in technology provide additional options to teachers. Here are some ideas for using technology in observing and assessing. Note taking might be easier for a teacher who uses a *personal digital assistant (PDA)*. This is a handheld computer that can be used for taking notes. Teachers can download notes from the device to a laptop or desktop computer via a cable or wireless connection.

A *digital voice recorder* is another device that some teachers find useful in observing children. It is hand held and small and a significant advance over older tape recorders because there is no tape and no rewinding involved to listen to a recording. Use a voice recorder to do an event sampling, for example. This device has a memory chip and can hold varying amounts of information in files, which makes them an extremely efficient tool for teachers. Voice files from a digital voice recorder can be downloaded to a computer. Some of these devices can convert the voice file to written text, very useful in writing summaries of observations.

Use a *digital camera* to record events in short movies or a series of photos. This would help teachers in reviewing an event. The teacher could then include a selection of the pictures or movies in a digital portfolio, including samples taken over time or at different times of the day or week.

Review and Reflect

A teacher uses observations to support children's social and emotional development, but first needs to review information gathered through observation and then to reflect on it, asking questions about how to support a child (Belinda, 2005). Here are some potentially helpful things to ponder about observations:

- What did I learn about this child's social and emotional development?
- Does this information change any of my ideas?
- What patterns were revealed in the observations?
- Do I need to change how I do something to help this child?
- Would it help this child if I changed something about the classroom's environment or the schedule?
- Do I need to consider making a referral to another professional or an outside agency?

Children's social development takes place in a variety of systems (Bronfenbrenner, 1994). Let's look at some of the things that affect this developmental domain.

MULTIPLE INFLUENCES ON SOCIAL DEVELOPMENT AND LEARNING

Easily observable differences exist in children's social competence. As with any area of development, we account for these differences by looking at the multiple factors interacting to bring about different paths in social development. Some of the major factors are

Go to MyEducationLab and select the topic "Technology." Under Activities and Applications, watch the video *Social Learning* (*with computers*) to see children working together and learning relationship skills as they work with computers.

- relationships with adults,
- individual developmental variations,
- culture, and
- media violence.

Relationships with Adults

Relationships with adults have a powerful impact on children's social development and learning, a concept supported with both theory and research.

Use Theory to Understanding Relationships

From Vygotsky's theory (Berk & Winsler, 1995; Vygotsky, 1978), children *construct knowledge*; we apply its logic to social development and competence by acknowledging that children build understanding about how to get along with others. A main organizing principle in this theory is that children construct social knowledge and competence by *interacting with more knowledgeable others (MKOs)—parents and teachers mainly but also other children*. These MKOs support children's construction of knowledge and skills about things such as how to make and keep a friend and how to deal with conflicts.

A teacher is scaffolding his students' understanding about printing and about how to use speech to guide themselves when they are printing.

The process takes place through shared problem solving, the person with greater knowledge assuming most of the responsibility in the early stages of learning. In the case of social learning, the MKO supports the child as she builds understanding and skills about getting along with others. Vygotsky emphasized the role of the MKOs language in this process, the adult talking with children. As children develop social understanding, the adult, or other child if the MKO is a child, decreases support and children gradually begin to use their own internal language to guide interactions and relationships with others. The following example with 6 year olds illustrates a teacher's effort to help Tim learn to wait for others to finish speaking before speaking himself.

Mr. Hernandez *modeled* waiting for someone to finish speaking, *coached* children, including Tim, and *reminded* them frequently at first. Gradually, with minor setbacks, Tim and the others acquired this social skill and successfully waited *most* of the time.

All children can benefit from learning how to use speech to guide their actions. For example, preschool children, even those considered at risk for behavioral problems, successfully used speech to guide their actions (Winsler, Manfra, & Diaz, 2007). This research follows classic research of Meichenbaum and Goodman (1971) who showed that children have better self-control when they talk to themselves as they work.

Helping children build such understanding is a slow process. A child might seem to "get it" and show the more appropriate behavior. Why, then, might a child regress and use one of his old unhelpful ways of interacting? Young children often remember an *incorrect* perception (interrupting others when talking with them or when someone in a group speaks), even when it has been replaced by a more accurate perception of events (Freeman, Lacohee, & Coulton, 1995). The incorrect idea, during the learning process, is held back or repressed for a short time so that a child can use a new idea. A child then might, to the great frustration of her teacher, use the less helpful idea again.

Gradually, small signs point to a child's budding and more permanent knowledge and skills. Tim, for example, at group time wound himself up to blurt out a question and then seemed to stop, blink, and stay quiet. This was evidence of Tim's newly formed **self-control** when waiting, his own internal language advising him to wait. In Vygotsky's framework, Tim had *internalized* his teacher's language about this social skill.

Self-control Voluntary, internal regulation of behavior, a part of executive function.

Use Research to Understand Adult-Child Relationships

Researchers have found that adult-child relationships influence children's perceptions of their value (Kernis, Brown, & Brody, 2000), how they get along with others, and how they adapt to school (Birch & Ladd, 1997; Hamre & Pianta, 2001; Pianta & Stuhlman, 2004). For instance, a highly conflicted teacher-child relationship during the kindergarten year is linked to negative academic and behavioral outcomes through eighth grade (Hamre & Pianta, 2001). Children whose parents use harsh discipline tend to have great difficulty interacting with peers. In one study of preschool children, boys were more aggressive when parents used physical force but girls were more aggressive when parents used psychological control (Nelson, Hart, Yang, Olsen, & Jin, 2006).

On a more positive note, a variety of adult characteristics and behaviors help children to develop social competence. One of these is the adult's level of education. Children's social development and competence tend to be stronger when their parents have education beyond high school (Loeb, Fuller, Kagan, Carol, & Carroll, 2004). Children also tend to have more effective social skills when parents play with their children in a nondirective way. The parent in this case models appropriate social skills that are observed and then adopted by their children. Unless it is necessary, parents of children with good social skills also avoid interfering when their children play with peers. This allows children the necessary give-and-take of sustained child-child play and the opportunity to practice social skills with peers (Mize & Abell, 1996).

Research about children getting along with others supports Vygotsky's belief in the value of adult-child dialogue. For example, children are better liked by other children if adults talk with them about getting along with others (Laird, Pettit, Mize, Brown, & Lindsey, 1994). Children gain social competence when adults help them interpret social events in a positive, resilient, constructive way (Mize, Pettit, Lindsey, & Laird, 1993), when the adults endorse friendly solutions that fit in with other children's interests or ongoing play (Mize & Abell, 1996), and when adults help children come up with multiple solutions to problems and then reflect on consequences of each (Mize & Pettit, 1994). For example, Mr. Hernandez helped second grader Willis who had been refused entry into a work group.

How many children are allowed to use Geoblocks at one time? (reminding child about classroom rule) . . . that's right, four.

Sam and James are there now, so, can you play, too? (reminding child that he has a right to work with blocks, too).

Let's figure out what to do. (invites child to do the problem solving).

What could you say to let them know about four children working at once? (encourages thinking about the solution).

Individual Developmental Variations

Individual developmental variations Factors influencing an individual child's social development and competence.

Every child's journey to social competence is somewhat similar as outlined in Figures 5.1 and 5.2. However, as with emotional and all other areas of development, teachers observe that children have taken different paths in the journey. **Individual developmental variations** influence children's social development and competence. Some of these are

- temperament
- disabilities
- ADHD, autism, and bipolar disorder
- chronic medical problems
- child abuse and neglect

Effect of Temperament on Social Development

Temperament The predictable way that a child responds to events; the biological part of personality.

Temperament refers to the predictable way that a child responds to events; the biological part of personality (Encyclopedia of Children's Health, 2004). It is clearly linked to a child's social development (Sanson, Hemphill, & Smart, 2004). Children have different ways that they might react to new situations and change. We should avoid labels as much as possible and focus on the idea that they simply have different styles.

Some children are slow to adapt to change, might react with stubbornness if forced to change prematurely, and withdraw from new events or stimuli, such as opportunities for interaction with other children and the chance to develop and practice social skills and to develop good relationships. Other children adapt well to change, have mild reactions to new events such as the chance to play with other children, and have primarily positive moods. They tend to develop good social skills and relationships with other children and, as a result, are viewed as socially competent. A teacher's goal is not to apply labels but to observe all children and reflect on what they might need. Then, the teacher's goal is to work with all children to help them develop the skills that they need for positive interactions and good relationships.

Effect of Disabilities on Social Development

A variety of children's disabilities or exceptional needs, mild cognitive delays and emotional disturbances for instance, affect different domains of development, including social development and competence. Some preschoolers with mild cognitive delays have problems with forming friendships and establishing relationships. Difficulties include entering peer groups, initiating activities (Wilson, 1999), and keeping play episodes going (Guralnick, Connor, Hammond, Gottman, & Kinnish, 1996). They can have difficulty resolving conflicts and often challenge other children in a hostile manner (Guralnick, Paul-Brown, Groom, Booth, Hammond, Tupper, & Galenter, 1998). This places the children at risk for less peer acceptance and fewer satisfying relationships.

Likewise, some children with emotional disturbances have difficulty establishing and maintaining relationships with other children or with teachers (Chen, 2006; National

Dissemination Center for Children with Disabilities, 2002). A child with emotional disturbance, along with all children, needs to learn social skills and to increase self-esteem and self-control.

Effect of ADHD, Autism, and Bipolar Disorders on Social Development

Attention deficit hyperactive disorder (ADHD) is seen in 3% to 5% of school-age children. Children with ADHD show some behaviors much more frequently and much more severely than do other children of the same age and developmental level. For example, they tend to blurt answers, fidget or squirm, are very easily distracted, talk too much, have difficulty playing quietly and paying attention, do not pay attention to details, interrupt or intrude on others, and are impatient (AACAP, 2004b). Children with ADHD symptoms are at risk for being disliked or rejected by peers and have trouble making and keeping friends because many children, like adults, are very likely annoyed when somebody interrupts them.

Autism is a developmental disability that significantly affects verbal and nonverbal communication and social interaction. It adversely affects a child's educational experience and is generally evident before age 3. Characteristics often associated with autism are engaging in repetitive activities and stereotyped movements, resistance to changes in daily routines or the environment, and unusual responses to sensory experiences.

Children with autism face challenges in social development. They initiate fewer social behaviors, and they are less responsive to the feelings of others. They are able to recognize facial expressions but have difficulty taking the perspective of another person. Many children with autism lack speech, and they are limited in the ability to use gestures to communicate (Sigman, 2006).

Children can be diagnosed with *bipolar disorder,* a mental illness characterized by depressive and/or manic symptoms. Some children can show both depressive and manic symptoms, but others might show one or the other mainly. The symptoms can cause problems with social development. Manic symptoms include extreme changes in mood, such as acting extremely happy or silly or extremely aggressive and irritable. There are also great increases in energy and talking. Depressive symptoms include extreme sadness, frequent crying, and depressed mood along with thoughts of death or suicide. The child might also cease to enjoy things and activities formerly treasured (AACAP, 2004a).

Bipolar disorder affects children to a greater degree than it does adults (Birmaher et al., 2006). This illness damages relationships with the child's family and with other children. The child is often socially isolated, extremely sensitive to rejection and failure, and might have difficulty communicating (NIMH, 2000). Psychiatric treatment aims to help children with bipolar disorder to develop socially as normally as possible. The goal of treatment is to help a child understand herself and build relationships (Carlson, 2008).

Effect of Chronic Medical Problems on Social Development

Chronic medical conditions are persistent, ever-present problems such as asthma, sickle cell anemia, and otitis media or middle ear infection. These problems may challenge children's social development as well as their physical health. For example, children with chronic otitis media in their first 3 years of life are at a distinct disadvantage for social development. They play alone more often and have fewer interactions, either

Attention deficit hyperactive disorder (ADHD) Much more frequent and severe behaviors than with other children of the same age and developmental level; showing behaviors such as blurting answers, fidgeting, talking too much, and difficulty playing quietly and paying attention.

Chronic medical condition Persistent, ever-present problems.

positive or negative, than do children without this medical problem in child care. Thus, they miss the play opportunities with other children, the foundation of developing skilled interactions, meaningful relationships, and acceptance in a group (Vernon-Feagans, Manlove, & Volling, 1996).

Effect of Child Abuse and Neglect on Social Development

Child abuse and neglect often has both short- and long-term effects on children's development. Observing abuse or family violence can have equally harmfully effects. The following listing illustrates some of the major effects of child abuse and neglect on children's social development and competence.

- Maltreated children have relationship problems with peers, being more withdrawn and passive (Crittenden, 1992).
- Maltreated children tend to have disturbances in how they view their "self" (Toth, Cicchetti, MacFie, & Emde, 1997).
- Emotional maltreatment can lead to poor peer relationships (Bolger, Patterson, & Kupersmidt, 1998).
- Physically abused children are likely to interpret, incorrectly, the actions of peers and then to respond aggressively (Dodge, Bates, & Petit, 1990).
- Children who *witness* family violence tend to engage in less social behavior, are less socially competent, and are often aggressive (Parkinson & Humphreys, 1998).

The effect of abuse on social development can start very early in a child's life and set that child up for poor interactions and rejection. Early research by Main and George (1985) documented the effects of abuse on 1- to 3-year-old children's social interactions. Infants and toddlers who had been abused physically assaulted peers and were the only children who assaulted or threatened to assault their teachers. They were far less likely to approach teachers who had invited interaction in a friendly way. If the abused toddlers did approach another person, they did so from the side or from behind—*a combination of approach and avoidance* when interacting.

Culture

We describe and explain emotional and social development in separate chapters. These two domains, however, are strongly linked and are affected by similar influences. Recall from Chapter 4 on emotional development that a child's cultural group expresses its rules and traditions through values, beliefs, and goals. In terms of social development, one culture, valuing cooperation, might express it in gathering to help one of its members build a barn.

Modeling social interactions and how to develop and maintain relationships powerfully influence children's social development. Children observe, for example, as adults greet others or as they deal with feelings of anger, jealousy, and pride within their relationships. Some children observe adults interact in friendly, civil ways while other children observe unfriendly, even rude interactions. Children take note of how adults treat each other by observing adult relationships. For example,

> Andy, a preschooler, observes the teachers in his school as they interact. He watches Mrs. Chang and the parent volunteers as they work together every day. Mrs. Chang is friendly and respectful with each parent, patiently explaining the parent's duties for the day.

Children learn about interacting with others within their culture.

One of the core standards for preparing early childhood professionals is *building family and community relationships*. Future teachers learn about children's families and communities and use this knowledge to build respectful and reciprocal relationships. Good relationships are based in part on how well teachers understand their own views on other cultures, which involves knowing about different ways that members of our diverse society view interacting within the larger society. These include (LaFramboise, Coleman, & Gerton, 1993):

- *Assimilation:* incorporation into the culture considered dominant. For example, a family moving into a different culture might want to blend totally into it and adopt the language, customs, and food as well as every other aspect of the new culture.
- *Acculturation:* becoming competent about a different culture but not adopting the culture. A teacher working with children and families from three different cultures might strive to become competent in each while not becoming a part of them. This concept of cultural competence was discussed in Chapter 3. (See Figure 3.8.)
- *Alternation:* competence in two cultures and able to function well in both. A child might have a family who maintains its distinct cultural identity. They still enjoy their culture's food, music, literature, and dance. He, however, adopts the new culture's language, customs, and food while he *also* continues to function well in his home culture.
- *Multicultural:* one social structure with different cultures still evident.

Media Violence

There is an overwhelming consensus in the research, public health, and early childhood communities that watching and participating in media violence threatens the development and well-being of young children. The Kaiser Family Foundation's report on the effects of electronic media on children from birth to age 6 (Center on Media and Child

Health, 2005) documents a variety of health risks to children who watch too much television or play too many video games. A significant health risk to social development is that a child becomes more aggressive from watching too much aggression (Huesmann, Moise-Titus, Podosky, & Eron, 2003).

Screen time The time that children spend watching a screen of any type.

Children have a lot of **screen time**, which refers to all the time they spend watching a screen of any type, such as television, game systems, handheld devices, and computers. Children watch violence quite frequently (Rideout, Vandewater, & Wartella, 2003). For example, 74% of children younger than 2 years have watched television, and almost 60% of these children watch for over 2 hours each day. Thirty percent of infants and toddlers have televisions in their bedrooms, whereas the figure is 59% for children 4 to 6. An interesting, very recent study showed that 2 year olds can certainly learn from video (Troseth, Saylor, & Archer, 2006) when the person on screen used social cues and personal references.

Physical aggression Intentionally hurting another person's or animal's body in some way, such as with hitting or biting; the main individual risk factor for antisocial, hostile behavior.

Physical aggression is the main individual risk factor for antisocial, hostile behavior (Brody et al., 2003), thus, threatening children's social development. Physical aggression involves intentionally hurting another person's or animal's body in some way, such as through hitting or biting. Children who are aggressive, therefore, are in grave danger of having *negative* interactions and *poor* relationships with other children and are *not* likely to be accepted by a group of children. There is a high probability that children with early-onset aggression, which is aggression developed *during* early childhood, are in greater danger of antisocial, behavior-related problems in adolescence and early adulthood than are children who become aggressive in later childhood.

Scripts The way that children organize their understanding of how to get along with others; information is conveyed to children through a variety of systems.

Watching media violence gives children unhelpful, negative **scripts** for how to get along with others and how they view hurting others. There is real value in all of the violence-in-the-media research of the last 40 years, including research from the early 2000s on playing violent video games (Anderson, 2004). This accumulation of knowledge alerts teachers to the well-developed and well-rehearsed scripts about unpleasant, even hurtful ways of dealing with other children. If the same children have not learned more competent social behaviors, then teachers can expect them to put their unhelpful learning and their aggressive scripts to work when they work and play with other children in school. Children can also learn scripts for other stereotypes through the media—commercialism and distorted views of girls and women, senior citizens, and other races and cultures—and this can affect how they perceive and interact with members of those groups.

Social competence depends, in part, on a child's support network, particularly the adults in his or her life. We now examine some of the things that teachers can do to help children develop social competence.

USING KNOWLEDGE ABOUT SOCIAL DEVELOPMENT TO CREATE A HEALTHY AND RESPECTFUL ENVIRONMENT

Becoming socially competent is a process for which all children need support. Some children's social development, however, has been hampered by any of the factors described in the previous section. There is a good chance that they have not learned how to get along well with other children as well as they can, one-on-one or in a group. This group especially needs support. Some children have learned *unhelpful scripts* for interacting with others. Early childhood teachers support these children best by assisting children in writing more helpful scripts for interactions, relationships, and for functioning in a group.

Teachers can foster all children's social development when they

- create a caring classroom community,
- build a socially responsible, democratic classroom, and
- help children learn to manage interactions and relationships.

Create a Caring Classroom Community

A **caring classroom community** is positive supportive school and classroom climate. Every child feels like a valued, contributing member of the classroom, where it is safe to take risks or ask for help. Children want to take care of each other and animals, and teachers encourage acts of generosity and compassion.

Caring classroom community A positive, supportive classroom climate.

McGuire (1998) reviewed school-based programs aimed at promoting social competence. He noted that programs succeeded only in schools with a real sense of community. An example is the Responsive Classroom model, described in Chapter 2, which focuses on developing caring classroom communities. This model base has seven principles, several of which target social development. It places equal emphasis on social and academic curriculum in the belief that it is as important to concentrate on how children learn as much as on what they learn. Developers of the RC approach believe that social development supports cognitive growth and emphasizes teaching key social skills such as cooperation, responsibility, and self-control. Children in a RC tend to do very well academically, and they also develop good relationships with their teachers (Rimm-Kaufman, 2006).

Recall that Vygotsky valued adult-child discussion. Teachers who discuss social concepts such as friendship and friendliness help children gain knowledge about their culture's view of these topics. Some teachers speak about all children in a class being friends, but Mr. Hernandez had a different idea when the class discussed classroom rules as illustrated in the Teach Intentionally box.

TEACH INTENTIONALLY

Friendliness to Everyone

What the teacher did: When reviewing classroom rules, Mr. Hernandez led a discussion about *friendliness to everyone*. The children gave their ideas of the definitions of *friendly and unfriendly*. Then, the teacher gave several examples of interactions and asked the children to supply a *friendly versus an unfriendly* response. Finally, he and the children developed an *acting friendly to everyone* rule for the classroom.

How the teacher was intentional: He deliberately focused on an important aspect of social development, understanding the concept of sociability. He also helped the children contrast friendly and unfriendly responses in the same interaction. Their rule states a clear expectation about considerate actions toward others.

Recall that the constructivist theory tells us that children build their own knowledge. Piaget noted that children build different types of knowledge, including *social knowledge*, which is learned as children interact with others in their culture and society. Mr. Hernandez has followed the constructivist tradition in helping children build their own knowledge about sociability—friendly and unfriendly responses.

Welcoming English Language Learners to a Classroom

Every child feels welcomed and valued in a caring classroom community, including, for example, English language learners. Teachers are in a good position to draw their classroom circle to include children learning a different language. There are many simple and practical ways to help English language learners feel welcome in their classrooms (Colorìn Colorado, 2007).

- Learn a child's name. This includes learning how to pronounce names accurately. To do this, listen to the pronunciation and repeat until you get it right. Model the correct pronunciation for other children.
- Offer one-on-one help. English language learners often do not request the help that they need because they do not yet have the words for asking. Observe carefully and offer assistance.
- Pair an English language learner with another child. The partner should be eager and able to assist his classmate. The partner's role is not to do the new classmate's work but to help him know what he or she is supposed to do, for example, (how to tell how many children can work in a center.)
- Display a daily schedule with pictures. English language learners, like all children, need to know about the flow of the day, and a schedule is a common aid. Pictures of daily activities, such as reading groups, center time, and outdoor play help the child predict upcoming events and decrease stress from not knowing what comes next.

CHECK YOUR UNDERSTANDING
Analyze the Preschool Vignette

Use the section that you just read, "Welcoming English Language Learners to a Classroom," to analyze the preschool chapter-opening vignette. Identify and explain two things that this teacher did to welcome Pedro, an English language learner, to his new classroom.

Build a Socially Responsible Classroom

Socially responsible classroom Classroom that applies democratic principles, such as self-rule, egalitarianism, includes everyone.

Kohn (1996; page 70) presented an early argument for helping children construct ideas about social responsibility. He said that children ". . . learn to make good choices by making choices, not by following directions." A **socially responsible classroom** is a place that applies democratic principles of including everybody, social equality, and self-rule. Children arrive at consensus and work collaboratively. Such a classroom fosters good social skills. All of these are a part of the Responsive Classroom model or any approach fostering social responsibility.

Early childhood teachers following a developmental model and wanting to foster socially responsible attitudes teach the concept of *fairness*, treating others justly, and helping children understand that the rules apply to everyone in the classroom. They also encourage cooperation in work and play, and this helps children learn that cooperation is actually enjoyable and that it prevents or decreases aggravation. Mr. Hernandez, for example, reminded Willis that his job was to work with Annie in cleaning the gerbil's house and that Willis and Annie could do the job more easily together than either would alone.

Teach Skills for Resolving Conflicts

Teachers foster social responsibility when they teach children how to resolve conflict and arrive at friendly, cooperative solutions. They teach the followings steps in resolving conflict:

- *Identify the problem as a shared one.* Use a nonaccusatory tone, "Looks like you both have a problem. You both want to take Sunshine out of her house so that you can clean."
- *Invite children to participate in fixing the problem,* "Let's think about how to solve this problem."
- *Generate possible solutions with the children, accepting a variety of solutions,* "Yes, you could both lift her out; Willis can take her out and Annie can put Sunshine in her temporary place while you clean; one can lift her out of her house and the other can put her back."

Teachers build a socially responsible classroom by encouraging children to work together to get things done.

- *Examine each idea for merits and drawbacks.* With the children, decide which to use. Thank the children for thinking of solutions. "I appreciate how you both thought of ideas that keep Sunshine safe. . . . OK, you've both agreed that Annie will lift her out and Willis will return Sunshine to her house."
- *Put the plan into action.* Help the children get started if they do not know this skill. "What do you need to do to carry out your plan so that Sunshine is protected?"
- *Follow up.* Evaluate how well the solution worked. "You worked so well together! I'll bet that Sunshine felt really safe and you got her house cleaned quickly. Tell me how your idea for solving your problem worked for you both."

Teachers can scaffold children's construction of ideas for resolving conflicts. Scaffolding involves giving more help when children are learning a new skill and then gradually withdrawing assistance as children demonstrate competence. At first, children need a lot of help in resolving conflicts, as illustrated in the steps just explained. After children learn and practice the steps, a teacher can decrease the amount of help given. The goal is to give children the confidence and skills they need to work out conflicts on their own, but this takes time. Eventually, a teacher would encourage children to use problem solving by themselves whenever possible.

Teachers can use the steps in resolving a conflict with toddlers but meet their needs by modifying the steps. Taking the *generating possible solutions* step, as an example, toddlers ask *yes* or *no* questions. For example, "Could you each pick up a block?" They will then only have to nod yes or shake their heads no. When putting the plan into action, give some ideas about how to get started instead of expecting a toddler to come up with the idea.

Help Children Learn Key Social Skills

Teachers can help children learn to manage interactions and relationships, and this involves acquiring and using social skills linked to school success. Children who do not learn key social skills have problems in school, with other children, and with adults. Children, especially those with challenging behaviors who do learn social skills have better self-control and better peer relationships (Center for Evidence-Based Practice, 2004). Children with specific disabilities such as emotional disturbance or autism need help in social skill learning (Chen, 2006). Both informal and formal approaches are effective in helping children learn social skills and competency.

Formal Approaches for Social Skills Learning

Children can learn social skills through formal instruction (LeBlanc & Matson, 1995). Some of the general strategies employed in a formal approach include modeling; role-playing for older, early childhood children and puppet play for younger children; cooperative learning that involves working together to accomplish some task (building with blocks, writing a story together); anger management; and self-control strategies, such as learning to monitor oneself (Chen, 2006).

Purchased, packaged programs are one way to do formal instruction. One example is the Dina Dinosaur program (Webster-Stratton, 2007). Another is the Second Step program, which has separate sets of materials for preschool and kindergarten and grades 1 through 5 (Committee for Children, 2007). Some teachers appreciate having all materials in one package. Others find these kits to be too expensive and too structured and simply prefer an informal approach.

Informal Approaches for Social Skills Learning

Children can also learn key social skills informally in everyday interaction with teachers and parents who model and encourage specific abilities and who provide an environment conducive to learning social skills (High/Scope, 2008). Teachers model social skills informally when they greet children cheerfully at arrival time, express adult emotions responsibly, politely request help from children, state limits well, and use a direct but validating style of communication.

The classroom routines also contribute to informal learning, such as learning how to greet other children during morning meeting and learning how to listen as another person speaks in group time. We can also set up the classroom so that children make some choices, move around when appropriate and work and play with other children. Vygotsky's model and constructivist approaches in general advocate time for children to work and play together.

Chapter 2 described different program models and explained how important play is in every model, and this text emphasizes the importance and role of play in several chapters. Play is also one of the best ways for children to learn and practice social skills. Children need opportunities and enough time to play with peers (Elkind, 2006), preferably in a stable peer group such as a classroom because they develop better and more sophisticated social skills when they play with other children (Mize & Abell, 1996). Teachers can also model good social skills when they actually play with children and obviously enjoy themselves. They let the child lead, avoid directing the play, have fun, and avoid criticizing the child.

Mr. Hernandez played the part of a customer at the post office. He bought stamps, saying "Thank-you" to the clerk, put one on his envelope, and handed it in for mailing. Kindergartener Andy said, "Thank-you, Sir. I will mail your letter right away!" (Notice the social skill of saying "thank-you," which mirrors the teacher's language.)

Go to MyEducationLab and select the topic "Child Development." Under Activities and Applications, watch the video *Family Style Dining: Lunch* to observe how children learn social skills in everyday situations.

All children can learn social skills and play is a good way to learn for most children. Some children, however, need special assistance in this regard. Children with autism, for example, tend to have difficulty in playing with other children. A recent study found that children with autism can learn social skills effectively from *virtual peers*, animated life-sized children who demonstrate the talking and behaving of a typically developing child. Researchers found that the goal is to teach social skills with the virtual peer but then to encourage children with autism to generalize the new skills. They were encouraged to practice their new social skills in their interactions with real, not virtual children (Northwestern University, 2008). See a description and a picture of the virtual peer at the web site in this citation in the reference list.

Children develop more sophisticated social skills when they play with other children.

SUMMARY

All children can develop social competence, which is a process, and its foundation is laid in infancy and toddlerhood. A secure attachment and consistent and loving care during infancy and toddlerhood helps children to develop a working model of how good relationships work, and this model influences their relationship style into adulthood.

- Children who experience high-quality child care (little turnover of teachers, small teacher-child ratios, and well-educated staff) do better on measures of social skills and tend to have better social relationships in as late as second grade.
- Continuity of care is important in an infant or toddler's well-being and social development.
- A socially competent child relates well to other children, is generally agreeable and acknowledges and responds to others, and has developed good social skills.

Socially competent children stand a good chance of succeeding in school. There are a number of different ways to assess social competence, such as with

- interviewing other children.
- brief notes known as anecdotal records or notes. This involves a teacher's writing very brief notes about an observation. Several observations often reveal a pattern in a child's behavior.
- event sampling. This method identifies one category of behavior, such as speaking respectfully to others.

The teacher then observes the child's stream of behavior, recording only instances illustrating the defined category.

- checklists. A teacher checks off whether a child shows a specific behavior. This is a quick form of observation but does not give much information, other than that the child did or did not show the behavior.
- a teacher's careful review and reflection of information gathered about children's social development and skills.

As with any area of development, we account for these differences in social development by looking at the multiple factors that interact to bring about different developmental paths. Some of the major factors include

- relationships with adults. Children know about how to get along with others. They construct helpful ideas when they interact with more knowledgeable others, such as teachers and more skilled peers. They learn about things such as making a friend, keeping a friend, and dealing with conflicts.
- individual developmental variations. Children differ in their style of interacting with others, and this affects their overall social development. Teachers need to acknowledge individual differences before they can help a child.

disabilities that might affect social development. Some children with learning disabilities, emotional disturbances, mild cognitive delays, ADHD, autism, and bipolar disorders are challenged when relating to other children. Teachers can help these children by working closely with special education teachers and mental health experts.

All children can become socially competent, and all children need a teacher's support. Some children, however, have not learned the skills that they need and, therefore, need help even more. Teachers can foster all children's social development by

- creating a caring classroom community in which every child feels valued. Children learn to take care of each other and animals, and teachers encourage acts of generosity and compassion.
- building a socially responsible classroom. This is a place that applies democratic principles of including everybody, social equality, and self-rule. Children learn how to resolve conflicts so that everybody's needs are met.
- helping children learn key social skills, through formal or informal methods. Informal methods include everyday interaction with teachers and parents who model and encourage specific abilities.

QUESTIONS FOR REFLECTION

1. Reflect on your ability to develop good relationships with children. Describe an instance when you were able to help a child because you had a good relationship with him or her.

2. Reflect on the differences between these two statements: "In this classroom, we are all *friends*" or "In our classroom, we are *friendly* with every other person." Which of these concepts is more realistic, given the information in this chapter?

APPLY YOUR KNOWLEDGE

What Should This Teacher Do?

1. Review the kindergarten vignette at the beginning of the chapter. Then, role play what Mr. Hernandez would *say and do* to help Juanita and Joseph resolve this typical conflict. Use the steps in resolving conflict described in the chapter, *teach skills for resolving conflicts*. Fill in each of the blanks with what you would be likely to say when following the guideline described.
   - Identify the problem as a shared one. Use a nonaccusatory tone. I would say, _____
   - Invite children to participate in fixing the problem. I would say, _____
   - Generate possible solutions with the children, accepting a variety of solutions. I would say, _____

- Examine each idea for merits and drawbacks. With the children decide which to use. Thank the children for thinking of solutions. I would say, _____
- Put the plan into action. Help the children get started if they do not know this skill. "I would say, _____
- Follow up. Evaluate how well the solution worked. I would say _____

2. Mrs. Chang winced when she saw Nellie sit at a table and scoop a handful of small plastic blocks from Sandra's pile. Name the social skill that Nellie needs to learn. Then use Vygotsky as a guide and say how the teacher can act as the more knowledgeable other to help Nellie acquire this ability.

KEY TERMS

WEB SITES

American Psychological Association
http://www.psychologymatters.org
Home page for a division of the APA, American Psychological Association. Many excellent links useful for teachers.

High Scope
http://www.highscope.org/Content.asp?ContentId=294
Good information on how this program focuses on social skill development.

The Incredible Years
http://www.incredibleyears.com
Home page for Webster-Stratton's social skill learning program. Sample lesson for the Dina Dinosaur program for young children at http://www.incredibleyears.com/Program/CP_sample-sessions.asp.

National Dissemination Center for Children with Disabilities (NICHCY)
http://www.nichcy.org
Links you to many ideas about children with disabilities. Resources in both Spanish and English.

Second Step Program
http://www.cfchildren.org/programs/ssp/overview
A packaged social skills education program. Follow the links to see video clips and for other information.

CHAPTER 6

Supporting Children's Cognitive Development

GUIDING QUESTIONS:

- What are some of the major characteristics and needs of children's cognitive development?
- What are some of the influences on children's cognitive development?
- What can teachers do to foster children's ability to think?

INFANT/TODDLER
Soft Cubes and the Itsy Bitsy Spider

Michael, 10 months old, crawled to the soft cloth cube that his teacher had placed on the carpet. He patted the cube and rolled it around, squealing with glee.

"More!" That was toddler Nick's request for another round of his favorite finger play. Mr. Bjornrud responded, "OK, Nick. Put your fingers together. The itsy, bitsy spider went . . ."

PRESCHOOL
Building Math Concepts with Blocks

Ralph worked steadily in the block area for 25 minutes, lining up unit blocks. Having laid out the longest unit blocks, he then gathered the smaller units, testing and retesting how different combinations of smaller unit blocks measured up against one of the longest. Mrs. Chang sketched some of his combinations for his portfolio.

KINDERGARTEN
Figuring It Out in the Flower Shop

The dramatic play center was buzzing with pretend play in the flower shop. Andy and Jake, heavily involved in their salespeople roles, negotiated about how to package the flowers for a customer. After tossing a bunch of plastic flowers in a bag, Andy heard Jake say, "No, no, no. You have to wrap the flowers first. Then you put them in the bag with the flower sticking out." Andy was clearly confused and asked, "Why?" "Because," Jake replied, "that's how the grocery store does it."

PRIMARY
Remembering Things in Morning Meeting

Greeting section of the daily morning meeting—the children, seated in a circle, passed around their greetings, looking at each other and using each other's name. Luis met Emma's eyes as she greeted him and he returned her "good morning." Then he turned quickly toward Clare and greeted her but forgot to look at her. After one of the children reminded him, Luis rolled his eyes in an exaggerated fashion and then fixed them on Clare and repeated his greeting.

I have attended many university graduations and always end up reflecting on cognitive development. The process through which the students arrived at their sophisticated ability to think still astonishes me. How did they get from infancy's gazing, listening, cooing, and playing to this point? How and when did they acquire the cognitive skills needed to do the work of their future professions: design computer architecture, bridges, and roads, develop good lesson plans, edit films and books, or investigate and write about the news? Their years of development before graduation included brain development, conversations with adults and other children, formal schooling, playing with objects and materials, and developing language and information processing skills. All of this results in an adult cognition that is fundamentally and profoundly different from their infant cognition.

Cognitive development refers to systematic changes in children's reasoning, concepts, memory, and language. This chapter does not describe everything about cognitive development in children: There is simply too much information on this domain for one chapter. We explore, however, the major cognitive characteristics and the cognitive needs children have. We briefly consider some of the influences on cognitive development and competence. Finally, we describe developmentally appropriate strategies teachers can use to support cognitive development and competence. As with the other chapters on development, each of the three major sections in this chapter emphasizes one of the following three concepts (NAEYC, 2001). To foster children's cognitive development, effective teachers of young children must

- know and understand young children's cognitive characteristics and needs.
- know and understand the multiple influences on cognitive development.
- use knowledge about cognitive development to create healthy, respectful, supportive, and challenging learning environments.

UNDERSTANDING CHILDREN'S COGNITIVE CHARACTERISTICS

Chapter 2 described the major tenets of children's cognitive developmental theories—with Piaget and Vygotsky as the focus. They described the qualitative changes and the increasingly complex and organized nature of children's cognition. Let's look at some of the major characteristics of children's cognitive development.

- Children construct their own understanding and knowledge.
- Children construct different types of knowledge.
- Children construct knowledge and skills by relating information to what they already know.
- Children process information.

Children Construct Their Own Understanding and Knowledge

Children are extremely curious, like to investigate things, ask questions, and thrive on play. They continually are active in their development and learning, building or constructing their own understanding of the physical and social world as they interact with people and work with objects (NAEYC, 2006), as 10-month-old Michael did with the soft cube in a chapter opening vignette. Children take in information, observe, make guesses about how things and people work, and test out their ideas, meaning that they build models about the world and its workings. A child who observes dogs, for example, figures out that dogs communicate with a distinctive sound, a bark, and have four legs, two eyes, a mouth, ears, and hair covering their bodies.

Constructivism is an approach to learning and teaching. In this view, children actively build or *construct* knowledge and skills (Bruner, 1990) and the child's constructed knowledge exists within the child's mind, not in the environment. A child who works

Cognitive development Refers to systematic changes in children's reasoning, concepts, memory, and language.

Constructivism An approach to learning and teaching in which children build or construct knowledge and skills.

with objects might build a concept about the objects, but the idea does not exist in the stimuli, the objects. The idea is in the child's mind where it was constructed.

For instance, 4-year-old Ralph observed that his friend John is shorter than Ben. He then compared other pairs of children and developed or constructed a concept that children can be different heights. This concept is not in the classroom itself but in Ralph's mind.

Another major tenet of constructivism contends that children adapt and learn because they process environmental information. They take in and mentally operate on information about physical objects or the social world, thus building new concepts from this processing.

Constructivism in education and child development has itself been under construction for well over 70 years. Theorists most closely connected with this perspective are Dewey (1933; reissued 1998), Piaget (1972), Bruner (1990), and Vygotsky (1978). Other researchers have applied constructivist theory to different areas of early childhood education. For example, teachers can help a child understand mathematical ideas with a constructivist approach. They would first identify an error that the child had made. Then, they would figure out what the child needs to understand before figuring out the "correct answer" (Kamii, 2000) as shown in Figure 6.1.

Children Construct Different Types of Knowledge

Constructivists believe in Piaget's ideas about children building three types of knowledge: social, physical, and logico-mathematical (Russell, 2004). **Social knowledge** is understanding things such as knowing how one's culture typically celebrates birthdays. Ideas that children create about how to behave during group time or about how to deal with angry feelings are also examples of social knowledge.

Physical knowledge refers to understanding physical qualities or traits of objects. Understanding that the paper in your textbook is smooth is an example of physical knowledge. Understanding that a marker has a soft tip or that many unit blocks have corners are examples of children's physical knowledge. This is the type of knowledge that children construct from sensory motor experiences and hands-on learning. They begin to understand the properties or qualities of items such as blocks, puzzles, pieces of fruit, vegetables, and sand by touching, feeling, and manipulating them.

Logico-mathematical knowledge is the understanding about relationships that children form in their minds. For example, a child who works with two types of markers begins to notice and understand differences between the two. One marker has a soft, slanted tip, but the other marker has a soft straight cut tip. His noticing the differences and seeing the relationship between the two items is logico-mathematical knowledge. He has constructed this relationship in his mind; thus, the relationship exists in his mind where it was constructed.

Children Can Make Mistakes About Concepts That They Construct

Children can be accurate or inaccurate in any of the types of knowledge that they construct. A child, for example, might make an error about the physical properties of paint when she says the paint is lumpy. One should not be surprised that, like all people, children make mistakes occasionally in how they view things, people, and relationships (Dreikurs, 1958). As social creatures, one of their great psychological needs is to feel accepted and to be a member of a group.

Children go about fitting into a group by interpreting the rules of the group; they construct ideas about what they have to do to belong. Some children interpret rules of

Social knowledge
Knowledge that humans create, for example, how a group typically celebrates a holiday.

Physical knowledge
Understanding the physical qualities of objects.

Logico-mathematical knowledge Understanding about relationships that children form in their minds.

FIGURE 6.1   Helping Children Construct Mathematical Ideas

Issue: A child makes this error: 3 + 5 = 5. What is the problem?

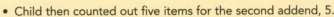

- Child counted out three items for the first addend, 3 (*addend* is a number to be added)

- Child then counted out five items for the second addend, 5.

- Error: when counting out the five items for second addend, 5, child included the three that she had already counted out.
- *She counted only five items, giving her an incorrect total.*

Think like a scientist: What do children need to understand to get the correct answer, 3 + 5 = 8?

- Idea or concept of "whole" and "part" ("I am a part of my class; my class is a whole thing")
- Ability to think about parts and a whole at the same time
- Ability to put two wholes together: Three is a whole and five is a whole
- Idea that two wholes, 3 and 5, can be combined into a higher-order whole, 8
- Addition requires children to understand *relationships* between wholes and parts (logico mathematical knowledge)
- Constructing this understanding is quite difficult for children; children can easily do addition *after constructing* these basic, difficult ideas

How can I use scientific knowledge about how children learn math to scaffold children's understanding?

- Avoid forcing children to memorize rules or using "tricks" about how to add.
- *Do* provide plenty of play with objects in different centers and small groups.
- Encourage manipulation, arranging, rearranging, combining, and breaking up combinations of the objects. This helps children construct understanding of wholes and parts and, finally, addition.

Source: Adapted from Kamii, C. (2000). Teachers need more knowledge about how children learn mathematics. *Mathematics Education Dialogues.* Copyright © 2000 by the National Council of Teachers of Mathematics, Inc. www.nctm.org. All rights reserved.

group membership inaccurately and base their behavior on these faulty interpretations (Marion, 2007). For example, older children who lack perspective-taking skills systematically misread or misinterpret the actions and intentions of others. They often attribute aggressive intent when, in fact, there was no aggressive intent (Chalmers & Townsend,

1990), for example, interpreting another child's facial expression as angry or aggressive when no such intent existed.

Children Construct Knowledge by Relating Information to What They Know

Children are like scientists in constructing knowledge and understanding. They persist in observing, manipulating objects, asking and answering questions, listening to adults, reading, watching television, playing, and forming hypotheses about (making guesses about) and thinking about things. Their curious, active approach gives them numerous bits of new information.

Children try to make sense of the data by relating it to something that they already know or understand. Thus, they build on their existing or prior knowledge. A child who has constructed a concept about dogs will have further experiences with dogs. For example, he observes a miniature version of a breed. After talking with his father, he concludes that the tiny terrier is indeed a dog but is smaller than a cat. This child has accommodated to new information and now has a more sophisticated concept of dogs. His model will continue to evolve. Similarly, a child who has had a brother bump into

Children are active and curious. They construct knowledge through activity and play.

him in an obviously intentional way might just store this memory with its emotional overtones and interpret future accidental run-ins at school inaccurately.

A major part of children's cognitive development lies in how their models change over time, as children continue to interact with people and things and as they interpret and transform their concepts. They revise and modify their knowledge by building on what they know. What a child learns from any new information or lesson depends on the knowledge that he brings to the experience. For example,

> The child who constructed knowledge of the relationship between two different markers brought his prior experience with markers to this experience: Markers have tips, they are used for writing, they come in different colors, some tips are pointed, and some tips are broad and thick. This knowledge base made it easier for him to construct the relationship between the two different markers.

Children Process Information

Information processing involves perceiving, taking in, remembering, and retrieving information. Children are capable of constructing concepts about objects and relationships because they can process information. This approach is in line with Piaget and Vygotsky's descriptions of children's cognitive development by explaining the processes that children use to perform mental operations. Recall from Chapter 2 that Piaget explained that children assimilate or take in information and transform existing schemas or concepts to accommodate the new information. It is a child's brain, in this procedure, that processes information.

Information processing
Perceiving, taking in, remembering, and retrieving information.

Three Units Used to Process Information

The complex processing goes on in three units: a sensory register, short-term memory, and long-term memory. The **sensory register** is a unit through which a child's brain registers auditory or visual sensory information from the environment. Children see and hear thousands of bits of information daily and obviously do not deal with each stimulus. They simply forget much of the sensory data and transfer other data to the next processing unit, short-term memory.

Short-term memory, a useful site, is like a way station, receiving information. First, the sensory register transfers information to short-term memory. Then short-term memory transfers it to the third unit or discards it. There is a greater chance of retaining the information if the child thinks that it is important.

Long-term memory is the third unit involved in processing information. It stores information that children register, send through short-term memory, and then make an effort to learn, such as when they rehearse their phone numbers. Information stays in long-term memory until a child needs to use it, for example, when his mother asks him to repeat the family's phone number. Long-term memory has an almost unlimited storage capacity. A child accumulates so many bits of information that it is almost impossible to comprehend. Long-term memory capacity is more than fifty-thousand times the amount of text contained in the Library of Congress (Marois, 2005).

Children's cognitive development links with other domains, such as the emotional domain. Information that is very important or tinged with strong emotion is much more likely to be transferred to long-term memory than is trivial information.

> Riley, for instance, registered information about the collie Max's, adoption day from the Humane Society in his sensory register and then sent that memory for long-term storage, very possibly because the circumstances in which he formed the memory were so happy.

Working Memory

Short-term memory, in addition to receiving data from the sensory register and sending it on, also has another job. Often, children need to get data from long-term memory so that they can work with it. For this, they use their **working memory**, which is a part of short-term memory. Working memory is the brain's way of providing working space to a child. A child uses working memory to store information temporarily so that he can use it to perform some other task (Tsujimoto, Yamamoto, Kawaguchi, Koizumi, & Sawaguchi, 2004). Working memory forms the base for a child's ability to plan and to do the mental operations that Piaget described. Here is an example, with Riley using the memory of his dog Max's adoption day.

> Riley can retrieve his memory of Max's adoption when he needs it. When Riley's teacher asked him to dictate a story about a very happy time, Riley searched through his long-term memory, retrieved the dog adoption memory, took it out of storage, and placed it in his working memory so that he could tell the story with it. Completing his dictation prompted him to shift the memory back to long-term memory.

Because working memory is so important in a child's cognitive development, researchers have examined it at the brain level, trying to understand this part of neural development (Huttenlocher, 2003). We now know that children and adults are quite similar in how their brain activity looks when they activate working memory. Recent research has found that parts of the prefrontal cortex in a young child's brain are activated

---

Sensory register Unit in the brain that registers auditory or visual sensory information from the environment.

Short-term memory Unit in the brain, a way station for receiving data from the sensory register and then sending in on to long-term memory or discarding it.

Long-term memory Unit in the brain with an enormous capacity for storing information that a child has made an effort to learn.

Working memory Part of short-term memory; space used for temporarily storing information so that a child can work with it.

when she uses working memory just as in an adult's brain. This part of a 5- to 6-year-old child's brain, then, is already functionally developed, allowing working memory to function fairly well (Tsujimoto et al., 2004).

As children get older, they gain more space for working memory. This allows children to work with and process more information for longer periods. A human brain, however, in spite of its wonderfully complex nature, is quite limited in capacity in short-term memory. We can keep only about four objects in short-term memory at any one time, and it does not matter how many objects we see. We remember only about four (Marois, 2005).

Go to MyEducationLab and select the topic "Child Development." Under Activities and Applications, watch the video *Memory—Early Childhood*, an interview of a young child explaining how he remembers things.

CHECK YOUR UNDERSTANDING
Luis Remembers

Before going to the next section, apply what you have just read. Read the chapter-opening vignette Primary Classroom: Remembering Things in Morning Meeting. How does this vignette illustrate Luis's *long-term* memory and how Luis used his *working* memory?

Social Information Processing

Children process information about interactions with others. **Social information processing** refers to perceiving, taking in, remembering, and retrieving information in *social interactions*. There are six steps in social information processing (Crick & Dodge, 1994).

1. Paying attention to social cues and remembering important information. For example, Jessie observes that two children are working together on a mural. He wants to join them and recalls his teacher explaining how to join a group.
2. Giving meaning to the social cues. Jessie thinks that the two children intended to work together.
3. Selecting a preferred outcome. Jessie decides that he will try to join their work.
4. Searching for an appropriate social response, either remembering a response or developing a new response. He decides to stand nearby for a short time and observe. He then decides to *ask* if he can paint too.
5. Deciding which social response might work. He decides that standing nearby and asking to join them is a good plan.
6. Acting out the selected response and monitoring the effect. The other two children make room for Jessie to paint.

Social information processing Cognitive processes essential in social interactions; involves six steps.

How children process information in general can predict some aspects of their social behavior, such as aggressive behavior (Dodge & Crick, 1990). Information processing, therefore, links closely with a child's social development. One area of research in social information processing studies how children with learning disabilities process information. All children can develop social competence, but some children with learning disabilities (LDs) are rejected by other children and find it hard to make and keep friends. In turn, this may lead to damaged self-esteem and feelings of loneliness (Raskind, 2005).

Some children with LDs have problems with several of the steps in processing social information. For example, kindergarten age girls with LDs performed quite low on the last two social information-processing steps. These girls found it difficult to decide which social response might work—they had trouble figuring out which of two ideas,

TEACH INTENTIONALLY

Learning to Notice Social Cues

What the teacher did: Mr. Hernandez realizes that a few children in his kindergarten have difficulty paying attention to *social cues* such as facial expressions. Therefore, he did a brief lesson on the meaning of facial expressions. He held up a picture of a child making an "angry" face, and the children identified the emotion. Then, he did the same thing with the emotion of "disgust," after which he encouraged the children to make these faces.

How the teacher was intentional: This teacher was intentional when (1) he deliberately used his knowledge of child development (some children have trouble with facial cues); and (2) he also used materials (the picture) purposely as well. Thus, he focused on a specific thing that some of the children needed to know so that they could process information in social settings more effectively. He will observe to see whether the children who needed assistance have indeed learned about watching faces for clues about how people are probably feeling.

for example, they should use. They also had trouble putting the selected response into action (Tur-Kaspa, 2004). Some of the problems that children with LDs have in the six steps of processing social information (Bauminger, Schoor-Edelsztein, & Morash, 2005) include

- Having a hard time paying attention to social cues. In a large group time, for example, a child with LD might not pay attention to another child's facial expression of disgust when the child with LD blurts out a question. If she misses a cue, she cannot give it any meaning.
- Coming up with fewer social solutions.
- Coming up with less appropriate social decisions. This seems logical if a child does not pay attention to social cues. Our child who missed his classmate's look of disgust (the social cue) would likely develop an inappropriate solution based on the information that he does have, and this does not include that important social cue.

Teachers can use this information when they know that a child has trouble with processing social information, as Mr. Hernandez does in the Teach Intentionally item.

Children's Perception Changes in Predictable Ways

There are many changes in children's thinking during early childhood, and changes in processing skills account for the shifts. One of these skills is perception, which undergoes great change during early childhood.

Cohen and Cashon (2002) reviewed perception and cognition of very young children, noting the considerable perceptual skills in infants. Infants have clear visual preferences. They prefer, for example, to look at patterned rather than uniform and complex rather than simple (Fantz, cited in Cohen & Cashon, 2002). Infants, especially very young infants, also seem to have an initial preference for familiar things. They do gaze on novel items if they have seen very familiar items repeatedly. For example, an infant who has gazed repeatedly at a familiar mobile might move her gaze to a different item over her crib. Older infants move on to prefer novelty after having had sufficient experience with the moderately complex items.

Children continue to develop perceptual skills as they get older. At 2 years old a child has many perceptual skills, and by age 5 has skills that are even better than when he was a toddler. However, young children still have problems directing their attention. First, *young children do not search or scan very well.* They may search for something but are not systematic in their search. They are not as accurate or efficient as an older child and many younger children do not seem to realize that they should stop searching at some point. This is illustrated in the next example.

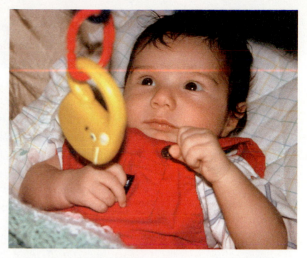

Very young infants seem to prefer to look at familiar things. They look at new things after they have gazed at the familiar item repeatedly.

> Ralph, 4 years old, watched as Mrs. Chang wrote his name on a name tag. He easily recognized his name when it was grouped with three others. However, the next day, Ralph's name tag was on the chart with 22 others. He looked for a long time, but became frustrated when he could not find his name tag.

Second, *young children have difficulty "tuning out" irrelevant information.* They are not skilled in controlling their attention and have difficulty tuning out (ignoring) meaningless information or stimulation. Their attention wanders when they hear or see some sudden, intense stimulus.

> Mrs. Chang, realizing that her preschoolers are easily distracted by things such as people coming into the room during story time, posted a sign on her door requesting *all* visitors to wait until group time was over before entering.

Third, *young children tend to focus on only one thing at a time.* When they have a disagreement with another child, for example, they tend to focus on their own viewpoint and are unable to see how the other child might see things.

As children get older, their more mature reasoning skills, more efficient memory, language abilities, and more experiences to draw on are some of the things that go along with their changing perceptual abilities (Figure 6.2). Children get better at selecting things they ignore or to which they pay attention (Maccoby and Itasen, 1965). They also spend more time *on task* and they get better at redirecting their attention as they get older.

Children Develop Language and Literacy from Birth

Early childhood teachers have always focused on language and literacy development. The No Child Left Behind federal law of 2001, however, requires that schools test children starting in grade 3 in three areas, one of which is reading, a part of language arts. This has resulted in a heightened focus on this area of the curriculum. The purpose of the testing is to hold states, schools, teachers, and children accountable for meeting the state learning standards in the content areas of mathematics, science, and reading.

Language and Literacy: Definitions

Language arts involves children learning how to read, write, listen, and speak. **Language** refers to communicating by listening and speaking, which is oral language. **Literacy** refers to communicating through print, which is writing and reading. Figure 6.3 shows these. Language and literacy develop together, from the moment a baby is born. Speaking,

Language Communicating by listening and speaking which is oral language.

Literacy Communicating through print, which is writing and reading.

FIGURE 6.2   Perceptual Issues and Changes in Perception as Children Get Older

- Young children do not search or scan very well.
- Young children have difficulty *tuning out* irrelevant information.
- Young children tend to focus on only one thing at a time.
- Young children who are impulsive have even greater problems with perception.
- Children get better at selecting things that they ignore or to which they pay attention.
- Children are better able to redirect their attention with age.
- Children can shift attention from one part of a problem to another part more quickly and easily as they get older.
- Children gradually spend more time *on task* as they move through the early childhood years.

Practical things that teachers can do

- Teach children to scan systematically.
- Help impulsive children to learn strategies to control impulsiveness (Meichenbaum & Goodman, 1971).
- Minimize disruptions (Buchoff, 1990).
- Screen for sensory impairments.
- Teach social skills (Williams, Donnely, & Keller, 2000).

Go to MyEducationLab and select the topic "Emergent Literacy and Language Arts." Under Activities and Applications, watch the video *Individual Story Time: Toddler* to see a literacy activity for a very young child.

listening, reading, and writing are tied so tightly together that focusing on all is wise as teachers plan for children of any age, including infants, toddlers, preschool, and kindergarten children.

Our goal as teachers, therefore, is to understand how language (listening and speaking) is connected to literacy (reading and writing) and then to commit to helping children develop in both areas. Another, and very important, goal is to focus on language arts (language and literacy) in developmentally appropriate ways.

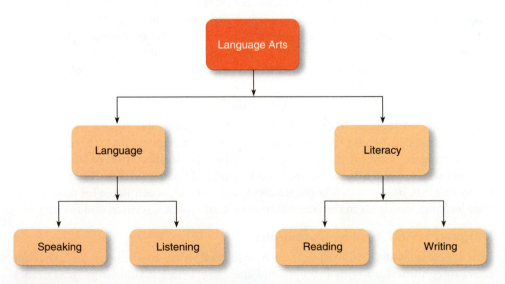

FIGURE 6.3   Language and literacy: Relationship to language arts.
Source: Based on Vukelich, Christi, and Enz (2008).

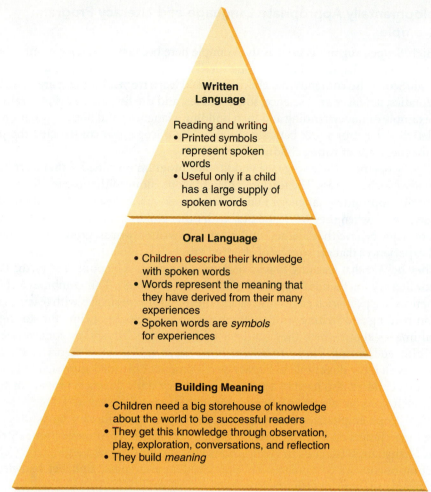

Written Language

Reading and writing
- Printed symbols represent spoken words
- Useful only if a child has a large supply of spoken words

Oral Language

- Children describe their knowledge with spoken words
- Words represent the meaning that they have derived from their many experiences
- Spoken words are *symbols* for experiences

Building Meaning

- Children need a big storehouse of knowledge about the world to be successful readers
- They get this knowledge through observation, play, exploration, conversations, and reflection
- They build *meaning*

FIGURE 6.4   Connection between language and literacy.

Source: Based on Vukelich Christi, and Enz (2008).

Relationship Between Language and Literacy

How, then, are language and literacy related? Children *construct* strong literacy skills of reading and writing. First, however, they construct the foundation of strong language development, speaking and listening skills. Strong language development grows from finding meaning from experiences (Vukelich, Christi, & Enz, 2008). Figure 6.4 shows this relationship—building up a storehouse of information through experience, then learning and using spoken words to represent that knowledge, and finally using written words, in writing and reading, to represent the spoken words.

Children need to have many meaningful experiences when they are very young. They need to play and interact with other children. They need to work with objects, puzzling over them. They need to talk about things with teachers and other children, building an understanding of their world. They need a content-, book-, and print-rich environment in which teachers focus on engaging children in appropriately challenging yet developmentally appropriate experiences that help them slowly develop a substantial knowledge base (Neuman & Roskos, 2005). They need to develop a large storehouse of words, a large vocabulary that they use to describe and explain experiences.

Go to
MyEducationLab
and select the topic
"Child Development."
Under Activities and
Applications, read the
strategy *Book Reading to
Children* and see how read-
ing to children develops
brain circuits for language.

**Blended approach to
literacy development**
Combining child-initiated
learning with developmen-
tally appropriate teacher
instruction.

Developmentally Appropriate Language and Literacy Program: An Example

The High/Scope program is used as the example here because its theory is one of several explained in Chapter 2. This is a constructivist approach, focusing on active learning. High/Scope also contends that children should learn from all content areas, such as
mathematics, language arts, science, social studies, and the fine arts. This program is a
good example of understanding and then building a language and literacy program acknowledging the strong link between the two. High/Scope also constructed the program for the needs of young children.

High/Scope built their language and literacy program on the idea that learning is
essentially a social process. The teachers at High/Scope, along with those in other developmentally appropriate language and literacy programs, believe that children learn
most effectively when they work and play with other children and with knowledgeable
teachers. They believe that literacy, understanding written words, grows out of meaningful experiences that are worthy of children's time.

They believe that learning to read and write is a process beginning at birth. Their
plan for literacy is a **blended approach** (Vukelich et al., 2008). This combines a child's
experiences in a print-rich environment and meaningful experiences with teachers and
peers in reading and writing with an emphasis on large blocks of time for storing up
mental images about which they can later talk and write. Thus, they concentrate on
child-initiated learning. They also believe, however, as in Vygotsky's theory, that teachers also have a more direct role in literacy development. A blended approach to literacy
means that children also need to learn specific literacy skills. Teachers provide instruction in such skills but always in a developmentally appropriate way.

High/Scope emphasizes four main components of early literacy in its program,
basing their choices on The National Early Literacy Panel's recommendations (Strick-
land & Shanahan, 2004, cited in High/Scope's web site on Language and Literacy). The
four components are comprehension, phonological awareness, alphabet knowledge,
and concepts about print (High/Scope, 2008).

Comprehension. This includes four skills. *Vocabulary building* involves helping children add to their storehouse of words and helping them to understand the meaning of
new words. It involves helping them to use the words in speaking to others as they describe and explain events. *Prediction* is the ability to say what will happen in a story.
Mrs. Chang asked her preschoolers to look at the cover of their new book and to predict what the story was about. *Saying what will happen next* in a story is the ability to
use information gleaned from what has already been read to predict the rest of the
story. After several pages of the new book, for example, Mrs. Chang asked, "So, every
person in this story has given advice to Henry. What do you think will happen when
he meets the next person?" *Retelling* involves telling about events and actions from the
story.

> Mrs. Chang encouraged her class to do this by asking, "Think about how
> our story started." Then, "How did Henry find out how to solve his prob-
> lem with his bike?"

Phonological awareness. This includes rhyming, alliteration, and segmentation.
Rhyming refers to saying, identifying, and producing pairs of words that rhyme.
For example, Mr. Hernandez reads poetry to his class and the children pick out
rhyming words—face/place, mice/nice, rosy/cozy, rose/nose. Then the children

think about other additional rhyming words—mice/rice, nice/rice, place/race, face/race. Mr. Hernandez used this opportunity to teach a new vocabulary word, splice. He had rhymed rice/splice and explained the meaning of the new word. *Alliteration* refers to saying, identifying, and producing words with the same first sound, such as fun, first, fist, five. The first sound, the f is called a phoneme. In *segmentation*, children learn about breaking words into their syllables (parts), such as "toe/nail."

Alphabet knowledge. This includes identifying and writing one's own name, letter recognition, and correspondence between letters and sounds. Teachers work on helping children *identify their own printed names* in many ways, such as labeling lockers or cubbies, writing names on artwork, watching as the teacher writes his name, picking one's name from a list of printed names. Children learn to *write their own name* when they sign in on the attendance sheet and other lists, for example, or when they print their name in sand or with other media. Early childhood teachers put much effort into helping children learn to *recognize and name letters of the alphabet* and they use a variety of instructional strategies and materials, such as magnetic or sandpaper letters, alphabet charts, and even computer activities dealing with letter recognition. Children also learn that there is *correspondence between letters and sounds*. They identify a specific letter's sound, such as the sound of an "m" or a "b." They also learn to listen to a sound and then to identify that sound's letter.

Concepts about print. This literacy skill involves identifying book parts, orienting books for reading, distinguishing between pictures and words, and understanding direction of text. To help children *identify parts of a book*—front cover, back cover, pages, title page—teachers might use direct instruction at large group time or they might also do this less formally as they read with small groups or individual children.

> Mrs. Chang, for instance, during the first week of school, read with Sam but before they started the story, she patted the front cover and said, "OK, let's start right here with the front of the book."

Orienting books for reading refers to holding a book for reading. Children gradually hold books so that a reader can use it correctly for reading. This progression is evident when we observe infants and toddlers holding a book upside down or sideways but observe preschoolers and kindergarten children holding a book correctly. Children also learn to *distinguish between pictures and words*.

> Mrs. Chang, for example, helped children with this literacy skill when they played in the dramatic play center, operating a taxi service. She pointed out the pictures of the taxi and then wrote the word "Taxi" on a sheet of paper. The children wanted to print their own sign and they copied hers. Then they placed their printed word next to the picture at their taxi stand.

Concepts about print also involve *understanding the direction of text*. Teachers help children understand that we read from left to right and, again, use a variety of strategies. Children observe as teachers hold their hand or finger under print in a chart or book, moving from left to right while reading. Children are encouraged to do the same thing when they read.

Children need a large store of vocabulary words. This child is learning starfish, a new word for him.

Along with the characteristics of children's cognitive development go the needs that children have for optimal cognitive development, which we now examine.

UNDERSTANDING CHILDREN'S COGNITIVE NEEDS

Teachers nurture cognitive competence by paying attention to what the child needs to advance in this developmental domain. Some of the most pressing of a child's needs in cognitive development include

- internal motivation,
- play,
- social interaction, and
- appropriately challenging and novel tasks.

Internal Motivation

Internal motivation An inner resource; drives cognitive development; process within a child that kicks off and sustains the search for knowledge and skills.

What is it that drives a baby to swing at the mobile over her crib? What drives 3 year olds to work so diligently at the sand table, and what drives a second grader to persist in trying to figure out a problem with Geo-blocks Motivation is the key but more specifically, **internal motivation,** the engine that drives cognitive development. Residing deep within a child, internal motivation is a part of the child's inner resources.

Children's built-in goal to seek knowledge and to learn is clear as a baby joyfully looks, listens, reaches, tastes, interacts, and touches. Toddlers, preschoolers, and kindergarten children eagerly search for meaning in their world as they work with physical objects, begin to build understanding about relationships, and interact with other children and adults. Somewhat older children demonstrate internal motivation when they work willingly and with pleasure at academic and personal activities. Internal motivation, then, is the process within a child that kicks off and sustains children's activities, which in turn, helps them quench their thirst for knowledge.

Benefits of Internal Motivation

Children tend to learn and retain much more when they are motivated from within (Carlton, 2003). Internal motivation is particularly helpful to children with specific challenges. For example, children with attention deficit hyperactivity disorder (ADHD) often have trouble concentrating but maintain focus more easily when they are highly interested and internally motivated (Carlton, 2003).

Characteristics of Internally Motivated Children

Suppose that you wanted to find out whether a child was internally motivated. You could observe the child over time for signs of motivation from within. Internally motivated children show these characteristics (Carlton, 2003). They are persistent, staying with an activity for quite some time, even if they think that the activity is a challenge. Children lacking internal motivation do not persist at tasks; they give up easily.

Children who are successful and internally motivated take on challenges. Early success increases their motivation and builds confidence in their abilities. This, in turn, increases the odds that they will be willing to take risks with moderately difficult tasks and to do the hard work often necessary in gaining knowledge. Children who have early successes are more willing to choose challenging tasks than are children who have not had very many early successes as we see in the next example with one of Mr. Hernandez's second graders.

> Ben zoomed to the spelling center where he found the "fuzzy wire spelling challenge"—to write at least one new spelling word with fuzzy wire (pipe cleaners). This internally motivated child wrote every new spelling word with the wire, persisting even when he had trouble bending the wire for one of the words. Later in the week, Ben, who met the "fuzzy wire spelling challenge," readily accepted another spelling center challenge.

Highly and intrinsically motivated children tend to be *independent learners*. They do not need constant reassurance from adults, although they are not averse to ask for assistance if they really are stuck. Ben, for instance, had worked independently with the spelling challenge, not requesting help, but willingly trying different solutions to his problem of bending the wire. Internally motivated children also like what they do and tend to *display positive affect*. They show contentment, joy, happiness, and pleasure, with their work or play. For instance, digital photos, taken for a documentation board, showed 7-year-old Ben's face, as he worked with fuzzy wire, contorted in concentration, frustration, determination, and pleasure. Children who are not so highly motivated might appear to be cranky, bored, or unhappy.

External Motivation

Children, as they get older, however, are not all motivated by the same forces. Some children remain internally motivated, but others, somewhere in their journey of development, lose the bright light of internal motivation. Their primary incentive shifts to an **external motivation,** in which they begin to do things for reasons outside themselves. For example, a child might read a book only when there is the promise of a reward for the reading.

External motivation
Doing things for reasons outside the child.

The type of motivation nurtured in childhood affects a child for a lifetime, and so knowing that by school age, many children begin to lose this internally motivated search for knowledge is distressing (Jablon & Wilkenson, 2006). Children who find no satisfaction in searching for knowledge are caught in a dance of failure. Just as early success breeds continued success, early failure feeds itself with diminishing self-esteem and subsequent unwillingness to try new things for fear of failing. Many children never escape from such a downward spiral. Poor intrinsic motivation worsens with age and might well be the culprit in many academic problems (Gandis, 2005).

Many teachers use praise when guiding young children but, in doing this, run the risk of damaging children's internal motivation. Teachers praise with words such as

- "Good job!" to a child succeeding in putting a puzzle together or completing any task (not a recommended thing to say). The child does not know why it was a "good job." It would be more meaningful to acknowledge the child's effort to complete the puzzle. "You really worked hard to figure out how to fit all the pieces together."
- "I really like how Sam is sitting," as a general comment at large group time, meant to motivate other children to sit as Sam is sitting (also, not recommended). There are a couple of problems with such a statement. First, the teacher thinks that the other children will automatically observe how Sam is sitting, check how they themselves are seated, and then correct themselves to sit like Sam which is too

much to ask them to do with such a vague statement. Second, the teacher has called attention to one child in the large group. He has already done what the teacher requests and seems to be internally motivated. The adult runs the risk of damaging Sam's internal motivation. The teacher could be more straightforward and clear if he said, "We need room for everybody in the circle today, so I want every person to sit so that you are not sprawled out. Remember the two ways that we figured out? Pick one of those."

- "I knew that you could find the solution because you are so smart," to a child who had solved a math problem (not recommended). This teacher has praised a child's intelligence, which has been linked to *decreased* enjoyment and persistence (Mueller & Dweck, 1998).

Praising children might seem logical, but praise as in the preceding statements are motivation from outside the child, extrinsic motivators. When children help a friend eagerly and willingly or work willingly at difficult tasks such as putting together puzzles, they are already demonstrating internal motivation. Teachers do not need to praise children for these things because such praise actually decreases their willingness to do these things again. Instead, a teacher should consider acknowledging and encouraging a child's *effort*. We can do this by asking open-ended questions and using scaffolding. Here are examples.

- "You kept on trying with that puzzle. How did you figure out which piece goes in the corner?"
- "It's a little crowded in our circle today, so how do you think that we should sit so that everybody has a spot?"
- "Looks like you've finished the problem. What is it that got you thinking after you got stumped a while back?" Here, the teacher focuses on helping the child reflect on his strategy for success. He does not praise intelligence.

Play

Children need classrooms conducive to active learning and exploration of ideas because cognitive competence is linked to play. Play is also voluntary and extremely satisfying to children.

Children Have a Right to Play

The consensus among early childhood professionals is that play is not a luxury but is an essential vehicle for children's development and learning (Elkind, 2006). Children need first-hand experiences in dramatic play, music, painting, reading, listening to and telling stories, drawing, and constructing models, clear-cut examples of what most professionals refer to as play (NAEYC, 2006). Play gives children an opportunity to communicate spontaneously and to express needs and feelings (International Play Association, 2007).

Play is considered a right of all children (Ginsburg, 2006; United Nations, 1989) and some organizations promote understanding of a child's right to play (International Play Association, 2007). State boards of education have incorporated this thinking into state learning standards. For example, the Illinois State Board of Education bases the preschool and kindergarten learning standards on the principle that children learn through activity (Illinois State Board of Education, 2008). This state group views children's play as supporting children's development and learning in areas such as math and physical education as the next example shows.

One of the preschool vignettes at the chapter's opening showed Ralph concentrating on building with blocks. He stayed with this for quite some time, comparing sizes of and measuring the blocks. Ralph was engaged in a moderately challenging activity, learning about the physical properties of blocks and about the relationship of one block to another. He was learning through play.

Similarly, the National Association for Music Education (1991), recommends in a position statement, that music education in early childhood be play based and involve active learning.

Play Affects Cognitive Development

Forty-five years of research documents the beneficial effects of play in all domains of child development including cognitive development (Kalliala, 2006; Seifert, 2004) and on the development of a child's brain (Frost, 1998).

Bergen (2002) reviewed the effects of high-quality, socially interactive **pretend play** on children's cognitive development. Pretend play, the classic play of childhood, brings pleasure to children and fosters their cognitive competence. Part of the reason lies in how extensively pretend play involves a child's brain. Social interactive pretend play involves children's emotions, language, sensorimotor, social, and cognitive skills. Thus, many different areas of the brain are activated during pretend play. High-quality pretend play may well facilitate the development of denser synaptic connections in a child's brain (Bergen & Coscia, 2001).

Pretend play Symbolic play in which children act out an idea; might take on roles involving other children.

Pretend play, especially taking on roles involving peers helps children to develop cognitive developmental skills such as **perspective taking**. This ability takes several years to develop and appears in a predictable sequence. It is the ability to understand how another person or animal views a situation. Pretend play requires that children learn to negotiate with other players and act out someone else's actions and ideas. Thus, the play-based verbal give-and-take and negotiations of pretend play helps children to begin to appreciate another viewpoint, although it will still take several years for high-level perspective taking to evolve.

Perspective taking The ability to understand how another person or animal views a situation.

Piaget would explain the pretend play, perspective-taking connection as children having to confront other children's ideas on how to do things and eventually having to come to terms with that other perspective. When children learn to take another's perspective, they also have to control their own impulses, and pretend play helps children achieve healthy self-regulation (Krafft & Berk, 1998), also an important element in social competence. Andy, in the kindergarten vignette opening this chapter, learned to take his friend Jake's perspective on how to package the flowers that they were selling in the dramatic play flower shop.

Pretend play also helps children develop memory and contributes to language arts. For example, one study found that children who actually play out a story line rather than just talking about the story are more likely to

Social, interactive pretend play contributes to the development of denser synaptic connections in a child's brain.

remember the order in which a story is presented, at least immediately after the play episodes (Kim, 1999).

Teachers can help all children get the most out of play by paying attention to those having difficulty expressing themselves during pretend play. English language learners, for example, might not engage in pretend play if they are not comfortable with the dominant language (Head Start, 2005). Children with speech and language disabilities can use symbolic thoughts in play but they seem to have difficulty in expressing their ideas during play. Consequently, for this disability, it is a matter of expression, not of competence (Bergen, 2002). Teachers can work with speech specialists to figure out how best to help children optimize pretend play.

CHECK YOUR UNDERSTANDING
Music, Art, and Creative Thinking

The No Child Left Behind federal law of 2001 mandates testing children starting in grade 3 in reading, mathematics, and science. Some schools now spend most of their time preparing children for these tests and have eliminated or severely cut back on music and art. What effect do you think that this will have on children's ability to think creatively?

Social Interaction

Children develop cognitive competence not in a vacuum but as they live and work with other people. Social interaction has an incalculable role in cognitive development, and children who miss appropriately stimulating social interaction are at a great disadvantage in the cognitive domain. Missing warm, stimulating social interaction has far-reaching effects, rippling out to affect more than just a child's cognition.

Good Teacher-Child Relationships

Teachers are most effective in any part of their teaching role, including fostering children's cognitive competence, when they have a warm and trusting relationship with children. This implies a validating and open style of communication (Pianta, 1996). They have an authoritative style (positive, warm, caring) in which they are highly responsive to what children need and in which they are appropriately demanding (Baumrind, 1996; Marion, 2007). The quality of a child's relationship with his first teachers affects his level of later academic success (Pianta & Stuhlman, 2004). Mr. Bjornrud demonstrated a warm and trusting relationship with toddler Nick in the chapter's opening vignette. He cheerfully repeated the favorite finger play, knowing that Nicked enjoyed it.

Bilingualism: Impact on Early Cognitive Development

Bilingual children speak two languages and are strong in both languages. They are not learning a new language. Monolingual children speak one language. There are benefits to bilingualism for children, and bilingualism does not damage children's cognitive development. On the contrary, both bilingual and monolingual children develop in the same way for things such as phonemic awareness in the linguistic domain and memory span development in the cognitive domain. When the two languages spoken share a writing system, such as Spanish and English, children's reading skill tends to be accelerated. Bilingual 4- to 8-year-old children tend to be better at solving problems requiring control and attention than are monolingual children (Bialystok, 2006).

Bilingual children engage in code switching, a sophisticated communicative tool in which a child switches from one language to the other in a conversation or an activity. This strategy helps children when they interact with others and when they face cognitive demands. Bilingual children successfully use code switching to do three things in school (Hurtado, 2005).

1. Code switching helps bilingual children work through difficult problems and understand concepts. An example is a child who switches from Spanish to English when working on math concepts.
2. Code switching helps bilingual children tell intent to someone when speaking. For example, a child starts out in a conversation speaking Spanish to another child but switches to English to make it clear, for example, what she intends to discuss.
3. Code switching helps bilingual children work with other children in a small group. They switch languages when they think it will help the group move along in getting the work done.

Teachers should encourage children who speak different languages to use code switching because it fosters good interactions and helps them to solve problems.

Go to MyEducationLab and select the topic "Emergent Literacy and Language Arts." Under Activities and Applications, watch the video *Peer Scaffolding* to see an example of scaffolding by a teacher with a bilingual child.

Appropriately Challenging and Novel Tasks

Children grow cognitively when they have to tackle reasonably challenging tasks. Moderately challenging and novel tasks require children to perform mental operations using new information so that they can reestablish equilibrium, a concept from Piaget's theory. For example, 8-year-old Paul had learned about how fish can breathe even though they live in water. He was faced with a moderately challenging idea when he first saw a seal, first on land and then in water. "How does she breathe?" was his first reaction.

If the teacher is alert, he will recognize this child's curiosity as an opportunity to help Paul refine some concepts and add to his knowledge base. Teachers need to adjust challenges to help children learn and become confident and successful thinkers and learners. A moderately novel experience challenges a child but is one that she can achieve with current knowledge or skills plus her teacher's assistance.

Vygotsky explains this as operating in the child's zone of proximal development, the space or zone where learning and development take place. At one end of the zone is a child's current ability, what he understands about some topic, such as which animals can breathe under water. At the other end is what the child can learn or accomplish with the help of an adult or more competent member of the culture. Paul, for example, can learn how seals breathe if his teacher helps him to understand this new idea.

In summary, children have specific cognitive needs—internal motivation, play, social interaction, and appropriately novel and challenging experiences. Moreover, a variety of factors play a part in a child's path of cognitive development and we now examine those influences.

INFLUENCES ON COGNITIVE DEVELOPMENT

Research has shown us that widely divergent events and conditions affect children's cognitive powers. Some of the major influences include

- abuse and neglect,
- nutrition,
- addictive substances,
- exposure to media, and
- auditory and/or visual processing disorders.

Abuse and Neglect

Other chapters on development in this text document the harmful effect of abuse and neglect on children's physical, motor, social, and emotional development. Abuse and neglect have similarly damaging effects on cognitive development. For example, neglect during childhood is associated significantly with delayed cognitive development (Hagele, 2005; Strathearn, Gray, O'Callaghan, & Wood, 2001). This shows up in lower scores on language skills and cognitive development (DHHS, 2003, cited in Child Welfare Information Gateway, 2006).

Nutrition

Undernutrition during infancy and early childhood has a negative impact on children's cognitive development. For example, a diet deficient in iron during very early infancy may cause brain abnormalities that are very difficult to reverse (Mendez & Adair, 1999). We see a different story with an adequate diet. For example, longer periods of breast-feeding seem to have a positive effect on cognitive development (Angelsen, Vik, Jacobsen, & Bakketeig, 2001). Some children malnourished during infancy improve in cognitive skills after they receive nutritional supplementation. They also benefit from an enriched environment. Benefits are greatest to children with the longest exposure to an enriched environment (Pollitt, 2000).

Addictive Substances

Many children are exposed to drugs during the prenatal period if their mother drinks alcohol or if she ingests drugs such as cocaine. Children exposed to alcohol during the prenatal period tend to have problems in many domains, such as with social and emotional development. Their cognition is affected greatly as shown in problems with memory, attention, and learning. Cocaine also causes problems. For example, 2 year-old children exposed to this drug while they were fetuses had higher rates of mental retardation than did children not exposed (Singer et al., 2002).

Exposure to Media

The many years and thousands of studies documenting the negative effect of watching excessive amounts of noneducative television and other media is described in other chapters in this text, especially those on social and emotional development. Researchers are also interested in whether and how media viewing affects children's brain and cognitive development. They are asking these questions about all young children, including infants and toddlers because children today live in a media filled environment.

The brain develops as infants respond to stimulation from the environment, such as playing, talking with parents or siblings, and playing with safe and appropriate toys. The current thinking is that watching television and other media would likely interfere with brain development for very young children because infants are so passive when they watch (Center on Media and Children's Health, 2005). One study has found that 1- to 3- year-old children engage in significantly shorter play sessions when a television is in the background. Their episodes of alert attention were also significantly shorter (Evans, 2003). Current recommendations call for *no time watching television or other media* for children birth to 2 years (American Academy of Pediatrics, 2007).

Auditory and Visual Processing Disorders

Recall that the sensory processor registers auditory (listening) and visual (looking) stimuli. Some children have diagnosable problems, however, with the auditory and visual systems (National Center for Learning Disabilities, 2007).

Auditory processing refers to what happens when a child's brain registers and interprets sounds. Sounds are changed into electrical information as they travel through the child's ear, and then her brain interprets the information. If she has an **auditory processing disorder,** she has difficulty processing auditory signals. The child can have several difficulties because of this, including trouble understanding speech, confusing words that sound the same, such as couch/cow or chair/hair. The child might also have difficulty learning to speak or remembering stories.

Visual processing refers to what happens when a child's brain registers and interprets visual stimuli. A child with a **visual processing disorder** has trouble interpreting visual stimuli. As a result, the child might have trouble with understanding written symbols, such as % or @. She might have trouble differentiating between similarly shaped letters or numerals, such as b/d, q/p, 9/6. This child is often distracted very easily.

Children need to feel their teacher's respect and genuine affection.

Auditory processing disorder Difficulty processing auditory signals.

Visual processing disorder Difficulty processing visual stimuli.

Teachers who know the characteristics and needs of as well as influences on children's cognitive development have used their knowledge to create an environment that optimizes children's development, a topic to which we now turn.

USING KNOWLEDGE ABOUT COGNITIVE DEVELOPMENT TO CREATE A HEALTHY ENVIRONMENT

We help children best by using evidence-based practices that are based on solid theory and research. This section presents such practices. *If-then* statements, for example, "If children learn best through activity and play, then . . . ," are followed by suggestions for developing a play-based classroom.

There are four major categories of suggestions:

- Teacher-child relationship
- Child guidance
- Classroom environment
- Constructing different types of knowledge

Teacher-Child Relationship

If children need a warm caring relationship with their teacher, then demonstrate abiding respect and genuine liking for children. Acknowledge every child every day and foster friendly interactions among children (Marion, 2007). Reflect on your relationships with every child in a class. Learn to recognize the signs that your relationship with a child might be deteriorating—perhaps you speak in a less than friendly way with a child, have started to avoid her, are seeing only the child's irritating traits or challenging behaviors. Teachers find challenging behaviors very threatening, and they often begin interacting in a less friendly way. Value children's active role in any interaction with you. Act on your conviction, though, that your adult role carries greater responsibility in any interaction with any child. Communicate in a direct and open way. Deliver messages simply, kindly, firmly, and consistently. Give reasons for what you want children to do or to stop doing. Teachers show children respect when they give explanations appropriately.

Child Guidance

Children construct social knowledge and concepts about relationships. Help them by having age- and individually appropriate expectations for behavior; clearly stating appropriate limits; and monitoring children and supervising them well. Use positive, helpful guidance strategies. Keep in mind the possibility that children make mistakes in constructing knowledge about how to get along with others. Help children to interpret events accurately. For example, if a child says that somebody hit him on purpose and you know that to be inaccurate, then use the Vygotskian strategy of talking with the child. This usually helps a child to reinterpret his conclusions. Resist the first urge when confronted with a child who is seeking power or undue attention and take a different approach. Try to figure out what he is getting from an interaction and help him figure out a better way of getting what he wants or needs.

Help a child understand when her actions have hurt someone. This will take courage, especially when dealing with a child with challenging behavior. Focus on specific skill development. For example, a child whose social skills are poor needs instruction in making friends, dealing with conflict, knowing how to ask for what he needs, or waiting his turn. Also, focus on fostering perspective taking, perceptual, and memory skills. See Figure 6.2 for suggestions for facilitating perceptual skills. Figure 6.5 gives suggestions on helping children develop good memory skills.

Classroom Environment

Children construct knowledge, are active learners, and need to be internally motivated, Therefore, construct a classroom where children can

- Play in blocks of uninterrupted time and make dramatic, pretend play a staple in the classroom.

FIGURE 6.5   **Helping Children Develop Memory Skills**

- Encourage children to use memory strategies: For example, divide long lists into smaller segments. Remembering names of a large group of new classmates is easier by thinking about smaller groups of the class, such as Mary and Michael, Samir and George, and so on.
- Teach children why memory strategies are so useful.
- Use familiar pictures, sounds, and objects (helps children with long-term memory).
- Plan activities, games, and lessons with fewer steps.
- Present only a few bits of information at one time.
- Think of different and creative ways to repeat things.
- Present information in a variety of ways: children form a large square, cut out play dough with square shapes, draw squares on playground with chalk.
- Actively involve children with things that they should remember (practice routines, such as how to wipe tables after art activities or snack).
- Label objects and experiences (labeling helps children remember things).

- Interact and collaborate with other children and adults.
- Move. Arrange learning centers so that children can move around the room easily. Encourage children to move around the room as they choose different learning centers.
- Make choices from among several options.

Constructing Different Types of Knowledge

Recall from Chapter 1 that children construct social, physical, and logico-mathematical knowledge. Foster this ability by looking to children as a major source of the curriculum and using projects to integrate curriculum areas such as math, science, language arts, music, and art. Present children with moderately challenging activities. Introduce novelty, but not overwhelming novelty, into classroom activities and materials. If, for example, children usually do the morning greeting in English, introduce the phrase "Good morning" in a second language. Use concrete, open-ended materials such as books, sand, water, paints, play dough, blocks, writing and drawing materials, puzzles, and other manipulatives. Help children link new information to what they already know. Ask them, for example, "You figured out how to walk down the hall *very* quietly yesterday. Can you figure out how our class can stay quiet in the school meeting, even if other classes are noisy?"

Ask children to engage in problem solving. "I'd like to hear your ideas on how you can both get a turn at the computer." Ask questions that prompt children to come up with solutions. "Can you think about one way of getting down the hallway really, really quietly?" Give children examples of strategies. "Here's one idea for fixing the pulley. See if it would work.'" "Try running your finger over the two blocks to see which is smoother." Model a skill or a way of approaching a problem, such as during a lesson on social skill development. "Watch as I greet Joe. I will look at him and then say 'Good morning, Joe." If a child has difficulty paying attention to social cues, show him how to look at someone's face to check the person's facial expression.

SUMMARY

Cognitive development refers to systematic changes in children's reasoning, concepts, memory, and language. Several characteristics of children's cognitive development are important for teachers to keep in mind. One core characteristic is that *children construct their own knowledge*.

- Children are extremely curious and active knowledge seekers who take in information, observe, make guesses about things, and build models about how the world works. They construct different types of knowledge, such as knowledge about physical properties of objects, about relationships between things, and about their culture's way of doing things.
- Children are like scientists when they build knowledge. They take in an enormous amount of data and make sense of it by relating it to something that they already know. Gradually, they change their understanding of how things work.

A child's ability to construct knowledge rests on another characteristic of cognitive development, that *children process*

information. Their brain takes in sensory information and stores some, but not all, of it in long-term memory, ready for future use.

- Children pull information from long-term memory and place it in their working memory where they can use it. For example, a child who has taken a walk to observe a stop light stores that information and later hauls it out of storage so that he can dictate a story about stop lights to his teacher.
- Domains of development are intertwined. For example, children use their information processing skills to sort out information in social situations, meaning that they process social information. Some children have difficulty getting along with others because they do not process social information very well.
- A child's perceptual abilities affect how well he processes information, and there are predictable changes in perception through the early childhood years.

Children's language and literacy development starts on the day that they are born. Schools are under a great deal of pressure to show that children are good readers, with children taking standardized tests in reading starting in third grade. Many teachers are now "teaching to the test" in an effort for their schools to meet adequate yearly progress on the tests. Early childhood educators, those teaching third grade and below, feel the pressure about the tests. Consequently, the early childhood field has been making a concerted effort to describe practices most likely to help children become good readers.

- Children become successful readers when they build up a storehouse of meaningful information about the world through active exploration and play, when they have the vocabulary to describe their experiences.
- Teachers who use a blended approach successfully combine child-initiated and teacher-directed activities in language and literacy development. For example, children might play gas station in the dramatic play center, but the teacher would print signs such as "Gas" and "$4.25," indicating the price of a gallon of gasoline.
- The main components of an early literacy program are comprehension (vocabulary development and prediction, for example), phonological awareness (rhyming, for example), the alphabetic principle (writing one's name and recognizing alphabet letters, for example), and concepts about print (such as identifying parts of a book).

We nurture children's cognitive competence by paying attention to what children need to advance in this domain. Four of the most pressing needs in cognitive development include the following:

- Children need to be internally motivated. School success builds on a child's ability and willingness to take on challenges, to work independently, and to take pleasure in working.

- Children need to play. Play is a necessity, not a luxury, for young children and has a positive effect on development. For example, social interactive pretend play builds denser synaptic connections in a child's brain. Pretend play helps children develop specific cognitive developmental skills such as how to take somebody else's perspective.
- Children need social interaction with other children, parents, and teachers. Warm, stimulating social interaction, a good teacher-child relationship in which a teacher scaffolds children's understanding of events and people, for example, affects later academic success.
- Children need appropriately challenging and novel tasks. Moderately challenging and novel activities require a child to perform mental operations using the new information. Children, through interesting activities, develop the extensive knowledge base and vocabulary that they need for school success in this way.

There are many influences on children's cognitive development, including but not limited to, abuse and neglect, nutrition, addictive substances, exposure to the media, auditory and visual processing disorders. Teachers can work to improve children's cognitive development in many ways, which fall into two categories.

- Teachers must develop a warm, caring, positive relationship with every child and communicate messages to children simply, kindly, firmly, and consistently.
- Teachers must use child guidance strategies that help children construct social knowledge and helpful concepts about relationships.

Because children build knowledge and need to be internally motivated, teachers should construct classrooms in which children can be active in learning, planning, making choices, and interacting with others.

QUESTIONS FOR REFLECTION

1. Reflect on your own ability to do *social information processing*. In your opinion, how good are you with the first step, paying attention to social cues? Give an example of when you paid attention very well to a social cue. Explain how paying attention well helped you decide what to do in that social situation.

2. Look at the chapter opener vignette Preschool: Building Math Concepts with Blocks. Which of the following types of knowledge that children construct does this vignette illustrate: physical, social, or logico-mathematical? Give your reasons.

APPLY YOUR KNOWLEDGE

What Should This Teacher Do?

1. Mrs. Chang's principal said that three parents had complained about the dramatic play center in her classroom. They are upset that their children are wasting their time in playing there. He asked that she somehow help them understand why that center is so important. List at least four things that she could communicate to the parents about the value of dramatic or pretend play.

2. Sharina, a kindergarten child, is transferring to Mr. Hernandez's K-to-2 class from another school. Sharina has a developmental learning disability, and Sharina's parents are concerned about their 6 year old's problem with making friends. Based on your understanding of social information processing, name at least three things that Mr. Hernandez should observe about Sharina when she joins his class.

KEY TERMS

Auditory processing
   disorder, 159
Blended approach to literacy
   development, 150
Cognitive development, 140
Constructivism, 140
External motivation, 153
Information processing, 143

Internal motivation, 152
Language, 147
Literacy, 147
Logico-mathematical knowledge, 141
Long-term memory, 144
Perspective taking, 155
Physical knowledge, 141
Pretend play, 155

Sensory register, 144
Short-term memory, 144
Social information
   processing, 145
Social knowledge, 141
Visual processing disorder, 159
Working memory, 144

WEB SITES

Early Reading First
http://www.ed.gov/programs/earlyreading/index.html
Information on the literacy program sponsored by the federal government, as a part of the No Child Left Behind Act of 2001.

International Play Association
http://www.ipaworld.org/
Home page of the International Play Association.

National Association for the Education of Young Children
http://www.naeyc.org/academy/standards site within
http://www.naeyc.org
Focuses on standards for child development centers wishing to be accredited by NAEYC. Click on "Standard two, curriculum." You will see several parts of the curriculum

standard focusing on cognitive development. This should give you a good idea of what a classroom or school that fosters cognitive development would look like.

Zero to Three
http://www.zerotothree.org/
Reputable source for evidence-based information on children birth to 3 years. Up-to-date with information on development, assessment, working with parents. The following is the site for professionals:

http://www.zerotothree.org/ztt_professionals.html
For example: type in "importance of play" in the search box, and you will get an excellent source on play.

CHAPTER 7

Supporting Children's Physical Development

- What are some of the major characteristics of children's physical characteristics and needs?

- What are some of the key influences on children's physical development?

- What can teachers do to facilitate children's physical development?

INFANT AND TODDLER
Everyone Is Walking!

Mr. Bjornrud looked at the records of the infants in his class, thinking about the differences in the timing of when three children walked alone for the first time. Ernesto walked without assistance or holding on when he was 14 months old. Sylvia walked alone at 12 months. Gabe, however, was only 9 and a half months old when his father said, "Hey, Mr. B., watch this!" Dad placed Gabe on the floor facing the teacher, and Gabe walked the three steps to Mr. Bjornrud.

PRESCHOOL
Graphing Heights

Mrs. Chang's class of 4 year olds made a large graph showing how many children were 38″, 39″, or 40″ in height. The chart did not have individual names but grouped the number of children at each height and showed that most of the children were about 40″ tall. Two children were 43″ tall, and two were 38″ in height.

In spite of these differences, every child in Mrs. Chang's class was within the normal range of height for age and gender.

PRIMARY
The Obstacle Course

Mr. Hernandez set up an obstacle course as an informal assessment strategy and noted the differences in motor abilities in his class. He observed that first grader Luis sailed smoothly through the course and recorded his observations. He also noticed Pete's difficulty with the balance beam but not with any other part of the course. He was genuinely worried about Trina, a child with developmental coordination disorder. He wanted to focus on Trina enjoying this activity, not on her problem with coordination. You will read later in this chapter how Mr. Hernandez helped Trina enjoy this challenge.

There is great beauty in all of child development. Throughout early childhood, children get taller, their bodies get longer, and they learn to run, jump, write, shoot baskets, and swim. Think about a child's development as a brilliantly designed knot with all domains of development flowing together to form a whole that is much more awe-inspiring and complex than any of the strands alone. Physical development, a wonder on its own, is intertwined with and is affected by other developmental domains. For example, being overweight or obese takes a toll on a child's emotional and social development just as it affects physical health (Dehghan, Akhtar-Danesh, & Merchant, 2005; Hughes, Farewell, Harris, & Reilly, 2007). Clumsiness and poor motor skills endanger a child's overall development, including social and emotional development (Leeds Consensus Statement, 2006).

This chapter describes and explains children's physical development—predictable changes in height and weight within a normal range and *windows of achievement* for key motor skills. We explore major influences on physical development and consider practical strategies teachers use to support children's physical development. As with the other chapters on development, each of the three major sections in this chapter emphasizes one of the following concepts (Hyson, 2003). To foster children's physical and motor development, effective teachers:

- know and understand young children's physical characteristics and needs,
- know and understand the multiple influences on physical development, and
- use knowledge about physical development to create healthy, respectful, supportive, and challenging learning environments.

UNDERSTANDING CHILDREN'S PHYSICAL CHARACTERISTICS AND NEEDS

There are clear differences, in any group of young children, in their height and weight. Teachers who work with young children see patterns in child development and recognize the predictability in children's physical growth and motor development. They understand how a child's brain influences growth and motor skills and that we document children's growth with growth charts.

Healthy Physical Growth Follows Predictable Patterns

Growth Rates for Young Children Are Predictable

A full-term infant, on average, weighs 7 pounds. The infant's weight doubles in 5 months to 14 pounds and triples by 12 months to 21 pounds. At age 4, he weighs about 35 pounds. The same average infant, 20 inches long at birth, is about 30 inches tall when he smashes his hands into his first birthday cake. At 4 years old, he is about 40 inches tall. Notice the pattern—rapid growth rates during infancy—10 inches in length during 1 year and a threefold increase in weight—and slower rates after age 2. During childhood years 3 through 8, children grow an average of 2.5 inches each year (Dawson, 2002).

Changes in Body Proportions Are Predictable

Knowing about and understanding children's growth rates make predicting the changes in body proportions as children grow possible. Infants have an appealing appearance that seems to give the impression of helplessness and seems to draw many adults to them. An infant's head is large compared to total body length. A toddler's body retains much of this appeal in spite of the rapid changes in weight and length. Toddlers' body proportions still give them a rounded, chubby, baby-like appearance with the head still large compared to height. Toddlers tend to have a rounded abdomen. During the preschool years, a child's body takes on a leaner, longer, taller look with baby fat decreasing dramatically and long bones in arms and legs getting longer.

Checking on Children's Growth

Children's growth, including weight, length or height, head circumference, and amount of body fat is monitored with growth charts (National Center for Health Statistics, 2002). They describe a broad sample of children in the United States. There are 16 charts, 8 charts for boys and 8 for girls. There are two major age categories in the growth charts, one for children birth to 36 months and another for children from 2 to 20 years. Some of the charts allow professionals to assess a child's likelihood of becoming overweight or obese. See an example of the 2000 Growth Rate Charts in Figure 7.1.

How are the growth charts useful to teachers? Like physicians and parents, teachers want to know if a child is growing normally. The growth charts can help teachers give an objective measure of how a child compares, in height for example, to other children of the same age and gender. Here is an example.

> Joshua is 5 years old and 43 inches tall. His nurse, during his checkup, used the growth chart and found the spot where these two numbers come together. They converge at the number 50, meaning that 50% or half of the boys his age are taller than and half are shorter than Joshua. It also means that Joshua is growing normally.

Healthy Motor Development Follows Predictable Patterns

Using groups of large muscles to roll over, stand, hop, run, walk, or maintain balance is gross motor development. Fine motor development, on the other hand, involves using fingers and hands to hold a bottle, squeeze a toy, hold a crayon or pencil, and copy shapes or letters. Children develop these abilities at the same time that their bodies are growing. Motor development and brain (neurological) development are linked. Gross and fine motor development, like physical development, follows predictable patterns.

Gross Motor Development Milestones

Healthy children develop gross motor skills in a reassuringly predictable pattern. Parents, delighted upon observing their infant's first steps, take pictures and show them proudly to family and friends to mark the event. Predicting exactly when any child will sit up, crawl, or walk unassisted, because of the variability in children's development, however, is difficult.

What we do know is that healthy children achieve motor skills within windows of achievement for gross motor skill development (WHO Multicentre Growth Reference Study Group, 2006b). A window of achievement for gross motor skills is the time span during which a typically developing child, for instance, sits without support, stands with help, crawls on hands and knees, walks with assistance, stands alone, and walks alone. There is a normal range for these and other motor skills, as Mr. Bjornrud's observations of the infants in his class revealed (see chapter opener vignette).

Each of the children in his class is developing normally and acquiring gross motor skills at different points in the normal range. Gabe walked at $9\frac{1}{2}$ months, very early but within the normal range. Sylvia walked alone at 12 months, about the average and within the normal range. Ernesto waited until 14 months to walk alone, and he, too, is in the normal range for this gross motor skill. These and all children use vision in developing gross motor skills. Vision problems can delay the time when a child walks, crawls, or runs. Children with blindness develop gross motor skills later than do sighted children (Brambring, 2006). Table 7.1 shows gross motor milestones.

Growth charts Charts used for monitoring children's weight, length or height, head circumference, and amount of body fat.

Gross motor development Using groups of large muscles to perform major movements.

Fine motor development Using fingers and hands to perform precise manipulations.

Window of achievement for gross motor skill development Period during which a typically developing child will, for example, walk alone or crawl on hands and knees.

CDC Growth Charts: United States

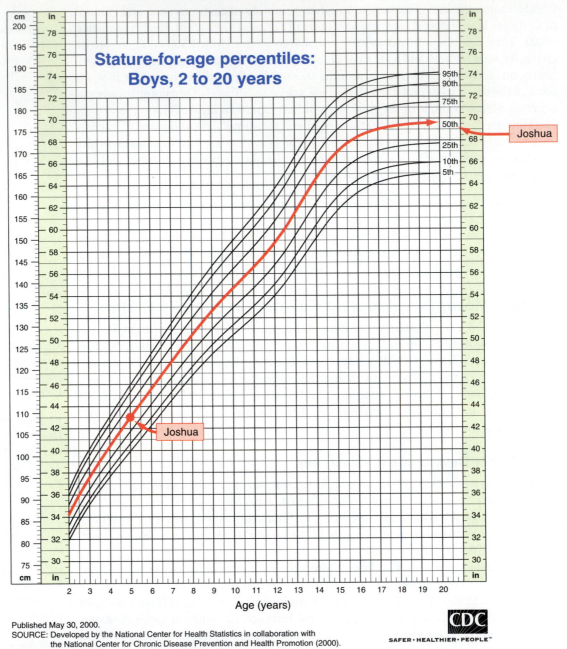

Published May 30, 2000.
SOURCE: Developed by the National Center for Health Statistics in collaboration with
the National Center for Chronic Disease Prevention and Health Promotion (2000).

FIGURE 7.1   Example of a Growth Chart

This chart determines whether boys ages 2 to 20 are growing normally in terms of height.
Source: http://www.cdc.gov/nchs/data/nhanes/growthcharts/set2/chart%2007.pdf

Fine Motor Development Milestones

Fine motor skill development is also highly predictable in children. They grasp, reach, open, and shut hands, for example, in a recognizable sequence. Table 7.1 shows this sequence. The phrase *by the end of* signifies that children master fine motor skills, not at the same exact time for each child but within a window of achievement, a time frame

TABLE 7.1   Developmental Milestones: Gross and Fine Motor Development

Child's Age (by the End of)	Gross Motor Development	Fine Motor Development	How Teachers Can Help*
3 months	Raises head and chest Supports upper body with arms	Shuts and opens hands Puts hand to mouth Swings at object dangling over crib Uses whole hand to grasp toys	Provide "tummy" time for practicing those head raises. Place mobile in spot where baby can swing at it.
7 months	Rolls from back to tummy Rolls from tummy to back Sits with support of hands, then sits without support of hands Supports whole weight on legs Reaches with one hand	Moves an object from one hand to other hand "Rakes" at objects with hand (fingers bent like tines in a rake)	Provide safe objects to grasp. Provide time and space for practicing motor skills. Provide safe objects for baby to move and to rake with hand.
12 months	Gets to sitting position without help Creeps on knees and hands Crawls on belly Gets from sitting to crawling Gets from sitting to lying on tummy Pulls self up to stand Walks holding on to things such as furniture Stands without support Walks without support for a few steps	Uses pincer grasp, uses thumb and fingers to pick up objects Uses index finger to poke at things Attempts to imitate scribbling Places objects in containers Takes objects out of container	Allow child to progress at own pace. Have many positive, low-key, face-to-face interactions centered on physical activity. Provide safe objects and toys for picking up, poking, and placing in containers.
24 months	Walks up and down stairs while holding on to person or railing Climbs onto and off furniture without help Stands on tiptoe Kicks a ball Runs Carries large toys while walking Pulls toy while walking	Scribbles Empties container Builds tower of four or more blocks Begins to use one hand more often than the other	Let toddlers use fine motor muscles in self-help activities: zipping, pouring, and washing hands. Encourage large muscle development by providing lots of room and time. Encourage climbing, running, and jumping.
36 months	Climbs very well Climbs and descends stairs, one foot per stair step Runs effortlessly Pedals a tricycle Bends over easily without falling	Uses crayon, marker, or pencil to make up and down, sideways, and circular lines Builds towers of more than six blocks Turns nuts, bolts, and jar lids Turns handles that rotate	Provide a variety of things with which to draw: markers, crayons, and paintbrushes. Provide blocks, stringing beads, and busy boards.
48 months	Hops Stands on one foot up to 5 seconds Climbs and descends stairs without support Throws ball overhand Moves forward and backward smoothly Catches ball bounced to him most of time	Draws and copies circles and squares Begins to copy some uppercase letters Uses scissors Draws person with two to four body parts	Provide space and time for play. Provide safe equipment for practicing large motor skills: balls, stairs, climbing gyms, and large blocks for stacking and carrying. Plan simple, noncompetitive games.
60 months	Stands on only one foot for at least 10 seconds Somersaults Hops Swings Climbs Might be able to skip	Draws person with a body Prints some letters Dresses without help Undresses without help Uses spoon and fork Might be able to use a table knife Usually can take care of own toilet needs	Provide paper, chalkboards, whiteboards, and other materials for painting and drawing. Encourage self-help skills. Provide a print-rich environment.

*Observe and keep records; challenge children's skills but avoid demanding too much; provide safe spaces for practicing skills.

Source: Based on data from Altmann (2006); Bredekamp and Copple (1997); PBS Parents (no date); and Shelov and Hanneman (2004).

of normal fine motor development. As with gross motor milestones, we can predict the sequence with accuracy but timing of the sequence varies for different children.

The Brain's Role in Motor Development

Understanding motor development includes describing when, for example, children crawl, walk, or pick up things. It also includes explaining development. For example, why does an infant use her hand to rake things before she can pick them up between two fingers? Researchers have explained the brain's impact on a child's motor development.

A Child's Brain Controls Movement

A child reaches for her favorite puzzle, a classroom event so seemingly commonplace and a voluntary and deceptively simple action. Closer inspection, however, reveals the movement's incredible complexity. Visual areas of the brain gave the child information about the location of the puzzle. Her limbic system reminds her that she enjoys playing with this puzzle or that the puzzle looks interesting, and her prefrontal association area motivated her initial decision to move. Her visual system uses her brain's posterior parietal cortex to send information about the puzzle to the premotor areas where plans for movement take place. Then, information is sent to her primary motor cortex. Finally, signals are sent to her motor neurons (Martin, 2003). A child reaches for a puzzle—a voluntary and *highly complex* movement.

The interrelatedness of developmental domains is deeply evident when examining motor and brain development. A newborn's brain, about 25% the size of an adult's brain, is most developed in the brain stem and the spinal cord. These brain areas control bodily functions such as breathing, circulation, sleeping, sucking, and swallowing, areas most important at a baby's birth. The regions of the brain responsible for thinking, planning, and control, including control of motor pathways, take somewhat longer to develop (Zero to Three, 2001).

The parts of the brain most closely aligned with motor development are the motor cortex and the cerebellum. The **motor cortex** is important to developing voluntary movements and exerts control over the spinal cord by directly controlling a group of motor neurons. The motor neurons direct the movement of muscles attached to the bones of the legs, feet, arms, hands, and fingers, allowing children to execute amazing motor skills such as reaching for puzzles or tying intricate knots.

The **cerebellum** is a large, extremely complex part of the brain. It consists of two peach-size masses of tissue near the base of the brain as shown in Figure 7.2. The cerebellum begins to develop before a child is born (Hashimoto, Shimizu, Shimoya, Kanzaki, Clapp, & Murata, 2001) and continues to develop after the birth. The main functions of the cerebellum are to control movement of arms and legs (limbs) and to help a child maintain balance and posture.

The cerebellum sends signals to a child's brain stem and pathways, which control muscles of a child's arms, legs, trunk, and eyes (Martin, 2003). The cerebellum also has a role in cognitive development (Diamond, 2000). A child whose cerebellum is injured usually has problems with coordination and movement. The cerebellum coordinates muscle movements by pulling together data or information from and communicating with many different sources, including the brain stem, the spinal cord, and muscles. New skills, such as throwing a ball overhand, might be learned in a hit-or-miss fashion, but the skill gets coded and stored in the cerebellum to wait for the next time the skill is needed (Society for Neuroscience, 2006).

Motor cortex One of two parts of the brain most closely aligned with motor development; involved in voluntary movements.

Cerebellum Part of the brain near the base of the brain; controls movement of arms and legs; helps children maintain balance.

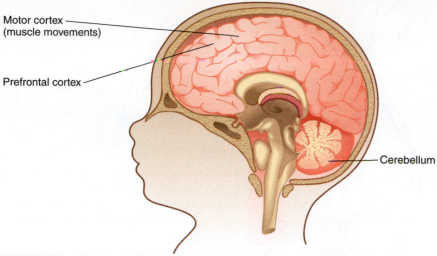

Motor cortex
(muscle movements)

Prefrontal cortex

Cerebellum

FIGURE 7.2   The brain showing the cerebellum and motor cortex.

CHECK YOUR UNDERSTANDING
A Child's Brain Controls Movement

Explain two things about the brain's development that allows a 4 year old to pick up and hold a paintbrush. Explain why he could not perform this fine motor skill when he was an infant.

Practice Improves Motor Skills

New motor skills result when muscles get stronger and the brain's neural circuits become better coordinated. Practice is another factor. Practicing motor skills leads to more skillful performance (Society for Neuroscience, 2006). A 5-year-old child might seem unsure in her first attempts to throw a ball overhand, but practice often leads to more skillful throwing movements. Motor skills, therefore, develop from skills that children already have. As another example, the infant who can raise her head when prone (on her abdomen) uses and practices that skill and later combines headlifting with a newfound ability to use her arms to push herself up as she lifts her head.

Myelination's Part in Motor Development

Another process, **myelination** contributes to the progress in motor development. **Myelin** is a compact, fatty, buttery-textured, whitish substance surrounding and insulating the axons of neurons, as shown in Figure 7.3. The axons are responsible for conducting messages, and the messages have to be able to get from one axon to another. Myelin is deposited gradually on the axons and has a role in the sequence of motor development. Myelin-coated axons send and receive messages more quickly and with greater velocity and accuracy than those without myelin. Myelination, then, allows information about movement much easier passage through the brain and motor pathways, enabling young children to move with increasing grace and coordination (Zero to Three, 2001). Figure 7.3 shows a myelin-coated axon in the brain.

Go to MyEducationLab and select the topic "Child Development." Under Activities and Applications, watch the video *Physical Development* to observe motor skills of two preschool children of different ages.

Myelination Gradual process in which axons are coated with myelin.

Myelin Fatty, whitish material surrounding and insulating axons.

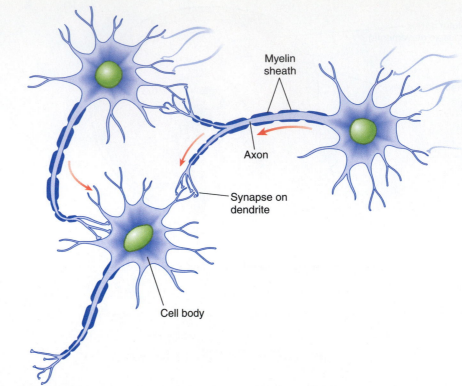

Myelin sheath

Axon

Synapse on dendrite

Cell body

FIGURE 7.3   Nerve cell showing the axon coated with myelin.

We now look at one motor development problem that teachers are very likely to see in some children. Mr. Hernandez, in the chapter opener vignette, knows that first grader Trina has been diagnosed with developmental coordination disorder.

Developmental Coordination Disorder

Developmental coordination disorder A problem in motor development characterized by clumsiness; evident in either large motor coordination or in fine motor skills or both.

Children with **developmental coordination disorder** have significant problems in motor skills and coordination compared with other children the same age. For example, the child who appears to be clumsy or awkward and have graceless coordination may have problems with large motor coordination such as uncoordinated running, throwing, or jumping and hopping. The child might also have problems with fine motor skills such as illegible handwriting, difficulty using scissors, or getting a zipper started. Some children face challenges in both large and small motor coordination, as Trina, in Mr. Hernandez's class and featured in the primary chapter opener vignette does (Ball, 2002).

Developmental coordination disorder, seen in approximately 6% of school-age children, is not a trivial problem. These children are at risk for repeated injuries, and they miss chances to engage in play and athletic events. Other children often tease them. As a result, they often develop an unfavorable self-concept and poor self-esteem. Developmental coordination disorder can exist alone or with other learning problems. Jongmans (2006) makes a convincing argument for early identification of this problem. Identifying this problem early whenever possible can prevent some of the problems that children with developmental coordination disorder experience once they are in school. Very young children with this disorder show significant delays in the basic motor skills such as sitting up or walking.

Teachers can best help children with this disorder by changing the child's environment (Missiuna, 2006). The goal, to focus on helping the child participate in motor

FIGURE 7.4   Children's balance improves as they get older and as their brains develop.

activities more easily and with greater pleasure, requires us to avoid focusing on the child's impairment. The rationale for this approach comes from research about what successful young adults who had a developmental coordination disorder as children, recalled about their childhood. These successful young people, when remembering their childhoods, did not focus on their coordination problems but instead described accommodations at home and in school that helped them (Missiuna, Moll, King, King, & Law, in press; cited in Missiuna, 2006).

Any intervention for a child with this disorder should focus on functional activities that are relevant to everyday living. Intervention should be meaningful to the child, and the child's wishes should be taken into account when designing an intervention (Leeds Consensus Statement, 2006). Mr. Hernandez followed that advice as shown in the Teach Intentionally box.

Assessing Motor Skills

The National Association for the Education of Young Children's (NAEYC) standards for preparing early childhood teachers (Hyson, 2003) requires that they learn to use *informal assessment strategies* as a good start in individualizing curriculum for children. Increasingly, early childhood teachers are required to implement standards and assess children's development and learning, including physical skills (Geist & Baum, 2005; Seefeldt, 2005). For example, early learning standards in many states require that teachers help children achieve standards in physical development (Illinois State Board of Education, 2006). Examples are, ". . . engage in active play using fine and gross motor control" and

Go to MyEducationLab and select the topic "Observation and Assessment." Under Activities and Applications, watch the video *Observing Children in Authentic Contexts* and observe as a teacher uses informal, authentic assessment strategies.

TEACH INTENTIONALLY

Trina's Success in the Obstacle Course

What the teacher did: He had each child go through the obstacle course with a partner, each giving the other hints for success. Trina and her companion helped one another go around the cones by saying, "OK, here's a cone . . . go way around!"

How the teacher was intentional: Mr. Hernandez did not focus on Trina's developmental coordination disorder but instead focused on helping her successfully and joyfully participate in the obstacle course. He also set things up so that all children gave and received assistance from their partners.

This teacher has followed Vygotskian theory by figuring out how he could properly support her participation and by encouraging the children themselves to work together, taking turns at acting as mentors and more knowledgeable others. He has also focused on Trina as a whole child who enjoys physical activity and social interaction when goals are achievable. His whole child approach will undoubtedly help her develop a positive view of herself. This positive self-esteem will grow out of seeing herself as *competent* in a motor activity and as *worthy* of her teacher's effort and time. This will likely help her develop a new level of *confidence* in herself. Competence, a sense of worth, and confidence are all parts of self-esteem, the judgment that children form about themselves.

Document Collecting, analyzing, interpreting, and displaying evidence of development and learning.

This teacher can assess how her student is progressing through the milestones of gross motor development by observing her.

"move with balance and control." The question is how should teachers assess children's achievement of the standards.

Informal, authentic assessment involves observing infants and combining observation with interviewing older children or asking children to perform a task such as going through an obstacle course. Developmentally appropriate assessment for young children is planned, has explicitly stated purposes, is an integral part of the curriculum, is free from stereotypic images and language, and comes from many sources, not just one (Seefeldt, 2005). Teachers **document** each child's abilities with appropriate assessment and then plan curriculum for the child, building on strengths and helping the child overcome challenges.

The Project Spectrum's obstacle course (Krechevsky, 1998) is an informal method for assessing large motor skills. This is a ready-made instrument developed at Harvard's Project Zero. Observers use it to assess

- power,
- agility,
- speed, and
- balance.

Figure 7.5 shows the obstacle course as a series of stations, each meant to assess one or more of these targeted skills. The obstacle course illustrates play-based assessment done as a part of the regular curriculum. Teachers decide how much of the course they are to use and where they set it up

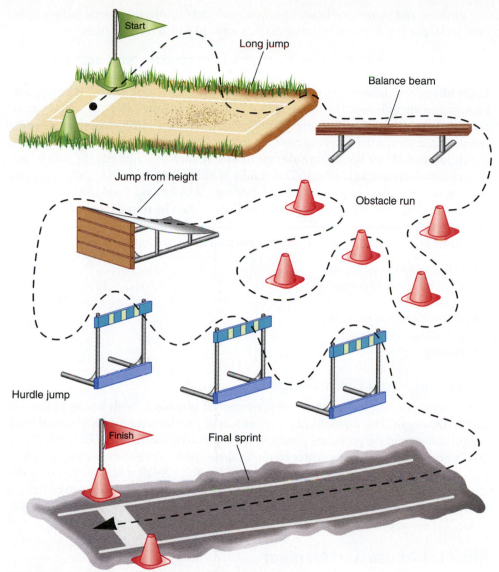

FIGURE 7.5 Obstacle Course from Project Spectrum

(Krechevsky, 1998). They model the skill at each station before beginning to observe children. Mr. Hernandez let the children use the obstacle course for a couple days before he even considered scoring anyone's performance. For each of the four categories children can score a 1, meaning that there are some problems with a category, a 2, indicating good performance with only minor issues, or a 3, signifying exceptionally good performance.

Mr. Hernandez accommodated Trina's needs by having pairs of children traverse the obstacle course, giving each other hints about how to perform well. Vygotsky's theory acknowledges the role of a more knowledgeable other and Mr. Hernandez has encouraged the children to act in this capacity with each other.

Physical and motor development follow predictable patterns. Several factors, however, influence this developmental domain, a topic to which we now turn.

INFLUENCES ON PHYSICAL DEVELOPMENT

Easily observable differences exist in children's physical development. All developmental domains are influenced by nature, a child's genetic potential, and nurture, the environment in which he lives. The interplay of genetic potential and environmental factors results in the stark differences in physical development in young children. For instance, if a child's parents are both above average in height, then the child has the genetic potential for above average height. The child's environment, however, also influences **stature.** If he gets sufficient and adequate nutrients, then he has a good chance of reaching his physical potential. If he is poorly nourished, then he is in danger of not reaching his genetic potential.

Stature Height, measured in inches or centimeters.

Some of the main factors influencing physical development include

- extremely low birth weight,
- physical abuse and neglect,
- pollution,
- chronic medical problems,
- nutrition, and
- obesity.

Extremely Low Birth Weight

A newborn who weighs less than 100 grams or 2.2 pounds at birth has an **extremely low birth weight.** This infant has a far greater set of problems than does a normal birth weight infant, and the problems persist into the early childhood years (Pediatric News, 2005). Some of the problems center on physical and motor development. Specific problems included cerebral palsy, asthma, vision of less than 20/20, and poor motor skills. Children who had extremely low birth weight tend during early childhood to be lighter, shorter, and have a smaller head circumference than normal birth weight children (Kilbride, Thorstad, & Daily, 2004).

Extremely low birth weight A weight of less than 100 grams or 2.2 pounds at birth.

Physical Abuse and Neglect

A child's early life experiences affect all areas of development, including physical development and mental health (McEwen, 2003). Some unstable child-parent relationships become abusive, with grave effects on a child's short- and long-term development. Other parents, for many different reasons, neglect children by not meeting their most basic needs. Neglect, like abuse also affects children's physical development.

Physical Abuse

Physical abuse is the *intentional* infliction of harm to a child's body and produces immediate injuries, such as bruises, lacerations, abrasions, broken bones, and internal trauma. These injuries often have a negative impact on a child's growing body. Chronic abuse alters a child's brain chemistry, leaving him excessively watchful and wasting precious time needed for playing, learning, making friends, and growing emotionally (Hagele, 2005). In terms of physical development, abuse often damages a child's long bones in arms and legs. The bones' growth centers are at the ends of the bones, and some forms of physical injury damage these growth centers. Child abuse is comparable

Physical abuse The intentional infliction of harm to a child's body to seriously endanger the child. Each state's laws on child abuse define physical abuse for that state.

to military combat, with a child constantly on guard, in danger, and missing the joy of a healthy childhood.

Physical Neglect

Neglect is the most common form of child maltreatment (Crossen-Tower, 2002). Children can be neglected medically, physically, and emotionally, and parents can fail to supervise them or even abandon them. Adults who **physically neglect** children fail to provide food, water, sanitation, or safe shelter. Thirty-eight percent of the fatalities from child maltreatment were from neglect (Child Welfare Information Gateway, 2006).

Children's development is threatened when children are neglected, and the effects are related to the type, severity, and timing of the neglect. Physically neglected children, very often malnourished with poor or no medical care, contract infectious diseases such as pneumonia more easily than well-nourished children and might have smaller brains. Poor nutrition or an inadequate amount of food often affects the way a child's body releases the hormones that regulate physical growth. Neglect, therefore, adversely affects a child's physical growth and development, including the growth of the brain (Perry, Colwell, & Schick, 2002).

Physical neglect The intentional failure to provide a child with food, water, sanitation, or safe shelter.

Pollution

Pollution is a worldwide problem that affects human growth. Many different pollutants exist, and they exert their effect through different pathways in a child's body. Pollutants can affect physical growth adversely, particularly during prenatal development. For example, lead, which is a soft and extremely toxic metal, enters a child's body if he breathes or eats it, for example, by chewing on a window sill or a toy coated with lead paint. Lead can lower a child's level of intelligence, even when he ingests or inhales only small amounts. Lead can be detected with a blood test.

The percentage of children with lead poisoning has decreased in the past several years because a variety of laws have removed lead from consumer products such as gasoline and paint for interiors of homes, but poor children still have higher levels. Young children are the most vulnerable to lead poisoning because of their rapidly growing brains and bodies. The highest blood level of lead is reported in children under 5, especially in 2 year olds because they put toys into their mouth (National Institute of Environmental Health Sciences, 2005). In 2007, there were many recalls of toys coated with extremely high levels of lead paint (Barboza, 2007).

Asthma, a Chronic Medical Problem

Asthma is a persistent medical condition in childhood and currently affects 6.2 million children. A child with asthma has a chronic inflammation of the airways because the airways have an extreme reaction to many different harmful stimuli such as secondhand smoke, roaches, pollen, mold, animal dander, feathers, dust, food, and irritating gases. These children have asthma attacks when their airways tighten and fill with mucus. Teachers often hear the wheezy breathing of a child whose asthma is gearing up for an attack. Acute asthma attacks often result in hospitalization among children under the age of 15 (American Lung Association, 2007).

A child with asthma has difficulty breathing in general and struggles mightily during any attack. The child has difficulty playing vigorously, running, climbing, and engaging in rough and tumble play of a normal childhood. In addition to missing some valuable social experiences, many children with asthma also miss the physical exercise so necessary in developing excellent motor skills.

Some of the highest rates for asthma exist in inner city, African-American children, many who do not get the proper medication. Many also do not know how to manage asthma properly, and they are exposed to asthma triggers such as pollution, cigarette smoke, and mold. Consequently, they have frequent attacks and use the emergency department of a hospital to deal with acute symptoms. One study done in Chicago found that a trained, culturally competent lay health educator, working one-on-one with children and families, contributed to a reduction in the number of visits to emergency rooms, better use of asthma medication, reduction of the allergens triggering attacks, and better asthma-related knowledge (Margellos-Anast, Whitman, Gutierrez, Seals, & Jajoo, 2006).

Asthma is an issue in schools, particularly urban schools (Freedman, 2004). It is the main reason for school absences linked to chronic medical problems. There were almost 13 million lost school days for children with asthma in 2003 (American Lung Association, 2007).

Adequate Nutrition

An adequate diet is necessary for a child's overall well-being and optimal physical development. The prenatal period and the first 3 years are critical in establishing proper nutrient levels and an adequate intake of calories. Poor nutrition before birth and during infancy and the toddler years places children at risk for brain development problems, growth problems, poor motor development, and a host of other ills.

As discussed in Chapter 6 on cognitive development, good nutrition is essential for healthy brain development before and after birth. A mother's nutrition, therefore, has an impact on prenatal brain development. Specific nutrients have a great effect on brain development, including protein, energy, certain fats, iron, zinc, copper, iodine, selenium, vitamin A, choline, and folate (Georgieff, 2007).

Some nutrient requirements are directly linked to a child's progress in physical and motor development. For example, the process of myelination of the brain and nervous system requires dietary fats, leading to recommendations that whole milk instead of reduced or nonfat milk be used (International Food Information Council, 2006). Nutrition also influences a child's bone development (Specker, 2004). Some of the nutritional factors that contribute to bone growth in infants and toddlers include how well nourished mothers are during pregnancy, the type of feeding during infancy, the calcium and phosphorus content of infant formula, and diet during the toddler years. When mothers do no get enough vitamin D during pregnancy, problems crop up with stability of calcium in newborns. Preterm infants are at risk for bone deficiency, and a high-mineral formula reduces but does not eliminate this problem.

There are several challenges brought on by poor nutrition (WHO, 2006). A deficiency of zinc is associated with diarrhea and growth retardation. Improper feeding of infants is responsible for one-third of the cases of malnutrition. Undernutrition in pregnant women can lead to infants born with low birth weight, which, noted in the section on extremely low birth weight, places infants at risk for poor health, less than optimal physical growth, and poor motor skill development.

Adequate nutrition, including vegetables that are *not* deep fried, contribute to children's healthy physical development.

There is another side of the nutrition coin—the intake of too much energy or calories, whatever the source.

Obesity

There has been a steady increase in obesity in children in the developed countries. Twenty-five percent of U.S. children are overweight, and 11% are obese (Dehghan, Akhtar-Danesh, & Merchant, 2005). An obese child has an excessive amount of fat. This means that his weight is too high in proportion to his height as determined with a specific growth chart. This ratio of weight to height is the body mass index (BMI). In a recent study, the number of obese children were underdiagnosed, largely because the body mass index growth chart was not used during their physical exam (Hampl, Carroll, Simon, & Sharma, 2007). The risk for obesity can be identified in early childhood. Children who are overweight in the preschool period are very likely to be overweight at age 12 (Nader, O'Brien, Houts, Bradley, Belsky, Crosnoe, Friedman, Mei, & Susman, 2005).

Obesity during childhood coexists with serious medical problems, such as type 2 diabetes mellitus (Hannon, Rao, & Arslanian, 2005). Children who are obese are at risk for developing this disease, which has been on the rise in the past 20 years. The complications of this disease include atherosclerotic cardiovascular disease (deposition of cholesterol in arteries), stroke, sudden death, kidney problems, nerve problems that threaten legs and arms, and problems with the eyes that can lead to blindness.

Two main environmental factors contribute to being overweight and obesity—level of physical activity and nutrition. Nutrition factors contributing to being overweight and obesity are excessive consumption of fast foods; a high-protein, high-carbohydrate, high-fat diet; sugared soft drink consumption (Nowicka, 2005); and increased portion sizes (Dehghen, Akhtar-Danesh, & Merchant 2005). Inactivity also contributes to excessive weight. Excessive *screen time*, time spent watching movies, television, DVDs, or computers of all kinds, takes the place of more active play and is one of the major contributing factors to the epidemic of inactivity among children (Council on Sports Medicine and Fitness and the Council on School Health, 2006).

Preventing overweight and obesity is best done by combining an emphasis on healthful, good-tasting food and increasing physical activity for children (Rodearmel, Wyatt, Barry, Dong, Pan, Israel, Cho, McBurney, & Hill, 2006). However, some parents do not acknowledge that their child is overweight. A recent study has found that very few parents with overweight or at risk for overweight children even realize that their child has too much fat and showed little concern about their child's weight (Eckstein, Mikhail, Ariza, Thompson, Millard, & Binns, 2006).

Body mass index (BMI) A measure; the index of weight adjusted to a child's height; determined with a growth chart.

CHECK YOUR UNDERSTANDING
Influences on Physical Development

Choose one of the influences on physical development just presented—extremely low birth weight, physical abuse, physical neglect, pollution, asthma, nutrition, physical activity, or obesity. Explain, to a classmate, how this factor affects children's physical well-being.

USING KNOWLEDGE ABOUT PHYSICAL DEVELOPMENT TO CREATE A HEALTHY AND RESPECTFUL ENVIRONMENT

Teachers can support children's physical and motor development in many different ways and on different levels. They can

- reflect on personal beliefs about nutrition and physical activity.
- provide opportunities for developmentally appropriate physical activity.
- foster children's understanding of healthful eating.

Reflect on Personal Beliefs About Nutrition and Physical Activity

Socrates and Plato, among the first philosophers to teach people how to think logically, advocated questioning things, and this influence is evident in teacher education's emphasis on reflection, thinking, and questioning one's own practices. Early childhood professional groups advocate focusing on teachers as thinkers (Hyson, 2000).

When thinking about issues of nutrition and physical activity, teachers must acknowledge their own beliefs that drive their practices in the area of healthy physical development in children. A teacher who believes in and practices healthful eating would be quite receptive to focusing on healthful eating and physical activity in his classroom.

We also know that a teacher's beliefs about appropriate practices, such as encouraging physical activity for children, can be at odds with official school policy. This places the teacher in the position of figuring out how to put beliefs about appropriate practices to work in a setting that discourages appropriate practices. Teachers who practice unhealthful eating and do not believe in the value of physical exercise are not likely to make good eating and physical exercise an important part of their classroom culture and curriculum. We create a supportive and challenging physical environment by reflecting on our own beliefs.

This teacher believes that physical activity is important for children and includes it every day in the curriculum.

TABLE 7.2 How Much Physical Activity Does a Young Child Need?		
Age of Child	Minimum Number of Minutes Daily of Structured Physical Activity	Minimum Number of Minutes Daily of Unstructured Physical Activity
Birth to 12 months	Daily physical activity aimed at developing motor skills and exploring a safe environment	
12 months to 3 years	30	60
3 years to 5 years	60	60

Source: Based on data from the National Association for Sport & Physical Education (2002).

Provide Opportunities for Developmentally Appropriate Physical Activity

Children need high-quality physical activities because some of them have far too much screen time, because of the high rates of obesity, and because there is simply an overall decrease in physical activity in our culture (University of South Florida, 2008).

Allow Time for Physical Activity

One way that schools and teachers can make sure that children get enough physical activity is to allot a reasonable amount of time for physical activity. Lawmakers in many states, aware that some schools are eliminating recess, have proposed and enacted laws mandating that children get physical activity as a part of the regular school day. See Table 7.2 for recommendations on the minimum number of minutes of exercise that children, birth through preschool, need every day.

Design the Classroom for Movement

Children need physical activity; therefore, we should design the room and schedule to encourage movement. First, reflect on what we do in classrooms. If we believe in the concept of the whole child, then we would not separate physical activity from the rest of a child's development. We would not depend exclusively on recess or outdoor play for physical activity, although they are very important in a child's day. We would not set a room up so that young children sit at tables or desks all morning and afternoon. Instead, we would use the environment and curriculum to encourage physical activity.

Chapters 10 and 11 focus on implementing curriculum and setting up a classroom. Here are suggestions for designing the room, schedule, and learning activities to incorporate physical activity as a natural part of daily classroom life.

- Set up learning centers accommodating four to five children each. Many daily learning activities take place in centers, with children choosing centers in which they learn and moving from one center to another when they are ready.
- Intentionally include a center focused specifically on physical activity, as the teacher in the next example did.

> Mr. Hernandez used a very small section of the room for physical activity. He changes the equipment there periodically, and the children especially liked the small stationary bike, the balance ball, and the bean bag toss. And he teaches content such as math and science with this center.

Go to MyEducationLab and select the topic "Curriculum/Program Models." Under Activities and Applications, watch the video *Supporting Different Learning Styles: A First Grade Mathematics Lesson* for an example of active learning.

- Focus on active learning. Help children to learn math in an active way, for example, as Mr. Hernandez did. Each child made a bar graph showing the number of times that he or she got beanbags through the target on 3 consecutive days.
- Allow large blocks of time for center activities. This allows children to work in several centers during a morning and/or an afternoon. Mr. Hernandez requires that every child choose the physical activity area at least once every day.
- Acknowledge and accommodate individual differences and needs among children. For example, if a child has difficulty grasping and then releasing things, then provide a variety of items in the small manipulatives area.

Gross Motor Equipment

Provide enough equipment so that children do not have to wait too long for a turn. Be sure that the equipment fosters many different motor skills such as climbing, running, throwing, steering, and balancing. Go a step farther and focus on skills at different levels (Harms, Clifford, & Cryer, 1998). Mrs. Chang, the preschool teacher, removed pedals from two tricycles to give children experience with and without pedals.

Fine Motor Equipment

Provide a variety of developmentally appropriate fine motor materials in centers—small building toys, art materials, manipulatives such as pegboards, and puzzles—for a good part of each day, and organize materials logically and well. Provide materials with varying degrees of difficulty, for example, both large and small plastic interlocking blocks. Rotate items so that children remain interested in them. Store fine motor materials so that children can help themselves (Harms et al., 1998). Table 7.1 describes how teachers can help children with gross and fine motor skills during the first several years of life.

Swirling, spreading, and smoothing finger paint helps these children develop motor skills and an appreciation for making art.

Foster Children's Understanding of Healthful Eating

Recall, from Chapter 2, Bronfenbrenner's ideas about different systems affecting children's development. A child's family, school, and culture all influence his eating habits and preferences. There is growing awareness about the need to work on healthful eating at the family and school level, and this has resulted in legislation aimed at reducing obesity through physical activity and more healthful eating in schools. For example, the state of California in 2005 enacted legislation that required elementary schools to sell only full meals and individual portions of items such as eggs, cheese, nuts, nut butters, and vegetables not deep fried. Check the *Childhood Obesity* web site at the end of the chapter for information on your state's efforts.

These are good changes, and schools need to involve families in any effort to teach children about eating well. This might involve changing our thinking and practices about things such as snacks that parents might supply for a classroom or birthday party foods. Many parents bring cupcakes, doughnuts, or cookies for snacks. Schools and teachers can work with parents to develop a list of readily available, inexpensive snacks such as whole grain crackers, ready-cut vegetables, and dried fruit.

Consider Children's Developmental Needs

As with physical activity planning, teaching about good-for-you foods is most effective when teachers consider the developmental needs of young children. For example, children prefer eating small amounts of food frequently. Servings of food should be quite small, about one or two small carrot sticks, a tablespoon of peas, and a quarter of a sandwich. One of the problems in recent years is the increase in portion sizes of many foods. Children should not eat adult-sized portions. Be prepared to serve a food several times before children accept it completely. Encourage children to drink water, and avoid serving too many fruit juices.

Make Nutrition Education a Regular Part of Children's Learning

Many states have laws requiring some form of nutrition education to prevent obesity (National Conference of State Legislatures, 2007). All teachers, however, can plan nutrition education activities as a regular part of the curriculum and integrate these activities into language arts, music, physical education, and even math and science. Teachers should not focus on mathematics or science or literacy as isolated topics, as Chapters 10 and 11 explain. Instead, children can see patterning in foods, can count different food items, and can classify foods into groups. Mrs. Chang's class, for example, toasted whole grain bread, noting the change in how the bread felt after it was toasted. This was a science and language arts activity. She incorporated alphabet knowledge, not with worksheets but with a more active approach by making a list of fruits at group time, noting letters used in making the words.

Consider the benefits of cooking with children. Cooking is a high-interest, highly motivating activity, whether the children simply toast bread or cut up and mix fruit in a salad. What matters is that they are actively involved in learning about a topic—healthful food—in an enjoyable way, the essence of developmentally appropriate practice. Any

Children like to cook, which helps them learn about healthful eating in an enjoyable, active way.

nutrition education activity should be accurate, evidence based, and free of bias. Gaining accurate knowledge requires that a teacher gain necessary information before planning a lesson and not just using a ready-made lesson plan if it contains material unfamiliar to the teacher (OFSTED, 2004).

SUMMARY

Children's physical and motor development is predictable. Some of the expected patterns that we see in this domain include.

- Distinct patterns in the children's growth rates and changes in their body proportions. The rapid growth rates during infancy are followed by slower rates after age 2. Regarding body proportion, an infant's head is a large percentage of his total body length, but by the preschool years his body has lengthened, with his head a smaller percentage of overall height.
- Windows of achievement, or normal ranges, for gross motor skill development during which a typically developing child, for example, sits with support, crawls, stands alone, or walks. Fine motor skill development is also predictable with windows of achievement for skills such as reaching, grasping, or picking things up with two fingers.

A child's brain has a major influence on gross and fine motor development. The development of the brain itself accounts for the predictable progression of gross and fine motor skills.

- A newborn's brain is only about 25% the size of an adult's brain and is most developed in the regions controlling bodily functions such as breathing, sucking, and sleeping.
- Control of muscles of the neck, arms, hands, and legs is possible only when other regions of the brain, such as those allowing control of motor pathways, develop. One part of the brain related to motor development is the motor cortex, which controls motor neurons that direct muscles attached to hand, feet, and leg bones. The cerebellum controls arm and leg movement as well as balance and posture.

- Myelination of axons connecting neurons also contributes to the orderly progression of motor development. This gradual process of insulating axons allows them to conduct messages about movement through the brain and motor pathways very quickly, allowing children to move with increasing grace and coordination.

In spite of its predictability, the quality and path of a child's physical growth and motor development can be affected by several factors. Two of the many factors explained in this chapter are

- Poor nutrition during prenatal development and the first several years after birth places children at risk for problems with brain development, growth problems, and poor motor development.
- Obesity and being overweight, having too much fat in proportion to one's height, places children at risk for poor physical health as well as for social and emotional problems.

Teachers can support children's healthy physical and motor development in many ways, including:

- Teachers should reflect on their personal beliefs about nutrition and physical activity because their beliefs influence what they actually do when working with children.
- Teachers encourage physical activity by designing their classrooms to encourage movement and by providing equipment for climbing, throwing, and other large motor skills. They can also help children develop fine motor skills with items such as pegboards, puzzles, art materials, and small items for building.
- Teachers can make nutrition education a regular part of the curriculum, helping children acquire healthful attitudes about food and eating.

QUESTIONS FOR REFLECTION

1. Mr. Hernandez arranged a small yoga and exercise center in the large group meeting space of his K-to-2 classroom. The children use this space for yoga during center time. The children know basic yoga poses, starting large group times with yoga or stretching and slow breathing. They also go to the yoga center and other exercise corner individually at least once each day. Some children use it even more frequently. Think like the teacher. What would he say are three good reasons for providing children with regular physical activity?

2. Explain, based on what you have read in this chapter, the effects of eliminating recess in schools.

APPLY YOUR KNOWLEDGE

What Should This Teacher Do?

1. A teacher who is interested in helping children develop healthful eating habits gets a note from a parent about bringing in birthday treats. The parent says that she will bring in cupcakes with frosting. What would you advise that the teacher do? How could the teacher have prevented this problem?
2. The school board has proposed taking away recess so that the kindergarten and first graders ". . . will have more time for academics." Teachers are opposed to this move. Write a statement including at least two benefits to children's physical and motor development from recess that the teachers could deliver to the school board. Give reasons for your statements.

KEY TERMS

Body mass index (BMI), 179
Cerebellum, 170
Developmental coordination disorder, 172
Document, 174
Extremely low birth weight, 176

Fine motor development, 167
Gross motor development, 167
Growth charts, 167
Motor cortex, 170
Myelin, 171
Myelination, 171

Physical abuse, 176
Physical neglect, 177
Stature, 176
Window of achievement for gross motor skill development, 167

WEB SITES

Center for Disease Control (CDC)
http://www.cdc.gov/ncbddd
Information about developmental milestones in all domains. Type "milestones" in the search box for a list of sites about developmental milestones mentioned in this chapter.

Childhood Obesity
http://www.ncsl.org/programs/health/ChildhoodObesity-2005.htm#raising
Web site for the National Council of State Legislatures.

Occupational Therapy Organization
http://www.otworks.ca/otworks_page.asp?pageID=611
This is a site written by an occupational therapist's professional group. Excellent site for teachers searching for ways to help children with developmental coordination disorder. Many suggestions and helpful links.

Preschool Activity Guidelines
http://www.aahperd.org/Naspe/template.cfm?template=ns_active.html
Preschool Activity Guidelines of the National Association for Sport and Physical Education.

Young Rembrandts
http://www.youngrembrandts.com/About/
An art education program. Search in this site for information on the link between drawing and a child's brain development.

Zero to Three
http://www.zerotothree.org
One of the most reputable sources on early brain development for teachers of very young children. Click on "hot topics" and then on "brain development." Highly recommended.

CHAPTER 8

Using Assessment to Support Children and Families

GUIDING QUESTIONS:

- **What are the goals, benefits, and uses of assessment?**
- **What are some appropriate forms of assessment?**
- **What do we mean by ethical and responsible assessment for young children?**
- **What is an assessment partnership with families?**

INFANT/TODDLER
Nick Makes Contact

Mr. Bjornrud recorded two observations about 2-year-old Nick. The first is that Nick went quickly to his father who arrived to pick up Nick. The second is that Nick observed the parent of a child new to the class. Then, Nick showed the new adult his book.

PRESCHOOL
Wet Sand Is Cool

Ralph zoomed to the trays of wet sand set on the writing center table. He worked in the sand for almost the entire morning work session, pressing his hands into the sand, drawing with his fingers, and finally, forming his name. Mrs. Chang took his picture as he worked and asked him to tell her about what he was doing. She recorded his words, later transferring them and the photo to a documentation panel about working with wet sand. She also posted a small sign that said, "Here are the State Standards that we met with our wet sand exploration" and then listed several standards.

KINDERGARTEN/PRIMARY
Authentic Assessment for Your Children

Mr. Hernandez was meeting with the parents of the children in his classroom. The parents had just completed a checklist of their child's interests. The teacher described the assessment methods that he proposed using, including gathering samples of children's work, writing selected anecdotal records, using a few teacher-made checklists, getting information from parents, and pulling all this together in a portfolio. Then he explained why he thought that getting samples of children's work was important and described how he would use the samples of actual work in talking with parents about children's learning and progress. Parents took an anecdotal record form home and were to observe their child and record what they observed.

Clearly we have entered an age of standards, testing, and accountability, resulting in ever-increasing testing of young children (FairTest, 2007; Guddemi & Case, 2005). **No Child Left Behind (NCLB),** Public Law (PL) 107-110, requires formal testing for all children in public school, including those in early childhood. Head Start, a program primarily for

**No Child Left Behind
(Public Law 107-110)** The reauthorization of the 1965 Elementary and Secondary Education Act. Its purpose is to ensure answerability and flexibility for education.

Assessment Systematic procedure for obtaining information from observations, interviews, portfolios, projects, tests, and other sources that can be used to make judgments about characteristics of children or programs.

children from low-income families, has also felt the push for accountability. Head Start was required, in its 1999 reauthorization, to implement learning standards in literacy, language, and numeracy skills. Starting in 2003, Head Start was required to test all 3- to 5-year-old children in the program on these skills at the beginning, middle, and end of the school year. Teachers, therefore, must understand the role of standardized testing, but they also need to know about more appropriate, performance-based assessment. Such knowledge enables teachers to use multiple sources of assessment, the most appropriate way to evaluate a child's development and progress (New Jersey Office of Early Childhood Education, 2005).

This chapter focuses on early childhood **assessment,** the ". . . process of observing, recording, and otherwise documenting the work children do and how they do it, as a basis for a variety of educational decisions that affect the child, including planning for groups and individual children and communicating with parents" (Bredekamp & Rosegrant, 1992, page 10). We examine and emphasize a teacher's role in the assessment process, the gathering of information about children. We also focus on a teacher's main assessment responsibility—to identify and build on a child's strengths (Utah Education Network, 2003). To that end, you will learn about forms of assessment that are particularly beneficial for young children and about how to include parents in the assessment process. To support young children and families through appropriate assessment, effective teachers of young children must (Hyson, 2003; NAEYC, 2001)

- understand the goals, benefits, and uses of assessment.
- know about and use appropriate assessment tools and approaches, including observation and documentation.
- understand and practice responsible assessment.
- know about assessment partnerships with families and other professionals.

GOALS, BENEFITS, AND USES OF ASSESSMENT

A teacher's overall professional mission is to support all areas of children's development and learning. To this end, teachers do everything in their power to nurture children's development and to help them become successful learners. Everything that we do as teachers should flow from this professional mission, including how we use assessment.

We begin this section focusing on the goals, benefits, and uses of early childhood assessment. The following types of assessment will be discussed in this chapter:

- Authentic assessment (also called performance assessment): performance-based; children apply their skills and knowledge in a real-world setting
- Developmental screening: initial screening/evaluation of developmental domains–health, motor, social-emotional, language, and cognition; done to make referrals for in-depth assessments
- Functional assessment: looking for each child's individual way of accomplishing specific purposes, such as mobility or communication
- High-stakes testing or assessment: testing in which some decision rests on the results of one test, such as when a child's entry into a gifted class depends on one test
- In-depth assessments: performed by trained individuals; follows up on initial, developmental screenings

- Informal assessment: using anecdotal and running records, checklists, rating scales, children's work samples, and interviews of children to evaluate children's progress
- Strength-based assessment: appraisal aimed at identifying and building on a child's strong points

Goals of Assessment

Assessment should be **strength based**, aiming to identify and build on a child's strengths (LeBuffe & Naglieri, no date). There are three major goals in responsibly used assessment in early childhood education. The first is to support every child's development and learning. The second goal is to communicate with and to support families. The third is to evaluate the quality of programs, curricula, and services offered to children.

Suppose, for example, that you observe that one of the children in your class shows advanced understanding of concepts in mathematics. You document your observations and communicate your observations to the principal, who advises that you speak with the parents. They tell you that they already know that their child is "smart," but that they had no idea about the "math thing." You want to support this child's gift and offer to get information about/assistance the school can offer their child.

Strength-based assessment Appraisal aimed at identifying and building on a child's strong points.

Benefits of Assessment

Appropriate assessment benefits every person involved in the process. Teachers work in a system with administrators, including principals or directors. They work with children and parents. Anything affecting one system member also affects other parts of the system. A change in one classroom system member affects other parts of the system. Children, teachers, administrators, and parents, therefore, are affected by and gain from appropriate assessment.

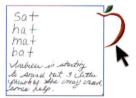

Go to MyEducationLab and select the topic "Observation and Assessment." Under Activities and Applications, view the artifact *Three Letter Phonetics Assessment (Preschool)* and observe how Isabelle's teacher uses assessment to plan curriculum.

Children Benefit from Appropriate Assessment

One of the biggest benefits for a child is to go to school, develop, and learn in an effectively planned environment. Appropriate assessment helps us to create such a setting. Policies and practices affecting assessment, curriculum, and teaching in effectively planned environments clearly focus on children's best interests and developmental abilities or limitations. The curriculum, for example, is entwined with assessment because teachers decide on what children need to learn by assessing what children already know and can do and what children still need to learn. Then teachers decide on how to teach, choosing instructional strategies based on what they know about their group's response to different strategies.

Children also benefit from assessment because they learn about **self-assessment** (Utah Education Network, 2003). Their teachers help them to evaluate their own work, feelings, and effort. A teacher might ask children, for example, to say how they feel or might interview a child about how difficult an activity was for that child. This sort of activity ultimately reinforces their critical thinking and decision-making attitude and skills.

Self-assessment Children learn how to evaluate their own work, feelings, and effort.

Mr. Hernandez followed up the PowerPoint presentation (Teach Intentionally box) with a request for the children to write the action/linking verbs that they got right in their journals. Then, he asked them to list the words on which they still needed to work.

TEACH INTENTIONALLY

Verbs, Zebras, and Computers

What the teacher did: Mr. Hernandez wanted to help his second graders understand different types of verbs, specifically action and linking verbs (Carnes, 2005; Illinois State Board of Education, 1997). Action verbs such as run, walk, or eat, convey actions received by an object. For example, zebras eat grass (the object). Linking verbs such as are, am, is, link a subject of a sentence with a word that completes it. For example, the zebra is an animal. He discovered, through assessment, that many of the children did not understand the difference between these verbs. He also knew that almost all of his children enjoyed working with the computers, and he wanted to weave instruction about verbs with the children's current project on zebras. Therefore, he and the second graders developed a PowerPoint lesson on the two types of verbs with zebras as the focus. They chose the clip art and worked with the teacher to write sentences containing the verbs.

How the teacher was intentional: He assessed the children's need to learn about the verbs guided by the learning standard in his state. He chose an instructional strategy, using the computers, because of high interest in this technology. He was intentional when he worked with the children to develop a PowerPoint presentation about the verbs. He deliberately integrated language arts learning about verbs into a project about which the children were extremely interested. He followed the advice of early childhood theorists Dewey and Piaget in purposely designing an active learning environment.

Teachers and Administrators Benefit from Appropriate Assessment

Teachers also benefit when they assess children appropriately—they *get a good picture of children's development*. Teachers who observe and document children's thinking, language, social skills, physical and motor development, and how they handle emotions can plan for a child's emotional development much better than if the teacher had not observed and recorded information. Good assessment, then, helps teachers to perform their teaching role more effectively.

Relationships do not just happen; they have to be nurtured. To their surprise and dismay, many teachers have a difficult time establishing or maintaining a good relationship with some children, especially those with challenging behaviors such as hitting or swearing. They feel threatened when a child seems to be extremely angry and aggressive. These disquieting feelings arise because the teacher is anxious and unsure about how to help the child or because normal good guidance strategies do not seem to work. Feeling threatened, a teacher is very likely to change the way that she interacts with a child, often pulling back from children with challenging behavior and might not even be aware of how her

Teachers often interview children as a part of assessment.

interaction has changed. Then the relationship might likely become conflicted, with very poor communication and with escalating bad feelings between teacher and child (Hamre & Pianta, 2001).

How can assessment help in a situation like this? Assessing children's behavior unemotionally and objectively gives information. It allows the teacher to think and to bypass, at least temporarily, the unpleasant emotions associated with observing a child's frequent aggression. It allows a teacher to focus and not to be so emotionally involved, and that is the key to remaining calm and positive in interactions. Observing and documenting challenging behaviors such as hitting, for instance, is the first step in developing a sound guidance plan for children with challenging behavior (Marion, 2004). A teacher can then use the information, thinking, ". . . OK, I can handle this. It is not fun but I can deal with it." Appropriate assessment, therefore, allows a teacher to maintain a closer relationship. *Not* gathering information and remaining embroiled in emotions almost guarantees that a teacher's relationship with a child will deteriorate (Black, 2006; Hamre & Pianta, 2001).

Good information allows teachers to make many other types of decisions and recommendations. They are better able to plan learning experiences tailored to children's interests and needs when they have assessed children's knowledge, skills, and learning-style preferences appropriately. Principals and other administrators also find appropriate assessment helpful in understanding how teachers are meeting state learning standards.

Teachers benefit from collaborating with children, parents, and other professionals in the assessment process. When a teacher interviews children, he begins to understand what children think they know and can do. Teachers gain insight about children by working closely with parents.

Regular education teachers participate in meetings to determine a child's need for special education services, required by the Individuals with Disabilities Education Act (U.S. Department of Education, 2004). This law requires that teams construct Individual Education Plans (IEPs) for children and that the teams include a regular education teacher (IDEA, 0224, section 300. 321, a, .2, rules on Individual Education Plan teams). Teachers gain valuable information about a child's specific needs through such collaboration and they are instrumental in ensuring that IEP outcomes are being implemented and achieved in their classrooms.

Appropriate assessment also helps teachers to live up to their code of ethical conduct. Teachers who believe in the National Association for the Education of Young Children's (NAEYC) Code of Ethics (inside front cover) know that their most important obligation to children is to do no harm in any way. Because high-stakes testing has such great potential for harming children, teachers who understand appropriate assessment essentially prevent harm by planning and using better, more appropriate ways to gather information.

Parents Benefit from Appropriate Assessment

Parents have a genuine interest in what their children are doing and learning, and appropriate assessment gives them a full, rich picture of their child's development and learning. Parents benefit when they collaborate with a teacher in assessing their child. Consider this. Parents know their child in many situations other than school and are, therefore, a valuable source of information about that child's development. For example, how does the child approach new things and people? What does their child really enjoy doing? What is going on in their child's life that might affect him or her in school? Parents know the answers to these questions and can help teachers better understand a child.

Parents who function as members of an assessment team, therefore, may well feel more confident in participating in school activities. They are also more likely to see improved learning and growth in their child (Bredekamp & Copple, 1997; CCSSO, 2004; Shepard, Kagan, & Wurtz, 1998). As partners in the assessment process, parents have a better idea of what they might do at home when working with their child. They know what the school is doing and are able to follow up on the school's activities.

Uses or Purposes of Assessment

Go to MyEducationLab and select the topic "Observation and Assessment." Under Activities and Applications, read the strategy *Understanding Reading Progress* for a look at how teachers can assess children's reading behaviors.

There are so many decisions to be made about choosing how we assess young children's development and learning. The key determinant, though, is this: What is the purpose of the assessment? The answer to this question drives all other decisions about what should be measured, what method should be used, what level of validity and reliability is necessary, and what stakes are involved. There are several purposes of assessments for young children (Shepard et al., 1998).

- To plan curriculum to meet children's individual developmental and learning needs
- To identify individual children who might need focused programs or interventions
- To evaluate effectiveness of services and programs
- To assess academic achievement and to hold individual children, teachers, and schools accountable

Plan Curriculum for Development and Learning

Here, the major purpose is to support children's development and learning. The main audience for the assessment is the teacher, but parents are also part of the audience. Some school systems use a readiness assessment test or a screening battery or set of tests that evaluates a child's readiness for kindergarten (Maxwell & Bryant, 2000).

For 3 to 5 year olds, teachers concentrate on using informal assessment strategies such as anecdotal and running records, checklists, and rating scales; examining children's work samples; interviewing children; and talking with other school personnel and parents about children. They use information gained to decide what to teach or how to help a child with a specific domain of development. For 5 to 8 year olds, teachers use both formal and informal methods of assessment but still concentrate on informal methods. Teachers in both groups communicate with parents about what children know and can do.

Informal assessment
Using anecdotal and running records, checklists, rating scales, children's work samples, and interviews of children to evaluate children's progress.

The major technical requirement for **informal assessments** is a working knowledge of child development, which allows teachers to see where a child's response might lie in a range of development.

For example, Mrs. Chang knew that her 4 to 5 year olds could recognize an array or group of items, but they can probably recall only three or four of the group of 12 items. This knowledge helped her to use a checklist to identify Serena as operating beyond the normal memory capabilities of this age because the child recalled seven of the items.

This developmental approach to assessment helped parents understand their child's good memory is an asset and they can work with their child to build on this strength.

Identify Children for Focused Programs or Interventions

This assessment is used to spot a child's need for additional help or services and then to get those services for the child. The audience is the teacher, others working with the child, and the parents who must know about their child's needs. There are two levels of assessment here: developmental screening and in-depth assessment.

Developmental screening ". . . is a procedure designed to identify children who should receive more intensive assessment or diagnosis, for potential developmental delays. It can allow for earlier detection of delays and improve child health and well-being for identified children" (Center for Disease Control and Prevention, 2005). The Individuals with Disabilities Act requires states to identify infants and toddlers who have developmental delays and to provide services to them. This acknowledges that severe disabilities are often evident very early in a child's life and developmental screening is the first step to identifying a potential problem.

Developmental screening is recommended for all children within 3 months of entering an early childhood program. Such screening is recommended for every developmental domain—health, motor, social-emotional, language, and cognition (NAEYC, 2006). Screening for health problems includes tests for vision and hearing, which are often mandated for children of different ages. The state of Michigan, for example, requires hearing and vision screening at several grade levels, including preschool and first and third grades, and makes it available to younger children through the special education department of local school districts.

Great care must be taken with developmental screenings. They should be used *only* to identify children who might need a more thorough assessment and to make referrals for more in-depth assessments. Screenings are far less reliable than more in-depth assessments and are usually administered by persons without special training in test administration or diagnosis of developmental problems. A technician who does hearing or vision screenings, for example, usually is not qualified to diagnose problems in this area. Likewise, teachers are licensed as teachers but usually *not* qualified or licensed to diagnose problems. For a teacher to make such a decision is unethical.

Also unethical is using developmental screenings as the main determinant for placing children in any special education program. Identifying children for special services is a serious matter. One must be as accurate as possible so that children are not placed in a special needs category when they are not in need of special services and that children with true special needs get the appropriate help.

A two-step process—developmental screening followed by an in-depth assessment—therefore, must be done with great care. An in-depth assessment should be done as soon as a potential problem is suspected, but developmental screening usually comes first (Shepard et al., 1998).

In-depth assessments must be done by trained specialists. A licensed speech pathologist, for example, would do an in-depth assessment to decide whether a child has a communication disorder (New York State Department of Health, 2002). Similarly, audiologic (hearing) in-depth assessments are conducted by credentialed or licensed audiologists (American Speech-Language-Hearing Association, 2004). These assessments must meet high standards for validity and reliability. They should be conducted in the family's primary language to avoid confusing a language difference with disability. In-depth assessments should also focus on gathering information on the child at home as well as in school.

Developmental screening Initial screening and evaluation of developmental domains—health, motor, social-emotional, language, and cognition; done to make referrals for in-depth assessments.

In-depth assessments Performed by trained individuals; follows up on initial, developmental screenings.

Evaluate Effectiveness of Services and Programs

The first two purposes focused on children themselves. Here, the purpose shifts to gathering, combining, and using data about children in groups. Because the data come from groups of children, the assessment information is used to make decisions about group or educational programs, not about individual children. The audience consists of professionals who make education and social policy decisions, and the combined information can help to document whether programs are meeting stated outcomes and standards.

Assessing Academic Achievement and Accountability

Here, the purpose is to hold teachers and children or schools accountable for specific outcomes in learning, mentioned about the No Child Left Behind Act at the beginning of this chapter. This type of assessment is usually ordered by the federal government, in the case of No Child Left Behind, a school district, or some other agency and usually consists of administering a **standardized test** to each child. Unlike authentic or informal strategies for conducting assessments, standardized testing is a different method for measuring children's progress and performance, which is usually also known as **high-stakes** assessment because *specific* people are affected. Teacher retention and salary raises may hinge on the results of a mandated assessment in which the results of that teacher's classroom are reported to the public. A child's placement in a special needs class or in a gifted class may depend on the results of the mandated assessment in which the results are reported for that individual child. The stakes in such testing and assessment are indeed very high.

There is and has been, for quite some time, general agreement within the early childhood profession that standardized testing of young children that is used to make high-stakes decisions is highly *in*appropriate (Genishi, 1992; Katz, 1997; Meisels, 1993) and should never be used to rank or sort children in any way (CCSSO, 2004). The three main concerns about standardized testing for young children are

1. Standardized tests are administered to groups of children, most often in paper and pencil format. There is a time limit for the test, and testers usually read questions only one time. Children are required to sit still, listen to questions or statements, and make marks on a paper, all highly inappropriate for children under the age of 8.

2. Standardized tests often have a negative effect on an early childhood curriculum. In the first purpose of assessment (described earlier), teachers use informal assessments such as observation and evaluating children's work samples to make curriculum decisions. Teachers who know that their class is to be tested with a standardized test might design the curriculum so that it prepares children *for that test*. Such a curriculum is not based on what children need, their interests, and their abilities. It is based, instead, on the content of the standardized test. This is often referred to as "teaching to the test."

3. Some people have used the results of standardized tests unethically. For example, the tests have been used to sort children for special education or gifted classes or to keep them out of a school.

Standardized test Test that is given, scored, and interpreted in a standard way.

High-stakes testing or assessment Testing in which a decision rests on the results of one test, such as when a child enters a gifted class.

CHECK YOUR UNDERSTANDING
Your Thoughts on Standardized Testing

You have read about the use of standardized testing in schools today. What do you think of high-stakes testing, and what do you think are the implications for the future?

APPROPRIATE ASSESSMENT: OBSERVATION

Authentic assessment involves observation (NAEYC, 2006). At times, when you observe, you want to write an account, a narrative, about what you see. Two major narrative methods for observing include anecdotal records and running records. At other times, you do not need to write an account about what you observe; this is a nonnarrative method. Two major nonnarrative methods of observing include checklists and rating scales. Checklists and rating scales do not tell a story, but they are very useful for gathering specific information quickly. This section focuses on each of these four methods for observing.

Authentic assessment (also called performance assessment) Performance-based; children apply their skills and knowledge in a real-world setting.

Anecdotal Records

An **anecdotal record** is a brief, open, narrative method for observing. This is a favorite method among early childhood teachers because it is efficient and easy to learn and to use. An anecdotal record is a *brief* record of some aspect of a child's development or learning. Teachers observe an incident and record essential elements with just enough detail to give a snapshot, a concise description. This narrative is like a short story, giving just enough detail to recall the incident easily.

Anecdotal record Usually consists of brief written notes about an incident; like a snapshot.

Anecdotal records are *open*, meaning that teachers may observe a variety of behaviors or interactions or almost any aspect of children's learning or development. One teacher might observe how children join groups, and another observes a child's ability to recall important facts.

An anecdotal record is a *narrative* form of observation. The teacher, the narrator, intends to tell a story, although a short one, with anecdotal records. The teacher describes a series of incidents or just one incident or some aspect of development in enough detail so that the record may be useful later when actually using the observation, say, for making a curriculum decision or for consulting with a parent. The whole purpose of writing anecdotal records is to be able, on some future occasion, to pick up the observation, read it, recall the incident clearly, reflect on it, and use it to plan for the child. The anecdotal record usually has a beginning, middle, and end with events being described in sequence.

This student teacher is observing, a form of authentic assessment.

Anecdotal records can be planned or spontaneous. A planned set of anecdotal records would be useful in many cases. For instance, a second-grade teacher planned to do anecdotal records of each child's grasp of the method for writing haiku poems. A kindergarten teacher, over a week's time, wrote anecdotal records of each of her children's ability to use words to express strong emotion.

Teachers make good use of anecdotal records when they have the opportunity to observe spontaneous incidents that they did not intend to assess but that would reveal quite a bit of good information about a child or the curriculum. For example, Mr. Hernandez noted that Lewis always gravitated to the books about animals on trips to the library. He made a brief note and placed it in Lewis's file. Then, he used information about Lewis's interest in animals to plan and started placing more animal-related books in the classroom library.

FIGURE 8.1   Anecdotal Record Format

Goal for this observation:

Setting:

Date/day:

Time of day:

Basic activity:

Focus child:

Others involved:

The anecdote:

Reflections/Interpretation:

Advantages and Disadvantages of Anecdotal Records

Anecdotal records have some clear advantages. Anecdotal records help teachers to do many things. They help teachers understand child development; assess a child's interests, needs, and abilities; make good decisions about guiding children; and plan or evaluate curriculum. Anecdotal records are *straightforward*, a time-honored and dependable observation method. Observation, to be realistic, must be woven seamlessly into a busy teacher's schedule and anecdotal records are favored for this quality. A teacher can do anecdotal records without being separate from classroom activities and without breaks. The flow of teaching can continue uninterrupted.

One can develop hardcopy forms for observing as shown in Figure 8.1, can record on a digital voice recorder, and can use a laptop or desktop computer. An even simpler method is also shown in Figure 8.2 in which a teacher uses sticky notes. As with any method, teachers need to protect children's privacy and keep all observation records completely out of public view.

Anecdotal records are easy to learn to use. Keeping key guidelines in mind makes it more likely that an anecdotal record is good and useful (Marion, 2004). Guidelines include writing observations as soon as possible after the incident, recording only data,

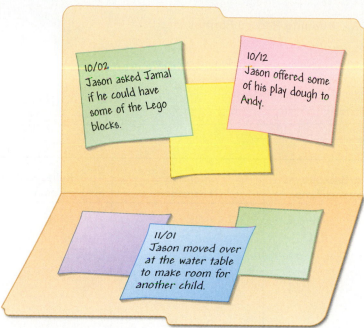

FIGURE 8.2   Anecdotal Record Done on Sticky Notes

describing the setting, writing enough detail to get a clear picture of the incident, striving for objectivity, and interpreting carefully and without bias.

There are potential disadvantages associated with anecdotal records. One shortcoming is that this method captures only a snapshot and is, therefore, not a complete reflection of the child's overall behavior. Another is that observers can make biased and opinionated statements. This usually happens when observers forget to look beyond their initial impressions of a child. A child who frequently grabs things from other children is worthy of observation. Suppose, though, that a teacher thinks that this sort of behavior is selfish and embarks on a series of anecdotal records. The teacher, predisposed to see any grabbing behavior through the lens of grabbing = selfish, would likely not even record evidence that the child also shares things. This adult would likely make a biased statement such as, "Gina is so selfish. Look at all of the examples of her taking things from other children that I've recorded."

Another disadvantage is that interpretations may be invalid. An observer might make several anecdotal records and then conclude what is simply not supported by the data. This problem is a real one, but teachers go a long way toward avoiding it when they stick to recording only facts or hard data and leaving opinion out of their observations.

Running Records

Figure 8.3 shows the format for a **running record** which, like an anecdotal record, is an open, narrative method. Unlike anecdotal records, however, as illustrated in Figure 8.4, a completed running record is a slightly longer observation and very useful when a teacher needs to record more detail than is possible with anecdotal records. More detail helps a teacher understand some aspect of development. The typical running record takes only about 5 to 10 minutes to complete. Notice that Figure 8.4's observation took 9 minutes and recorded much information about Kenny's play.

Running record A longer, open narrative method for observing; tells a longer story; gives more detail.

FIGURE 8.3   Running Record Format

Running Record

Focus: _____

Date: _____

Context/Background Comments/Time	Intensive Observation	Reflections or Comments

Interpretation:

Running records are more effective when the observer has a clear focus. Looking at the entire classroom can be overwhelming—one must start with a clear focus. A clear focus centers the observer's attention, allowing her or him to pay attention to some specific aspect of classroom life and less attention to others. Observers can focus on one child, the overall group, one activity, interest center, or play material, or the teacher. The teacher in Figure 8.4 focused on the play and social interaction of one child.

The format for a running record shows three main columns: the context and background comments, the intensive observation, and reflections or comments. The context and background section give a clear idea of the setting. Include information about the setting, people involved, your impression of the mood of the group, and the child's activity. Include starting and ending times.

The intensive observation column provides space for an accurate, objective, detailed description of an incident, describing children's actions and speech as well as how they *seem* to feel. The third column is for reflecting. Analyzing every comment or action is not necessary or desirable, but making sensible and well-thought-out reflections is advisable. Avoid making judgments or interpreting here.

The interpretation section at the bottom of the page is left blank until the observer completes all other parts. Even then, making an interpretation is not always advisable. The teacher in Figure 8.4 did not write an interpretation but did write very brief, objective reflections. One must look for patterns in behavior, which may take more than one running record to do so.

Writing Objective Observations

It is important to be objective in all parts of an observation. Therefore, the goal is to write objective statements and to avoid subjective statements, when describing the setting, writing the intensive observation, reflection/comments, or the interpretation sections. An *objective* statement gives the facts or data. The descriptive language in an objective statement describes or tells the reader what the observer saw or heard. A *subjective* statement, on the other hand, gives the observer's opinion which is not an appropriate observation strategy. Here are examples of each.

Subjective: "Sam is always so happy when he arrives at school." The observer has not recorded any data supporting this judgment. Contrast this with the next, more objective statement.
Objective: "Sam smiled and waved hello to the teachers and to every child in the room when he arrived today, just as he has done every other day this week." This statement gives data and not opinion.

Subjective: "Josiah was disruptive during story time today." What does "disruptive" mean? The writer has given no data to support such a conclusion and has been judgmental as well.
Objective: "Josiah stood up suddenly during the story. This was not a part of the story and the children had not been asked to stand up. He said, 'Pop goes the weasel!' and then sat down. This, too, was unrelated to the story."

Subjective: "Ralph dislikes carrots." The writer has not given any data. What gave him or her the idea that Ralph dislikes this vegetable?
Objective: "Ralph looked at the carrot sticks on his napkin. He picked one up with thumb and forefinger, holding it up and far away from his face. His eyes were closed and his face was scrunched up. He said, 'Yuck!' " This statement gives facts, clues about words, facial expressions, and statements which are all consistent with the emotion of disgust.

FIGURE 8.4   Running Record Observation (Focus: One Child)

Focus: _____

Date: _____

Context/Background Comments	Intensive Observation	Reflection/ Comment
8:02 a.m. Background comments/context: Kenny is a slim but solidly built 4-year-old. He is one of the tallest children in his class. His dark brown hair is very short all over. He has bright dark brown eyes. I would say that Kenny appears to be a healthy, strong, sturdy child. Yet, he moves gracefully. He seems to be alert all the time and he smiles easily. Today, he wore clean shorts, a tee shirt, sneakers, and socks. His dad told him to leave his cap in his cubby. This incident took place indoors, at the water table, just after arrival time. It was August and was hot. About half the class was there and children chose an activity after saying good-bye to parents. (8:04, end of background comments.)	8:04 Kenny's dad had just left after bringing Kenny (K) to school. K kept his cap on. Dad had told K, "A gentleman does not wear his hat inside, K. Put your cap in your cubby." K complied with this limit and then waved good-bye to his dad. He then made a beeline to the water table, which contained several boats. Ritchie (R) and Sam (S) were there. S was already playing in the water with a boat and R, also wearing an apron, was watching S play. K quickly put on an apron and stationed himself on one side of the table. "I'm gonna play with this boat," he announced to the other children. "It's a ferryboat. Toot, toot . . . it has to go pick up the people on the island." After that announcement, Kenny said nothing as he slowly steered his ferryboat through the water, from one end of the water table to the other end. He turned from the table, went to a nearby shelf to get some small plastic figures of people, and then returned to the water table. "Time to get into the ferry! Time to go to the mainland. Toot, toot." He ferried the passengers to the other end of the water table. "Everybody out, please. Watch your step. Careful there, Sir." K picked up each figure and placed it carefully on the ledge of the water table. The teacher (T) had heard this whole episode and now smiled. "Did you visit your Grandma this weekend, Kenny?" (K's grandmother lives on a nearby island and K and his family visit her often, riding a ferry to and from the island.)	Did not argue with Dad. Complied with the limit. Kenny seemed to be eager to get to the water table, to play. Unlike Ritchie, K did not hesitate to play. He jumped right in and then became absorbed in his play. K seems to understand the role of ferryboat captain.

FIGURE 8.4   (cont.)

8:11 (K and R continued to play ferryboat captain for several more minutes and then K left the water table for the dramatic play area where he put on a ferryboat captain's jacket. He then sat at the steering wheel and piloted the ferry to the mainland.)	"Yep, we did. We rode on the ferry. The captain saluted at me and I saluted back! My Grandma gave me a cookie that was still warm. The chocolate chips were all gooey!" He looked away from the T and bobbed the boat in the water. "Toot . . . toot. We have to make another trip now. Bye." K looked over at S and said in a deep voice, "Wind's blowin' up. Do you have any passengers over there for my ferry? We're leaving soon for the island. All aboard!"	K's play is based on a real experience, an experience that seems to have been a pleasant one for him.
	K piloted the ferry across the water table a few more times and seemed to be absorbed in this play. Ritchie, a child with Down syndrome, had moved closer and closer to K. K looked surprised (and angry?) when R reached for K's ferryboat. "No, Ritchie! I'm playing with the ferryboat now. I had it first. You have to wait until I'm done." K looked at R who had backed away quickly and who looked as though he might cry.	K imitated the captain's voice. His memory seems to be well enough developed so that he remembers the exact words as well as the sound of the captain's voice.
	K did not just go right back to playing but stopped and talked to R. "I'm sorry, R. Here's a good boat for you to play with. It's just like mine." R perked up when K picked up the other boat, gently took R's hand, and placed the boat in R's hand. K; "Let's make boat sounds together, toot . . . toot!" Put your boat right next to mine, R. That's good. Now, make the boat sound, toot . . . toot!" R never did make the sound but steered his boat along with K's boat, R looking at K frequently. Whenever K said, "Toot-toot!" R smiled.	K's expression of his frustration was positive and nonaggressive. K showed empathy. K even put the boat in R's hand. K did not get frustrated with R when R could or simply did not make the boat sounds. K just played with R in the way that R seemed able to play.
Interpretation:		

Source: From *Using Observation in Early Childhood Education* (pp. 74–75), by M. Marion, 2004, Upper Saddle River, NJ: Merrill/Prentice Hall. Copyright 2004 by Pearson Education. Reprinted with permission.

Writing even the *interpretation* section objectively is important, too. An observer who chooses to write an interpretation of the events remains objective in this section. For example, after observing Sam with several anecdotal and two running records, his teacher concluded:

> "Sam seems to enjoy most activities at school. He anticipates outdoor play, participates cheerfully in art and music, and leads his cooperative work group."

Advantages and Disadvantages of Running Records

Running records, like anecdotal records, have understandable advantages. With an ample amount of observing time and its sharp focus, a running record includes a couple of major advantages. First, *more details are possible*. Carefully observing for several additional minutes enables observers to record more facets of a child's behavior than is possible with shorter methods. Second, *a variety of behaviors can be documented*. More time for observing allows observers to see unfolding of behavioral sequences. Figure 8.4 shows that Kenny chose his activity, complied with a limit, interacted with his teacher, interacted with other children at the water table, reenacted a real ferryboat ride, and asserted himself nonaggressively. The observer also saw Kenny behave in a way that most reasonable people would label as compassionate.

The major disadvantage of this method is that *the teacher cannot interact with the children* and someone else must work with the children. A second disadvantage is that the *observer's attention is divided*. Writing a running record requires observers to write, type, or speak into a digital video recorder while continuing to observe. As the observer records, he or she also watches and has to remember what is seen. While this might seem like a simple thing to do, it is not: The observer is actually dividing attention between looking and recording, possibly affecting what the observer recalls about an incident (Iidaka, Anderson, Kapur, Cabeza, & Craik, 2000).

Checklists and Rating Scales: Nonnarrative Methods for Observing

Often, teachers do not need to write an account or give much detail, but must assess quickly some behavior or characteristic. Checklists and rating scales are useful in this case.

Checklists

Checklist Nonnarrative method for observing; an inventory of characteristics or behaviors that can be checked as observed.

A **checklist** is an inventory, a *shortcut* method because it bypasses most of the details in an incident (Genishi, 1992). A checklist merely checks development and progress; it takes an inventory of a child's or a group's development and progress.

When observing young children, the teacher looks over the list of characteristics or behaviors. As the teacher observes a group of children, he or she notes whether each child shows a listed characteristic or behavior. The teacher records a check if a child shows the behavior or leaves a blank space if the child does not yet show it. A checklist is an efficient way to determine the presence or absence of a behavior (Beatty, 2005).

Teachers can observe one child, an entire group, or several children on a single checklist. Checklists can be used to observe every domain of children's development.

For example, Mrs. Chang documented children's gross and fine motor development with a checklist and Mr. Hernandez documented his first graders' ability to use emotion words to express their feelings. Checklists can also be used to observe children's progress, such as with handwriting, uses of commas, or question marks. In this case, a checklist may be used several times to track children's progress. The Work Sampling System (Meisels, 1993) is a prime example of a checklist used three times during the year. Using checklists like this allows a teacher to document children's strengths and success as well as curriculum areas needing improvement. Figure 8.5 is an example of a checklist documenting how a child expresses stress.

FIGURE 8.5   Example of a Checklist for Observing Stress

Checklist: How _____ Exhibits Stress

Children can show stress in a number of ways. Check any boxes that pertain to this child and give a brief explanation for each choice.

Date: _____

☐ **This child's reactions to stress seem to be passive**
    Excessive fatigue
    Withdrawing and putting head on table or desk
    Excessive fears

Explanation:

☐ **This child's reactions to stress seem to be more active, with behaviors that involve only the child**
    Nail biting
    Manipulating one's hands or mouth
    Repetitive body movements

Explanation:

☐ **This child's reactions to stress seem to show up when s/he interacts with others**
    Stuttering
    Bullying, threatening, or hurting others
    Nervous, inappropriate laughter

Explanation:

☐ **This child's reactions to stress seem to show up as s/he works with objects**
    Excessive squeezing or tapping of pencils, markers, crayons
    Clumsy or fumbling behavior

Explanation:

Source: From *Using Observation in Early Childhood Education* (p. 265), by M. Marion, 2004, Upper Saddle River, NJ: Merrill/Prentice Hall. Copyright 2004 by Pearson Education. Reprinted with permission.

Advantages and Disadvantages of Checklists

There are several advantages to using checklists. A teacher can readily observe several children and children would not be aware that they were being observed. Checklists are easy to implement and specific developmental or skill-based areas can be targeted. Teachers can readily see an individual child's experiences and abilities.

The disadvantages are that teachers may rely on a checklist as the only indicator of a child's progress. Checklists do not give information about the quality of a behavior. For example, it might indicate that a child can run but does not say how he ran—gracefully or awkwardly—or if he enjoys running. Checklists do not give information on how frequently a child does something. A teacher checks, for example, that a child plays circle games outside with other children, but that does not tell how often the child plays this way with others. There is also a risk of personal bias because there are no data supporting the judgment. Finally, a teacher cannot get a true picture of a child's developmental level.

Rating Scales

Rating scale Nonnarrative method for observing; a listing of activities or characteristics; calls for a summary judgment.

Like a checklist, a **rating scale** is a shortcut method in observing young children because the adult summarizes observations and makes a *summary judgment* about a child's performance. Rating scales do not call for recording original data. Rating scales are a very good choice when teachers simply need less information and do not need original data.

A rating scale is a listing of characteristics or activities such as how a child expresses anger. The observer marks the observation sheet to show how she or he rated that child, for example, on how often he "strikes out when angry." Ratings can be numerical or descriptive. Figure 8.6 shows a descriptive rating scale, because it uses words such as *always* or *occasionally* rather than numbers to indicate the teacher's judgment. A teacher using a rating scale cannot show the quality of a child's performance but can show how much of something he observed. For example,

> Mr. Hernandez had done a brief series of anecdotal records on how each child dealt with anger. He prepared for parent meetings by developing and using a rating scale to show his judgment.

Figure 8.6 is also an example of a *forced-choice rating scale*. An observer reads each descriptor of a child's behavior or performance and then chooses the *one* phrase that most accurately describes how a specific child does something. The observer, therefore, has been forced to choose one of the descriptors. The observer indicates the choice by circling the chosen phrase as Mr. Hernandez did in Figure 8.6.

Advantages and Disadvantages of Rating Scales

The advantages are similar to those for checklists. A rating scale is a timesaving, efficient method. It is easy to use and a very good way to pull together a series of observations to arrive at an overall judgment.

The disadvantages are that rating scales carry the risk of personal bias when there are no data supporting the teacher's judgment and that many raters simply rate children at the midpoint on the scale. When this happens, the rating scale is useless. Still another potential issue lies in the descriptors in the scale: They might be unclear, making them open to interpretation by whomever is using the rating scale. For example, one rater might see the descriptor "often" in one way while another rater would see the same word in a different way.

FIGURE 8.6   A Rating Scale on How a Child Manages Anger

Graphic Rating Scale: How ___Tim___ Manages Anger

Reflecting on your observations of this child, rate how she or he manages the emotion of anger. For each statement, choose the rating that best describes this child and circle the appropriate spot on the scale. Write a brief narrative in the *Comment* section. Use this information when you write your observation report of this child's development.

Child's Name: _____

Date: _____

	Always	Often	Occasionally	Seldom	Never
Uses words appropriately to express anger				⊙	
Strikes out when angry		⊙			
Name calling when upset			⊙		
Expresses anger appropriately toward teachers			⊙		
Expresses anger appropriately toward other children				⊙	
Generates word labels for frustration and anger				⊙	

Comment:

Source: From *Using Observation in Early Childhood Education* (p. 271), by M. Marion, 2004, Upper Saddle River, NJ: Merrill/Prentice Hall. Copyright 2004 by Pearson Education. Reprinted with permission.

Event Sampling

Event sampling is a formal method of observing children's behavior. Teachers use this method most effectively when they are interested in one specific aspect of the curriculum or a child's development. The observer identifies the specific category such as "participates in center time" and then carefully defines the category. For

Event sampling Formal method for identifying specific categories of behavior.

example, a teacher defines *participates in center time* as showing focused attention on one or more centers in the time allotted and using helpful social skills. The teacher then observes the child's stream of behavior and records only instances illustrating the defined behavior. Event sampling gives teachers information about a child's developing abilities (Brassard & Boehm, 2007).

The teacher uses a preconstructed form to record a narrative in enough detail about the event to give an accurate portrayal (Bentzen, 2004). Figure 8.7 shows that the form

FIGURE 8.7   Event Sampling Form for Recording Observations

Focus of the observation. The "event" that I am looking for is:	
Date: day of week/date	
Time:	
Antecedent event: what happened before the event?	
Describe the event	
Results: what happened after the event?	

contains space for recording the time, what came right before the event, the behavior, and what happened because of the behavior. After gathering several examples over a reasonable period, the teacher has a better view of this aspect of the child's social and emotional skills. Then, the teacher has vital information for planning how to help the child.

Advantages and Disadvantages of Event Sampling

The major advantage with event sampling is that teachers focus on something quite specific. They tend to concentrate on only this aspect of the curriculum or development, which gives their observation a sharper focus. In addition, they can comment on the quality of what they see. Disadvantages include possibly unclear definitions of the category, which could lead to inaccurate observations. Event sampling is, however, still the teacher's written view of an event and can be biased if the teacher simply ignores data.

Time Sampling

Time sampling is a methodology that deals with a smaller sample of a child's total stream of behavior. The teacher records only a small part of the behavior (Bentzen, 2004). It is often used to record the types of activities in which a child engages or his interactions with other children or adults in a typical day at school (Olmsted, 2002).

An observer uses a form similar to that in Figure 8.8. The objective is to choose the total time allotted for the sampling period, for example, 10 minutes. That block of time is divided into segments of equal length. The observer then observes the child for a designated portion of the segment. The observer sets a limit on the number of seconds (or minutes if observing that long) for each of the observations.

> **Time sampling** Observes uses a limited time period for a specific behavior, recording whether it occurred.

Advantages and Disadvantages of Time Sampling

Time sampling requires less preparation than event sampling and requires less writing than running records or event sampling. The teacher does not have to pay attention to the same child for an extended period. This method also gives an estimation of a behavior rather than documenting every instance. After, an observer who completes a number of sampling periods would be able to graph the designated behavior and would have a good idea about a specific child and this observed behavior. A clear disadvantage is that in time sampling, an observer can miss important examples of a given behavior if it occurred outside of the designated time for watching. The teacher also has to stay focused and pay attention to timing so that he observes at the correct time for each interval.

APPROPRIATE ASSESSMENT: DOCUMENTATION

One of the basic tenets of the Reggio Emilia philosophy of early childhood education, explained in Chapter 2, was **documentation**, which refers to using evidence of children's work and thinking. Photos and interview notes, for example, authenticate or provide "proof" of what exists. Documentation, an essential and logical companion to observation, is an important element in the learning and assessment process that focuses on how children get to their understandings of concepts (Bennett, 2001; Fu, Stremmel, & Hill, 2002; Gandini & Goldhaber, 2001).

> **Documentation** Using evidence of children's work to reflect on what children are thinking and where they need to go next.

Methods for documenting children's development and learning include children's work samples and products, documentary displays, observation reports, and portfolios. Teachers use the material gathered to reflect on what children are thinking and where they need to go next as well as where any gaps in children's understanding exist (Chilvers, 2005; Hertzog, 2001; Katz & Chard, 1996; Stegelin, 2003).

FIGURE 8.8   Time Sampling Form

Observer's Name: __Jim Hernandez_____

Child's Name: __Tim_____

Date: January 24   Start time: 8:45 a.m.

Behavior Observed: Talking to another child during the first 30 minutes of choice time.

Total observation time: 30 min.	How long is each interval? 3 minutes	How long will I observe in the interval? 10 seconds, at the beginning of the interval
Interval#	Did the behavior occur? (Record Yes if the behavior occurs and No if it does not occur)	Total number of times that the behavior occurred for this observation time period
1	Yes	
2	Yes	
3	Yes	
4	No	
5	No	*Tim spoke with another child 6 times during the first 30 minutes of choice time.*
6	No	
7	Yes	
8	Yes	
9	Yes	
10	No	

Source: Based on *Special Connections.* Retrieved on July 7, 2008, from http://www.specialconnections.ku.edu/cgi-bin/cgiwrap/specconn/index.php.

Children's Work Samples

Work sample A child-produced item serving as evidence of performance.

A **work sample** is a child-produced item. Work samples are an example of *performance assessment* (Meisels, 1995) with the actual item produced by the child as evidence of her performance. Work samples include children's writing, their poetry, artwork, examples of their math work, photographs of children's work (block structures, writing or drawing in sand, math manipulatives), reading logs, audiotapes, dictations or transcriptions of children's conversations or interviews, self-portraits, songs written by a child, and videotapes. Teachers usually include those items that seem most relevant for each child. Any item should help a teacher understand and reflect on the child's thinking and progress. Teachers should collect samples of children's work from all curriculum areas.

Teachers occasionally collect the same work sample from each child when they want to document the same aspect of development for every child (Gullo, 2004). For example, Mr. Hernandez collected writing samples from all of his second graders at the beginning of the school year and then periodically throughout the year. He wanted samples from each child so that he could document change in writing over time. At other times, teachers collect work samples from individual children to document some aspect of that child's development or progress. Mr. Hernandez collected Josiah's drawings of polar bears, the work sample, after the teacher realized that this child was so interested in this particular animal.

Documentary Displays

Schools in the Italian municipality of Reggio Emilia have rekindled interest in displaying children's work and documenting children's thinking and understanding (Rinaldi, 2001). A **documentary display** visually represents children's past and current experiences in the classroom. The Reggio documentation panels attest to the view that the *classroom is a teacher*. A Reggio-inspired documentation panel uses the wall space in a classroom to convey a visual, artistic message about the room—that every part of the room should be an important part of the child's education.

In contrast, every inch of many classrooms in American schools is covered with precut, craft-type items or cartoonish figures. The walls in a Reggio classroom, with carefully constructed documentation panels, are both beautiful and a vital part of discussion, thinking, and reflection on classroom learning and activities (Tarr, 2004).

Teachers might display photographs, video prints or video tape, teacher notes explaining the illustrations, samples of children's work and transcripts of interviews with children, and children's comments about their work. In one school, carefully planned documentation panels promote staff inquiry and a sense of collaboration among teachers. They viewed their experience of incorporating documentation into their classrooms as an emotionally and intellectually challenging experience, requiring reflection from individuals and the group of teachers (Goldhaber & Smith, 2004).

Creating documentary displays tells children that teachers value their work. Preparing and displaying children's work and words encourages teachers and children to revisit the experience, clarifying and strengthening understandings in the experience. Such displays also make it easy to convey solid evidence to parents about the mission and curriculum of the school. Showing is much easier than telling a parent how a school is meeting state standards with visual evidence through a documentary display.

Documentary display
Photograph of childrens' work and interviews with children that represent their experiences in the classroom.

CHECK YOUR UNDERSTANDING
Using Documentation

Before proceeding with your reading, apply what you have just read. Look at the chapter opener vignette, "Preschool: Wet sand is cool!" How has the preschool teacher engaged in documentation? Name three ways in which this type of assessment is likely to benefit the child involved.

Observation Reports

Observation report
Written summary of observations of a child.

An **observation report** is a written summary of observations of a single child (Carbonara, 1961; Cohen, Stern, & Balaban, 1996). The teacher brings together all anecdotal or running records, checklists and rating scales, as well as any other form of observation. He then reflects on different aspects of the child's development and progress and summarizes them in the form of a report. A well-done observation report conveys a concise, clear picture of a child's development.

Observation reports *summarize and document development*. Teachers observe different domains of development. The report summarizes the observations and enables teachers to focus on and convey information to parents about many aspects of their child's development, such as how their child works with materials, how she or he approaches other children, and how the child deals with pleasant and unpleasant emotions. A summary report requires that a teacher read and reflect on the many observations and bring coherence to them in the form of a summary report.

Observation reports *document positive aspects of a specific child's growth*. Good assessment implies making a judgment and a carefully done observation report includes a teacher's written judgment about a child's growth in different developmental domains. Teachers do not ignore areas in which a child needs help, and they avoid just saying, "Everything is fine." Instead, they report findings, document positive change, and say it in a nonjudgmental way. For example, Mr. Hernandez wrote this as a part of second grader Patrick's observation report.

> At the beginning of the school year, we observed that Patrick did not seem to enjoy independent reading. We noticed a major change after he started writing in his journal. His journal started to include little notes about books that we read as a group.

Observation reports can also *document problems and challenges*. Children face different issues and problems as they grow and develop. Teachers use observation as the first step in helping children deal with problems. A periodic or final observation report should include information about such problems. You met Trina, a child in Mr. Hernandez's primary class. Trina has developmental coordination disorder, and her teacher observed the following example of her problems with small motor skills:

> Trina has trouble gripping writing instruments, such as pencils, pens, chalk, or markers. She grips them in her fist and writes or draws with jerky movements.

Observation reports *should make recommendations*. A child's new teachers and parents can benefit from reading summaries of development, but they also need to get well-reasoned recommendations from a child's teacher (Cohen et al., 1996). Parents and teachers can then work together to help a child with such recommendations. A child's new teachers can follow up on work begun the year before to continue to help a child. For example, Mr. Hernandez recommended the following for Rico:

> Rico has shown good progress in the "stop and think" strategy. We still remind him to stop and think and he does this willingly and now comes up with the words to say how he feels. We are convinced that Rico will continue to manage his emotions well if adults continue to help him.

Observation reports *should point out exceptional or extreme behavior or development*. Teachers are not licensed to diagnose major problems, but we can observe and document behaviors indicating that a child might have some troubling issue. Teachers gain confidence in thinking about extremes in behavior if they work with school specialists such as guidance counselors or school psychologists. Extremes in behavior such as cruelty to animals, excessive expression of anxiety or fear, pretending to set fires, extreme aggression, or extreme passivity often signal that a child needs help. Documenting the behavior is the first step in getting help for the child.

Portfolios

Portfolio assessment is a form of authentic assessment using a collection of a child's actual work along with teacher assessments. Teachers should consult with children about artifacts, items that the child wants to place in the portfolio to show what he knows and what he can do. The teacher reflects on the contents of the portfolio to evaluate the child's development and progress and to make decisions about the curriculum and guidance for that child. Portfolios are an authentic or performance-based method of assessment because they contain real-world observations and documentations of children in multiple settings—the observations having been done over time.

Portfolio assessment is beneficial for children, teachers, parents, and administrators. Children learn how to evaluate themselves in the course of portfolio development, and this ability is important in positive and realistic self-esteem. Getting to choose one's own work samples for the portfolio, learning to evaluate one's own performance, and having a teacher who takes the time to construct a good portfolio contribute to a sense of control, a sense of competence, and a sense of worth, all building blocks of self-esteem (Marion, 2007). Teachers who use portfolio assessment for children gain better knowledge about their students, have a good base for developmentally appropriate practice, and gain a good starting point for talking with parents. Parents see good evidence of their child's development and progress when they look at their child's portfolio. Portfolio assessment is also meaningful for principals and other administrators. It shows that teachers have documented children's meeting of curriculum goals and district standards.

Portfolios contain child-produced materials and teacher-produced materials. Child-produced materials are the work samples described earlier. A portfolio is not simply a scrapbook stuffed with all sorts of drawings and writing samples. Portfolio contents should be chosen wisely, focusing sharply on the "end" or major goal of documenting the child's development and progress. While children's work samples are the core of a portfolio, a teacher's reflection on the items gives the portfolio coherence. Teacher-produced portfolio items include the adult's analysis of the work samples and transcribed interviews of children on their work as well as the teacher's observations or observation report. To make the portfolio immediately understandable to parents, teachers organize the portfolios with a brief statement of purpose and a table of contents.

Portfolio assessment
Authentic assessment using a collection of a child's work samples along with teacher assessments.

Go to MyEducationLab and select the topic "Observation and Assessment." Under Activities and Applications, watch the video *Portfolios* for an example of a child who analyzes her own progress in writing with her teacher scaffolding her understanding.

ASSESSING INFANTS AND TODDLERS

Assessing infants and toddlers is as important as it is with older children during early childhood.

Reasons for Assessing Infants and Toddlers

Reasons for assessing very young children are the same as for the older group (Dichtelmiller & Ensler, 2004). Assessment allows teachers to understand an infant or toddler's development, an essential step in developing a positive and warm relationship with a child. For example, careful observation would reveal the things that upset a specific toddler and would allow a teacher to help the child.

Understanding what infants and toddlers are capable of doing also allows teachers to make individual plans for them. For example, a teacher who documents that an infant's independent walking, walking without holding on to anything, would plan individual activities for him, such as sitting facing him and encouraging the child to walk to the teacher.

Developmental information is also useful to parents who want to know if their child is developing normally. As noted in this chapter, monitoring development allows teachers and parents to identify areas of concern that might need in-depth assessment.

Effective teachers build partnerships with parents. Acknowledging parents as partners in observation and assessment communicates a teacher's willingness to work together for their infant or toddler's welfare. It also tells them that the teacher values them as team members dedicated to documenting their child's strengths and to optimizing his development.

Problems with Assessing Infants and Toddlers

Teachers who understand child development also understand the challenge in assessing very young children. Infants and toddlers, even though they are competent and capable, have limited language, attention, memory, emotional, social, and mobility skills. Very young children do not talk, so interviewing them is out of the question. Even a toddler's emerging language does not allow him to verbalize thoughts, feelings, likes, and dislikes as older children can. Likewise, they simply cannot pay attention to directions and requests as an older child might. They experience emotions but do not know how to manage them yet, increasing the chances of their becoming extremely upset if a teacher asked them stop playing for an assessment.

Functional assessment
Looking for each child's individual way of accomplishing specific purposes such as mobility or communication.

The problem, then, is to assess infant or toddler abilities with these challenges in mind. We do not get good information by asking them to perform specific tasks. For example, an adult asks a very young child to put a cube in a container, a specific task. While this might sound like a good idea, it relies on asking a child with limited language and self-control to perform a task requiring both.

Many developers of infant and toddler assessment systems prefer to focus on a different approach—the **functional assessment** that involves observing and documenting children's abilities in natural settings as they go about their day. The children are not asked to do a specific task, but observers record information about how individual children achieve their purposes, for example in communicating their needs or in connecting with others (Dichtelmiller & Ensler, 2004; Meisels, Marsden, Dombro, Weston, & Jewkes, 2002).

Appropriate assessment of infants and toddlers is done in natural settings.

The Ounce Scale

The Ounce Scale is an example of functional assessment that assesses social and emotional, cognitive (including language), and physical development (Florida Children's Forum, 2004; Meisels et al., 2002). It is an ongoing assessment, meaning that teachers observe an infant or toddler over time, not just for one or two times. Teachers observe the child's functional accomplishments in the domains listed with the observational record, a method for recording brief notes about the child's development. Teachers then use data and information to plan individual activities for the child or to plan activities to build a relationship.

Another part of the Ounce Scale is the family album in which parents record their observations of their child's development. The third element is the developmental profile, derived from the observations in the observation record and the family album. The Ounce Scale, therefore, provides multiple sources of information, observes over time, and includes a child's family in the assessment.

CHECK YOUR UNDERSTANDING
Assessing Infants and Toddlers

Explain what is meant by *functional assessment*. How has the teacher in the toddler vignette at the beginning of the chapter used functional assessment? Why do you think that this is an appropriate way to assess infants and toddlers?

RESPONSIBLE AND ETHICAL ASSESSMENT OF YOUNG CHILDREN

Our goal as teachers is to engage in responsible and ethical practice in all phases of our work with children and families. This goal certainly applies as we consider methods of assessing children's development and progress. This section focuses on how a federal law affects our commitment to ethical assessment and on guidelines for ethical and responsible assessment of young children.

Federal Law Affects Assessment Practices

Public schools for young children are currently required by federal law to use standardized testing with young children. The No Child Left Behind act requires standardized testing as the only method of assessment of a school's progress toward meeting *adequate yearly progress* described in the act. Thus, whatever a teacher or a school might believe about appropriate assessment, they might also be required to assess children in a way that violates recommendations from major professional organizations and study groups.

The NAEYC feels that authentic, performance-based testing is preferable to standardized testing for young children. NAEYC's Code of Ethical Conduct, P-1.5 states, "We shall use appropriate assessment systems, which include multiple sources of information . . ." The Code of Ethical Conduct is in the Appendix. One of the leading teacher's organizations has challenged the testing requirements of No Child Left Behind. They propose that schools use more than test scores to measure student learning [National Education Association (NEA) 2006].

Guidelines: Responsible and Ethical Assessment of Young Children

The NAEYC's 2003 Position Statement gives specific guidelines on appropriate, responsible, and ethical assessment of young children. The main recommendation is to make valid, reliable, and appropriate assessment a regular feature of all early childhood programs. NAEYC (2003, 2005), CCSSO (2004), and Gullo (2004) give critical indicators of responsible assessment.

Assessment practices are *based on ethical principles.* For example, a child's placement in a class for gifted children would not be made based on one standardized test. Assessments are not used to sort children in any way. Assessment instruments are *used only for their intended purpose.* Teachers do not use assessment instruments for other purposes if the assessment has not been validated for such a purpose.

Assessment instruments are *age appropriate* and are *linguistically and culturally appropriate.* Native speakers of an English language learner's home language review and translate assessment instruments published in English into a child's home language. The translators should understand the complexities of assessment and translation. Translation must be done with care and the understanding that the results may not be accurate.

Assessments must be *appropriate for children with disabilities.* Such assessments must also include decisions about whether to assess children with disabilities and any accommodations necessary to meet the test of fairness (Destafano, Shriner, & Lloyd, 2001).

Assessment instruments *meet strict and high standards for technical quality.* When a school does decide to use screening tools or individual norm-referenced assessments, the items chosen must meet the highest standards of professional groups, which set standards for assessment instruments. Good assessments minimize chances of misinterpreting results—they are valid, reliable, and fair. *Valid* assessments measure what they are supposed to measure. For example, a valid assessment for vocabulary does not assess spelling. *Reliable* assessments yield the same outcome every time that they are given, produce the same outcome with a similar group, and produce the same result regardless of who does the assessments. All of this means that the assessment can duplicate the results. Assessments that cannot do this are not reliable. *Fairness* implies an evenhanded approach to assessment. Any child assessed, therefore, would have an equal opportunity to get a good assessment. All children assessed should have had an equal opportunity to gain the knowledge or skill assessed. The assessment should be free, to the extent possible, of gender or cultural stereotyping (North Central Regional Educational Laboratory, 2007).

Teachers assess *educationally and developmentally significant topics.* Irresponsible assessment examines a narrow sets of skills. Responsible assessment is associated with learning standards and curriculum goals, and these are based on the teacher's observation of children's needs, abilities, and interests.

We *use evidence from assessment* to understand learning, to improve children's knowledge, and to identify children's learning style. We acquire greater understanding of all children in our classes, including children who face challenges such as those learning English or who have special needs. Our assessment-based knowledge can and should be translated into curriculum and activities appropriate for specific children in our classes.

Responsible assessments are *done in realistic settings*, come from many sources, and are done over time. Responsible assessment relies on systematic and ongoing observation and documentation of children in the classroom setting.

Screening assessment is *always tied to follow-up.* As discussed earlier, screening and in-depth assessments are quite different and a screening assessment is never used to diagnose problems.

Use of individually administered, norm-referenced tests is limited. A **norm-referenced test** (standardized test) compares a child's score on the test against the score of a group who has taken the test, often called the *norming* group. Any time scores are reported in this way, "Janie scored in the 95th percentile," the score is from a norm-referenced test. Examples of norm-referenced tests often used in kindergarten, primary, and elementary schools are the Cognitive Aptitude Test, Comprehensive Test of Basic Skills, and Iowa Test of Basic Skills.

Screening assessment
Used to identify children who might need a more thorough assessment.

Norm-referenced test
Standardized test comparing a child's score on the test against the score of a group who has taken the test.

BUILDING ASSESSMENT PARTNERSHIPS WITH FAMILIES AND OTHER PROFESSIONALS

Strength-based assessment focuses on identifying and building on children's strong points or assets and communicating with and supporting families. Real assessment partnerships with families include parents in the whole process of assessment (NAEYC, no date), as Mr. Hernandez demonstrated in the kindergarten/primary chapter opening vignette.

Parents are actively involved in assessment partnerships. The school communicates with parents about all aspects of assessment. Parents are encouraged to share observations of their child's behavior and interests from home, and teachers offer observation reports to parents periodically. The school regularly schedules parent-teacher conferences, which allow teachers and parents to discuss a child's development, learning, and progress. They use conferences to make plans for meeting a child's specific needs.

The school-family partnership develops an assessment plan that best meets a child's needs and that is culturally and linguistically sensitive. Families have accurate information about all assessment methods and know the specific methods used.

For example, in the kindergarten/primary vignette Mr. Hernandez discussed with parents how he would write anecdotal records in his classroom. The parents had a copy of an anecdotal record form and would do an anecdotal record on their child at home.

The parents understood what an anecdotal record was, how Mr. Hernandez would use anecdotal records, how he would interpret them, and how he would use the observations to communicate with them and to plan for their child's specific needs. The teacher developed a handout on the advantages and disadvantages of anecdotal records and on how he would attempt to use this method in the best way possible. Schools provide parents with clear information on confidentiality. Mr. Hernandez, for instance, explained how he kept his anecdotal records confidential and explained to parents who could and who could not read his notes. The school discloses regulations about who has access to a child's files and about a family's rights in this matter. The school explains how any screening or assessment information would be used and interpreted.

SUMMARY

The field of early childhood education has entered an age of standards, testing, and accountability. The focus of this chapter is appropriate assessment, which is a systematic way of getting data from many sources including developmentally appropriate observations, portfolios, and projects.

- Assessment should be strength-based and aim to identify and build on a child's strengths. The goals of assessment are to support children's development and learning, to communicate with and support families, and to evaluate the quality of programs, curricula, and services offered to families.
- Children, teachers, parents, and administrators all benefit from appropriately conducted assessments.
- Assessment is used to plan curriculum, to identify individual children who might need focused programs, to evaluate effectiveness of services and programs, and to hold different parts of the system accountable for meeting standards.

Observation is a form of authentic assessment. There are many ways to observe, some involving telling a story and others not. Each method has advantages and disadvantages.

- Anecdotal and running records are narrative types of observation. They tell a story with a teacher observing and then recording the observations. Anecdotal records are quite short and running records are longer, allowing more detail to be recorded.
- Checklists and rating scales are nonnarrative types of observation. They do not tell a story but simply check when a behavior occurs or make a judgment. A checklist is an inventory listing specific characteristics or behaviors that a teacher wishes to observe. Rating scales allow teachers to make a summary judgment about a child's performance.
- Event sampling refers to identifying a specific category of behavior and then observing a child's stream of behavior for occurrences of the behavior. Time sampling allows a teacher to observe for specified behaviors within a specified period.

Documentation is a part of appropriate assessment and refers to using evidence of children's work and thinking.

Documentation is a logical and essential companion to observation. Teachers use material gathered to reflect on what children are thinking and where they need to go next. Methods of documentation include children's work samples, documentary displays, observation reports, and portfolios.

Teachers assess infants and toddlers for the same reasons that they assess any other age group; however, infants and toddlers present challenges to teachers in assessment because of their limited language and other aspects of development.

- Functional assessment involves observing and documenting children's abilities in natural settings as they go about their day. They are not asked to perform a specific task, but observers record information about how individual children achieve their goals, for example, in communicating.
- The Ounce Scale is an example of functional assessment for children birth to 42 months. Teachers and parents both observe, and teachers use the information to plan individual activities for each child

Valid, reliable, and appropriate assessment should be a regular feature of all early childhood programs. Some of the critical indicators of responsible assessment are that they

- are based on ethical principles and are used only for their intended purpose.
- are age, linguistically, and culturally appropriate.
- are appropriate for children with disabilities. They must include decisions about accommodations to meet the test of fairness.
- meet high standards for technical quality. They must be constructed to minimize the chances of misinterpreting results.
- are used to assess educationally and developmentally significant topics.
- are done in realistic settings, come from different sources, and are done over time.

Parents are an important part of the assessment process. They should understand all parts of assessments and be encouraged to share observations of their child.

QUESTIONS FOR REFLECTION

1. From your perspective, what are two of the most important benefits from using portfolios in assessing young children?

2. When would a screening assessment be appropriate, and when would an in-depth assessment be appropriate?

APPLY YOUR KNOWLEDGE

What Should This Teacher Do?

1. Read the kindergarten and primary vignette at the beginning of the chapter. Mr. Hernandez has described a good assessment system to the parents. Write an ending to his presentation: "This type of assessment will benefit your child in three ways: 1._____, 2._____, 3._____."

2. Mr. Hernandez wants to assess whether or not each of his first graders can name letters of the alphabet. Explain whether a running record observation or a checklist would be the most efficient and effective tool for this assessment. Give the reason for your choice.

KEY TERMS

Anecdotal record, 195
Assessment, 188
Authentic assessment (also called performance assessment), 195
Checklist, 202
Developmental screening, 193
Documentary display, 209
Documentation, 207
Event sampling, 205

Functional assessment, 212
High-stakes testing or assessment, 194
In-depth assessments, 193
Informal assessment, 192
No Child Left Behind (Public Law 107-110), 187
Norm-referenced test, 215
Observation report, 210
Portfolio assessment, 211

Rating scale, 204
Running record, 197
Screening assessment, 215
Self-assessment, 189
Standardized test, 194
Strength-based assessment, 189
Time sampling, 207
Work sample, 208

WEB SITES

National Association for the Education of Young Children (NAEYC)
http://www.naeyc.org
Main page for the National Association for the Education of Young Children. View the position papers cited in this chapter and other information on assessment.

National Center for Fair and Open Testing
http://www.fairtest.org/facts/nratests.html
Good site for information on different types of tests and assessments and rationales for using or not using them.

National Education Association (NEA)
http://www.nea.org
Home page for the National Education Association. Good site for information on progress of the next reauthorization of the Elementary and Secondary Education Act (renamed No Child Left Behind when it was reauthorized in 2001).

No Child Left Behind (NCLB)
http://www.ed.gov/nclb/overview/intro/guide/guide.pdf
The No Child Left Behind Act is the 2001 reauthorization of the 1965 Elementary and Secondary Education Act.

CHAPTER 9

Supporting Children with Guidance

GUIDING QUESTIONS:

- What are the goals in guiding young children?
- What are some of the major influences on children's behavior?
- What are some of the positive guidance strategies available to early childhood teachers?

INFANT/TODDLER
Emilio Calms Down

Mr. Bjornrud had noticed that 1 year old Emilio was somewhat agitated when he arrived with his dad that morning. Dad said, "There was a fire in the house across the street from us last night, and the sirens and flashing lights scared Emilio."

Mr. Bjornrud realized that Emilio needed help in managing the stress he was feeling from the night before. He spoke soothingly to Emilio, took extra time in helping him eat his snack and lunch, and requested that the assistant teacher accompany Emilio throughout the morning. About halfway through the morning, Mr. Bjornrud noticed that Emilio had stopped biting his lower lip and had relaxed enough to enjoy playing next to his friend Alyssa.

PRESCHOOL
Information for Long-Term Memory

Mrs. Chang had taken digital photos of the children making happy, sad, and angry faces. At large group time, she showed the photos on a monitor, asking the children to identify the emotion on each face.

PRIMARY
Tim Uses Words

This is a mixed age primary classroom, with some kindergartners and first and second graders. "You know, Tim, I heard you use words to tell Luis that your name was next on the list and that it was your turn." Tim gave only the slightest nod upon hearing his teacher acknowledge his efforts but heaved a big sigh as he sat down in front of the computer. As you saw in Chapter 4, Mr. Hernandez has been working diligently on helping Tim learn to manage his anger responsibly and has observed that he is talking more and hardly ever striking out in anger now.

Facing different guidance issues—an infant who is clearly stressed, preschoolers needing information on what facial expressions communicate, and a second grader needing help in getting along with other children—the teachers have all used the developmental approach to deal with each concern. The teachers used their knowledge about children in arriving at guidance decisions, and each was effective because of a positive, trust-building style of interacting with children (Day & Kunz, 2001). They believe in helping children construct their own ideas about things, and they rely on their knowledge of early childhood education theory to develop appropriate learning activities. They do *not* believe in controlling children because of the potential for this to damage the child's own developing self-control. They believe that children are capable and competent. Mr. Hernandez, in the primary grade vignette, believes that Tim *is* capable of learning about emotions and constructing more responsible ways of expressing negative feelings.

In this chapter, we examine essential elements of appropriate child guidance and the major goals in guiding children. We also apply information from Chapter 2 on theories of early childhood education to guiding children. Then, we focus on some of the influences on children's behavior. Finally, we examine some of the most essential, and positive, guidance strategies that competent and ethical teachers use. Effective early childhood teachers believing in the developmental approach

- achieve the goals in guiding children,
- use theories of early childhood education as their base for guiding children,
- understand major influences on children's behavior, and
- understand and use positive guidance strategies.

A TEACHER'S GOALS IN GUIDING CHILDREN

Guiding children is an essential component of effective classroom management. Teachers using the developmental approach have three essential goals in mind when guiding children:

1. Develop positive and supportive relationships with children.
2. Encourage positive social interaction among children.
3. Support children in developing self-esteem, self-motivation, and self-control.

Develop Positive and Supportive Relationships with Children

Teachers build child guidance knowledge and skills, and one of the most important building blocks is our relationship with children. Research tells us that we help children succeed in school and in getting along with peers when we have a warm and caring relationship with them (Pianta, 1992). Vygotsky's theory also suggests the value of a good teacher-child relationship in guiding children. Positive and supportive teachers are highly responsive to what children need and attempt to influence children's behavior in a developmentally appropriate way.

Respond to What Children Need

Teachers responding to what children need are warm, understand child development, and communicate well with children. A warm teacher, whatever the gender, culture, or personal manner, is kind and friendly, communicating genuine liking and respect for children. For example, he or she greets children warmly, expressing sincere interest in their well-being.

We also build positive relationships by understanding child development and having realistic expectations of what children can do. We could expect 4 year olds to be able to verbalize the word *mad* when expressing angry feelings while we would never expect infants to express emotions with words. A primary teacher, on the other hand, might well expect second graders to know several different words to describe the emotion of anger. Mr. Bjornrud, in the infant vignette, realized that Emilio was simply too young to calm himself. The teacher did not expect him to be able to do this.

Finally, responsive teachers communicate effectively, delivering messages simply, kindly, firmly, and consistently, again demonstrating respect for children (Bishop & Rothbaum, 1992). For example, to a child forgetting to pass a snack basket, the teacher might say firmly but kindly, "Vinnie, Carlos is waiting for the apples. Please pass the basket."

Influence Behavior in a Developmentally Appropriate Way

Teachers who develop a positive, supportive relationship with children influence their behavior appropriately. Effective teachers use **limits** to help children understand the idea of boundaries; thus, they state expectations helpfully. For example, at group time, Mrs. Chang showed a picture of a child washing his hands and verbally reminded each preschool child to wash his or her hands before eating. Mr. Hernandez, working with second graders, used a list of written health rules, not pictures, including one about hand washing and asked the children to reread and recap the rule about hand washing. Effective teachers help children cooperate with limits by **explaining reasons for limits**. For example, Mrs. Chang said to Serena who left small plastic pieces on the table and went to the reading area, "I'll hold onto the book you've picked out while you put the plastic pieces back in the tub, Serena (the limit). That way, the next person has a nice clean area for working" (the reason). Finally, teachers *monitor and supervise* children well. They actually prevent many guidance problems because they know what goes on in all parts of the classroom and they provide continuous monitoring with appropriate supervision. Effective teachers are able to *anticipate* possible behaviors as they plan and think ahead.

Limits Boundaries; in child guidance refers to stating expectations for appropriate behavior or using nonverbal boundaries.

Explaining reasons for limits Giving a rationale for why a child should or should not do something.

Encourage Positive Social Interaction Among Children

Teachers can meet this goal by creating a classroom community with a pervading sense of respect, by modeling positive interaction, and by teaching social skills that children need.

Create a Sense of Community in a Classroom

Positive social interaction among children springs from feeling respected and belonging to a classroom community (Bickart, Jablon, & Dodge, 1999) and prevents many discipline encounters (Marion, 2007). Supportive teachers create a community of learners. Children feel at home in their classroom, and their families work as partners with the teacher. The teacher plans the first days of school carefully. For example, Mr. Hernandez contacted families and children and welcomed them, learned children's names, and planned interesting but nonthreatening activities for the first day of school. They help children understand their classroom's organization and routines. Occasionally, they use group time for discussing social skills and for solving problems.

Model Respectful Social Interaction and Teach Social Skills

Supportive teachers understand the power of modeling (Bandura, Ross, & Ross, 1963) and encourage positive social interaction by demonstrating respectful interactions with parents, other teachers, children, and animals. The teacher speaks and interacts with children respectfully and encourages polite and courteous interactions with everyone, including animals.

Go to MyEducationLab and select the topic "Guidance." Under Activities and Applications, watch the video *Promoting Socially Appropriate Behavior in Kindergarten* to see teachers reflecting on how to help children with social skills.

> Aviva and Mrs. Chang fed the hamster together, the teacher talking reassuringly to the animal as they worked. "We have some fresh food and water for you, Fluffy. Excuse me while I remove your bowls."

Chapter 5 explained how to teach social skills, a good way to encourage children's positive interactions (Editors, 2003/2004). Teaching strategies include demonstrating a skill with puppets or with people, discussing with pictures as a starting point, giving direct instruction, providing practice and coaching, and encouraging children for their efforts.

Develop Self-Esteem, Internal Motivation, and Self-Control

Socially competent children have a positive view of themselves, are internally motivated, and are self-controlled.

Self-Esteem

Self-esteem The judgment that a child makes about him- or herself; consists of feelings of competence, control, and worth.

Authentic **self-esteem**—positive, healthy, confidant, and balanced—provides a secure foundation for further growth and development. Early childhood teachers have an opportunity to help children form a healthy and balanced view of themselves (Bakley, 1997). Self-esteem refers to a child's self-evaluation (Coopersmith, 1967; Tafarodi & Swarm, 1995). Initial self-esteem develops slowly in early childhood and tends to be stable (Verschueren, Marcoen, & Buyck, 1998). A child who evaluates herself as competent, in control, and worthy will likely develop a healthy, balanced judgment; she is likely to have predominately positive self-esteem. A child who evaluates herself as unworthy, unloved, and not competent will likely develop a negative view of the self.

The three parts or dimensions of self-esteem are competence, control, and worth.

Competence Ability to meet demands for achievement; an element in self-esteem.

Competence is the ability to meet demands for achievement (Tafarodi & Swarm, 1995). People with healthy self-esteem know that they cannot just wish for competence but that they must work for it. They have earned a positive self-evaluation through the hard work that results in increased competence (Lerner, 1996).

Control Degree to which a child thinks that he is responsible for how things turn out; element in self-esteem.

Control is the degree to which a child thinks that he is responsible for how things turn out (Wong, 1992). High–self-esteem children believe that they do have control and that their actions influence whether or not they achieve a goal. Teaching children how to deal with minor setbacks is a good way to strengthen a sense of control.

Worth Child's general sense of his significance to others; element in self-esteem.

Worth is a child's general sense of his significance to others (Tafarodi & Swarm, 1995). In judging their worth, children evaluate how much they like themselves and whether they think that others like or love them. Children judge themselves worthy when they feel accepted by and deserving of attention from others, such as when a teacher takes the time to help them learn things.

TEACH INTENTIONALLY

A Great Chance to Figure Something Out

What the teacher did: Andy, a kindergartner, doing a science experiment, added food color to white play dough to try to match the sample light blue dough, but he added too much color and got an intensely dark color. Mr. Hernandez asked, "Let's figure this out. What can you do, Andy, to get the color indicated?"

How the teacher was intentional: He took the time to help Andy learn something, which tells a child that his teacher thinks he is worthy of the attention. He did not solve the problem but helped Andy think about it. Thus, he deliberately focused on treating this minor setback as a learning opportunity. This contributes to Andy's sense of competence, that he will make mistakes but that he can also fix them.

Internal Motivation

Teachers also have the goal of helping children develop **internal motivation** or motivation inside one's self. Such motivation drives the rest of cognitive development because a curious, self-motivated child wants to know more about his world and enthusiastically works to discover all that he can. He makes an effort to learn about the people, animals, goings-on, and physical environment that he comes across.

An internally motivated child, therefore, is primarily interested in understanding something new or in acquiring some new skill and is oriented toward learning. In a second-grade classroom, for instance, children encounter a new math manipulative for the first time. Some of the children might become nervous about using this new material. Other children, self-motivated, have confidence that they can use the new item and they expect to perform well on challenging tasks. They gradually develop the ability to realistically analyze tasks and become able to estimate accurately the difficulty of a task (Elliott & Dweck, 1988).

As noted in Chapter 6, many teachers mistakenly believe that lavish praise boosts internal motivation, but it often backfires. Rewards like stickers seem to have the same backfiring effect (Kohn, interviewed by Brandt, 1995). Kohn believes that rewards seem so logical on the surface as they say to a child, "Do _____, and you'll get a _____ (pizza or gold star, for example)." Kohn believes that this approach, however, comes to be viewed as punishment by children in the end. Why would this be so? Kohn notes that nobody likes to have their favorite things controlled by somebody else, and it is this sense of being controlled that children eventually see as punishing.

Internal motivation An inner resource; drives cognitive development; process within a child that kicks off and sustains the search for knowledge and skills.

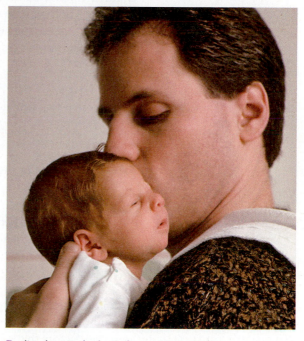

Feeling love is the basis for positive self-esteem.

Self-Control

Self-control or **executive function**, voluntary, internal regulation of behavior, is one of the most significant changes taking place during early childhood. It is an essential part of how children learn, is important in a child's growth and development, and is fundamental in preserving social and moral order (Harter, 1993). Children demonstrate self-control or executive function when they can step back, examine a situation, and then decide how to act. They resist acting impulsively. They refrain from doing something that is inappropriate to the situation, such as talking in a movie. They remember classroom limits and accept them willingly. They can initiate a plan and carry it out.

Two second graders drew a control panel of an airplane and then constructed a panel from recycled materials. The project required 3 days to complete.

Self-control develops slowly, emerging at around the age of 2, and takes several years to develop fully. During this time, children's developing cognition enables them to understand things, their perceptual abilities mature, and they become better able to express themselves. All of this allows them to understand things from a different perspective and gives them access to better skills for controlling their impulses. Self-control evolves haltingly with children demonstrating good self-control on occasion but not always. Finally, self-regulation develops gradually as adults transfer control to children.

Self-control Voluntary, internal regulation of behavior.

Executive function The ability to regulate one's own behavior.

The younger the child, the more a teacher must remind the child to do and remember things, for example, to wear gloves or to wash hands after using a tissue.

Play in Developing Self-Regulation

Play is one of a child's basic needs, as discussed later in this chapter. We have also seen in every other chapter of this book how important play is in children's development. For example, children can learn about their feelings when they play. High-quality pretend play also influences children's cognitive development. Play is also a good way for children to develop executive function. Both structured and unstructured games, a more freewheeling type of play, can encourage children to stop and think, control impulses, regard someone else's view, and understand their part in a group. See Figure 9.1 for play that encourages self-regulation or self-control.

CHECK YOUR UNDERSTANDING
Self-Esteem and Self-Control

Explain to a classmate the difference between self-*esteem* and self-*control*.

Teachers have a better chance of achieving their child guidance goals by understanding factors influencing children's behavior. Let's look at some of those influences.

INFLUENCES ON CHILDREN'S BEHAVIOR

It can be difficult to target specific causes of a child's behavior, such as why one child hits another or why another constantly interrupts group meetings. However, there are some key factors that can *influence* such actions. Some of the major influences on children's behavior include the following:

- child development, including brain development,
- disabilities,
- basic needs, whether and how they are met, and
- adult's caregiving style.

Child Development

Chapters 4 to 7 describe and explain growth during early childhood, including the role of brain development of emotional, social, cognitive, and physical development. Teachers who achieve the goals of guiding children build on that knowledge, believing that child development affects guidance. For instance, a preschool teacher might want to support children in learning how to work through disagreements with others. She knows that preschoolers get better at looking at things from different perspectives as they get older and if someone teaches them how to deal with disagreements. Although all aspects of child development affect a teacher's guidance, some developmental trends are especially helpful when making guidance decisions, including abilities to

- listen,
- remember things, and
- take another's perspective.

FIGURE 9.1   Play: A Great Way to Develop Executive Function

Play is not a luxury in early childhood. It is essential to children's health development in all domains. Play is a good way to help children develop self-control. Listed are some types of play.

Social, Interactive, Pretend Play

- Requires planning, concentration, decision making, sticking with something, imagination, and occasionally complying or agreeing with something important to somebody else.
- Child-devised props encourage creativity and planning.
- Teachers can certainly provide some props as well.

These children are learning to stop and think, control impulses, and see different points of view as they play.

Reading and Acting Out Stories

- Shows good print examples of impulse control as children observe perseverance in stories.
- "Mike Mulligan and His Steam Shovel" or "The Little Engine That Could" are examples.

Games

- Games such as "Duck, duck, goose" require that children think about actions. For example, a child has to think about whom to tap for the "goose" role.
- "Simon Says" requires that a child *not* do something, which is very difficult for children to do, but this game is a safe and enjoyable way to practice.

Other Play Activities Requiring Planning

- Young children plan when they put things together such as building a Lego structure.
- Older children can build from patterns that are more complex. For example, the older children in Mr. Hernandez's class met the challenge of putting together a prefabricated play structure for cats. This had many different parts with written instructions and drawings. They later donated the structure to a cat rescue group.
- Cooking and following recipes requires self-control and planning.
- The Responsive Classroom model described in Chapter 2 uses Academic Choice with primary-grade children. Children engage in a *plan-do-review* sequence for work time. This is an active learning and play-based approach to learning and teaching. Children make specific plans, carry them out, and then review what they have learned.

Source: Based on Spiegel (2008).

Ability to Listen

Listening Paying attention and trying to understand what a speaker says.

Listening refers to paying attention and trying to understand what a speaker says. It is fundamental in guidance, for example, when a child listens to a teacher's directions or limits. Listening skills develop gradually during childhood with young children not really understanding what good listening is. Older children realize that good listening requires trying to understand what another person says, but during early childhood, children assume that sitting quietly is good listening (McDevitt, 1990; McDevitt, Spivey, Sheehan, Lennon, & Story, 1990). Young children do not know how to clarify their understanding of what they hear (McDevitt, 1990), as illustrated in the next example in a kindergarten group.

> "Listen carefully," said Mr. Hernandez as he told the 5 year olds the procedures for a fire drill. Though they sat still and seemed to be listening, the teacher discovered during a practice fire drill only 5 minutes later that several of the children did not seem to have understood what he had said.

A child who cannot clarify a speaker's meaning is very likely to act on his flawed understanding. We adults and older children might ask a question to clarify a speaker's meaning, such as "Did you want every person in each group to turn in a separate paper or do you want the group to turn in one paper?"

As with most skills, children must learn and practice good listening skills. Teachers can do some practical things to help children get better at listening. Mr. Hernandez focused on these developmental issues in learning to listen as you can see in Figure 9.2.

FIGURE 9.2   Understanding Developing Listening Skills: What It Means for Guiding Children

Teach Children What "Paying Attention" Means

- Mr. Hernandez taught the kindergarteners that part of paying attention means to focus on what someone is saying.
- "I want you to listen to my words because I have to tell you something important."

Present Small Amounts of Information

- Young children remember guidance information if they are not overwhelmed by too much information.
- Mr. Hernandez gave them only three, but crucial, things to remember after they heard a fire bell: stop what you are doing right away; line up at the classroom door; follow the teacher.

Teach How to Clarify What a Speaker Says

- He said to the group, "I just showed you three pictures of what we do when the fire bell rings.
- "What's the first thing?" Pang, "Go to the door?" Teacher, "That's one of the steps but not the first."
- "Look at the chart. The first thing is . . . ?" He also told the children that "it was good to ask him a question if they did not understand something that he said."
- Pang then asked, "Do we have to have a partner when we stand near the door?"

Ability to Remember Things

"Oh, no. Here we go again," thought Mrs. Chang as she watched an angry Ian shove Vinnie for pushing ahead of Ian in line. As she turned to the two boys, she wondered once again if her lessons about "using words when you are angry" would ever sink in for Ian.

Memory, explained in Chapter 6, is the basic cognitive process by which children store information and then later retrieve it, as Mr. Hernandez's kindergarten children do with fire drill information and as Mrs. Chang's class does with the skill of using words when angry. A child's memory capacity and skills are critical pieces of the guidance puzzle for teachers because they want children to remember many things, such as using words when upset.

A child's memory develops gradually. Newborns are equipped to recognize familiar objects, and young infants can recall a familiar object like a mobile but usually only when they get a reminder about the object such as Dad moving the mobile. Memory improves between the ages of 1 and 3 years (Howe & Courage, 1993) but develops dramatically for children who are 4 to 12 years old. Children's memory improves as space for short-term memory increases in their brains and as they gain more knowledge about the world (Schneider & Pressley, 1989).

Long-term memory, as explained in Chapter 6, is the storage area for knowledge and skills acquired during a lifetime. In terms of guidance, children draw on their accumulated knowledge and skills in interacting with others. Children's long-term memory, evident in infancy and the toddler years, becomes even better as children acquire knowledge about the world and simply have more information to store in long-term memory. Individual children in classrooms have had different experiences, some of them having learned and stored helpful ways of interacting with others and others having acquired and stored unhelpful or even aggressive knowledge and skills.

The preschool vignette at the beginning of the chapter illustrates Mrs. Chang's intentional teaching aimed at helping her 4 year olds with their memory. She shows them visual images of different facial expressions of emotions and this helps them to acquire helpful knowledge about emotions. They will be able to draw on that knowledge when they interact with others in the future.

Teachers have many opportunities to guide children well by focusing on memory development. A child's ability to recall things from long-term memory is a plus because, as we teach children helpful ways to interact with others, they store each memory and then later call forth and use what they learn. At the same time, some children who have acquired *un*helpful knowledge and skills, such as hitting when angry, call those memories forth as well. These unhelpful skills are very strong, often overshadowing new, more helpful teacher-taught skills like using words to express anger (Freeman, Lacohee, & Coulton, 1995).

Mrs. Chang, clearly frustrated that Ian is still remembering and then using the harmful strategy of hitting when angry, also knows that it will take more time and practice to help him.

Figure 9.3 gives suggestions for early childhood teachers who want to make it easier for children to remember helpful ways of relating to others. Mrs. Chang uses Vygotsky's advice about the importance of teacher-child discussion in helping children construct new ideas.

FIGURE 9.3   Understanding Developing Memory: What It Means for Guiding Children

Discuss Things with Children

- Mrs. Chang has used several different ways of talking about "using words" with her preschoolers—conversations with individuals and small or large groups and dictation of their successful use of words to express irritation.

- Vygotsky believes that talking about issues helps children develop internal language that they later use to guide themselves when faced with the need to express strong emotion.

- Talking about how using words to express emotions helps children recall the appropriate strategy later because they have stored the lesson in verbal form (Reese & Fivush, 1993; McDevitt & Ormrod, 2004).

Actively Involve Children with Things That They Need to Remember

- Mrs. Chang did a puppet show in which one puppet learned to use words when angry, and then she left the puppets in a learning center for children's practice.

- Mr. Hernandez's class practiced the fire drill procedure.

Teach Children to Use Memory Strategies Like Rehearsal or Repetition

- Mr. Hernandez taught the children to rehearse the steps in responding to the fire bell by repeating: stop, walk, follow.

- The children repeated the three steps several times: Stop what you are doing, walk to the classroom door, and follow the teacher. Stop, walk, follow.

Ability to Take Someone Else's Perspective

"When you stepped in front of Ian in line, Vinnie, he got really angry. How could you tell that he was angry? That's right; he made a face." Mrs. Chang encouraged Vinnie to look at things from Ian's perspective. **Social perspective taking** is the ability to consider how something looks to another person or animal, the ability to take someone else's point of view even when one's own perspective is different. In the example, Vinnie wanted to be first in line (Vinnie's perspective), but Ian was there first and wanted to stay first (Ian's perspective).

Good perspective taking is important because it helps children to regulate aggressive impulses. Vinnie or Ian's ability to take another's perspective will take several years to develop, but this skill has roots in early childhood (Dixon & Soto, 1990). The boys must get older before they are capable of true perspective taking; however, getting older is not enough. They must also learn how to look at things from somebody else's viewpoint.

Arguments. Anger. Aggression. Often, the origin of these issues in a classroom is a child's inability to take another child or animal's perspective. Think about Vygotsky's theory here. Children are in the process of constructing or building many skills, including their ability to take another's perspective, and teachers who provide the scaffolding help children with the building of perspective-taking skills. Figure 9.4 presents three practical examples of scaffolding or supporting a child's growing ability to consider other viewpoints.

Disabilities

Figure 3.3 lists the disabilities defined by the Individuals with Disabilities Education Act (IDEA). A disability might well affect a child's behavior and a teacher's guidance. Here are some examples.

Social perspective taking Ability to consider how something looks to another person or animal.

Go to MyEducationLab and select the topic "Guidance." Under Activities and Applications, watch the video *Facilitating Peer Interaction* in which the teacher helps Bri'Asia understand Haven's perspective.

> **FIGURE 9.4   Understanding Perspective Taking: What It Means for Guiding Children**
>
> **State how others think, feel, or view things.**
>
> - State the other's view in everyday instruction or conversation with children.
> - State the other's view when children are arguing or acting aggressively.
>
> **Encourage children to communicate their views to others.**
>
> - Mrs. Chang's class was passing a ball around a circle when Ralph hit Carlos with the ball. Carlos was not hurt but was surprised. He did not cry.
> - Her response, "How do you think that we could keep from hitting someone?" encouraged each child's perspective.
> - She then said, "You had lots of ideas. Carl's idea was different from Vinnie's but they were both good ideas," communicating that different perspectives are worthy of respect.
>
> **Begin to ask young children to say how another person or animal might view things.**
>
> - After children understand the concept that different viewpoints exist, teachers can begin to ask them to say how someone might feel or think.
> - Mrs. Chang told a story about a kitten who was lost and then asked, "How do you think that the kitten might have felt when she was lost?"

If typically developing children have developmental limitations on how well they listen, then consider the challenges that a child with hearing impairment would likely face. Hearing impairment and hearing loss put a child at risk for problems with self-esteem, communication, and behavior problems. Children wth hearing impairments use up much more energy in communicating than do hearing children. Listening, so important in communicating, is especially energy consuming for children with hearing loss, and they often need help with self-expression and in working with peers (Kaland & Salvatore, 2002).

A child with autism (see Figure 3.3) has difficulty processing information, communicating, with social skills, and with playing. The challenge to a teacher lies in how to communicate effectively with a child with autism. The goal is to help such a child learn how to manage his own behavior, just as we do with all children. Children with autism have difficulty processing language but seem to understand visual supports much better. See examples of visual supports in Figures 9.5 and 9.6. Teachers use the visual supports as a part of the child's Individualized Education Program (IEP). Visual supports help a child with autism focus on an activity, give him good prompts, and allow the child to say how he feels (Rao & Gagle, 2002).

Some children have specific learning disabilities, meaning that they have difficulty in using or understanding written or oral language. Different children with learning disabilities will show this difficulty in dissimilar ways. For example, some might have trouble with mathematical calculations, reading, or spelling. Learning disorders appear in others as an unsatisfactory capacity to speak, think, or listen (National Dissemination Center for Children with Disabilities, 2008). A teacher, therefore, would need to work with the IEP team to develop a plan that would identify the specific problem and outline a plan to support the child in getting what he needs.

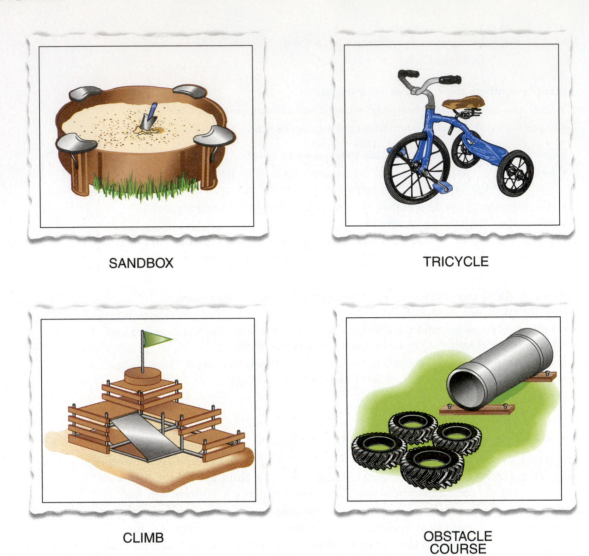

FIGURE 9.5 Children with autism benefit from using visual supports such as this planning sheet for outdoor play.

Whether Basic Needs Are Met

All children have specific basic needs for

- safety,
- security,
- love,
- acceptance,
- adequate nutrition,
- exercise,
- sleep, and
- play.

They feel loved and cared for with their basic needs met, making it much easier for them to see themselves as loveable, to get the most from learning activities, and to get along with others. Unmet basic needs, however, frequently have negative effects on children.

BLOCKS

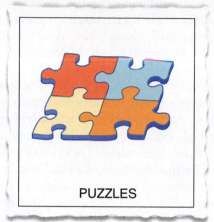

PUZZLES

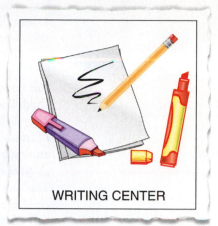

WRITING CENTER

MUSIC AREA

BOOKS

COMPUTER

CLIMB

YOGA CENTER

FIGURE 9.6 Visual supports for indoor center time

For example, some children consistently do not get enough rest and sleep or they have a sleep disorder. There is a relationship between lack of sleep and behavior problems or adjustment in school (Bates, Viken, Alexander, Beyers, & Stockton, 2002).

All of the systems in which children exist—for example family, school, neighborhood, society—have responsibilities to satisfy those basic needs. Some systems meet this responsibility admirably but others do not, such as when a parent neglects or abuses a child. The extreme stress of abuse or neglect alerts a child's body to defend itself from danger, placing him in a state of high alert, his body producing an excessive amount of stress hormones, high levels of which kill brain cells and reduce the number of connections among brain cells, the synapses. The brain of a child who is abused can be up to as much as 30% smaller than the brain of a child who is loved and cared for (Lowenthal, 1999). Teachers are mandated reporters of suspected child abuse. *A teacher who suspects that a child has been abused or neglected is required by his state law to report his observations.* Schools have procedures for reporting in place, and teachers must follow those procedures.

Teachers meet some basic needs by structuring classrooms well. Developmentally appropriate classrooms, built around children's needs, provide options and encourage choice, movement, activity-based learning and play, interaction, and they emphasize positive guidance. There are, for example, more stories, music, and center activities in developmentally appropriate classrooms, and there are more worksheets, waiting, and transitions in developmentally *in*appropriate classrooms (Burts, Hart, Charlesworth, Fleege, Mosely, & Thomasson, 1992). Several studies suggest that children who attend developmentally appropriate programs have better academic achievement and fewer behavioral problems than those in developmentally inappropriate classrooms (Marcon, 1993). The higher levels of stress behavior in developmentally inappropriate preschool and kindergarten classrooms contribute to guidance problems (Hart, Burts, Durland, Charlesworth, DeWolf, & Fleege, 1998).

Observe children carefully to determine whether their basic needs have been met. Ask some simple questions when concerns about children's behavior send signals. Has this child eaten today? Does she get enough sleep? Has my class had enough physical exercise? Answers to these most basic questions give clues about how to support children.

For these two students, the need for connection with others is met in their classroom "community."

Adults' Caregiving Style

Adults' caregiving style influences children's development and behavior. For example, some caregivers are chronically angry and irritable, a potentially damaging pattern for children. Persistently angry adults model anger, extreme irritation, and aggression. The children in their care or classrooms often become very angry and aggressive themselves (Jenkins, 2000). The main caregiving styles describing how we relate to children are the authoritative, authoritarian, and permissive. Two features stand out in each style: first, how the adult makes demands of children and second, how responsive the adult is to their needs. (Baumrind, 1996; Darling, 1999).

Authoritative adults have high but reasonable expectations and do make expectations for children's behavior known. They are also aware of and highly responsive to what children need to construct ideas about how to behave well. For example, they set clear standards, are assertive without being intrusive, and use positive, supportive guidance strategies. They explain why they want children to do something. Researchers have rated children of authoritative caregivers as socially competent, having healthy self-control, and tending to take responsibility for their own actions.

Authoritarian adults or caregivers are not very responsive to what children need but are highly demanding and directive. When they give an order, they expect children to obey quickly and without questions. Some authoritarian adults are very intrusive and maintain high levels of psychological control over children. Children from authoritarian systems tend to have poor social skills, lower levels of self-esteem, and higher levels of depression.

Permissive caregivers set few limits and use unhelpful discipline such as nagging. Some adults who set few limits are quite warm toward their children, but they are *indulgent*, simply not believing in setting limits or making demands. Their children perform less well in school, have higher self-esteem, better social skills, and lower levels of depression. However, they are also more likely to have problem behavior. Other adults who set few limits are less warm toward their children; they are *uninvolved*. Observers tend to view them as uncaring, uninvolved, and unresponsive with children. They often do not understand their child's development. They might be depressed or otherwise feeling overwhelmed with responsibilities. They frequently lack the interactional skills necessary to interact well with and to guide children effectively. In extreme cases, uninvolved caregivers can neglect children. Children cared for by uninvolved adults are very likely to have difficulty with normal classroom limits because they have never really focused on limits. These children tend to perform most poorly in all domains.

Recall from Chapter 2 that Bronfenbrenner believed that good relationships between microsystems such as family and school can benefit children's learning and development. Teachers might want to consider the caregiving style of the parents of the children in their class as well as their own caregiving style. In many cases, a teacher might have one style and a parent a different one. For example, a child with an indulgent parent would very likely not be good at living within classroom limits developed by an authoritative teacher and the class. A teacher who understands caregiving styles and who sees a mismatch between his or her own and a parent's style would have good information on which to build a good relationship with the parent. The teacher would also have assessed the child's individual needs for learning about limits.

Effective teachers use a set of ideas, a framework, to guide their work with children and families. This framework consists of the major theories of early childhood education as explained in Chapter 2, a topic to which we now turn.

Authoritative Caregiving style characterized by high reasonable demands and high levels of responsiveness to what children need.

Authoritarian Caregiving style marked by high, often *unreasonable* demands and low levels of responsiveness to what children need.

Permissive Caregiving style characterized by very low level of demands and varying amounts of responsiveness to what children need.

HOW THEORIES HELP TEACHERS WITH CHILD GUIDANCE

The theories of Dewey, Piaget, Vygotsky, Bruner, Bronfenbrenner, and Family Systems Theory, explained in Chapter 2, are central to our work as teachers. Their theories have helped teachers to understand that

- children construct knowledge; they are not sponges or blank slates.
- children have many questions about how the world works.

- children need to be actively involved in learning.
- children need to interact with people and things when they are learning.
- children build new understandings on previously acquired knowledge.
- children are affected by different systems, some close to them and some farther away but still influential.

We will look at one of the theories, Vygotsky's, as an example. Early childhood teachers use concepts from Vygotsky's constructivist theory when guiding children (Marion, 2007): scaffolding, the zone of proximal development (ZPD), and adult-child discourse (Berk & Winsler, 1995).

Scaffolding is a teaching strategy. It refers to a teacher's changing level of support during a discipline encounter or series of interactions. Teachers offer more support when a guidance task is new and less as a child acquires skills. Scaffolding in guidance assumes that teachers should intervene in a child's interaction with peers when it would help a child acquire the skill he needs to control his own behavior. Scaffolding also assumes that teachers view discipline encounters as problems to be solved and tha t teachers help children construct the solution to the problem. Good scaffolding assumes a good teacher-child relationship because effective problem solving occurs best when a teacher has developed a good relationship with children in a class. In addition, children often help one another with peer mentoring done as they scaffold each other's learning and as they solve problems together.

The concept of the Zone of Proximal Development (ZPD), when guiding children, refers to the space where guidance learning takes place. At one end of the zone is a child's current understanding of a guidance skill, such as managing anger well. Suppose, for example, that a kindergarten child knows only the word *mad* for the emotion of anger. At the other end of the ZPD is what the child can learn or accomplish with expert help from a parent, teacher, or some other skilled member of the culture, including children possessing the targeted skill. This child's teacher might decide to teach the child how to use one or two different words for anger.

Any guidance strategy based on Vygotsky's theory relies heavily on *adult-child discussion or dialogues*, talking about tasks that a child can accomplish with adult help (File, 1993). Understanding children's development is particularly helpful here—what is a typically developing 2, 4, 6, or 8 year old capable of understanding, for instance, when it comes to controlling his own behavior? Additionally, a teacher would consider an individual child's experience with the issue at hand. For example, has this child ever had an opportunity to think and talk about how to control his own behavior?

In the developmental approach to guidance, teachers scaffold children's understanding of getting along with others. The dialogue or conversation works by inducing children to use self-directed, private speech to guide their actions (Berk & Winsler, 1995). Suppose, for example, that a child is having trouble choosing new activities after finishing in an area. A teacher might design a contract or planner, drawing available centers on the card (Bickart, Jablon, & Dodge, 1999). When making choices about centers, the teacher would model self-directed speech by saying, "Look at your card and choose your next center . . . the reading area? You can say, 'Now I'm going to the reading area.'"

As you might guess, a teacher's guidance strategies grow out of his beliefs, which in turn, have come from theories. We now examine some of the major guidance strategies based on the theories explained in this text.

DEVELOPMENTALLY APPROPRIATE GUIDANCE STRATEGIES

The most important principle in an early childhood teacher's code of ethical conduct, then, deals with protecting children. The implication for teachers when choosing guidance strategies is clear; teachers are bound by their code of ethics to choose positive guidance and problem-solving strategies and reject any guidance strategies that harm children or have the potential to harm children.

Guidance strategies are specific actions that adults use to support children. Authoritative adults use positive strategies, focusing on teaching, never on punishment. They explain limits, redirect behavior, and teach behaviors that are more helpful. For example, Mr. Hernandez emphasized problem solving and negotiating. They help children *construct* knowledge about getting along with others and then encourage practicing new approaches. Learning how to use these strategies makes it possible for teachers to meet the needs of individual children and groups of children. This section lists, describes, and briefly explains the major positive guidance strategies. Figure 9.7 lists the strategies.

Guidance strategies
Specific positive actions adults use to support children.

Set Limits Well

The purpose of this strategy is to state expectations for desired behavior, to clarify boundaries or limits. Appropriate *limits,* based on needs and abilities of children, focus on important matters. Involving children in developing some of the classroom limits helps them accept limits more readily. Effective limit setting involves helping children focus on a task, giving good cues, using concrete words and short statements, telling a child what to do, and giving clear reasons for limits. Mrs. Chang used limits effectively with Carlos:

> Mrs. Chang hands a block to Carlos saying, "You used a lot of blocks today. I'll help you put them away but you have to work too." After Carlos had put away most of the blocks, Mrs. Chang said, "We need the block area for our group time, and that's why all the blocks have to go back on their shelves. Thanks, Carlos."

FIGURE 9.7   **Developmentally Appropriate Guidance Strategies in Early Childhood Education**

- Set limits well
- Teach helpful behavior
- Set up practice sessions and give on-the-spot behavior
- Give signals or cues for newly constructed behavior
- Change something about a context or setting
- Redirect very young children with diversion and distraction
- Redirect older children with substitution
- Give meaningful feedback to children
- Ignore behavior (only when it is appropriate to do so)
- Listen actively
- Deliver I-messages
- Teach conflict resolution and negotiation skills
- Help children save face and preserve their dignity

Source: Based on Marion (2007).

Teach Helpful Behavior

The purpose of this strategy is to help children learn the behaviors that they do not know. Children have so many things to learn about getting along with others and being a productive member of a class, for example, good social skills, how to deal with and resolve conflicts, or knowing how to put things away when they complete a project. Teaching such helpful behaviors gives children options that they might otherwise not have learned.

First, observe a child or a group to determine the skill that needs to be taught. Next, use Vygotsky's advice and ascertain what a child knows and what he might need to know about the skill. (Levi knows that there is a snack time but does not know how to pour his own juice.) Then, apply Vygotsky's principle of the ZPD to help the child learn this skill. Mrs. Chang demonstrated juice pouring, later observing that Levi successfully poured juice.

Set Up Practice Sessions and Give On-the-Spot Guidance

The purpose of this strategy is to give the chance to practice a newly learned skill with expert guidance from the teacher, a concept from Vygotsky. After learning the new skill of using a normal voice instead of whining, a teacher practices with the child by letting her ask for something in a normal voice. The teacher gives appropriate feedback and then gives on-the-spot guidance as a child works and plays. Mrs. Chang observing, for example, that Rosa whined when she wanted paint, gave on-the-spot guidance, "Remember, Rosa, use your normal voice for asking."

Give Cues for Newly Constructed Behavior

This strategy's goal is to help children remember to use a behavior that they have recently learned. Cues are hints or suggestions that remind children about a limit in a low-key way and can be verbal, nonverbal, pictorial, or written (for older children). Mrs. Chang uses two cues to remind children about washing hands, a song at group time and a picture of children washing hands.

Change Something About a Situation

The purpose of this strategy is for a teacher to figure out what she can do about a situation that helps a child be safe or enables the child to use a more helpful behavior. Because behavior occurs in a context or setting and that context has a powerful effect on behavior, a teacher asks, "What can I do about this context, this situation? Do I want to keep telling these two children to stop arguing over the blocks? Alternatively, can I change something to help them accept the idea of cooperating?"

There are three major ways to change a situation:

1. *Change the physical environment and time schedule.* Mr. Hernandez found that children had a great deal of difficulty staying in a group time that was almost 30 minutes long. He changed the situation by revising the schedule so that group time was around 10 minutes long. Another teacher discovered that the long space through the classroom encouraged running. She rearranged the room to eliminate that space.

2. *Increase options available to the child.* Introduce new ideas or materials to children engaged in an activity, for example, when it would extend the plan or help children start to solve an argument. Mrs. Chang brought out new accessories for the play dough table, encouraging the children to choose one of the three items.

Go to MyEducationLab and select the topic "Guidance." Under Activities and Applications, read the strategy *Limits*, which gives practical ideas about using limits with children.

Go to MyEducationLab and select the topic "Guidance." Under Activities and Applications, read the strategy *Transitions* for practical suggestions about using good transitions in a schedule.

3. *Decrease options when children seemed overwhelmed by too many choices.* Clear the science table of things not pertinent to the focus topic, for example. This gives children the opportunity to focus on one thing. Help a child who is easily distracted by too many choices during choice time. "Tom, you started on a painting yesterday. Would you like to finish that or would you like to work in the block area?"

Redirect Children

The overall purpose of redirection is to give a child positive alternatives to dangerous or unacceptable behavior. There are two forms of redirection, (1) *diversion and distraction*, which is appropriate for very young children, and (2) *substitution*, which is appropriate for children beyond toddlerhood.

Redirect by diverting and distracting is appropriate for very young children and is an effort to distract the child from a dangerous activity and then to divert her to a different activity. It is based on the idea that infants, toddlers, and young preschoolers do not understand danger inherent in activities like touching hot items or playing with electrical outlets. Teachers identify dangerous situations and then immediately do something to distract a child. Mr. Bjornrud, for example, rolled a ball to Emilio the instant that he saw him crawling near an outlet, even though the outlet was covered. Diversion and distraction is *not* appropriate for children older than 2 years.

Use *substitution to redirect* older children (over 2½ to 3). Its purpose is to show a child how to perform the same activity but in a more acceptable and safer way. Mrs. Chang saw Levi and Aiko zigzag through the crowded sand box. She developed the substitution of doing a zigzag pattern through four tires set on the ground. When Aiko ran back through the sandbox, the teacher responded to this testing by saying, "Aiko, zigzag through the tires, not the sandbox."

Alternatively, teachers can redirect a child who is not being safe to a completely different activity. For example, Ralph had removed his jacket and was swirling it around in a circle over his head nearly hitting others. Mrs. Chang caught the jacket and stopped the swirling. She redirected Ralph while she also restated a safety limit. "Tell me what you want to play with today, Ralph. I cannot let you whip your jacket around because it is not safe."

CHECK YOUR UNDERSTANDING
Reflecting on Redirection

You have just read about two different ways to redirect children. Diversion and distraction is appropriate for very young children but not for older children. How do you think that a 5 year old, for example, would react if a teacher tried to divert or distract him? Why?

Give Meaningful Feedback

The purpose of this strategy is to give helpful information to children. Feedback is critical to constructing new skills and competencies and is a part of good scaffolding, a concept from Vygotsky's theory. Good feedback can help children make changes.

Suggestions for giving meaningful feedback include expressing appreciation directly related to a child's effort or interest, for example, "You and Carlos really cooperated in putting away the books." It also means avoiding empty praise and flattery like constantly saying, "Good job!" (Kohn, 2001). Teachers can also use their expert knowledge and skills

The teacher on the left used diversion and distraction when she scooped up the child to get him away from the outside door. "Look, I have a toy!"

Redirect by using substitution: "Reach in and get the spoon. You can use that instead."

to give information so that a child can make a better choice about how to do something; for example, "Aiko got angry when you laughed at her."

Ignore Behavior (When Appropriate)

This strategy's purpose is to change the teacher's behavior, to help the teacher stop paying attention to a child's unhelpful behavior. Do *not* ignore behavior that endangers anyone, including the child herself, that might damage or destroy property (e.g., whacking a tree with a stick), or which is rude, embarrassing, intrusive, or unduly disruptive.

Teachers ignore behavior effectively by pinpointing the behavior to which they have given inappropriate attention and by explaining to the child that they will stop paying attention to the behavior. Then the teacher is prepared for the behavior to actually get worse before it decreases because of all the previous attention. She teaches and encourages a more helpful skill along with the ignore strategy. Mrs. Chang realized that Nandini's whining would increase after she started ignoring it because Nandini had received so much attention in the past for whining.

Listen Actively

The purpose of this strategy is for a teacher to listen carefully to a child's feelings. It is best used when a child is having a problem. It tells a child that his teacher recognizes and accepts her feelings and that the teacher trusts her ability to solve the problem with the teacher's help.

What does it take to "listen actively"? Pay attention, listen carefully, do not interrupt, listen for what the child seems to be feeling, and suspend judgment. Resist the urge to preach, give advice, or persuade the child to feel differently. Finally, merely reflect perception of the child's feelings, as Mrs. Chang, the preschool teacher, did when talking with 4-year-old Samir:

Samir was building with small plastic blocks and said, "This is fun!" Mrs. Chang replied, "You really like building with these blocks." Samir said, "Yes, but I don't like building when my brother is around." Mrs. Chang questioned, "You like building with blocks but not with your brother?" Samir answered, "Yeah." Mrs. Chang said, "H-m-m, you don't like playing with your brother." Samir answered, "Uh-huh. He calls me stupid." Mrs. Chang said, "You don't like it when your brother calls you names." Samir kept his head down and nodded.

Deliver I-Messages

The goal in this strategy is to give information, communicate feelings in a respectful way, give a child a chance to change behavior. Some teachers use I-messages when a child does something that unduly disrupts an ongoing activity or when the child has not taken responsibility for cleaning up. Other teachers use I-messages when a child has embarrassed or hurt someone. Mrs. Chang observed that Carlos had left the puzzles on the table and ignored the signal for cleanup. She wanted to help him take responsibility for cleanup and decided to use an I-message.

First, she gave observable data about the incident but did not accuse Carlos, "I see that the puzzles you used are still on the table." Then she told Carlos that his behavior would mean that someone else would have to put the puzzles away, which would cost that person time and effort, ". . . and that means that the parent volunteer would have to put the puzzles away just before snack when he has other work to do." She told him how she felt, again without accusing him, "I feel a little frustrated when the things are left out." Finally, she clearly told Carlos how to change things by essentially restating the classroom rule about putting one's own things away, "I want you to put the puzzles on the shelf after you've worked with them."

Teach Conflict Resolution and Negotiation

The purpose of teaching conflict resolution is to achieve a mutually agreeable solution to a problem without resorting to the use of power. This approach supports children as they construct ideas about alternatives to arguing and fighting, for instance, instead of punishing them for the behavior. Chapter 5 explains the steps in conflict resolution.

Help Children Save Face and Preserve Dignity

The goal of this strategy is to treat children respectfully apart from any other positive strategy used. An excellent way to show respect is to take a child's perspective in any guidance situation and let an episode become history when the guidance situation is over. Teachers show respect by not flaunting power and by avoiding saying, "I told you so."

Mrs. Chang realized that Carlos was very upset when he arrived at school, and she watched as he snapped at a child when she offered him some help in the listening center. The teacher listened actively and recognized Carlos's stress. She did not lecture him about shouting but instead helped him calm down and then ended the interaction quickly, simply, and gracefully. She quietly said to Carlos, "Let's go back and play now."

CHECK YOUR UNDERSTANDING
Guidance Strategies

Choose a guidance strategy that you have just read about but with which you are *not* familiar. Explain why this strategy is useful and why it is positive.

SUMMARY

Guiding young children has *nothing* to do with controlling, manipulating, or playing mind games with them. Control, manipulation, and mind games are unethical and unprofessional and have no place in our relationship with children.

A teacher's main purpose in guiding children is to support them as they construct knowledge and skills about getting along with others and about themselves. We view children as strong and competent individuals, quite capable of building helpful ideas with support from important adults in their lives. We have three main goals in guiding children.

1. The first goal and most essential element in guiding children well is a warm and caring relationship with

them. Responsive teachers are nurturing, understand child development, and communicate well with children. They demonstrate respect for children and deliver messages kindly, firmly, simply, and consistently.

2. The second goal in guiding children is to encourage positive social interaction among children. We do this by creating a sense of community in classrooms, by modeling respectful social interaction, and by teaching social skills.

3. The third goal in guiding children is to support them in developing self-esteem, internal motivation, and self-control or executive function. Teachers do this by encouraging play and interaction with peers as children learn.

Many people want to know what *causes* children's behavior. While this is a natural and normal question, it is an extremely difficult one to answer because it is nearly impossible to pinpoint accurately any one cause of a behavior. We can acknowledge, however, that many factors *influence* children's behavior.

- Some aspects of child development influence children's behavior. For example, a child's developing ability to listen, to remember things, and to take another's perspective affect how the child benefits from our guidance.
- Some disabilities affect how well children can listen, process information, communicate, play, and understand social skills.
- Another factor is whether a child's basic needs for safety, security, love, acceptance, adequate nutrition, exercise, sleep, and play are met. Children who feel loved and cared for, with basic needs met, find it much easier to see themselves as loveable, to get the most from learning activities, and to get along with others.

- An adult's caregiving style influences children's behavior. Authoritative (*not* authoritarian) teachers have high but reasonable expectations. They are also highly responsive to what children need. These adult traits help children to become competent, with healthy self-control and good executive function, and to take responsibility for their own actions.

The theories of Dewey, Piaget, Vygotsky, Bruner, Bronfenbrenner, and Family Systems Theory have helped teachers understand that children construct knowledge, have many questions about how the world works, need to be actively involved in learning, need to interact with people and things while learning, build new understandings on previously acquired information, and are affected by different systems.

The most important part of an early childhood teacher's code of ethics deals with protecting children.

- Teachers are bound by this code of ethics to choose only positive guidance and problem-solving strategies.
- They are bound by the code to reject any strategy that harms children or has the potential to harm children.
- Guidance strategies are specific actions that adults take to support children. They center on good limit setting, teaching helpful behavior, helping children practice the new behaviors, giving signals or cues for newly constructed behavior, changing something about the context, redirecting children, giving meaningful feedback, ignoring behavior (only when it is appropriate to do so), and teaching children how to resolve conflicts and how to negotiate.
- The most important guidance strategy, however, is to help children save face and preserve their dignity. This demonstrates our abiding respect and willingness to take their perspective, whatever the circumstances.

QUESTIONS FOR REFLECTION

1. How did Tim, in the chapter-opening primary grade vignette, demonstrate *self-control*?
2. From your reading of the chapter, how has Mr. Bjornrud, the infant and toddler teacher, helped Emilio decrease his level of stress (see chapter-opening vignette).

3. The preschool children in the chapter-opening vignette learned about different facial expressions. How does learning about emotions evident in facial expressions help children?
4. From the section on self-esteem in this chapter, describe how one of your childhood teachers did something to help you develop a sense of worth.

APPLY YOUR KNOWLEDGE

What Should This Teacher Do?

Vignette: Mr. Hernandez observed Max leaning over the gerbil house and hooting loudly, frightening the two animals. Using information from this chapter, complete the following.

1. Write an I-message for the teacher to use as he supports Max in treating the gerbils with more respect.

2. Max is 5 years old. List and explain two ways in which the teacher can help this child learn about perspective taking. Justify your response with information from this chapter.
3. Explain why the teacher should *not* ignore Max's behavior.

KEY TERMS

Authoritarian, 233
Authoritative, 233
Competence, 222
Control, 222
Executive function, 223

Explaining reasons for limits, 221
Guidance strategies, 235
Internal motivation, 223
Limits, 221
Listening, 226

Permissive, 233
Self-control, 223
Self-esteem, 222
Social perspective taking, 228
Worth, 222

WEB SITES

American Academy of Pediatrics
http://www.aap.org/parents.html
The parenting corner of this site. Search for topics related to guidance.

Center for Evidence-Based Practice
http://challengingbehavior.org
Technical Assistance Center on Social/Emotional Intervention provides information on positive behavior support.

Positive Behavior Support
http://www.apbs.org/new_apbs/earlyDesc.aspx
An explanation of the positive behavior support philosophy for early childhood education.

Zero to Three
http://www.zerotothree.org/site/PageServer?page name=key_keytopics
This is the *key topics* page for this site. Search through the list of topics of interest to early childhood professionals. Good information about child development.

CHAPTER 10

Developmentally Appropriate Curriculum

GUIDING QUESTIONS:

- How would you describe a developmentally appropriate curriculum for young children?
- What do teachers need to know in order to construct developmentally appropriate curriculum?
- What are the principles that teachers follow in developing early childhood curriculum?

TODDLER
Two Cars!

Mr. Bjornrud and the toddlers were playing outside when Nick, nearly 2 years old, turned to the sound of two cars turning into the driveway across the street. He stopped peddling his tricycle to watch and the teacher said, "Let's go to the fence to look at the cars, Nick." "Two cars!" said Nick. "Yes, I see two cars," replied his teacher.

PRESCHOOL
Parking the Cars

Mrs. Chang had posted photographs of different types of buildings in the block area. Four year olds Ralph and Ray, entering the area, looked closely at each and then tapped the parking garage photo, agreeing, "You can park a LOT of cars here!" After working with blocks for the entire morning work session and designing a garage for parking cars, the boys gathered all the cars that they could find and guided each to its parking space.

KINDERGARTEN
Observing and Building a Car

Clutching clipboards, the 5 year olds circled the car in the school's parking lot. They drew pictures, wrote notes, and asked questions about the car. There was a great deal of interest in the control panel and the "under the hood equipment." Back in the classroom, they constructed their cardboard car with the real car as their model. Two trips back to the real car clarified questions and refreshed memories about different parts of the car. Her teacher is fluent in Spanish and helps Juanita, who is learning English, by labeling car parts in Spanish first and only then in English.

PRIMARY
Guess How Far This Car Will Go!

Mr. Hernandez had set up a floor activity in the "discovery area." He placed a ramp on the tile floor and set several small cars next to the ramp. Working with their teacher, Luis and Trina eagerly sent one car at a time down the ramp, first speculating on how far each car would go. They marked the spot where each car stopped and later recorded their findings on a graph. Then, they repeated the experiment in exactly the same way and got the same results.

Each of these teachers has constructed a curriculum based on the abilities, needs, and interests of the children in their classes. They acknowledge children's development in planning, focus on individual needs, and consider culture when planning curriculum. They know and use instructional strategies appropriate for helping young children learn. Planning curriculum to support children's development and learning is one facet of an early childhood teacher's complex professional role (Bredekamp, 2004; Bredekamp & Copple, 1997; Day, 2004; NAEYC, 2006).

In this chapter we will explore curriculum focusing on the whole child and fostering children's intellectual skills that they will use to make sense of things and to analyze and synthesize information (Bruner, 1960, 2006; Katz, 1999; Rimm-Kaufmann, 2006). We will see how to develop an integrated early childhood curriculum, defined later in the chapter, and how specific instructional strategies support that approach. We will examine principles of building developmentally appropriate early childhood curriculum.

PEDAGOGICAL CONTENT KNOWLEDGE

Curriculum Goals for what children should know and be able to do as well as the methods through which they will acquire this.

Curriculum is defined by NAEYC (2006) as "the goals for knowledge and skills to be acquired by children and the plans for learning experiences through which such knowledge and skills will be received." This professional organization advises children's programs to develop and put into operation a curriculum "that is thoughtfully planned, challenging, engaging, developmentally appropriate, culturally and linguistically responsive, comprehensive, and likely to promote positive outcomes for all young children" (NAEYC, 2003).

Child-centered curriculum Based on children's development and designed to help children love learning.

This is a **child-centered curriculum** that should help children's programs meet the three main goals for early childhood curriculum, which are to:

- promote children's development in all domains,
- support children's learning, their knowledge and skills, and
- nurture their passion for learning (Bank Street, 2005; NAEYC, 2006).

Pedagogical content knowledge Consists of three forms of knowledge—subject matter knowledge, pedagogical knowledge, and knowledge about the context or setting.

A teacher needs **pedagogical content knowledge** to help children learn and to construct a developmentally appropriate curriculum (Shulman, 1986). This brings together three different types of knowledge—subject matter knowledge, pedagogical knowledge, and knowledge about the setting.

Subject Matter Knowledge

Subject matter knowledge Understanding content of academic disciplines and child development and early childhood education.

In early childhood education, **subject matter knowledge** refers to understanding theories and research in child development and early childhood education as well as different programs, as explained in Chapter 2. Teachers must also know about the content of academic disciplines such as art, music, mathematics, science, social sciences, language arts, and physical education. Teachers who understand these **content areas** more confidently and competently introduce children to the fundamental parts of their culture through curriculum.

Content areas Mathematics, literacy, science/technology, social science, the arts, physical development, and health, social/emotional development.

Two parts of subject matter knowledge are extremely important in early childhood curriculum development. The first is child development and how children learn (Branscombe, Castle, Dorsey, Surbeck, & Taylor, 2003). Teachers also need to understand that positive relationships and supportive interactions with children and families are the most essential elements in working with children (McMullen & Dixon, 2006a, 2006b). For example, effective teachers of infants and toddlers believe that these youngest children see teachers as a safe base for exploring their expanding world. Their beliefs, something that they accept as true, influence their decisions. Therefore, if they act on the belief, they would build a warm and positive relationship with each child (Deniz, 2004; Wheatley, 2003; Wilcox-Herzog & Ward, 2004).

In the toddler vignette at the chapter's opening, for example, the teacher demonstrated his understanding of appropriate curriculum for toddlers who acquire language and social skills rapidly. He noticed Nick's interest in the cars, observed with him, modeled good interaction, and then expanded on Nick's two-word statement. Nick and his teacher seem to have developed a warm and trusting relationship.

This child has a warm relationship with his teacher, which will give him the confidence to use her as a safe base from which to explore.

Pedagogical Knowledge

Pedagogical knowledge refers to understanding the science of teaching needed to help children learn. Teachers need to know how young children learn—through active learning and social interaction, for example—and to use effective instructional strategies. Teachers must also be able to *use* pedagogical knowledge to design environments and specific learning activities to help children understand the content. Effective teachers make intentional decisions—purposeful, careful, and methodical decisions—about every aspect of curriculum (McMullen & Dixon, 2006a, 2006b; NAEYC, 2007).

Pedagogical knowledge
Understanding how to choose and use effective instructional strategies.

Specific teaching strategies are explained later in this chapter, and Chapter 11 focuses on early childhood environments and organizing learning activities for children.

Knowledge About the Setting

Knowledge about the setting refers to a teacher's understanding of the settings affecting children. This acknowledges Bronfenbrenner's theory, which was explained in Chapter 2.

TEACH INTENTIONALLY

Kindness to Animals

What the teacher did: Mr. Hernandez organized learning activities on kindness to animals. The children read a magazine, *Kind News*, discussed reasons for taking good care of Sunshine, the class's pet hamster, sponsored a cage at the Humane Society, and participated in the school's food drive for the Humane Society. He and the children wrote an article for the school's newspaper about kindness to animals.

How the teacher was intentional: He designed this part of the curriculum so that children would learn to treat animals kindly, one of his beliefs. He was deliberate and he used specific teaching strategies to help children construct ideas about kindness to animals. He also explained his specific reasons to his principal and the children explained their work with a newsletter article for parents.

He believed that children's development is affected by several different systems in which they exist. For example, as a child's family, peer group, neighborhood, school, and larger societal attitudes, directly or indirectly influence his or her learning and development. Teachers are better prepared to develop effective curriculum when they understand the effect of different systems and interaction between systems, such as between home and school.

There are different sources of curriculum, a topic to which we now turn.

SOURCES OF CURRICULUM

Teachers use different resources when deciding what to teach. Three major sources of curriculum are the infants and children themselves, learning standards, and the teacher's knowledge, talents, and skills.

Children as a Source of Curriculum

Emergent curriculum
Learning activities become evident when teachers observe children's needs, interests, and abilities.

In a child-centered, **emergent curriculum,** children are an important source of the curriculum (Wien, 2006). Teachers listen to and observe children's questions, understandings, and misunderstandings. They observe as children manipulate objects and interact with people and animals. They observe children's concerns and joyful responses and use these things as one of the starting point for developing curriculum. The curriculum *emerges* or becomes apparent when teachers observe children carefully.

For example, as second-grade children practice spelling words with fuzzy wire (pipe cleaners), two of the children use the words to create a poem. The curriculum would emerge as the teacher guides children's delight with words into writing poetry (Jerome, 2006). The teacher, therefore, has negotiated a part of the curriculum based on something he observed about children.

Another teacher might notice that many of the children in his kindergarten class are captivated by the fishing boats that they see every day in their town at the docks. This teacher could very easily use the children's natural interest in fishing boats to frame a part of the curriculum. The children's hometown would provide a wonderful way to understand people and the community, a part of social science.

Infants as a Source of Curriculum

Relationships, as we saw in Chapter 5, are at the center of every child's life experience. An infant's survival depends on adults who observe and respond appropriately to his signals and engage in loving, respectful interactions. Infants and toddlers need these relationships to get their physical and psychological needs for nurturance, affection, stimulation, and play met. Even though there is mutuality in interaction between adults and infants or toddlers, the adult always has greater responsibility in exchanges and in the relationship. Infants and toddlers, therefore, need teachers and caregivers who are responsive to their unique needs (Wittmer & Petersen, 2006).

The curriculum in this classroom encourages his passion for learning.

Any planning for infants and toddlers should reflect the distinctive learning and care needs for this age group. Curriculum for infants should be *relationship-based* and focused on active learning. Programs should also emphasize continuity of care as discussed in Chapter 5. **Responsiveness** refers to how well an adult understands child development and, in this case, how infants and toddlers develop. A highly responsive infant and toddler caregiver understands the idea of the whole child but also knows about each developmental domain, such as language and motor development for very young children. He has a good grasp of the developmental milestones for infant and toddler.

Responsiveness also refers to how effectively an adult tunes in to what children need (Marion, 2007). Highly effective infant and toddler programs hire teachers who have studied infant and toddler development, who observe children closely, and who act on what they know that very young children need. They plan key experiences for a child's sensory-motor needs (Post & Hohmann, 2000) always in the context of their relationship with him (Program for Infant/Toddler Care, 2007). Thus, the adult's sense of greater responsibility encourages him to focus on his part in helping an infant or toddler move forward in development, as the next example shows.

Mr. Bjornrud understood that 4-month-old Ali could raise his head and shoulders when he was in the prone position, on his stomach. He responded by making sure that Ali had **tummy time** every day. This meant that he placed Ali on the carpet with soft toys nearby and stayed close to watch him and talk to him. In tummy time, Ali practiced raising himself up, thereby strengthening his head and neck muscles, all a part of motor and cognitive development.

Activity-Based Approach

Chapter 2 described several early childhood program models, and one of the defining features of all was a focus on children's need for an *activity-based approach* for infants and toddlers. Some of the models, such as High/Scope and Reggio Emilia, focus on infants and toddlers as well as on older children and emphasize active learning. Teachers in developmentally appropriate infant and toddler centers plan the program to meet a very young child's need to move, touch, and explore. Soft, cozy areas, small climbing structures and ramps, puzzles with knobs, blocks, sensory materials, books, appropriate outdoor equipment, and musical instruments are a few of the items in activity-based programs for infants and toddlers (Program for Infant/Toddler Care, 2007; Reggio Emilia Study Tour, 2008).

Standards as a Source of Curriculum

A **learning standard** is a statement about children's development and what children should know or be able to do (Scott-Little, Kagan, & Frelow, 2003). The learning standards web site in the list of web sites at the end of the chapter provides a chart identifying different levels of learning standards in all states and provides links to existing standards. All states have standards for grades 1 through 12. Many, but certainly not all states have them for kindergarten. Many states, as well as Head Start (Head Start Bureau, 2001) have also developed learning standards for preschool. A standard does not tell teachers how to teach: It merely says what children should know. Thus, learning standards should serve merely as guidelines (Gronlund, 2006). They are not a curriculum. Teachers build their own curriculum and choose their own teaching strategies, using the standards as a reference.

Responsiveness How supportive an adult is with children and if she or he understands child development and tries to meet children's needs.

Tummy time Giving an infant practice time for head- and shoulder-raising; infant placed in prone position (on tummy).

Learning standard Statement about children's development and what children should know and/or be able to do.

FIGURE 10.1   Professional Groups: Sources of Standards for Content Areas

International Reading Association (IRA)

Web site: http://www.ira.org

National Council of Teachers of English (NCTE)

Web site: http://www.ncte.org

Focus: developmentally appropriate literacy learning for children of all ages and guidance to teacher education programs on effective instruction in language arts

Standards: http://www.reading.org/downloads/publications/books/bk889.pdf

National Council of Teachers of Mathematics (NCTM)

Web site: http://www.nctm.org/about/default.aspx?id=166

Focus: Provides leadership to teachers who teach mathematics so that children have high-quality instruction

Standards: http://standards.nctm.org/document/chapter4/index.htm

National Science Teachers of America (NSTA)

Web site: http://www.nsta.org

Focus: Provides leadership to teachers in the area of science education so that children can become scientifically literate

National Council for the Social Studies (NCSS)

Web site: http://www.ncss.org/about/

Focus: Provides leadership to teachers regarding teaching social studies

Standards: http://www.socialstudies.org/standards/strands/

National Art Education Association (NAEA)

Web site: http://www.naea-reston.org/aboutus.html

Focus: To promote art education

Standards: *The National Visual Arts Standards*. What every young American should know and be able to do in the visual arts

Effective state learning standards originate in professional organizations for the different content areas as shown in Figure 10.1. For example, the International Reading Association and the National Council of Teachers of English provide standards for the content area of language arts. A professional organization's standards state what the group values in their field. Professionals in the English language arts area value proficient reading, writing, listening, and speaking. Therefore, the standards of these two groups guide states as they develop learning standards for language arts. The main example in this section is language arts.

The English language arts standards define, clearly and specifically, what children should learn in the English language arts. The long-term purpose is to assist teachers in developing evidence-based, comprehensive, and integrated curriculum. The curriculum should help children develop the language skills that they need to function well in school and in life (IRA/NCTE, 1996; see the link to the English language arts standards in Figure 10.1).

These standards serve as a foundation of most state language arts standards, illustrated in the next set of examples. We start with two of the 12 English language arts standards. These two help children understand texts, communications in different forms—printed, oral, or visual (DVDs, for example).

- **Standard 1:** Children read a range of print and nonprint texts to build an understanding of texts . . .
- **Standard 3:** Children apply a wide range of strategies to comprehend . . . texts.

The Illinois learning standards for language arts reflect the two professional groups' language arts standards. Here are examples from the Illinois language arts learning standards for preschool, kindergarten, and the primary grades standards.

Preschool

The state's goal here is to help children write to communicate for a variety of purposes. One of the preschool learning standards calls for children to, "Compose well-organized writing and coherent writing for specific purposes and audiences." An example is to *dictate stories*.

Kindergarten

There are many ways in which kindergarten teachers can use the standard calling for children to understand different types of reading material. One way for children to do this is to demonstrate understanding of concepts about books, such as the information conveyed on the title page of a book. Teachers can help children understand such concepts about books with individual children, small groups, or with whole groups.

Primary Grades

The state's goal for primary grade children is the same as it is for preschool children, to compose well-organized and coherent writing. Primary grade children, however, can now demonstrate meeting this standard much differently than can preschool children. Both preschool and primary children meet the same standard but in a way appropriate for their age and developmental abilities. For example, primary grade children might use prewriting strategies to generate and organize ideas. An example is to organize writing using a beginning, middle, and end.

Learning Standards for Infants and Toddlers

Chapter 1 described the whole child, using developmental milestones. Chapters 5 to 7 described each developmental domain in some detail, again focusing on developmental milestones. Teachers, parents, and medical personnel have used the milestones for many decades as a way to tell if a baby or toddler were progressing normally in the different domains of development, keeping in mind that there is a window or range of time during which the very young child might meet any developmental milestone. For example, the range for walking for typically developing children is between 9½ and 17 months. Teachers have used the milestone indicators to help them plan appropriate programs and activities for these children.

Indicators In learning standards for infants and toddlers, how they exhibit the learning.

Recently, however, there has been a movement toward developing learning standards for infants as shown in the same end-of-chapter web site about state learning standards. These standards are based on the familiar developmental milestones. Then **indicators** are listed. Finally, suggestions for adults interacting with the infant are given so that the parent or teacher knows what to do to foster the baby's development at a specific age. Figure 10.2 is an example from the Pennsylvania learning standards for infants and toddlers. Infant and toddler learning standards often focus on somewhat the same content areas as do standards for older children but the areas are adapted for use with this age group. The Pennsylvania standards, for example, focus on

- Approaches to learning and cognitive development
- Communication and emerging literacy
- Creative expression
- Physical and motor development
- Social, emotional, and personal development

Developers of the Pennsylvania standards emphasize that the standards should not be used as a curriculum and should not be used to assess infants and toddlers. They emphasize that the standards are to be used to guide caregiver interaction with very young children.

FIGURE 10.2   Excerpt from Pennsylvania Learning Standards for Infants and Toddlers

INDICATOR	EXAMPLES	SUPPORTIVE PRACTICE
PM 10.4 a Move limbs reflexively (non-voluntary movement)	**The infant will:** • Move arms and legs freely and randomly when not swaddled.	**The adult will:** • Allow infants opportunities to move arms and legs freely. Place toys in crib/playpen at infants' feet. Play tickle games and/or shake infants' feet with toys to draw attention to them.
PM 10.4 b Lift head when on stomach	• Move head to observe surroundings.	
PM 10.4 c Begin turning head from side to side when on back	• Kick and stretch arms and legs; push with legs against firm surfaces; bring hands to mouth.	• Provide ample tummy time when infants are awake once they have learned to roll over. (When sleeping, infants should always be placed on their back to reduce risk of Sudden Infant Death Syndrome.)
PM 10.4 d Move limbs voluntarily	• Hold head steady while being held in an upright position (e.g., during burping).	
PM 10.4 e Begin to control and lift head when held in an upright position		• Always support the infants' heads.

Source: Pennsylvania Department of Education and Office of Child Development and Early Learning, Pennsylvania Learning Standards for Early Childhood: Infants and Toddlers (2006), used with permission.

CHECK YOUR UNDERSTANDING
Learning Standards

How do you think that learning standards will help you as a teacher?

What does this statement mean to you? Learning standards are not a curriculum?

Teachers as a Source of Curriculum

Along with children and standards, teachers are a good source of curriculum. All certified teachers have taken general education courses which have helped them develop knowledge and skills relating to mathematics, science, social sciences (history, geography, economics, for example), language arts and communication, and the arts. Teachers, therefore, understand basic concepts in the content areas such as language arts.

Early childhood education teachers also learn about child development, a main component of *content* during early childhood. They are required to demonstrate that they know about and can use their knowledge of child development in their work with children and families (Hyson, 2003). For example, teachers who understand child development know about cognitive and language development. They understand the stages in developing language, and they can use that knowledge to help families understand how to foster their child's language skills (Oesterrich, 2004).

In addition, teachers come from different cultures and have a variety of hobbies, talents, and skills. They can use all of their abilities to develop curriculum. One teacher might be proficient in Italian. Another might be a master gardener, while one plays several musical instruments. A wise teacher uses his knowledge and talents to develop an appropriate and enjoyable curriculum for the children in his class. A teacher committed to healthy exercise, for example, would infuse physical activity into his curriculum and not just rely on recess or a physical education class for this content area.

> Mr. Hernandez has set up his classroom so that children have access to different forms of exercise throughout the day. During choice time, for example, the children have to pick one physical activity to mix in with their more academically oriented work. Phillip, for example, chose to do three yoga poses and Samantha chose to jog in place.

The next step is to understand how to organize a curriculum so that it meets state standards *and* includes every content area.

INTEGRATING EARLY CHILDHOOD CURRICULUM

An essential element of No Child Left Behind act is **accountability** for results. Teachers, in this era of accountability, must demonstrate that they are helping children to meet specific outcomes. Public schools are under pressure to show results on standardized tests. Some teachers are also under pressure to "get in" a specific number of minutes of instruction in literacy because a school receives federal funds for such programs.

The pressure for accountability has led to practices that are not in the best interests of children. For example, some schools, in a frantic attempt to boost test scores divide children into three groups—children who learn easily, children who could learn with extra help, and, a cynical, mean-spirited phrase to label their third group—hopeless cases. Teachers then, driven by the need to get results and bump up scores on the No Child Left Behind standardized tests, aim resources, questions, and attention primarily at the middle group (Booher-Jennings, 2007). Teachers believing in developmentally appropriate practices will face enormous challenges in constructing a curriculum reflecting children's need for activity and social interaction and including all content areas (Copple & Bredekamp, 2006).

The challenge is to plan a curriculum reflecting all developmental domains, including all content areas while paying attention to state learning standards. How can we meet this challenge? The answer might appear to be counterintuitive, not in accordance with what one would expect, but it is simple and the idea has been around for quite some

Accountability Required under No Child Left Behind; requires schools and teachers to show that children can demonstrate specific outcomes in mathematics, reading, and science.

Integrated curriculum
Includes all content areas; content areas combined in learning activities.

time. The answer is to develop an **integrated curriculum** (Shoemaker, 1991; Wood, 2002). An integrated curriculum combines content areas focusing on learning centers and projects, as it also weaves in technology. The content areas include:

- Social and emotional development
- Language development
- Physical development and health
- Mathematics
- Literacy development
- Science, including technology
- Social science (understanding ourselves, families, and communities)
- The arts: visual arts, music, dance, and theater

Combine Content Areas

Combining content areas is one of the two main features of an integrated early childhood curriculum. For example, a group of kindergartners made a graph showing how many of the children have different pets. This activity united math with language arts. Math is evident in the graphing part, and language arts are evident in the children's listening, speaking, and writing during the activity. Third-grade children who learn to square dance combine social, emotional, and physical development with learning about patterning in mathematics and language arts by listening to directions and learning new vocabulary related to the dance form.

An integrated curriculum avoids chopping up the curriculum into discrete content areas. It does not separate one content area, science, for example, from the others. A third-grade teacher, for example, might place a simple machine such as a pulley in a learning center. This activity certainly deals not only with science but also with language arts (speaking and listening) and social development as children work together with the pulley.

Until recently, the No Child Left Behind Act of 2001 placed a great deal of emphasis on testing two of the content areas, mathematics and literacy. These are, of course, important content areas, but so are all others. An unplanned outcome of the math/literacy emphasis was that other content areas are not included or get very little attention in a curriculum (McElroy, 2005). Recently, testing in the content area of science was added. Teachers under pressure to improve math and literacy, and now science, can still focus on all the other content areas by combining content areas with the tested areas.

Teachers who combine content areas structure both the classroom and schedule to accomplish their agenda. They set up the classroom and design a schedule with large blocks of time for children's learning and play. They give children choices, emphasize active learning, and deliberately focus on social interaction as a learning strategy. They document children's learning, noting learning standards met with projects and through center work.

Go to MyEducationLab and select the topic "Curriculum/Program Models." Under Activities and Applications, watch the video *Integrated Curriculum* to see how one teacher created an integrated curriculum.

Focus on Projects and Learning Centers

Teachers who integrate the curriculum tend to use projects and learning centers.

Projects

Young children are not very good at sitting at desks and doing workbook pages. However, they are very curious and they ask many questions and investigating things. Effective teachers acknowledge their need to play and to work with other children when learning. They combine content areas by organizing *projects* in the curriculum. Teachers can actually focus on even more content areas by using the project approach, which is based on the work of Lillian Katz (Katz, 1994; Katz & Chard, 2000).

A **project** is a method for providing learning experiences for children. Projects satisfy children's curiosity-driven, question-asking, investigative approach to seeking knowledge. Well-chosen and well-developed projects are intellectually stimulating for children. Children get to work closely with other children and to interact with different experts with this approach (Capezzuto & Da Ros-Vosels, 2001).

A project is structured (Project Approach, no date), *not* an "anything goes" situation. The structure helps children to organize their time and to plan. Projects have a beginning, middle, and end. Phase 1 is the beginning phase. Phase 2 is the development phase, and phase 3 is the concluding part. Here is what teachers would do in each of these phases of any project that they develop.

Phase 1: Beginning of the project

The teacher's role in phase 1, the "start-up" part of any project, is to devise ways for children to describe, represent, and explain what they already know about the topic. During this phase, the children:

- discuss and talk about prior experiences with the topic.
- might draw, write about, dramatize, or make up a poem about prior experience.
- share these *representations* with the class.
- raise questions based on what they already know about the topic.

Phase 2: Developing the project

The teacher's role in phase 2, the development part of any project, is to help children to do field work and investigations. This is the phase in which children build or construct new knowledge and understandings about the topic at hand. In phase 1, they explained what they already know. Teachers follow Vygotsky's advice and scaffold children's understanding of new concepts connected to the project's topic. During phase 2, the children:

- prepare for their fieldwork by talking about it and learning from books or other resources.
- go to the field site to investigate.
- interview experts, either in the classroom or in the field.
- investigate their original questions (from phase 1).
- do library research on the topic.
- record brief sketches and notes at the field site often using clipboards.
- represent field site findings through writing, painting, drawing, drama, dance, diagrams, or some other means.
- display the record that they are making of their investigations.
- choose to do dramatic play or build models based on what they have learned in their investigations.

Phase 3: Concluding the project

The teacher's role in phase 3 is to help children conclude the project. During phase 3, the children:

- review and evaluate what they have learned.
- summarize the project.
- represent their new knowledge.
- prepare some method of letting others know what they have learned. They make their learning public. This could include inviting parents to come to school to see the displays or to invite other children to come to their classroom.

Project Three-phase method for organizing learning experiences.

Go to MyEducationLab and select the topic "Curriculum/Program Models." Under Activities and Applications, watch the video *Emergent Curriculum Built on Children's Interests: A Hospital Project in Preschool.* You will see a good example of planning for a project.

Learning Centers

Teachers structure their classroom into learning centers so that small groups of children can make choices, work with other children, and work independently. Learning centers create the space in which children work on projects. A project focusing on color change would use different learning centers to help children move along in their understanding. There might be color-mixing items in the discovery and science area or two colors of finger paint in the art area. Learning centers are explained and illustrated in Chapter 11.

Teachers also use learning centers to help children learn specific skills in any of the content areas in an active way. Suppose, for example, a third-grade teacher wants to help children understand that paragraphs and stories have a beginning, middle, and end. He could use a learning center such as the writing or computer centers to focus on this knowledge. For example, he might write four or five paragraphs and place them in the computer. Children would have access to this activity during choice time.

The teacher could easily integrate his curriculum in this center by writing paragraphs focusing on specific content areas. For instance, a paragraph explaining how to do watercolor painting would focus on the arts content area. Another paragraph could focus on how snakes move because the children are studying the snake family, which is science content. Another paragraph might focus on a health concept. Thus, what would look most like the language arts content area is combined with several other content areas. The teacher has included many content areas by combining them into one learning activity in a learning center.

Teachers with good pedagogical content knowledge using teaching strategies that support an integrated curriculum is a topic to which we now turn.

SELECTED TEACHING STRATEGIES SUPPORTING AN INTEGRATED CURRICULUM

A state's learning standards serve as guides but are *not* the curriculum and do *not* dictate teaching strategies. Teachers choose the teaching strategies that help them carry out their curriculum. Effective teachers choose strategies in keeping with how children learn (Mindes, 2005). In short, effective teachers use their pedagogical content knowledge combined with good ideas about *how* to teach.

On one hand, there are the inappropriate strategies that work against an integrated curriculum and against children's learning. For example, relying on using workbook pages for each separate content area, all children doing the same workbook page at the same time, or teaching everything with large group direct instruction is not developmentally appropriate. These inappropriate strategies do not allow choice. There is no active, hands-on learning. The teacher has separated content areas and children do not get to work very much at all with other children.

On the other hand, our pedagogical knowledge offers many developmentally appropriate teaching strategies that go hand-in-hand with an integrated curriculum. This next section explains three of these:

- Creating choice times for children
- Planning productive group meetings
- Planning productive discussions

Creating Choice Times

Children need to learn to make choices and teachers are responsible for creating an environment in which children can practice making good choices. The schedules you will examine in chapter 11 provide choice times for children. The long periods for choice time are a mainstay of an integrated curriculum and a developmentally appropriate classroom.

Choice times are periods when children choose and work in learning centers. The teacher structures the centers based on what children need and provides materials for the centers. Children work in the centers for as long as they need to, such as during choice time, and teachers do not force them to move to a different center. Children move to different centers when they are ready. Teachers plan centers so that children learn from all content areas.

Academic choice, for primary grade children, is an example of how to do choice time (Denton, 2005) and a key strategy in the Responsive Classroom model, explained in Chapter 2. It is also an excellent way to structure lessons and activities in an integrated curriculum.

Academic choice involves three steps: planning, working, and reflecting. In *planning time for academic choice*, teachers decide on what to include in the curriculum, after they have observed children and assessed their needs and reviewed the state standards. They develop a number of alternative ways through which primary grade children can learn specific knowledge and can develop necessary skills.

For example, primary grade children must learn the conventions of writing, such as how to write a paragraph or a story in a logical order with a beginning, middle, and end. In academic choice, the teacher structures a number of learning activities all focusing on the same content, in this case, learning about beginning, middle, and end of stories and paragraphs. When presented with choices, children decide which learning activities they will do and if they work alone or with another child. Many times, children also choose how they show what they know. Some teachers have children fill out a printed planning sheet (Figure 10.3) when getting ready for academic choice.

In the *working part of academic choice*, children complete one or more chosen tasks. Teachers check on children's progress, often including a brief "check in with the coach, the teacher" as a part of academic choice. During academic choice, teachers work one-on-one with children or with small groups, scaffolding children's understanding as well as in checking work.

In the *reflecting part*, children think about what they have learned and document what they know. Some children choose to document their learning publically through a presentation. For example, they might read the ending that they had written to a story to the entire class during a meeting. Others might decide to show their work only to other members of their working group or even to their parents. Other children prefer private reflection shared only with the teacher. That, too, is their choice during academic choice. The whole point in academic choice is to teach children to become independent, reflective learners.

Nandini, in third grade, decided that she would meet with her teacher and demonstrate her knowledge of parts of a paragraph.

Planning Productive Group Meetings: Morning Meeting

Morning meeting is a major teaching strategy in the Responsive Classroom model, explained in Chapter 2. Morning meeting is a gathering of the whole class and an opportunity to use a large group meeting time to blend many content areas. The basic idea with a morning meeting is to blend academic and social development. This gathering blends a social curriculum while it also serves as a forum for learning and reviewing academic content.

Choice times Periods when children choose and work in learning centers.

Academic choice Choice time for primary grade children; involves three steps: planning, working, and reflecting.

Go to MyEducationLab and select the topic "Technology." Under Activities and Applications, watch the video *Technology in Classrooms* for a look at using technology during choice time.

FIGURE 10.3   Sample Planning Sheet for Academic Choice: Third Grade

Write your name here: _____

Today, we will learn about: *beginning, middle, and end in paragraphs and stories.* Choose two of the four activities from this list. Circle your choices.

1. Finding Beginnings and Endings

- Use the highlighter or computer to mark beginnings and endings in paragraphs.
- Highlight beginnings in paragraphs on laminated cards in one color marker and endings in a different color.
- Use the computer to do the same thing with paragraphs in the file labeled "Mark these paragraphs."

2. Unscrambling Paragraphs

- Pick a basket of index cards with sentences, or pick a basket of magnetic strips with sentences.
- Arrange the sentences so that your paragraph tells a story from beginning to end.

3. Writing Endings

- Work by yourself or with one other person.
- Choose one of the stories on the table in the art area and read it.
- Write an ending for the story.
- Use the large whiteboard, one of the individual chalkboards, a sheet of poster paper, or the laptop for your writing.

4. Picking the Best Ending

- Work with two other people.
- Read the story in the folders on the library table.
- Then, open the mystery box and remove the index cards.
- Each card has a different ending for the story.
- Choose an ending for the story.
- Say why you picked this ending.

There are four parts to a morning meeting:

- Greeting
- Sharing
- Group activity
- News and announcements

The *greeting section* involves children greeting someone else, using a specific greeting. For example, each child might shake one other child's hand as he says, "Good morning, _____." A class learns many different greetings and often enjoys choosing the greeting for the day. The greeting section of a meeting can include social studies content, for example, when a greeting is in a language other than English. The greeting directly focuses on social skills, one of the major content areas in early childhood curriculum. Teachers can focus on other content areas in the greeting as well. For example, greeting the person "to your right" focuses on vocabulary development, a part of language arts. Rolling a beach ball to the person directly across from you focuses on physical development as well as social and language development.

The *sharing section* of the meeting gives children a chance to share information about things going on in their lives. Others listen and ask questions for clarification.

The *group activity section* of the meeting is also a good time for introducing or reviewing academic content through singing, playing a game, or dancing. For instance, Mrs. Chang's preschool class sang a song about splashing in puddles as a part of their project on puddles and water. Mr. Hernandez showed on a large screen and then read a poem by children's poet Jack Prelutsky, *Be Glad Your Nose Is on Your Face*. This poem, soon became a favorite, with almost every child having memorized it. It became the "class poem," contributing to a real sense of community. This simple activity, therefore, focused on language arts—listening, speaking, and reading—but also on emotional development and the joy of learning. It focused on cognitive development, especially developing memory skills.

In the *news and announcements section* of the meeting, the teacher and children read the daily message. The teacher writes the message on a large piece of newsprint before the day begins and posts it where the children can see it during morning meeting. Figure 10.4 is an example of a midyear daily message in a kindergarten.

The daily message is an excellent forum for integrating the curriculum and reinforcing content areas. Most people would see the message itself as a part of the language arts content area. Notice that the teacher has written the sample message in Figure 10.4 in letter format. Also notice that the bottom of the message invites children to put a mark in the

---

FIGURE 10.4   Example of a Daily Message During Morning Meeting: Kindergarten

Wednesday, March 28, 2008

Good Morning,

Today is Wednesday. Sammy leads us to lunch. Herb will feed Sunshine, the hamster. We have many choices today. We have some new blocks. We will read a new story today.

Sincerely,
Mr. Hernandez

Do you have a pet?
Write your name under "Yes" or "No"

Yes   *No*

_____   _____

column indicating whether they have a pet. The teacher, therefore, has deliberately targeted academic content and has made sure that the children were actively involved. In this case, the teacher focused on mathematics. The next day, the teacher used the data gathered in the message to help the children develop a graph, another mathematics focus.

Teachers choose the strategies they think help children learn. In choosing the morning meeting format, a teacher has helped children learn math and language arts. The teacher has also chosen, deliberately and intentionally, not to teach any of the content areas involved in the morning meeting through workbook sheets.

Planning Productive Discussions: Guided Discovery

During a short group time, third grader Natalie's teacher held a metal cookie sheet (recycled item used as a magnet board and the sentences attached to magnets. "Today, some of you might want to work with these sentences on magnets during academic choice. But first, tell me how you have seen cookie sheets used before. How have you used magnets at other times?" The children responded. This is the beginning of a **guided discovery**, a teaching strategy for introducing materials (Bechtel & Denton, 2004).

Guided discovery
Teaching strategy employed to help children understand how to use a new material or perform a new routine.

The teacher acts as the leader in guided discovery, helping children construct new ideas in general. *Guided discovery* helps children understand the specific focus item(s). They begin with some existing ideas and construct an even deeper understanding with the help of the more knowledgeable other, the teacher. Guided discovery is a responsive classroom teaching strategy helping children to develop inquiry skills and fostering a thoughtful approach to using the materials at school. Teachers introduce new vocabulary words during a guided discovery and have a good opportunity to assess children's knowledge, for example about recycling and magnets. Guided discovery also intensifies the children's interest in a material or a learning center.

One of the central ideas in guided discovery is to help all of the children understand the same thing about the material at hand. The strategy is so successful because the teacher uses *open-ended questions*, questions that cannot be answered with yes or no. For example, "How have you seen cookie sheets used before?" "Tell me one thing that you know about magnets." Children get to tell the group what they know. It is their knowledge that they describe.

Then, the teacher invites children to describe how they could use the new materials, generating new ideas, or *brainstorming*. When children seem to run out of ideas, the third-grade teacher said, "I wonder if you have any other ideas." Then, a teacher often asks a child to model her idea. "Natalie, please show us how you would move the magnetized sentences around on the cookie sheet." At times, the children work with the material immediately to try out their ideas. At other times, they work with the material in a learning center when they go to that learning center, which was the case with the sentence strips and the recycled cookie sheets. Often, the children show their work to the class or to a small group of children (Bechtel & Denton, 2004).

Guided discovery is a good strategy to use with learning centers. Consider using guided discovery when you have developed a new center or when you have changed a center. For example, if you change the dramatic play center's focus, then use guided discovery to help the children understand how to use the new equipment or material. Use guided discovery to help children learn how to return materials to their designated spot. This helps children to be responsible for taking care of and cleaning up after themselves and for keeping the classroom orderly and neat.

From the information presented so far, we can derive some principles for developing early childhood curriculum, which we will examine next.

PRINCIPLES OF EARLY CHILDHOOD CURRICULUM

In six principles for early childhood curriculum development (Figure 10.5), there is a "what we know" statement followed by an explanation about how to apply that knowledge to make decisions about curriculum. There is a real-world example of how teachers with a developmental perspective apply some of the principles.

Principle 1: Plan a Curriculum Reflecting All Developmental Domains

What we know. Early childhood educators focus on the whole child but are well aware that children develop in many domains: cognitive, emotional and social, physical and motor, and aesthetic. State departments of education also focus on domains of development as they assist administrators and teachers in planning curriculum (Barnett, Hustedt, Hawkinson, & Robin, 2006; California Department of Education, 2006; Gronlund, 2006).

Changes in any domain of development might well affect other areas. As a child's prefrontal cortex matures (physical/brain development), he gains self-control (social-emotional development). As motor skills increase, a child can engage in different types of art activities (aesthetic development). Some preschoolers with mild cognitive delays tend to have problems with forming friendships and establishing relationships. They have difficulty keeping a play episode going with another child (Guralnick, Connor, Hammond, Gottman, & Kinnish, 1996).

Apply this knowledge to curriculum. Develop curriculum reflecting all areas of children's development. Daily interactions with children, developmentally appropriate curriculum, and the classroom itself can foster all areas of development. Here are a few examples.

- Focus on social development by encouraging children to work in groups on projects and in learning centers.
- Focus deliberately on emotional development by teaching the word labels for emotions (Dunn & Brown, 1994).
- Focus on language and literacy with stories and conversation and in every part of the room and throughout the day.

FIGURE 10.5   Guiding Principles of Early Childhood Curriculum Development

Principle 1: Plan a curriculum reflecting all developmental domains

Principle 2: Develop a curriculum with intellectual integrity and regarded as appealing and important to children

Principle 3: Plan a comprehensive and integrated curriculum focusing on recognized content areas

Principle 4: Plan a curriculum encouraging children's social interaction

Principle 5: Plan a curriculum with appropriately challenging and novel learning activities

Principle 6: Plan a curriculum to meet the needs of all children

- Focus on cognitive development by having children solve problems, remember things, or summarize a story.
- Focus on aesthetic development by examining and describing paintings or pieces of sculpture or by creating paintings or writing songs.

Focus on the whole child when planning the room's layout or when you organize and plan activities. The block area is a good case in point. Blocks, used mainly in preschools and kindergartens, would also be appropriate in primary grade classrooms. Most people would probably agree that the block area is an excellent vehicle for physical development but might not see its value for other domains. Notice how Mr. Hernandez, the kindergarten to second-grade teacher, focused on the whole child through block play.

First graders Trina and Luis, working in the block area, develop in every domain. They lift and move large blocks (physical development); plan the design for their farmyard (cognitive development); confer with another person (social development), deal with frustration when things do not go as planned (emotional development), and talk with each other while making a sign for the garage (language development and literacy). They create a thing of beauty (aesthetic development).

CHECK YOUR UNDERSTANDING
Focus on the Whole Child

Look again at the primary grade chapter-opening vignette. Explain how the experiment with cars focuses on the whole child. For example, how does it enhance children's development in physical, cognitive, social, and emotional development?

Principle 2: Develop a Curriculum with Intellectual Integrity and Regarded as Appealing and Important to Children

What we know. Children have a built-in thirst for knowledge. They are internally motivated to try to make sense of their world. Children ask questions. They explore. Children wonder. Children learn through play, and they actually *need* to play (Elkind, 2006; Gronlund, 2001). Children construct knowledge best through active engagement and play (Dewey, 1902; NAEYC, 2003) with materials, other children, and knowledgeable teachers.

Apply this knowledge to curriculum. Organize a classroom's space, activities, materials, and schedule for activity and play as a central defining feature of the curriculum. Provide options, choice, and movement. These change with development but should focus on children's direct experiences. This does not always mean manipulating actual physical objects but does mean that the child is actively engaged in learning. For example, he might create a graph using data that he has gathered in an investigation.

Be a well-informed consumer. Carefully scrutinize advertisements for educational products. Ask questions. Does the product or commercially produced curriculum meet rigorous standards? Is it rooted in child development? Are children actively involved in learning? Are the suggested materials or activities worthy of children's time? Alternatively, are they time wasters, focusing primarily on entertainment? For example, the *Curriculum on Wheels* requires that children sit and simply watch cartoon characters describe historical events (Schemo, 2007). Technology can certainly supplement children's

Children can learn about all content areas in classrooms organized for activity and play-based learning.

active involvement and investigations but should not substitute for children's involvement in their own learning.

Effective early childhood educators reflect children's eagerness for learning in a developmentally appropriate curriculum. They refuse to obliterate a child's enthusiasm with mind-numbing workbook pages and reject any strategy or room arrangement that destroys the joy of learning for children. They refuse to do harm to children's intellect and they follow a code of ethics in all of their work with children. Their first obligation is to do no harm to children (NAEYC, 2005).

Children should perceive the curriculum as engaging, relevant, and meaningful (Dewey, 1902; NAEYC, 2003). Curriculum should have intellectual integrity and should be worthy of children's time (Branscombe et al., 2003). Avoid a watered-down, boring, workbook-driven approach to curriculum, which is known widely as a top-down or **push down curriculum.** This refers to the tendency to *push down* a curriculum for much older children to the kindergarten and even the preschool (Katz, 1999).

Push down curriculum
Tendency to use a curriculum for much older children with kindergarten and preschool children.

Principle 3: Plan a Comprehensive and Integrated Curriculum Focusing on Recognized Content Areas

What we know. The physical sciences, mathematics and computer sciences, technology, literature, history, languages, and language development "represent all the cumulative strivings, experiences of all the generations" and experts in the academic disciplines have taken part in logically forming, summarizing, and arranging their discipline over time (Dewey, 1902). Mathematicians, scientists, and historians continue to move their disciplines forward through research, creating new knowledge, and publishing their results. Thus, building the world's knowledge is an ongoing process.

Apply this knowledge to curriculum. Teachers are the guides for children to the world's knowledge. We do this by developing a **comprehensive curriculum,** which includes all of the academic disciplines (Copple & Bredekamp, 2006; NAEYC, 2003).

Comprehensive curriculum
Brings together different content areas and focuses on learning centers and projects.

Teachers use their pedagogical knowledge to make mathematics, for example, accessible to children. Teachers realize that children can grasp basic concepts of the disciplines (Bruner, 1960, 2006) only if the curriculum is developmentally appropriate. Therefore, they use instructional strategies appropriate for early childhood learners. Effective teachers understand that counting, measuring, and arranging things in a series involves mathematical scholarship for young children.

Principle 4: Plan a Curriculum Encouraging Children's Social Interaction

What we know. Human beings are social creatures (Barnes, 1995; de Waal, 2000) and children, as social beings, crave companionship and acceptance in a group. In a constructivist framework, children also need social interaction to learn. Recent research, for example, has documented that children learn effectively when they play and work with other children (Rimm-Kaufman, 2006). They need to talk to each other and even challenge one another's ideas, a concept from Piaget's theory (Piaget, 1932; Russell, 2004). Whether they work on math, write poems together, come up with rules for a game, or resolve a disagreement, children construct knowledge by working with other children and with adults.

Apply this knowledge to curriculum. Set things up so that children work with other children throughout the day, at meeting time and in small groups playing together as well as working on activities and projects together. Emphasize treating others in a friendly way even if the other person is not a friend.

Principle 5: Plan a Curriculum with Appropriately Challenging and Novel Learning Activities

What we know. Children construct different forms of knowledge (Russell, 2004). When children play and work with objects, they come to understand and learn about the tangible qualities of the objects. Pinecones feel rough, play dough feels smooth, and sand is gritty. These are examples of the *physical knowledge* that children construct when they manipulate and explore concrete items.

As children observe other children and adults, whether in person on or a screen, they begin to understand the knowledge created by humans. This is *social knowledge*, ideas learned by observing and interacting with others. For example, a child learns how males and

Children learn effectively and develop good social skills when they play and work with other children.

females in his culture interact. He will learn about different jobs and professions in his culture through observation and interaction with adults who can help him understand the jobs. Children construct this knowledge more effectively by watching and interacting with other people than by manipulating objects.

Children develop *logico-mathematical knowledge* when they figure out relationships, as explained in Chapter 2. In terms of curriculum, children learn about relationships both formally and informally, building knowledge by connecting the familiar with the new. Figure 10.6 illustrates the three types of knowledge that children construct. In the arts, for example, children learn many different concepts in preschool, kindergarten, and first grade and then, by interacting with art educators, build on this knowledge.

Painting is a part of the visual arts and, in about third grade, children learn about the relationship between foreground and background in a painting (Klein, 2007; Utah Education Network, no date). The relationship of background to foreground is the idea that they construct in their mind; it is not in the painting. Still later, in upper elementary grades, for example, they will learn the techniques for creating background and foreground in their art.

Apply this knowledge to curriculum. Set the stage for learning. Provide time, materials, and appropriately challenging and novel experiences for projects. Scaffold children's understanding and provide enough time for children to build different types of knowledge. Figure 10.6 illustrates the three types of knowledge that children construct. Structure the schedule so that children have large, uninterrupted blocks of time for play and learning.

Provide materials. Children, whatever their grade level, benefit from working with manipulatives such as bristle blocks and other safe materials. Primary grade children

Go to MyEducationLab and select the topic "Curriculum/ Program Models." Under Activities and Applications, watch the video *Conducting an Investigation: Small Group 'Taste Test' Activity.* Observe as this teacher helps children build on their existing knowledge about apples.

This child will develop **physical knowledge** by manipulating the pinecone.

The child develops **logico-mathematical knowledge** when she sees the *relationship* of the pinecone to the tree that produced it.

She will develop **social knowledge**, such as the name of the object, when her teacher introduces the word *pinecone*.

FIGURE 10.6   Children Construct Different Types of Knowledge

learn many math concepts with manipulatives. Children can also work with interactive materials in computer programs and with raw data that they gather such as data on how many pinecones fill increasingly larger boxes. Children, in many cases actually handle objects, turning, feeling, smelling, and manipulating them to understand their qualities. In other cases, a child can develop physical knowledge when interacting with computer-generated items as she, for example, draws the pinecone on a screen.

Scaffold children's learning. Provide the experiences through which children begin to understand relationships. Observe children as they work. Ask questions. Help children learn labels for items. Help them understand relationships. For example, children learning about stop signs in a kindergarten class could take a walk to observe, at a safe distance, drivers coming to a halt at the sign. This is first-hand experience in observing the relationship between the stop sign and behavior of drivers.

Provide reasonably novel and challenging tasks for children. Cognitive growth revolves around facing questions about what we know, figuring out how to answer the questions, and finally understanding something new on that topic. For example, two of the second graders in Mr. Hernandez's class had focused in on circular objects divided into equal sections, the wagon wheel, grapefruits and oranges, a pumpkin pie, a pie chart on a poster, the wheel on the *Wheel of Fortune* game show. He recorded their learning with a documentation panel, a photo exhibition of the objects, the class observing and working with the objects, and the children's comments. He also included a note briefly listing state standards met with the experience. The children had learned quite a bit in their work. It was time for the next step.

The teacher challenged his second graders with this task. He placed a device for dividing pies into six equal segments on a table and placed large sheets of paper nearby, along with chalk, markers, and other writing instruments. As children worked, Mr. Hernandez observed that they traced the segments onto paper with chalk. They linked their work with the pie divider to the documentation panel, "Look, just like the wagon wheel!" Moderately challenging and novel tasks require children to perform mental operations using new information to go further in understanding their world.

Later, the teacher challenges these children again when he asks them to put together evenly divided cardboard segments of a large circle, a geometry lesson that met Illinois state standard 9As for mathematics for grade 2. He also challenges them to draw and label their own version of the shapes as shown in Figure 10.7.

Experiences such as these help children to gain a broad knowledge base about their world and develop, gradually, abstract ideas about the objects that they have manipulated. For example, a wagon wheel with its spokes is like a grapefruit with its sections. Children begin to see connections between things in their world. They think. Understanding starts with physical knowledge.

Principle 6: Plan a Curriculum to Meet the Needs of *All* Children

The National Association for the Education of Young Children defines the phrase *all children:*

> All children means *all*: children with developmental delays or disabilities, children who are gifted and talented, children whose families are culturally and linguistically diverse, children from diverse socioeconomic groups, and other children with individual learning styles, strengths, and needs. (Hyson, 2003, page 25)

What we know. Teachers have the responsibility to meet the needs of each and every child through the curriculum. Children who are developing typically show a range of

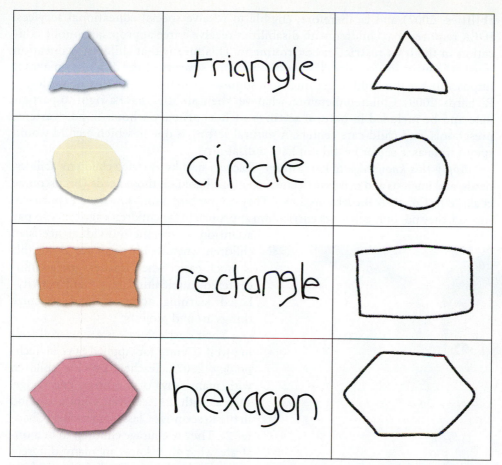

FIGURE 10.7 Children Observe Shapes (left) and Draw Their Version (right).

abilities within any developmental domain. For example, some children in a kindergarten classroom move with agility and grace but other children's large motor skills are not as smooth. Some children regulate emotions well, but others do not. Some children know how to approach groups for play, but others lack necessary social skills. Some children work independently while others cannot regulate their play. Many converse with others easily and have sizeable vocabularies, but others do not know how to have a conversation and might have much smaller vocabularies. Thus, typically developing children have individual learning needs.

Children who are learning a language different from their home language have special learning needs. Teachers must understand the culture from which children come and then need to understand the pedagogy involved in teaching children who are learning a new language while they are also learning material from the content areas. This is where a teacher's pedagogical content knowledge comes into play. She must know and use strategies demonstrated to help English language learners. In addition, teachers must keep in mind that a child learning a second language might have additional individual learning needs because he or she can be developing typically, have a disability, or can be gifted.

Similarly, other groups of children have individual learning needs. A **child with a disability** has one of the 13 disability categories defined in the Individuals with Disabilities Education Act, IDEA, PL 108-446 (National Center for Learning Dis-

Child with a disability A child who has one of the 13 disability categories defined in IDEA.

Least restrictive environment Educating children with disabilities in a regular classroom unless they cannot get the level of support that they need in that context because of how severe the disability is.

Natural settings The setting where a child would have spent time if she or he had not had a disability.

abilities, 2007) and is, therefore, eligible to receive special educational services. IDEA requires that children with disabilities receive a free appropriate public education in the **least restrictive environment**. This means that children's education must take place in a regular classroom unless the severity of the disability makes it impossible for the child to get intensive support in that setting (Taylor, Smiley, & Richards, 2009). Children therefore, whatever their abilities, have a right to participate and be included in **natural settings** such as primary schools, kindergartens, preschools, and child-care centers. A natural setting is one in which a child would spend time as if she or he did not have a disability.

Apply this knowledge to curriculum. Teachers start by assessing children's abilities, needs, and interests and make curriculum decisions based on those needs (Branscombe et al., 2001; Copple & Bredekamp, 2006). They do not take a one-size-fits-all approach. Instead, they not only construct curriculum appropriate for children's age but also pay attention to specific individual needs of children, whatever the needs are. Doing this is much easier when teachers use a child-centered curriculum, play- and activity-based learning activities, and organize things around projects.

Their curriculum has a universal feeling to it (Center for Applied Special Technology, 2007). Teachers provide children with many ways of acquiring knowledge, such as with the Academic Choice method in the Responsive Classroom model (Chapter 2). They encourage children to demonstrate what they know in many different ways, as the Reggio Emilia schools have done so beautifully (Chapter 2). Reggio schools are based on the idea that children have a hundred languages, a graceful way of expressing their respect for children's almost unlimited ways of showing us what they think, know, and can do. They also zero in on children's interests and build curriculum from there, as in the Project Approach.

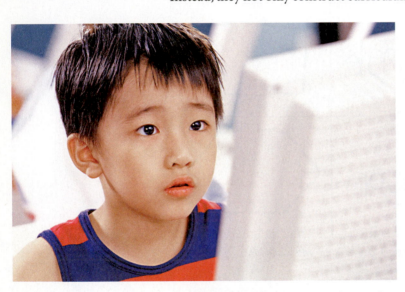

Construct a curriculum to meet the needs of all children, including those who are learning English.

Inclusion Supporting every child's right to participate in natural settings.

They build an inclusive classroom. **Inclusion** is a value that supports every child's right of participation (DEC, 1996) in natural settings, with children very close to his or her age, and with essential and suitable supports and services (Cross & Dixon, 2004). One of the best ways to meet the needs of all children is in inclusive classrooms (Odom, Schwartz, & ECRII Investigators, 2002). Children reap the benefits from inclusive classrooms. They "demonstrate increased acceptance and appreciation of diversity; develop better communication and social skills; show greater development in moral and ethical principles; create warm and caring friendships; and demonstrate increased self-esteem" (NAEYC, 1996, modified 2006).

Adaptation Way of changing something about a lesson or some aspect of the environment so that every child can benefit from activities.

Adaptation is a process of fine-tuning or changing teaching strategy, materials, the environment, or equipment so that every child gets the most from learning activities. The goal should be to use the least intrusive adaptation possible that helps a child participate in an activity. There are several practical and effective ways to adapt a lesson or curriculum (Cross & Dixon, 2004). Figure 10.8 lists different types of adaptations.

Nine types of adaptations.

LEVEL THREE
Alternative Goals: Identify an individual goal or outcome for the child within a learning activity that has a different focus for the other children. **For example:** Ask the child to hand individual bears to other children who are matching yellow and blue bears to color cards. The child's activity goal is to interact with others.

LEVEL TWO		
Difficulty: Adjust the skill level, complexity, or rules of how the child approaches the activity. **For example:** Ask the child to find all of the cars rather than asking for the little cars only.	**Participation:** Adapt the manner or way in which the child is actively involved. **For example:** A child can participate in a play by holding up a sign with the title or carry a special prop while others act out their parts.	**Alternative Teaching Opportunities:** Use other opportunities in the day to teach the child concepts and skills presented in planned activities. **For example:** When children are learning to count objects, ask the child to count the napkins, plates, cups, and crackers needed for a snack.

LEVEL ONE				
Environment: Adapt the flow of the room, seating, and positioning options. Adapt materials to meet the child's needs. **For example:** Add cups and spoons with large, thick handles to the sand table for the child who has difficulty holding smaller items.	**Time:** Adapt the time allotted for learning or task completion. **For example:** Call the child to be first to put on a coat for outdoor play so that he has the time to do it independently.	**Input:** Adapt the way you present information and materials to the child, including the way you talk. **For example:** Use picture cues along with your spoken words to help a child understand what the next activity is.	**Output:** Adapt the way the child communicates, including the way he responds to what is to be learned. Adjust how much you expect to be accomplished. **For example:** Arrange two objects in positions that help the child choose a play activity by looking at one or the other.	**Level of Support:** Vary the amount of personal assistance needed. **For example:** Put your hand over the child's to guide his movement for placing puzzle pieces and then lessen your help as the child begins to show independent ability.

FIGURE 10.8   Nine Types of Adaptations

Source: From *Adapting Curriculum and Instruction in Inclusive Early Childhood Settings* (rev. ed., p. 14), by A. F. Cross and S. D. Dixon, 2004, Bloomington, IN: Indiana Institute on Disability & Community. Copyright 2004 by Indiana Institute on Disability & Community. Adapted with permission.

Adaptations from the first group, Level one, give a child the greatest chance of participating in an activity in much the same way as every other child in the class. This involves something simple to enable his participation, such as adding knobs to puzzle pieces so that he can grip the pieces, an adaption of the environment. Level two adaptations allow you to help children who need a bigger change to learn. The adaptation in Level three is very useful when the others have not helped a child participate in an activity.

SUMMARY

The main goals for early childhood curriculum are to promote children's development; support children's learning, knowledge, and skills; and to nurture children's passion for learning. Teachers need pedagogical content knowledge to develop an appropriate curriculum. This means that they use their knowledge of subject matter such as social studies, language arts, or multiculturalism. They combine this with pedagogical knowledge, the teaching methods and strategies that are appropriate for young children and with knowledge about the setting in which young children learn.

There are three main sources for early childhood curriculum: children, teachers, and learning standards.

- Children are an important source in an emerging curriculum. Teachers observe and listen to children's understandings, questions, and misunderstandings. The curriculum emerges in response to what children need.
- Teachers, who understand child development and different content areas, such as mathematics and social sciences, are another source for the curriculum. They use their knowledge and their individual skills to build appropriate learning experiences.
- Learning standards are statements about how children develop and what children should know or be able to do. Effective standards come from professional organizations for the different content areas, such as science and language arts. They serve as guidelines as teachers develop curriculum but they do not dictate teaching strategies.

This is an era of accountability with teachers under pressure to demonstrate that they are helping children to meet specific outcomes. Teachers meet the challenge of planning a curriculum reflecting all developmental domains and which includes all content areas. They can meet the challenge by developing an *integrated curriculum*.

- We integrate curriculum by combining the content areas. Teachers organize learning activities focusing on different areas, such as math, creative arts, and science all at the same time, in the same activity.
- An integrated curriculum focuses on projects and learning centers. Projects satisfy children's curiosity and activity-driven approach to seeking knowledge. Learning centers encourage small groups of children to learn as they work with others or independently and as they make choices.

Teachers with good pedagogical content knowledge use teaching strategies supporting an integrated curriculum. Three examples of effective teaching strategies include:

- Teachers create choice times for children. These are extended periods in which children work on projects or in learning centers.
- Teachers also plan productive group meetings, in which children learn from the content areas and learn social skills.
- Teachers plan productive discussions, acting as the leader in helping children construct new ideas and understandings.

Teachers use several guiding principles to develop curriculum. They:

- plan a curriculum reflecting all developmental domains. They focus on the whole child, acknowledging all areas of development—social, emotional, physical and motor, cognitive and language, and aesthetic.
- develop a curriculum with intellectual integrity and regarded as appealing and important to children. They help children learn literacy and other content through play- and activity-based learning. They help children to satisfy their natural curiosity and need for knowledge.
- plan a comprehensive and integrated curriculum focusing on recognized content areas. They include all content areas and not just those on which standardized yearly tests focus.
- plan a curriculum that encourages children's social interaction. Effective teachers understand that learning is social and set up the room and schedule, as well as specific learning activities to foster positive and productive child-child interaction.
- plan a curriculum with appropriately challenging and novel learning activities. They believe that cognitive growth revolves around facing questions about what we know, figuring out how to answer the questions, and finally understanding something new on that topic.
- plan a curriculum to meet the needs of *all* children. They assess every child's abilities and do *not* take a one-size-fits-all approach. Instead, they attend to what each child needs at a specific time. The curriculum has a universal feel to it. That is, teachers provide children with many ways of acquiring knowledge, adapting the curriculum so that each child may participate fully in learning activities.

QUESTIONS FOR REFLECTION

1. Explain how the primary grade vignette at the beginning of the chapter, the "car and ramp" activity, opening the chapter, shows an integrated curriculum?

2. How does the preschool "parking the cars" vignette illustrate the principle of social interaction in curriculum development?

APPLY YOUR KNOWLEDGE

What Should This Teacher Do?

1. The "yeah, but . . ." Recall that Mr. Hernandez's class worked with circles divided into sections, including a pie divider. A parent observed his child working with the divider and asked the teacher, "Yeah, looks like fun, but what are they learning?" How should the teacher respond?

2. In a conference, a parent of one of the first-grade children asked Mr. Hernandez, "The children really seem to like talking to other children as they work. But doesn't the talking get in the way of academics?" How should the teacher respond?

KEY TERMS

Academic choice, 255
Accountability, 251
Adaptation, 266
Child-centered curriculum, 244
Child with a disability, 265
Choice times, 255
Comprehensive curriculum, 262
Content areas, 244

Curriculum, 244
Emergent curriculum, 246
Guided discovery, 258
Inclusion, 266
Indicators, 250
Integrated curriculum, 252
Learning standard, 247
Least restrictive environment, 266
Natural settings, 266

Pedagogical content knowledge, 244
Pedagogical knowledge, 245
Project, 253
Push down curriculum, 261
Responsiveness, 247
Subject matter knowledge, 244
Tummy time, 247

WEB SITES

Bank Street Children's Programs
http://www.bankstreet.edu/cp/
Site for the children's programs at the Bank Street College of Education. You read about this model in Chapter 2. It follows the principles of curriculum development in its children's programs.

National 4-H
http://www.n4hccs.org/
Main page for the National 4-H Curriculum, an informal yet professionally developed curriculum for children, including those in the K to grade 3 age range. Click on the 4-H Curriculum catalogue to see specific examples of DAP

curricula for young children, such as preflight adventures, a curriculum for grades K to 2.

Project Approach
http://www.projectapproach.org
Learn about the phases in projects. Many examples of real projects done in real classrooms for different age groups. Highly recommended.

Project Construct
http://www.projectconstruct.org
Main page for Project Construct, a program in the state of Missouri. Approach to teaching in preschool and primary grades that is based on how children develop and learn.

CHAPTER 11

Early Childhood Environments

GUIDING QUESTIONS:

- What are the different environments that early childhood teachers need to know about?

- What specific things do I need to know and be able to do in order to create these environments?

- How can I organize appropriate learning activities for children in these early childhood environments?

INFANT/TODDLER
Time to Paint

For outdoor play, Mr. Bjornrud placed four small buckets of water with a paintbrush in each near the wall on the playground, a new activity for the toddlers. Nick, 2½ years old, stood nearby gazing at the buckets. Observing that Nick might be interested but also somewhat hesitant, Mr. Bjornrud calmly picked up one of the paintbrushes, dipped it into the water, and demonstrated how to paint the wall. Nick followed his teacher's lead and painted the wall, too.

PRESCHOOL

A Good Transition

At the end of story time, Mrs. Chang asked what came next as she pointed to the daily schedule. "Choice time!" called out the children. She said, "Watch me!" and then wrote the letters *M, K* on the white board. "If your first name begins with M or K, you can go to choice time. She continued until all children had made the transition.

KINDERGARTEN
What Is on a Title Page of a Book?

At the beginning of the school year, Mr. Hernandez's kindergarteners sat in a half-circle around his chair for a story, staring at the large purple sticky note attached to one of the pages of his book. "What do we have here?" he said. "You're right. It's marking this page, this special page called the title page." The class went on to examine, very briefly, the content of a title page before reading the story.

PRIMARY
Ben Plans for Academic Choice

Ben, a second-grade child in Mr. Hernandez's class, checked his planning sheet for academic choice (planning sheets and academic choice were explained in Chapter 10. He had one hour to work and intended to go to the sensory table to practice new spelling words by writing them in sand and then to the whiteboard to use them in sentences. He also planned to work in the discovery center to mix *light* and *dark* blue paint. His class is working on understanding opposites and mixing paint is one of the four ways that they can choose to learn this concept.

Children thrive in healthy, safe, and appropriately challenging environments. They need a healthy interpersonal environment in which teachers show respect for children through words and actions. They need a physical environment in which they can learn actively and can develop social skills along with knowledge of mathematics, science, social studies, language arts, or the arts. They need a temporal environment, a schedule that allows for extended periods for work, play, and learning. They also need teachers who know how to organize learning activities.

This chapter will help you build on your knowledge of curriculum development from Chapter 10. You will learn specific skills for creating environments appropriate for young children. We will examine several ways for creating a healthy interpersonal environment. Then, we will observe how effective teachers design the physical environment so that it supports children's learning through activity, making choices, and social interaction. We will look at how to construct an appropriate temporal environment, the schedule for an early childhood classroom. You will see that such a schedule goes hand in hand with an appropriate physical environment in setting the stage for children's learning. Finally, you will study the essential elements of lesson planning, a way of organizing for children's learning in their healthy and safe environments.

INTERPERSONAL ENVIRONMENTS

Interpersonal environment
The interaction between teacher and child and between children; the relationships evolving from the interactions.

Feeling safe, secure, and cherished. How important are these for children? Moreover, what happens to development and learning when children do not feel safe and respected? These might seem like strange questions in a chapter on environments in early childhood education but are really at the heart of all effective teaching and learning whose foundation is a teacher's relationships with children and families (Hyson, 2003). Our positive relationships create the safe **interpersonal environment** that each and every young child needs.

A safe interpersonal environment helps children meet many needs, which were described by Maslow (1954). Figure 11.1 shows Maslow's hierarchy of needs with implications for early childhood teachers. This figure shows that a child's most basic bodily or physiological needs, such as for sleep and food, must be met before we can attempt to help him learn in school. Meeting needs for safety and security provides the foundation on which the social and esteem needs at the upper part of the illustration can be met. Maslow's hierarchy is also useful in our work with parents because they have the same needs. They have a right to feel like valued members of the classroom community.

Healthy interpersonal environments support children's development and learning. Their curiosity paves the way for exploring, discovering, practicing, and understanding, but children's curiosity-exploring-learning cycle is possible only when they feel safe and when they have appropriately affectionate and safe relationships. If children do not feel safe at school, then they will have a great deal of difficulty playing and learning. They do not feel safe if they are fearful or feel threatened. Fear destroys curiosity (Perry, 2000).

Healthy and safe interpersonal environments, a child's secure relationships, have powerful effects on his developing brain, personality, and ability and willingness to learn (Perry & Szalavitz, 2007). Predictable, structured, and familiar surroundings help young children to feel safe and secure. At school, children in all phases of early childhood, from infancy through grade 3, need predictable physical and temporal (time) environments. More important, though, teachers need to be predictable because they have a major part in creating the interpersonal environment. Children need teachers whose personalities convey genuine affection, caring, and respect (Marion, 2007). These consistently respectful behaviors create a cocoon, a safe interpersonal environment in

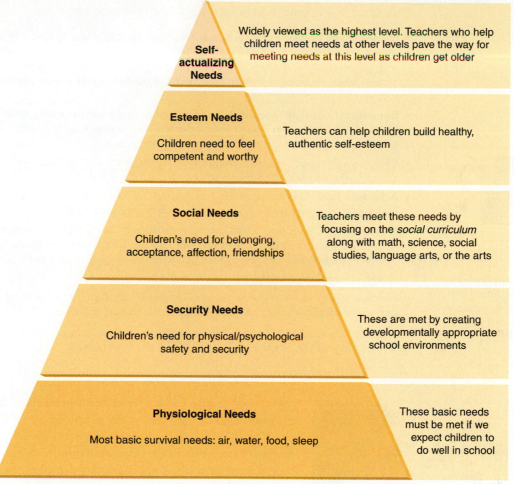

Self-actualizing Needs
Widely viewed as the highest level. Teachers who help children meet needs at other levels pave the way for meeting needs at this level as children get older

Esteem Needs
Children need to feel competent and worthy
Teachers can help children build healthy, authentic self-esteem

Social Needs
Children's need for belonging, acceptance, affection, friendships
Teachers meet these needs by focusing on the *social curriculum* along with math, science, social studies, language arts, or the arts

Security Needs
Children's need for physical/psychological safety and security
These are met by creating developmentally appropriate school environments

Physiological Needs
Most basic survival needs: air, water, food, sleep
These basic needs must be met if we expect children to do well in school

FIGURE 11.1   Maslow's Hierarchy of Needs: Implications for Teachers

which children spend time exploring, learning, and making friends. Figure 11.2 lists some of these practical strategies.

PHYSICAL ENVIRONMENTS FOR INFANTS AND TODDLERS

A teacher's role includes constructing a calming, productive, pleasant **physical environment** for children throughout the early childhood years. We focus on two things here. First, we look at classrooms for infants and toddlers through a video tour of one center. Then, we shift focus to classrooms for preschool, kindergarten, and primary grade children. In this latter section we will study a floor plan and learn about why it is appropriately arranged.

Program for Infant/Toddler Care

The *Program for Infant/Toddler Care* (PITC) is a California program dedicated to developmentally appropriate care for infants and toddlers. The group has developed several demonstration sites for showing those working with very young children how to set up an environment conducive to optimal infant and toddler development. This approach follows principles of developmentally appropriate practice. PITC emphasizes that

Physical environment
The material setting, inside and outdoors for a classroom; includes, for example, arrangement of space and furniture and materials used for children's learning.

FIGURE 11.2   Create a Safe Interpersonal Environment

- **Demonstrate Respect and Genuine Affection for Children:** Speak with respect, always. Be calm and composed. Children need to see you as a person who smiles and laughs easily and often. They need appropriate touch, such as gently holding a hand when restating a limit or touching a shoulder as you request attention for a story.

- **Consistent, Positive Teacher Behavior:** Behave in a consistent and positive way: Children will see you as a trustworthy person who is predictably positive, even when dealing with things such as aggression or distress.

- **Children's Perspective: How things look to children:** Get to their eye level, look at them when speaking to them; spend time on the floor with them.

- **Acknowledgement:** Acknowledge each child every day; acknowledge their pleasant and unpleasant emotions; acknowledge what they do.

- **Observation:** Observe children carefully; recognize their styles and temperaments; know their overload point; prevent conditions contributing to overload. Help an overwhelmed child find time and breathing space to get back in control.

- **Quiet Times:** Provide solitude—quiet, reflective times.

- **Guidance:** Take time to guide children's behavior appropriately; focus on teaching and never on punishment or any strategy that can hurt children.

Sources: Carlson (2006), Marion (2007), Perry (2000), and Tanner (2005).

Go to MyEducationLab and select the topic "Early Environments." Under Activities and Applications, watch the video *Infant and Toddler Setting* to observe how this school set up the classroom for this age group.

Toddlers need to move, touch, and explore.

infants and toddlers have special needs in terms of the physical environment and view the setting as crucial.

The PITC has several demonstration centers, which are designated as places where infant and toddler caregivers can get a first-hand view of an appropriately designed space for very young children. One outstanding feature of the whole PITC is the emphasis on relationships and an activity-based approach.

Videos of the centers show the design, a floor plan, and photos of individual classrooms. One of these centers is at Grossmont College, near San Diego in southern California. This center cares for children 6 months to 3 years old. View a video of this infant and toddler center at this college at the PITC web site listed at the end of the chapter. The center remodeled its classrooms and shows before and after photos of the major changes. In addition, please see the video on setting up an infant and toddler classroom in MyEducationLab (see margin note).

CHECK YOUR UNDERSTANDING
Time to Paint Vignette

For the infant/toddler vignette at the opening of the chapter, complete these two sentences:

Mr. Bjornrud has focused on relationships by _____

He has focused on an activity-based approach by _____

PHYSICAL ENVIRONMENT FOR 3 TO 8 YEAR OLDS

The design of the classroom in Figure 11.3 is based on principles of developmentally appropriate practice with a focus on three things:

- What are some of the features that make this room appropriate for young children?
- What messages does the room send to children?
- How is the classroom likely to affect children's development and learning?

FIGURE 11.3 Drawing of Early Childhood Classroom, Bird's Eye View.

Developmentally Appropriate Room Arrangement

The classroom arrangement makes this room appropriate for young children because it demonstrates a teacher's knowledge of and respect for how children develop and learn. The teacher practices what he believes about children's development and learning. This arrangement tells us that the teacher believes that children are curious, resourceful, and competent.

- **Sense of Order**
  It conveys a sense of order and provides a comforting place for work and play (Greenman, 2006). The room is arranged well and is tidy and organized. Children know that items have their own place in the room and that the basic structure will be the same from day to day even though the teacher might change materials and activities within the centers.

- **Making Choices**
  The arrangement gives children many chances to make choices. Children need to learn to make wise choices, and this room gives them plenty of practice. Consider the learning centers and materials. During choice time, children work alone or most often work with other children. Each center has a variety of materials directly related to that center, and children get to choose from available materials. For instance, children in this room can choose a computer, chalk and small chalkboards, colored pencils and recycled paper, fat markers and small whiteboards, or trays of damp sand for writing in the writing center.

  > Ben, from the primary grade vignette at the beginning of the chapter, is in a multiage K to 2 class. Therefore, his teacher has designed the environment for kindergarten, first- and second-grade children. The children work in centers. Ben has chosen two centers, the sensory table and the discovery area.

- **Active Learning**
  Active learning is encouraged in the centers, with all materials, and even through teacher-initiated activities such as guided discovery. Children manipulate physical objects, they gather data, and they develop new ideas or deepen their understand of old ideas in centers, such as when they are actively involved in making decisions about how to mix colors in the discovery area.

What Messages Does This Room Send to Children?

A well-designed classroom has a voice, sending messages to children (Tarr, 2001).

- *"You can learn many things here."*
- *"You can play and work with other children here."*
- *"You can make many choices here."*
- *"You can work on many different projects here."*
- *"When you are done working in one area, you can go to a different spot and work there."*
- *"When you want to, you can work by yourself."*
- *"There is a good space where all the children in your class can gather."*

Effect on Children's Development and Learning

There are many benefits for children when their teacher designs a developmentally appropriate classroom such as the one in Figure 11.3. They have far lower levels of stress and fewer discipline problems. They also tend to interact with others in a more positive way (Bovey & Strain, no date; Hart et al., 1998; Steinhauer, 2005). They tend to be more independent and self-controlled. They also display greater feelings of competence and confidence, both elements of authentic self-esteem. Therefore, a well-designed physical

These students are meeting their state's science standards through active learning in an outdoor learning center.

environment supports children's efforts to meet the higher order needs, such as esteem needs, in Maslow's hierarchy. Children in a well-developed environment develop better decision-making skills and ability to take initiative than children in developmentally *in*appropriate physical environments (Howes, 1991; Johnson, 2006; Stallings, 1975).

CHECK YOUR UNDERSTANDING
Take a Child's Perspective

Suppose that you were a child in the classroom in Figure 11.3. The research cited in this section reports that you would very likely feel far *less* stress than if you were in a poorly designed room. Offer two reasons that might explain why you would feel far less stress in this room than in a poorly arranged classroom.

Guidelines: Developmentally Appropriate Room Design

Effectively arranged classrooms acknowledge that children learn through play, active involvement, and social interaction. Teachers organize the classroom into learning centers, they provide enough centers, arrange the centers logically, and provide appropriately stimulating materials for the centers (Marion, 2007).

Organize the Classroom into Learning Centers

There are several different types of **learning centers.** Some are small, some large; some have seating and others do not. Specific materials are stored in some centers, but other areas have no materials stored there. Developmentally appropriate classrooms usually contain individual or small group learning centers, a large group area, and some sort of private area. This grouping is appropriate for preschool, kindergarten, and primary grade classrooms. Materials and activities within centers vary, of course, at different grade levels, but the structure would allow the teacher to provide an integrated curriculum with all content areas.

- **Small group learning centers** may include areas such as the block, dramatic play, science/math/discovery, art, puzzles/manipulatives, math, writing, and sensory (water or sand) table. Each is large enough for five to six children, and each has a specific function that helps the teacher meet program goals. Each contains materials logically related to that school's goals.

Go to MyEducationLab and select the topic "Early Environments." Under Activities and Applications, watch the video *Using Centers to Foster Learning* and view centers in a real classroom.

Learning centers Division of classrooms into play/work spaces; can be for small groups, the entire class, or individuals.

- **Large group center** is a space large enough to accommodate the entire class. This area should be large, open, and flexible to accommodate group activities related to different content areas such as music, dance, or drama, and language arts. The large group area serves many purposes; therefore, specific materials are not stored there but are brought to group time by the teacher. An exception is that you might consider storing items, such as a set of children's name cards, in the large group area that help you make transitions from group to some other activity.

The large group center accommodates the entire class.

- **Individual learning center** gives children a chance to work alone in a busy classroom. The writing center and the reading-library center would serve nicely for individuals or for two children to work side by side. In Figure 11.3 the reading-library area is set in a quieter area of the room.
- **Private space** is a small, partially enclosed space with room for only one or two children, visually isolated from other children but easily supervised by adults. This is a place for solitude, for children to recharge by taking time for themselves away from the group.

Arrange Learning Centers Logically

Help children understand the type of play and work in each center by using signs designating each center. Group centers that are more quiet together and group less quiet centers together. Examples of less quiet centers include blocks, dramatic play, and music. Create good physical boundaries for learning centers. Some older research showed that children tend to be more cooperative and far less disruptive when they understand where one area ends and the next begins (Olds, 1977).

Define an Effective Traffic Pattern

Traffic patterns Flow of movement in the room; children need open pathways clearly leading to learning centers.

Traffic patterns refer to the flow of movement in the room. Create open pathways that clearly lead to centers and that make it easy for children to move between areas. Trace the traffic pattern in Figure 11.3 and reflect on whether it meets these criteria for an effective pattern.

TEMPORAL (TIME) ENVIRONMENT: DEVELOPMENTALLY APPROPRIATE SCHEDULES

Temporal environment The time environment; the scheduling of activities in a classroom.

Teachers using the developmental approach understand that children differ in how they react to change (National Association of Child Care Resource and Referral Agencies, 2006). Knowing that children need predictability, effective teachers create a **temporal environment**, a predictable and appropriate schedule.

What Is a Schedule?

Schedule An organizing tool; involves deciding who will do what and when they will do things in a classroom.

A **schedule** is an organizing tool for teachers. Scheduling involves deciding who does what and when they will do things in a classroom. For a teacher, the schedule is a written document listing times and activities. For children, the schedule is a set of pictures, words, or even objects that tells them about activities that occur at different times during the day (Conroy, 2004). For parents, depending on their needs, the schedule can be written, an audio item, or even a photograph of the children's schedule.

Value of an Appropriate Schedule

Classroom schedules influence children's development, motivation, and learning. For example, children in developmentally appropriate practice (DAP) classrooms learn more effectively than do children in developmentally inappropriate classrooms (Project Construct, 2001), and children are more secure when their schedule is predictable and they understand the expectations in their environment. Children also tend to be less aggressive when a classroom schedule is predictable and appropriate (Ostrosky, Jung, Hemmeter, & Thomas, 2003). An appropriate schedule simply creates less stress for children than does an inappropriate schedule with numerous and poorly done transitions and inappropriate activities (Burts, Hart, Charlesworth, Fleege, Mosley, & Thomasson, 1992). A schedule helps children understand the flow of the day and fosters children's independence. Good schedules also prevent some challenging behavior (Alter & Conroy, no date; Conroy, 2004).

Guidelines: Developmentally Appropriate Schedules

Effective schedules acknowledge that children learn through play, active involvement, and social interaction and reflect children's need for extended time to develop ideas. Appropriate schedules in early childhood classrooms vary depending on factors such as a school's goals, length of time that the school is in session, and meals eaten at school. Half-day programs, for example, have a different schedule than a full-day program. All DAP schedules, however, are built on the following guidelines of balance, time, choice, transitions, and visibility (Bredekamp & Copple, 1997; Ostrosky et al., 2003).

Balance

There is a sense of order and harmony in a well-developed classroom schedule. Short periods for large group activities balance small group activities. Rest and quiet periods balance periods of physical activity (Corbin & Pangrazi, 2003). Balance also exists between teacher-directed and child-initiated activities and between indoor and outdoor activities.

Time

Children need expanded periods to learn and develop creatively. All developmentally appropriate schedules, whether for third graders or preschool children allow plenty of time for children's play, work, and learning. The schedule's pace or tempo supports children's development and learning (Hopkins, 2007; Wood, 1999). The duration of a choice time affects children's cognitive development and social play, with play/work periods longer than 30 minutes resulting in higher levels of cognitive and social play (Ostrosky et al., 2003).

The need for extended play and work sessions implies that we create schedules with extended work and play periods. Work sessions should be longer than 30 minutes, preferably for at least 1 or 1½ hours. It suggests that we avoid rushing children from one activity to another. It suggests that we let children use their choice times to delve deeply into an activity and carry it through if they wish. This strongly suggests that teachers not rotate centers. It suggests flexibility in scheduling; for instance, the schedule should be flexible enough to allow children to complete activities.

> Mr. Hernandez allowed plenty of time in the daily schedule for children to make choices and to complete their work. Ben, for example, in the primary grade vignette at the beginning of the chapter, had 1 hour to complete the two learning activities that he chose.

Choice

Developmentally appropriate schedules give children choices within limits. Given an array of centers or activities, children choose what they do for a good part of the day. Teachers schedule several indoor and outdoor choice periods, using this time to present content to children through well-designed center activities. Teachers use choice time for educational interaction with children, scaffolding children's understanding of ideas through appropriate and well-timed questions or comments. Teachers take the lead in arranging the classroom and materials for choice times (Harms, Clifford, & Cryer, 2005). Children in DAP classrooms often collaborate with other children as they learn because they have so many chances to work closely with other children (Telluride Mountain School, 2007).

The first and second graders in Mr. Hernandez's class, for example, could choose to work with Geoblocks as one of the many math activities for the week, and the exercises required that they work with a partner and have their work checked by the "coach," the teacher.

Transitions

Teachers in developmentally appropriate classrooms make decisions intentionally and deliberately (NAEYC, 2007). Understanding that transitions are potentially stressful for children, they minimize the number of teacher-directed transitions in the children's day. Teachers in DAP classrooms also know that some transitions are necessary and if done well might help children learn to deal with change well.

Transition Process of helping children move from one activity, such as a group meeting, in a classroom to another activity, such as outdoor play.

One such routine and necessary daily **transition** occurs between large group and choice time. Teachers give advance notice that a transition is "just around the corner" (Downs, Blagojevic, & Labas, 2006). They help children through the transition in a low-key, calm, orderly, and smooth way that wastes none of the children's time. They often use simple cues or reminders. For example, the teacher might hold up a picture of children getting things from cubbies or packing backpacks to cue children about the transition to going home.

Many teachers use transitions in a low-key way to foster social emotional skills. For example, a teacher might ask a child to make a sad, happy, or angry face before going to the next activity. At other times, teachers use transitions to teach something from a content area or recap what children are learning (McCart & Turnbull, no date).

Mrs. Chang, from the preschool chapter opening vignette, for example, focused on fostering self-control by having children wait a short time during the transition. She did not waste their time, however. She also focused on identifying letters of the alphabet, specifically the first letter in each child's name.

During choice time, these children have many options for learning.

The Columbus Magnet School in Norwalk, Connecticut, explained their view of transitions in their kindergarten and primary classrooms. The school follows the Bank Street model, explained in Chapter 2, minimizing the number of transitions needed because the room is set up in learning centers. Children in the primary classrooms as well as children in kindergarten have plenty of time to work on math, science, and the rest of the content areas within the learning centers. The schedule, even for the primary grades, resembles that in Figure 11.4. Necessary transitions between activities are viewed as "reasonable and flexible" because children are encouraged to direct their own learning (Columbus Magnet School, no date).

FIGURE 11.4   Daily Schedule: Early Childhood Classroom. The children's version of the schedule uses drawings.

Making Schedules Visible

All members of the system—children, teachers, and parents—need to know about, are able to see, and to have access to a classroom's schedule.

For Children

Using a pocket chart or magnetic strips, for example, develop a large sturdy replica of the schedule that children can use. The goal is to pair a written schedule with pictures illustrating each part of the schedule. For example, write *recess* on a card, place it in its pocket, and then place a photo of the children on the playground in the pocket next to the word. Then, place the schedule at children's eye level and make the schedule as interactive as possible (Kaser, 2007; University of Texas, 2004). For example, if recess has to be held in the gym, ask a child to make a change in the schedule by placing a picture of the gym next to the word *recess*. This helps children adjust to minor schedule changes.

Consider a schedule within a schedule. Some activities have several parts and children benefit from having a picture schedule of the steps involved in the larger activity (Alter & Conroy, no date). This is a particularly useful guidance strategy when the school year first starts and children are learning new routines, for children who need assistance with remembering steps in activities, for children who are learning English, and for teaching any new multistep project.

> Mrs. Chang, the preschool teacher, created a schedule within a schedule, a permanent set of laminated cards to use with all cooking activities. These simply drawn line pictures showed the steps—the beginning, middle, and end—in any cooking project: wash hands, come to cooking area, read recipe, cook, clean up, wash hands. She taught the steps for cooking projects in a large group time.

For Parents

Parents need a copy of the daily schedule preferably in their home language. Use the format most useful to them—hard copy or as an email attachment. Some parents appreciate a business-card–sized schedule that they can carry or pin easily to a bulletin board. A visually impaired parent would probably appreciate receiving a copy in Braille or as an audio copy, either via tape, digital voice recorder, or the computer. Consider taking a digital photo of each child standing next to the schedule. Send that photo to parents as an attachment to an email message or simply send a copy of the photo home.

The essential elements in appropriate early childhood daily schedules include the following: a clear sense of balance in the schedule, ample time for children to develop ideas, giving children choices, well-executed transitions, and making schedules visible and accessible to children and parents.

After thinking about the curriculum, integrating it, arranging the classroom, and developing an appropriate schedule, teachers organize for children's learning. This is also known as lesson planning, a topic to which we now turn.

ORGANIZING LEARNING ACTIVITIES: WRITING LESSON PLANS

Lesson plan An organizing tool; a teacher's general map for a learning activity.

A **lesson plan** is an organizing tool, a teacher's general map for a learning activity. Organizing for learning, including writing lesson plans, can be done in a developmentally appropriate way when we focus on children's needs and abilities and when the plans are a part of a child-centered, emergent curriculum.

There are many formats for writing lesson plans. Whatever the format or grade level, all effective and appropriate lesson plans contain the same organizing elements.

Selection of a Topic

Chapter 10 described three sources of the curriculum: children, standards, and teachers. Teachers select topics for lesson plans after observing children and what they are interested in or areas in which they need help. They pay attention to state or national standards and they also weave their own knowledge and talents into the curriculum.

Mr. Hernandez, from the chapter opening kindergarten vignette, selected the content area of language arts based on his state's kindergarten learning standards. He followed up the introduction to the title page with a center devoted to creating the cover for each child's book of dictated stories and observations.

Statement of Purpose or Goal

This is a brief statement about why you are doing the activity. Mr. Hernandez's purpose is to help children gain knowledge about books because he discovered that the children in his kindergarten liked books and art activities. Learning about books was also a part of the state's learning standards. The children had dictated or written their own stories and observations and made a blank front and back cover. He decided that they might now be interested in designing the front cover for the books. Teachers should be able to justify their reason for any lesson plan and it should always include the children's interests and needs.

Alignment with Content Standards or Benchmarks

These can be state or national standards for the different content areas. State learning standards list the state's major *goals* for each content area. Under each goal, the state lists one or more *learning standards* related specifically to that goal. Under each learning standard, the state lists *benchmarks*, the markers of a child's learning and development. See the Learning Standards web site at the end of the chapter to access the kindergarten standards for Illinois because these are illustrated in this chapter's lesson plan example. Consider examining your own state's learning standards. What is the language that your state uses in presenting its learning standards for preschool, kindergarten, and first, second, and third grade?

Mr. Hernandez has aligned his plan with benchmarks from his state's early learning standards for kindergarten. Specifically, he focused on these content areas:

- *Language arts.* The benchmark was for the children to demonstrate understanding of concepts about books, such as front cover or title page
- *Physical development.* The benchmark, engage in active play using fine and gross motor skills, such as using scissors
- *Visual arts.* The benchmark, participate in the visual arts and identify media and tools used in painting, drawing, and constructing

Learner Background

The teacher needs to take into consideration children's prior experiences and knowledge. The teacher, therefore, helps them to build upon this understanding with experiences that support and enrich their learning.

All of the children in Mr. Hernandez's class have been to the public library and all have read books in preschool and at home. He is helping them to build new understandings that are aligned with his state standards. Their new learning is based on their prior experiences with books. He had also documented their willingness to engage in creative arts activities.

Learning Objectives

These are also known as outcomes. The teacher writes two or three objectives to be attained with this activity. **Learning objectives** should be clearly measurable, child-centered and child-directed. They should be written with observable *verb terminology*. For example,

Learning objectives
Outcomes for the learning activity; child-centered and child-directed; written with observable verb terminology.

"Children will observe, investigate, write, draw, or identify," rather than "Children will enjoy, know, understand." The latter are not measurable and they are subjective. Mr. Hernandez's objectives: The child will

1. *Identify* art materials and techniques used in decorating the cover of his or her book.
2. Grip regular or grip-activated scissors correctly and *cut* paper with scissors.
3. *Identify* the front cover of his or her book.

Materials

A lesson plan is an organizing tool and the list of materials should be specific and thorough. If you are ill on the day for this activity, any substitute teacher should be able to do the activity because you have listed all necessary materials. Mr. Hernandez's list:

- Children's dictated stories and observations bound in its cover
- One book from the library area (to show as an example)
- Scissors: the regular children's scissors as well as the easy to grip style, which can be used by children who are either right- or left-handed
- Art supplies for decorating the covers: recycled paper for collage, glue sticks, and markers
- Digital camera: for documenting children's work
- Notepad and pen for recording interview remarks from children
- Clean wet sponge for cleaning the table

Lesson Procedure

The teacher describes how the lesson proceeds. It consists of initiation and lesson content.

Initiation

Initiation Way in which a teacher introduces a learning activity.

Initiation refers to the ways in which the teacher introduces the activity. There are many ways to introduce a lesson, for example, by reading a story, showing examples, puppet play, children's role-play. Teachers can also use inquiry techniques, such as those described in the first stage of a project. This involves asking open-ended questions to elicit children's understanding about the topic.

Mr. Hernandez, as previously done, introduced the activity at morning meeting. He placed a basket with each child's book of dictated stories next to him. He held one up, patted the front cover and asked, "Tell me the name of this part of this book." Then, he held up the library book and said, "H-m-m, look at one of our books and then at this library book. Tell me one thing that is different about the two covers." The children offered several differences, among them that the homemade book's cover had nothing on it. The teacher moved on to introducing the specific activity. "Today, you can create art for your cover in the creative arts center during center time."

Lesson Content

This can be a difficult part of the lesson plan because the teacher needs to record a step-by-step sequence of how the lesson proceeds. There should be evidence of modeling, scaffolding, and inquiry in the procedures. This is easier for many teachers if they break it down into logical parts:

- *Set up learning center:* Arrange four chairs around the table. Place the basket of children's homemade books nearby to be prepared for any child who chooses this center today. Place scissors at each of the four spots at the table. Place a basket of clean and safe recycled paper and the basket of markers on the table. Wear camera around your neck.

- *Children do the work.* When children come to this table, remind children about the activity, which was explained at morning meeting, "Tell me what you'll do with your books today." "That's right, make art on the *front* cover." He asked each child to show him the front cover and contrasted it with the back cover.

- *Observe children as they use scissors and offer assistance when needed.* Remind children that they can choose the easy to grip[1] or the regular scissors. *Demonstrate (model)* how to use scissors for children who need assistance. Observe as they demonstrate the skill. Help others make minor adjustments and then observe their technique. (You will have *scaffolded* their acquisition of using either type of scissors more effectively.) Listen for the word "scissors" and supply it if needed. Introduce the new vocabulary word to describe the art technique used, collage. It is ". . . when we paste things such as paper onto a surface. What is our surface?" Take photographs of and interview each child at work. The photos and notes will be used to make a documentation panel.

- *Closure.* When each child completes art for the cover, he or she places the book on the ledge so that the glue can dry thoroughly. Children clean up their spot when they are finished and then go to their next chosen activity. If children need help, ask them to name the center that they will visit next. Some teachers check here for children's understanding to see if they have learned what was intended for the content of the lesson and to see if objectives have been achieved. This is a review or way of tying things together. Mr. Hernandez checked for understanding during the interview of each child.

CHECK YOUR UNDERSTANDING
Initiating a Learning Activity

Use what you learned in this section to analyze the kindergarten chapter opening vignette. Explain how the teacher in that vignette *initiated* the lesson about title pages of books.

Assessment

List the type of **assessment** for a specific lesson. Mr. Hernandez has used authentic, performance-based assessment, explained in Chapter 8. He took pictures of every child as they used scissors or as they tore paper. He analyzed the photos and wrote notes on each child's ability. He analyzed his interview notes from the lesson. For example,

> Trina (a child with developmental coordination disorder): difficulty gripping regular scissors; same with grip-activated scissors; tore paper with little difficulty; used word *collage* to represent the new art technique; correctly identified front of her book.

> Terry: no difficulty with scissors; gripping correctly both types of scissors; cut more efficiently with easy to grip scissors; did not remember the word *collage*; said "gluing paper on paper"; identified front of his book correctly.

The assessment should contain the key performance proficiencies, in this case— gripped scissors correctly; cut paper with scissors; used "collage" to refer to the new art technique; identified front cover of book. These would reflect and directly align with the learning objectives or outcomes for the lesson, as listed in the lesson objective part of the plan.

Assessment In lesson plans, refers to the method for judging whether the learning objectives have been met; contains key performance proficiencies; aligned directly with learning objectives of the activity.

---

[1]Easy to grip scissors are available from different sources, such as from medical supply companies. Here is one source: http://www.medplususa.com/list-product_info-p-Mini_Easy_Grip_Scissors-pid-7356.html.

Adaptations

Children have varied abilities and our instructional strategies should meet the needs of all learners in a class. Using **differentiated instruction,** therefore, is essential in lesson planning. This refers to modifying or adapting a plan so that *each and every* child can benefit from the lesson's concepts. Differentiated instruction helps teachers engage in *individually appropriate* practices, one of the three elements in developmentally appropriate practice.

Mr. Hernandez adapted the plan effectively for Trina, a child with developmental coordination disorder, who has difficulty with both gross and fine motor tasks, including cutting with scissors. He gave her and every other child a choice of type of scissors used, providing the grip-activated type as an alternative to the regular, somewhat difficult to manipulate children's scissors. He also modified the plan by encouraging some children to tear paper. Trina chose to tear some paper but then chose the easy to grip scissors to successfully cut paper.

Other children might be learning a different language. Mr. Hernandez adapts *all* his lessons for the Spanish speakers in his class who are learning English because he is fluent in both languages. He easily supplies Spanish words to help children grasp concepts before he supplies the English word.

Some children are gifted and we need to differentiate instruction for them as well. For example, Shelly is a gifted child, whose family is highly interested and involved in the arts and takes her to museums. Mr. Hernandez knew, from having observed her in the art center that her art tended to be more sophisticated and detailed than that of the other children of the same age. For this lesson, he realized that she knew the word collage and had taken a class on collage in the children's section of the museum. Her book's cover, not surprisingly, was fairly intricate. She asked for help in folding small pieces of paper with which she produced a cut-out design to glue on the front cover of her book. She elaborated even more by gluing contrasting colors in the cut-outs.

SUMMARY

A part of a teacher's role is to construct a calming, productive learning environment, whether it is for infants and toddlers or second graders. This involves paying attention to the three different types of environments: interpersonal, physical, and temporal (time).

A safe and healthy interpersonal environment supports children's development and learning. Teachers create a healthy interpersonal environment by

- Demonstrating respect and genuine affection for children
- Consistent, positive teacher behavior
- Taking children's perspective
- Observing children carefully and acknowledging each child every day
- Providing quiet times
- Using positive child guidance

Teachers create developmentally appropriate physical environments, which convey a sense of order, help children make choices, encourage active learning, all of which sends clear messages to children.

- "You can learn many things here."
- "You can play and work with other children here."
- "You can make many choices here."
- "You can work on many different projects here."
- "When you are done working in one area, you can go to a different spot and work there."
- "When you want to, you can work by yourself."

Effective teachers, understanding that children need predictability, create an appropriate schedule which provides for

- Balance between large and small group activities, quiet and more vigorous activity, teacher- and child-initiated activity.
- Extended sessions for play, work, and learning, preferably for at least 1 or 1½ hours.

- Choice of activities during the extended periods for work and play.
- A minimum of transitions. Necessary transitions are done calmly, and in a low-key, orderly, and smooth way that wastes none of the children's valuable time.

Teachers organize for children's learning, when working with children from 3 to 8 years, by writing lesson plans. In a plan, the teacher selects a topic, states the purpose or the goal, aligns the lesson with content standards or benchmarks, considers the learner's background, writes learning objectives, lists materials needed, specifies lesson procedures, assesses whether children meet the learning objectives, and adapts the plan so that each and every child can benefit from the activity.

QUESTIONS FOR REFLECTION

1. Here is the morning schedule for a kindergarten:
   - 8:00 a.m. to 8:45 group time.
   - 8:45–9:45 seatwork. Kindergarten children do workbook pages from the language arts and math series.
   - 9:45–9:55 story.
   - 9:55–10:10 snack.
   - 10:10–11:00 seatwork. Workbook pages dealing with handwriting or writing words and sentences.

   Name three ways in which this schedule is *different from* the schedule in Figure 11.4.

2. Explain how the schedule in Figure 11.4 is appropriate for children in kindergarten or primary grades.

APPLY YOUR KNOWLEDGE

What Should This Teacher Do?

1. Mr. Hernandez was meeting with the parent of a first-grade child new to the school. The parent looked around the classroom and asked, "Why is the classroom divided in these small areas?" (as in Figure 11.3). What would you advise the teacher to say to this parent?

2. Mr. Hernandez, from the lesson plan about creating art for the cover of the homemade book, has photos of each child working with scissors or tearing paper. How can he use these examples of documentation to help parents understand their child's fine motor development?

KEY TERMS

Assessment, 285
Differentiated instruction, 286
Initiation, 284
Interpersonal environment, 272

Learning objectives, 283
Learning centers, 277
Lesson plan, 282
Physical environment, 273

Schedule, 278
Temporal environment, 278
Traffic patterns, 278
Transition, 280

WEB SITES

Community Playthings
http://www.communityplaythings.com
A commercial site. Good guides to planning the physical environment of an early childhood classroom.

Infant and Toddler Classrooms (Part of the PITC program in California)
http://www.pitc.org/
Home page for the Program for Infant/Toddler Care. Gives an excellent overview of one state's concerted effort to attain high-quality care for infants and toddlers.

http://www.pitc.org/pub/pitc_docs/grossmont.html
Site shows the infant and toddler care center of Grossmont College, near San Diego, California. It is one of the sites designed to demonstrate a developmentally appropriate environment for infants and toddlers. This site shows before and after photos of this center's remodeling and its move to an even more developmentally appropriate physical environment for this age group.

Learning Standards
http://www.ccsso.org/content/PDFs/State_ECstandardsMATRIX11.27.07.pdf
This is a good resource. It is a chart listing learning standards for every state.

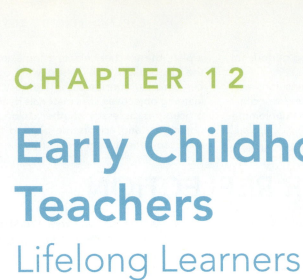

CHAPTER 12

Early Childhood Teachers

Lifelong Learners

- In what ways does professional development help someone grow and develop as a teacher?

- What is reflection and how does it contribute to a teacher's sense of professionalism?

- What are some of the major critical issues that you will encounter as an early childhood teacher?

CASE STUDY
Circle of Teaching

We met Emy in Chapter 1 in the opening vignettes. Here is her story of growing in professionalism during her first 5 years of teaching.

Year One: Right after she completed her undergraduate program, Emy's first teaching assignment was in kindergarten and she was eager to put her philosophy into action. When her mentor, Mr. Hernandez, assured her that she should look to him for assistance, she was relieved and did call on him several times during this first year for on-the-spot help. After the first week, she confided that being a teacher was "such a change from being a student." She had many questions about things such as how to deal with all the paperwork, how to get the items that she needed to structure good learning centers, and how to order materials. She also said that she was unsure about her role in staff meetings.

Year Two: Emy felt much more confident at the beginning of her second year about things such as the school's routines and managing her classroom. She continued working with her mentor, and their conversations shifted slightly from management-type issues to how to help specific children and about new teaching and guidance strategies. She met with the special education leader to become more proficient in preparing for Individualized Education Program (IEP) meetings. Knowing the benefits of hands-on learning, she also met with a math education professor about developing appropriate math manipulatives for her children to use in the math center. She also sought information from different sources on working with an extremely shy child, the guidance counselor and two reputable web sites about shyness.

Year Three: Emy was ready for new challenges. Her comfort level had risen and she felt like a full-fledged member of her school's faculty. She had outlined a professional growth plan with her principal and worked on it with her mentor. What she really wanted to learn about was the Reggio approach to documentation, an authentic assessment system. To do this she read several articles, saw the Hundred Languages of Children display, and visited a Reggio-inspired school that used documentation panels extensively. Emy also applied to graduate school and took formal coursework in child development and early childhood education.

Year Four: The graduate work continued with Emy doing action research in her classroom for two courses. She visited the schools in Reggio Emilia, Italy, as a part of a study tour and attended a national conference for the first time. There, she attended sessions on assessment and documentation of children's development and learning. She presented a session at a local conference on documentation in her classroom.

Year Five: Emy completed her master's degree. Her professional development goal for this year was to assess and reflect on how well she helped children develop the social skills and emotional competence they needed for success. To do that, she and the other kindergarten teachers used the *Inventory of Practices for Promoting Children's Social Emotional Competence* (CSEFEL, 2003). The team used the Inventory to identify their training needs and developed an action plan to help them acquire the necessary skills. This year, Emy would serve on the early childhood professional group's state-level committee on assessment, advocating for appropriate assessment. The school had hired a new kindergarten teacher, who had just graduated from college. Emy had taken on a new role. Emy greeted him, "Hi George! My name is Emy, and I'll be working with you as a mentor."

Emy's first year of teaching combined eagerness with concerns and questions, a normal combination for new teachers. On her journey of development as a teacher, she has grown in knowledge, skills, and confidence. Like all development, a teacher's progress does not happen overnight but proceeds slowly and steadily over time, as you will see in this chapter. A teacher is a lifelong learner who continually builds on a background of ideas rooted in research and theory and continually reflects on new ideas and approaches. Teachers' developmental path through the stages is better if she deliberately and intentionally focuses on reflection and professional development activities most likely to help her at each stage, as Emy has done in her first 5 years of teaching.

In this final chapter, we see that lifelong learning is essential for continued good teaching. We examine the stages of teaching and the issues about which teachers are concerned during each stage and what it means to build collaborative relationships with colleagues. Because reflection is central in professional growth, we focus on it in a relationship-based type of supervision. We close the chapter, and this textbook, with a brief look at some of the critical issues that you will face as a member of the early childhood profession and where the profession goes from here.

The National Association for the Education of Young Children (NAEYC) standards for preparing early childhood teachers state that teachers who demonstrate professionalism:

- engage in continuous, collaborative learning that informs practice,
- establish and maintain positive, collaborative relationships with colleagues, and other professionals, and
- reflect on their practices, give logical reasons for decisions, and use self-assessments for planning and modifying programs and for continuing professional development. (Hyson, 2003)

STAGES OF TEACHER DEVELOPMENT: CONTINUOUS, COLLABORATIVE LEARNING

Professional development
A continuous process of growth in knowledge, skills, and attitude through a variety of learning activities and resources.

Professional development offers teachers many different ways to increase their knowledge and teaching or guidance skills through professional organizations, professional literature such as research articles or books, other resources, and experiences. Professional development is a continuous process throughout a career, from teacher education programs until retirement with even the most experienced teachers engaging in learning and reflection (Baptiste, 1995; Moeini, 2008; Villegas-Reimers, 2003). Professional development, however, should not be the typical in-service days or one-time workshops or seminars. Effective programs offer what teachers require, that is, they assess and analyze

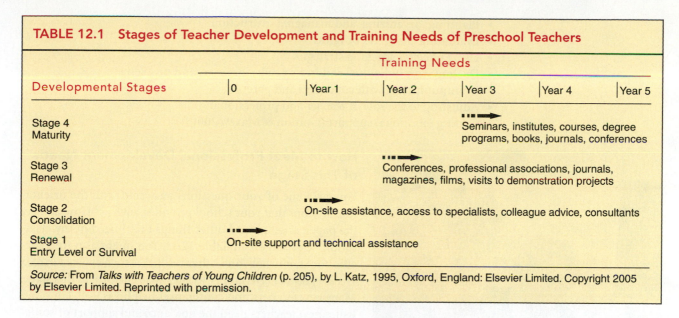

TABLE 12.1   Stages of Teacher Development and Training Needs of Preschool Teachers

Developmental Stages	Training Needs					
	0	Year 1	Year 2	Year 3	Year 4	Year 5
Stage 4 Maturity				Seminars, institutes, courses, degree programs, books, journals, conferences		
Stage 3 Renewal			Conferences, professional associations, journals, magazines, films, visits to demonstration projects			
Stage 2 Consolidation		On-site assistance, access to specialists, colleague advice, consultants				
Stage 1 Entry Level or Survival	On-site support and technical assistance					

Source: From *Talks with Teachers of Young Children* (p. 205), by L. Katz, 1995, Oxford, England: Elsevier Limited. Copyright 2005 by Elsevier Limited. Reprinted with permission.

needs. The organization would survey teachers to discover their specific areas of growth and would only then develop a plan to meet those identified needs (Moeini, 2008).

Becoming a teacher is an ongoing process, and there are different **stages of a teacher's development.** Teachers grow in confidence, knowledge, and skills during the stages, and different developmental tasks and training needs associated with each stage (Frede, 2003; Katz, no date) are shown in Table 12.1 and described in the following discussion.

Stages of a teacher's development Ongoing process in which teachers grow in confidence, skills, and knowledge; stages are survival, consolidation, renewal, and maturity.

Stage 1: Entry Level or Survival

The first stage, entry level, is often referred to as a *survival stage*, and usually coincides with your first year of teaching.

What This Stage Is Like

A teacher at this stage is acutely aware of all of the demands of this profession—planning curriculum, choosing appropriate teaching strategies, deciding about guidance strategies, and working with parents and other teachers. Many novice teachers do indeed wonder if they will survive. They observe more seasoned, mature teachers and wonder if they have what it takes to teach young children. A new teacher might not even realize that those mature teachers were once first-year teachers themselves with apprehensions and questions. A novice teacher begins to develop a professional identity in this first stage, especially after being immersed in the school culture (McKenzie, 2005).

Professional Development Needed at This Stage

Research suggests that beginning teachers have several high-priority needs and that several specific things help new teachers grow in confidence and competence. An *induction program* is a coordinated plan in which a school district or center gives coordinated support to new teachers (New Teacher Center, 2007). Most new teachers have similar questions and concerns, and they build success at this first stage when they receive guidance and support for things such as:

- Managing a classroom, including how to structure the classroom and schedule
- Getting accurate information about the school
- Finding materials and resources for teaching

- Planning, organizing, and managing instruction
- Evaluating children's progress
- Using effective teaching strategies
- Dealing with individual children's needs, interests, and problems
- Communicating with colleagues and parents
- Adjusting to the role of teacher and professional
- Getting emotional support (Gordon & Maxey, 2000)

An experienced teacher mentors a first-year teacher.

How to Meet Professional Development Needs of This Stage

You get some of your questions answered with the orientation sessions that your school provides, such as "How do I get the paper, scissors, and other things that I need in my classroom?" (see stage 1 in Table 12.1). You might also find specific books, journals, and other resources such as *The First Six Weeks of School* (Denton & Kriete, 2000) helpful in this stage. Many new teachers find conferences helpful as well. For other issues new teachers need the guidance and support of someone who is available to answer questions and deal with issues as they arise. Mr. Hernandez, for example, has been teaching for many years and has been mentoring Emy, the new kindergarten teacher. At lunch one day, she expressed a concern about the upcoming parent-teacher conferences.

"I'm not sure," she said, "how I'll deal with it if a parent becomes angry during our parent-teacher meeting. I expect things to go well, but you never really know . . ."

Stage 2: Consolidation

The second stage is evident after a teacher has answered many of the questions from the survival stage and feels more confident about managing a classroom and dealing with parents and other teachers.

TEACH INTENTIONALLY

Role Playing an Angry Parent

What the teacher did: Mr. Hernandez, mentor to new teacher Emy, offered to role-play a parent who comes to a conference angry or gets angry during a parent-teacher conference. For each example, he coached her on how to respond calmly.

How the teacher was intentional: Mr. Hernandez was intentional in his mentor role because he understood that new teachers have concerns about communicating with parents in general and that dealing with an angry parent can be an especially anxiety-inducing event. He helped Miss Sanders (Emy) practice an unruffled yet professional approach in the face of angry emotions. He helped her acquire the specific communication skills that she might need when dealing with a person feeling angry.

What This Stage Is Like

Teachers in stage 2 have different questions and concerns. They tend to shift their focus to begin to search for information on dealing with the needs of individual children (Katz, no date) and on different strategies for teaching. They feel some confidence in their ability to access information and might now begin to search for material, say, on how to help English language learners learn high-frequency words in first grade. They have enough confidence in general aspects of managing their schedule and classroom that they can seek information on helping children with challenging behaviors, for example.

Professional Development Needed at This Stage

Teachers who are growing in confidence still must increase their knowledge base and develop additional skills. They are ready to go beyond basic classroom management and guidance skills to more finely tuned skills. The teacher needs to keep building an understanding of children and families in that school and district or center. The teacher also benefits from reflecting on classroom routines and teaching strategies that he or she used during the first year.

How to Meet Professional Development Needs of This Stage

Teachers now feel a little more secure about the basics of their work. Still, they are relatively new to the profession and, as Figure 12.1 shows, benefit from working with an on-site mentor. Adult learners, such as the newer teacher, are goal oriented and want relevant and practical information (Knowles, 1998). A teacher in the consolidation stage, for example, might feel somewhat secure about stating limits but now wants to turn attention to limit setting for children with challenging behavior. On the other hand, a teacher who has developed a basic morning group routine might wonder if he can improve on it.

The on-site mentor can help a newer teacher reinforce and increase his knowledge base. This can happen very naturally in a simple conversation in which the two teachers discuss the problem or question. The give-and-take is important for a novice teacher. Recall from Chapter 1 Vygotsky's emphasis on the teacher-child discourse in children's learning and development. In this case, discussion helps the newer teacher reflect on his current understanding of a problem such as the limit setting, discuss it with the mentor, hear a different perspective, take it in, mull it over, and get to higher levels of understanding.

Teachers at this stage also benefit from branching out and searching out information from other colleagues. For example, a teacher who wants to incorporate more technology into the curriculum might now consult with the school's or district's computer teacher about incorporating technology effectively into her curriculum and about guidelines for choosing software for young children. She might also speak with the guidance counselor or school psychologist about group programs for children who are experiencing some crisis in their family, such as a death or divorce.

Go to MyEducationLab and select the topic "Professionalism/Ethics/Standards." Under Activities and Applications, read the case study *Case Report: Interaction and Reactions* for one teacher's reflections on how to help a child.

CHECK YOUR UNDERSTANDING
Stage 2 of Teacher Development

Describe the resources that Emy used to get the information she needed to help the shy child in her class. How does her approach tell you that she is in stage 2 of teacher development? Figure 12.1 might be helpful here.

FIGURE 12.1 **Professional Participation in Meetings**

Demonstrates Respect in Relationships
- Demonstrates civility
- Maintains rules of confidentiality
- Avoids gossip; does not judge others
- Gives credit to others for their ideas and work

Demonstrates Reciprocal Relationships with Colleagues
- Contributes to give-and-take atmosphere of the group
- Focuses on group's goal

Participates Well in Group Meetings
- Enters discussions
- Does not dominate the discussion
- Offers ideas without fear
- Adheres to ground rules of the group
- Supports other group members
- Does a fair share of the work
- Avoids disruptive behavior, such as having side conversations
- Focuses on ideas, not on people in the group

Communicates Well
- Listens actively
- Focuses on a speaker
- Does not interrupt

Stage 3: Renewal

Stage 3 occurs quite often between the third and fourth years of teaching.

What This Stage Is Like

Teachers enter this stage with confidence in their ability to manage their classroom and choose appropriate teaching strategies. They are also more confident about guiding children, including children with mildly challenging behaviors. They often yearn for new insights and information related to their profession, and they are ready to branch out and learn even more. For example, Emy said to her mentor, "I really want to use my small groups better. I've been thinking about that a lot."

Professional Development Needed at This Stage

Teachers at this stage are quite willing and should be encouraged to say what they need to know, as Emy did about small groups. Specific needs depend on a teacher's self-identified requirements. Some might want to delve into guidance strategies, and others might want strategies for opening the day at school. Still other teachers might want to join a debate on whether to use food in art activities, for example. Some teachers at this stage, however, get comfortable with one way of doing something and might not even realize that there are other equally good, research-based ways of doing the same thing.

How to Meet Professional Development Needs of This Stage

Teachers at this stage find it useful to diversify and broaden their knowledge and skills. Stage 3 teachers discover that conferences and workshops on topics of interest are valuable. Likewise, talking to colleagues from different settings about different approaches contributes to teacher renewal. The many resources of the professional organization, such as journals, magazines, and DVDs can give a teacher just the boost that he needs. Some teachers benefit greatly from visiting a demonstration school such as a Reggio-inspired school or a High/Scope program.

Stage 4: Maturity

Teachers reach stage 4 at different points. Some might enter it after as few as 3 years and others after 4 or 5 years or even slightly later.

What This Stage Is Like

At this point, teachers are veterans in the profession. They demonstrate a high level of comfort in their professional role, and their understanding of the curriculum, teaching and guidance strategies, assessment, and working with parents is usually excellent. Veteran teachers also have a far greater comfort level in adapting the early childhood education curriculum (Cross & Dixon, 2004). They have usually developed their own *teaching styles* that suit them as professionals.

Professional Development Needed at This Stage

This teacher has succeeded; nevertheless, such a teacher still has room to grow and desires information and skills at a much deeper level about a variety of topics. For example, he might ask questions about policies at the federal level that affect education in his state. He might want to know about the differences between different philosophical approaches to early childhood education, or he might start asking deeper questions about how children's cognition develops.

Teachers benefit from gaining knowledge at all stages of teacher development.

How to Meet Professional Development Needs of This Stage

Stage 4 teachers enjoy learning in formal courses or advanced-degree programs. When they attend conferences, they often attend the research sessions. They derive both pleasure and learning from reading journals and web sites devoted to evidence-based early childhood education. They continue to value discussions with other teachers.

Often stage 4 teachers act as mentors to new teachers. Effective mentors possess personal attributes that contribute to their success in mentoring. They tend to be supportive and attentive. They are comfortable when they help the younger teacher feel confident and positive, and they help the mentee build skills in reflection (Hudson, 2005).

Mentoring is a form of professional development for this level, increasing the veteran teacher's perception of his own competence (Saffold, 2005). Mentors get training in how to help new teachers most effectively, and mentors are usually veteran teachers who are teaching at the new teacher's same grade level. Mentoring is as beneficial to the mentor as it is to a new teacher. Psychological benefits include a sense of giving back to the profession and an increased level of professional self-esteem from having helped a new teacher. Veteran teachers also improve their own teaching skills through mentoring. For example, successful mentors practice good listening skills and helpful, nonjudgmental ways of giving feedback (Huling, 2001), as Mr. Hernandez did when mentoring Emy.

Beyond the First 5 Years: Motivation for Professional Development

This chapter calls for lifelong learning for teachers, not just in the first 5 years, because a teacher's career can encompass 30 or 40 years. They need to continue to learn throughout that career with their perceived professional development needs changing over time. Some teachers are eager lifelong learners while others show less interest. Teachers, then, vary in their willingness to learn and grow, with *motivation* a key factor in whether a teacher develops knowledge and skills throughout his or her career. Some of these key motivators include the desire

- to serve children and families and to help children develop and learn.
- to acquire skills and knowledge in specific content, such as child development or technology.
- to know more about educational philosophy. This helps teachers to deal with trends in the field. Early childhood teachers, for example, have studied the Reggio Emilia philosophy in the past decade, many of them teachers in midcareer, and this has influenced their understanding of developmentally appropriate practice and documentation of children's thinking.
- for career advancement. This seems to motivate teachers in early and midcareer but logically not during the later years of a career. (Harvey, 2005)

Motivation affects the effort that a teacher puts into any professional development activity. Acquiring new knowledge and skills, such as those learned in a Responsive Classroom week-long workshop, for example, requires much effort and practice. A highly motivated teacher is more likely to put forth the effort to learn than someone who did not want to learn about the method. In addition, a teacher's emotional state, her beliefs, and her habits of mind or attitude all influence her motivation to engage in professional development at any part of her career (American Psychological Association, 1995, updated 2000).

BUILDING POSITIVE, COLLABORATIVE RELATIONSHIPS WITH COLLEAGUES

Relationships are at the heart of a professional's practice. As explained in earlier chapters, early childhood teachers establish good relationships with children and with families as the basis for planning, teaching, guidance, and working with parents. Effective teachers also know how to build **positive, collaborative professional relationships** with other teachers and other professionals such as school psychologists, special educators, and administrators.

Positive and collaborative relationships enable an early childhood teacher to function effectively as a member of a team of professionals, whatever the stage of teacher development. Collaborative skills are essential for teachers, for example, when they participate in professional groups developing individual family service plans (Bruder, 2001), when they discuss a controversial issue such as eliminating recess, or when they work on a project such as developing a curriculum map. Good professional relationships contribute to a teacher's confidence and sense of competence as a professional, and this, in turn, moves a teacher forward in the stages of teacher development.

Working well with others requires specific knowledge and skills. One example is the set of effective communication skills, including skills in speaking, listening, and writing. Another example is the conscious avoidance of specific behaviors (University of Iowa, 2007). Figure 12.1 describes the qualities that a teacher needs to participate effectively in a professional group.

We now turn to the role of reflecting on one's practices in developing a sense of professionalism.

Positive, collaborative professional relationships
Professional interactions characterized by civility, respect, and working closely together.

REFLECTING ON PRACTICES

Effective teachers reflect on and give coherent reasons for their practices. They assess and then use self-assessment to make decisions about their professional development needs. Teachers find it helpful to their careers when they learn how to reflect productively on issues in the early stages of teaching. Teachers who reflect well tend to get the maximum benefit from professional development activities (Martin, 2005).

All humans, whether they are adults or children, as explained in Chapter 6, *construct or build* new ideas, *relate new information to what we already know*, and *process information*. When humans process information, the brain takes in data and admits some of it to a sensory register. Then, some of that information travels to long-term memory for storage. We retrieve information from long-term memory when we need to work with it. We call forth that information and place it, temporarily, in the space allotted for working, the *working memory*.

Good relationships are at the center of a teacher's practice.

For example, a teacher learns that young children are preoperational thinkers who learn by working with concrete objects. She sees how math manipulatives support a 6-year-old's ability to count. This enters her sensory register and is stored in long-term memory. When the teacher later sees a child having difficulty with counting, she retrieves the knowledge and places it in working memory so that she can use it.

What Is Reflection?

Reflection An active, intentional, problem-solving process; involves remembering an issue and then analyzing the memories.

A teacher who reflects uses his adult cognitive powers to tackle a problem or an issue. He actively searches his long-term memory for existing ideas about the issue and calls forth those memories. He then places the memories about the issue in his working memory so that he can actively focus on them. **Reflection,** then, is an active and intentional problem-solving process. Teachers who reflect go far beyond mere remembering: They remember something about an issue, and then they analyze those memories (Dewey, 1933; Epstein, 2003).

Reflection Takes Many Forms

Humans who think, examine, and contemplate things are well equipped to reflect. All reflection involves linking together different ideas about a problem, but there are many different ways to reflect (Tartell, Klein, & Jewett, 1998) and many different topics for reflection.

Teachers Reflect Alone and with Others

Self-assessment Reviewing and reflecting on one's own practice.

Teachers engage in **self-assessment** when reviewing their own practice and then pondering some aspect of their professional role. For example, "How well did I document the children's work? Could I have involved the children more in writing the captions in the documentary display? Could I have done anything more to more clearly illustrate their learning?"

At other times, a teacher reflects with one other person. For instance, a new teacher might reflect on her room's physical layout with her mentor. Teachers often reflect in larger groups, carefully identifying a topic and challenges as well as feelings about the topic.

> Jim and Emy, along with all other preschool and kindergarten teachers in their district, met monthly to develop the preprimary curriculum map for math and science.

Teachers Reflect at Different levels

The levels of reflection (Larrivee, 2006) are

- surface reflection,
- pedagogical reflection, and
- critical reflection.

Surface reflection Tendency to concentrate on practical issues in teaching.

In **surface reflection,** a teacher might concentrate on practical issues related to classroom management, such as, "How long should the group time be?" This is a necessary type of reflection and all teachers engage in it, more so at a career's beginning but at different times by more experienced teachers as well. For example, suppose that an experienced second grade teacher attends a seminar on the Responsive Classroom and the teacher learns about *academic choice,* a strategy for the primary grades. This mature teacher might well ask, "I've never done anything like this. How long, in general, is an academic choice period?"

This teacher has used pedagogical reflection in deciding how to set up her classroom.

In **pedagogical reflection,** a higher level, a teacher reflects on the connections between theory and practice and uses the connection to become more consistent in her practices. For example, a teacher says that she believes in Vygotsky's idea of scaffolding children's learning but, upon reflection, discovers that she often misses opportunities for scaffolding.

With **critical reflection,** a teacher is concerned about the ethical consequences of teaching practices on children. She might, for example, reflect on the issue of *time-out*. A teacher removes a child from a place in which he is getting attention for what the teacher perceives as misbehavior and places him in a place where he no longer receives this attention. This is a misunderstood and very often misused strategy and is *not* recommended. The teacher at the critical reflection level might ask, "How do children feel about time-out?" Contrast this with lower-level surface reflection where a teacher, not yet focused on how children feel, might only ask, "How long should a child stay in time-out?"

Pedagogical reflection
Tendency to think about connections between theory and practice in teaching.

Critical reflection
Concern expressed about ethical consequences of teaching practices on children.

CHECK YOUR UNDERSTANDING
The Teacher as a Reflective Practitioner

Explain how the case study teacher, Emy, used *surface reflection* during her first year of teaching. Explain how Emy used *pedagogical reflection* when dealing with the issue of using math manipulatives during her second year of teaching.

Teachers Can Use Many Formats for Reflecting

A teacher can simply think through an issue or perhaps put it in words. Others create and reflect on a written or electronic portfolio to document their best teaching activities. Some teachers find that using a voice recorder is helpful in reflection, while others might opt for presenting their reflections with photographs or even drawings. As already noted, teachers reflect by talking with other teachers, such as when teachers in Reggio-inspired schools use documentation that includes teacher collaboration and reflection (Edwards, 2002). Groups might meet at schools or in the community. Many teachers combine formats in reflecting.

> The school board notified teachers in Mr. Hernandez and Miss Sander's district that they planned to eliminate recess and use that time for "more academics." One of the teachers proposed that they respond in writing and in person before the school board. Emotions were high, but the teachers focused on gathering evidence-based documentation about the value of physical activity for young children. They ended up with a brief but coherent written statement approved by the entire group.

Teachers Reflect on Different Topics

Early childhood teachers have a broad knowledge base. They must know about child development, curriculum, working with parents, guiding children, professionalism, and assessment. Each of these elements has many parts. This presents teachers with an exceedingly long list of topics for reflection. For example, teachers reflect on ethical responsibilities to children and families as explained in Chapter 1. Use Figure 12.2 for some practice in using the Code of Ethical Conduct (NAEYC, 2005) to reflect on responsibilities, in this case, to colleagues, community, and society.

Reflective Supervision

Schools and centers or other settings are organizations with a recognizable culture with rules of operating, norms of behavior, and roles for different members of the organization.

FIGURE 12.2   Using the Code of Ethical Conduct: Reflecting on Ethical Responsibilities to Colleagues, Community, and Society

Consult the Code of Ethical Conduct in the Appendix of this text. Use the principles in Sections III and IV to reflect on and make decisions about your ethical responsibilities to your colleagues in the following situations.

- A male teacher, licensed to teach children from birth through age 8, applies for a teaching position at your school. You are on the hiring committee and hear a colleague make negative comments about hiring men to teach preschool children. Consult section P–3A and complete this sentence: My ethical responsibility is _____.

- One of your colleagues rarely washes her hands before serving snacks to her kindergarten class. You have talked privately with her about this issue, and she continues to ignore the hand-washing rules. Consult section P–3B. My ethical responsibility is _____.

- You are the director of a large preschool, and you have recently completed performance evaluations for the entire staff. One of the parents asks you for some personal information about one of the teachers. Consult section P–3C. My ethical responsibility is _____.

- Jessica is a 6 year old in your first-grade class. You hold an early childhood education teaching license, but you do not have a license to diagnose disabilities. Jessica's father has asked you to tell him whether she has attention deficit disorder. Consult the *individual* P–4 section. How can the Code help you in this case? What should you tell the father?

A school or center's culture affects a teacher's professional development, reflection, and progress through the stages of teacher development. There are, within any organization, including schools, persons whose role is to supervise. For example, in schools, the supervisors are usually directors, assistant principals, or principals. There are many styles of supervision from a strict hierarchical, top-down, often-authoritarian style to a more relationship-based style. **Reflective supervision** is a relationship-based style. It is based on the concept that supervision can be a good setting for a teacher's learning as well as for the professional development so important to advancing through stages of teacher development. There are three major elements in this style: reflection, collaboration, and regularity (Parlakian, 2001).

Reflection here takes place in a supervisory setting with a director or principal, for example, meeting with a teacher. It is a time for both to listen and to ask questions about any number of issues, such as working with children who are learning a new language or working with a very angry parent or even curriculum matters. The foundation for reflective supervision is mutual trust, open communication, and honesty combined with tact. The supervisor's role is not to give therapy, and, in this model, a principal does not shy away from making decisions. The principal, however, encourages teachers to reflect on their practices with the goal of learning from the reflection and to correct things if needed without feeling pressured or forced.

Collaboration, in reflective supervision, means that teachers and supervisors act as a team, sharing responsibility for some of the matters affecting children, the program, or the faculty and staff. However, the supervisor maintains supervisory responsibilities and works closely with teachers to examine issues and come up with solutions. Regularity refers to making the time for reflection and collaboration. Supervisors and teachers think that these meetings are important, set them up, do not allow meetings to be cancelled or postponed unless there is a real emergency, and plan well for them. The most significant thing about reflective supervision is that it creates the same type of relationship between supervisors and teachers as teachers are expected to create with children and families.

One thing that affects teachers and supervisors alike and on which they all reflect are the critical issues facing their profession, a topic that we will examine next.

> **Reflective supervision** A relationship-based style focusing on reflection and collaboration between a supervisor and the professional who is supervised.

WHERE DO WE GO FROM HERE? CRITICAL ISSUES IN THE EARLY CHILDHOOD PROFESSION

Chapter 2 described the history of the field for the last 100 years and focused on the many forces shaping a country's response to children's needs and to setting up early childhood programs. Reflective early childhood teachers who concentrate on continually building on their background of history, theory, and practice are well equipped to deal with the many current and critical issues within the early childhood profession that arise for a variety of reasons.

For example, decades of research in child development, starting with the child study movement of the 20th century, have helped our profession and society understand how important children's development and learning is in their long-term learning and well-being. We also know that high-quality early childhood education has a beneficial effect on children's development and learning (Karoly, Kilburn, & Cannon, 2005; Schweinhart, 2006). Factors such as these, combined with recent policy decisions, such as the No Child Left Behind act, discussed in other chapters, have moved the profession to reflect on current critical concerns. Here are some, but certainly not all, of the serious issues that we face as a profession.

Financing a System of Affordable Early Childhood Education

How will the profession bring together elements such as all the different program types (for example, public school–based prekindergarten, Head Start, and child care), licensing, facilities, planning, and training into a coherent "whole" or system? How can we best use some of the major direct revenue sources such as property, sales, and gaming taxes? How can we use indirect revenue sources such as tax credits for funding early childhood education that is affordable for families?

Compensation for the Early Childhood Workforce

Staff turnover in child care and preschools is a problem because of low wages. Publicly financing salaries of early childhood professionals, as is the case in public school kindergartens and primary grades, is highly desirable and, as we know from studying the history of our field, has occurred in the past. Currently, the general model is to link increased compensation to specific education in either early childhood education or child development (Mitchell, 2002). Use the web site in the Mitchell (2002) reference to get a good picture of how different states have constructed a system of compensation awards for increasing one's competence in early childhood education and child development.

Emphasis on Standardized, High-Stakes Testing

Chapter 8 focused on authentic assessment of young children by using methods such as work samples and observation. Many children, however, are subjected to standardized testing that does little to enhance their development or learning (Solley, 2007). Professional organizations such as NAEYC and the Council for Exceptional Children (CEC) have produced position statements about the need for authentic assessment (see the web sites for these organizations at the end of the chapter). The issue, then, is to advocate for authentic assessment and to make policy makers within and outside of our field aware of the need for authentic assessment for young children.

Maintaining Settings in Which Children Learn in a Developmentally Appropriate Way

Our profession has made a concerted effort to foster an understanding of developmentally appropriate practices (Copple & Bredekamp, 2006; Geist & Baum, 2005). State early learning standards describe what children should know and be able to do in the content areas of language arts and literacy, mathematics, science, social sciences, health, foreign language, and the arts. The standards do not tell teachers *how* to teach but do suggest developmentally appropriate approaches (Illinois State Board of Education, 2006).

Many teachers, however, recognize the discrepancy between what we know about developmentally appropriate practices and what we see in some public schools and other traditional forms of education. We know that children are active, curious learners who need to work and talk with others, but what we too often see is large group, workbook-driven instruction. Children experience a lot of stress in such developmentally inappropriate classrooms (Hart, Burts, Durland, Charlesworth, DeWolf, & Fleege, 1998). The need for developmentally appropriate learning environments, therefore, assumes heightened importance. For example, how can teachers foster literacy development

Go to MyEducationLab and select the topic "Emergent Literacy and Language Arts." Under Activities and Applications, watch the video *Teaching Reading* for an overview of this topic.

(IRA & NAEYC, 1998; Neuman & Roskos, 2005) in a developmentally appropriate way? How do we maintain a developmentally appropriate approach to children's mathematical thinking in the face of the push for workbook instruction (NAEYC & NCTM, 2002)?

Using Technology in Programs for 3- to 8- Year Old Children

Appropriately used, technology can enhance children's development and learning (Murphy, DePasquale, & McNamara, 2003; NAEYC, 1996, 2008). Weaving technology into the regular curriculum and using it as a tool to support children's construction of knowledge is wise. For example, primary grade children working on a project about plants might take digital photos of plants at different stages of growth. They would store the images and later put together a show of all photos. They might present their work to parents as a slide show on the computer and projected for all to see. In this instance, technology helps children in their quest for knowledge. The teacher avoids presenting working with computers and camera as a separate activity, divorced from any content. He connects it to learning in science, social studies, and language arts.

We should work to make sure that all children have equitable access to technology. As professionals, we must advocate for developmentally appropriate software and for programs that avoid stereotypes and violence. To be truly effective in dealing with this critical issue, teachers need appropriate professional development related to technology.

Where do we go from here as a profession? We move forward, but keep our rich history firmly in mind, knowing that our knowledge and skill base was forged in decades past. We build on our knowledge base and refine our skills. We think about issues and new programs critically and with a healthy skepticism, refusing to adopt just any program offered to us. We focus on evidence-based practices. We keep our eye on the prize—the best education possible for *all* children.

Go to MyEducationLab and select the topic "Technology." Under Activities and Applications, watch the video *Tablet Computers in First-Grade Math* to see how technology can be woven into the regular curriculum.

SUMMARY

Becoming a teacher is an ongoing process, and there are different stages of a teacher's development. There are developmental tasks and educational needs associated with each stage.

- The *entry or survival level* coincides with a teacher's first year in the profession. A new teacher is aware of the demands of the profession and might be apprehensive and have many questions. The teacher needs guidance and support in the practicalities of teaching such as finding materials and resources and assessing children's progress.
- The *consolidation level* is evident after the teacher feels more confident about managing a classroom and dealing with parents and other professionals.

Teachers now shift focus to refining teaching strategies used during the first year. Reflecting on pedagogical, or teaching, skills with an on-site mentor is very helpful at this stage.

- The *renewal level* often occurs between the third and fourth years of teaching. The teacher is now confident about classroom management and his or her ability to choose teaching and child guidance strategies. Professional development at this stage depends on the specific needs that individual teachers identify. Workshops and conferences are good ways to get this information.
- The *maturity level* occurs at different times, with many teachers reaching it after about 5 years. Teachers,

now veterans in the profession, have developed an individual teaching style that suits them. They search for information and skills at a deeper level and enjoy learning through formal courses or advanced degree programs.

- Teachers develop beyond the first 5 years with motivation a key factor in whether they pursue professional development activities. Highly motivated veteran teachers seek knowledge because of their commitment to helping children and families.

Good professional relationships contribute to teachers confidence and sense of competence as professionals, and this moves them forward in the stages of teacher development. Teachers need effective skills in speaking, listening, and writing. They need to know how to participate in a professional group, such as focusing on the group's goal. They also need to avoid intentionally specific behaviors such as gossiping.

Reflecting on one's practices is essential in developing a sense of professionalism in teaching. There are different levels of reflection:

- Teachers use *surface reflection* when trying to understand practical issues related to classroom management, such as "How should I set up snack time?"

- They use *pedagogical reflection*, a higher level, to consider the connections between theory and practice. The outcome is usually more consistency in how the teacher does things.
- Teachers use *critical reflection* when concerned about the ethical consequences of teaching practices on children. For example, the push down curriculum so evident today in kindergartens might be a topic for critical reflection.

Reflective lifelong learners continue to build on their knowledge of history, theory, and practice. This helps them to deal effectively with the many current and critical issues within the early childhood profession. Two of the many significant and current issues that we face as a profession are

- The emphasis on standardized, high-stakes testing with young children. Teachers serve children and families by advocating for authentic assessment.
- Maintaining settings in which children learn in a developmentally appropriate way. Teachers serve children by advocating for settings in which children can be active and curious learners.

QUESTIONS FOR REFLECTION

Using Figure 12.1 as a guide, reflect on your developing ability to participate successfully in professional group meetings.

1. At this point in my career, I feel most confident that I show the following quality of a successful professional group member: _____. An example of when I demonstrated this quality is _____.

2. Access one of the NAEYC position statements on an identified critical issue in the last section of this chapter. Make your choice from the statements on the NAEYC Web site, http://www.naeyc.org. Explain why this issue is important to you as a future early childhood teacher.

APPLY YOUR KNOWLEDGE

What Should This Teacher Do?

1. Emy Sanders, the case-study teacher, was sitting next to another teacher at a speech by the superintendent of schools for the district. Emy's colleague tried to engage her in a side conversation. Use Figure 12.1 to guide you in deciding what Emy should do. Give a reason for your response.

2. Greg has just completed his first year as a teacher. His principal approaches him and says, "What would

you say about mentoring the new third grade teacher we've just hired? She's brand new to teaching and could use your help." What are the potential problems for a teacher so new to the profession, such as Greg, mentoring another new teacher? What advice would you give to Greg?

KEY TERMS

WEB SITES

NAEYC critical issues
http://www.naeyc.org/ece/critical.asp
This part of the NAEYC web site has a very large amount of information on different critical issues in the profession, with links to relevant documents, including the critical issues discussed in this chapter.

NAEYC position statements on standardized testing and assessment
http://www.naeyc.org/about/positions/pdf/pscape.pdf
Joint statement of NAEYC and the National Association for Early Childhood Specialists in State Departments of Education (NAECS/SDE).

http://www.naeyc.org/about/positions/pdf/ELL_Supplement_Shorter_Version.pdf
Statement about assessment of English language learners.

http://www.naeyc.org/about/positions/pdf/ELL_Supplement_Shorter_Version.pdf
Statement about appropriate assessment for children with disabilities.

Reflective supervision
http://www.zerotothree.org
Home page for Zero to Three. Enter "reflective supervision" into the search box to access many excellent sources on this topic.

NAEYC Code of Ethical Conduct and Statement of Committment

PREAMBLE

NAEYC recognizes that those who work with young children face many daily decisions that have moral and ethical implications. The NAEYC Code of Ethical Conduct offers guidelines for responsible behavior and sets forth a common basis for resolving the principal ethical dilemmas encountered in early childhood care and education. The Statement of Commitment is not part of the Code but is a personal acknowledgement of an individual's willingness to embrace the distinctive values and moral obligations of the field of early childhood care and education. The primary focus of the Code is on daily practice with children and their families in programs for children from birth through 8 years of age, such as infant/toddler programs, preschool and prekindergarten programs, child care centers, hospital and child life settings, family child care homes, kindergartens, and primary classrooms. When the issues involve young children, then these provisions also apply to specialists who do not work directly with children, including program administrators, parent educators, early childhood adult educators, and officials with responsibility for program monitoring and licensing. (Note: See also the "Code of Ethical Conduct: Supplement for Early Childhood Adult Educators," online at http://www.naeyc.org/about/positions/ethics04.asp.) NAEYC (2005) Code of Ethical Conduct (2005 rev. ed.). Washington, DC: NAEYC. www.naeyc.org/about/positions/pdf/PSETH05.pdf. Reprinted with permission from the National Association for the Education of Young Children. Copyright © 2005 by the National Association for the Education of Young Children.

Core Values

Standards of ethical behavior in early childhood care and education are based on commitment to the following core values that are deeply rooted in the history of the field of early childhood care and education. We have made a commitment to

- Appreciate childhood as a unique and valuable stage of the human life cycle

- Base our work on knowledge of how children develop and learn
- Appreciate and support the bond between the child and family
- Recognize that children are best understood and supported in the context of family, culture,[1] community, and society
- Respect the dignity, worth, and uniqueness of each individual (child, family member, and colleague)
- Respect diversity in children, families, and colleagues
- Recognize that children and adults achieve their full potential in the context of relationships that are based on trust and respect

Conceptual Framework

The Code sets forth a framework of professional responsibilities in four sections. Each section addresses an area of professional relationships: (1) with children, (2) with families, (3) among colleagues, and (4) with the community and society. Each section includes an introduction to the primary responsibilities of the early childhood practitioner in that context. The introduction is followed by a set of ideals (I) that reflect exemplary professional practice and a set of principles (P) describing practices that are required, prohibited, or permitted.

The ideals reflect the aspirations of practitioners. The principles guide conduct and assist practitioners in resolving ethical dilemmas.[2] Both ideals and principles are intended to direct practitioners to those questions which, when responsibly answered, can provide the basis for conscientious decision making. While the Code provides specific direction for addressing some ethical dilemmas, many others will require the practitioner to combine the guidance of the Code with professional judgment.

---

[1]Culture includes ethnicity, racial identity, economic level, family structure, language, and religious and political beliefs, which profoundly influence each child's development and relationship to the world.
[2]There is not necessarily a corresponding principle for each ideal.

Source: National Association for the Education of Young Children. 2005. *Position Statement: Code of Ethical Conduct and Statement of Commitment.* Washington, DC: Author. Online: http://www.naeye.org/about/positions/pdf/pseth05.pdf

The ideals and principles in this Code present a shared framework of professional responsibility that affirms our commitment to the core values of our field. The Code publicly acknowledges the responsibilities that we in the field have assumed and in so doing supports ethical behavior in our work. Practitioners who face situations with ethical dimensions are urged to seek guidance in the applicable parts of this Code and in the spirit that informs the whole.

Often, "the right answer"—the best ethical course of action to take—is not obvious. There may be no readily apparent, positive way to handle a situation. When one important value contradicts another, we face an ethical dilemma. When we face a dilemma, it is our professional responsibility to consult the Code and all relevant parties to find the most ethical resolution.

SECTION I: ETHICAL RESPONSIBILITIES TO CHILDREN

Childhood is a unique and valuable stage in the human life cycle. Our paramount responsibility is to provide care and education in settings that are safe, healthy, nurturing, and responsive for each child. We are committed to supporting children's development and learning; respecting individual differences; and helping children learn to live, play, and work cooperatively. We are also committed to promoting children's self-awareness, competence, self-worth, resiliency, and physical well-being.

Ideals

I-1.1   To be familiar with the knowledge base of early childhood care and education and to stay informed through continuing education and training.

I-1.2   To base program practices upon current knowledge and research in the field of early childhood education, child development, and related disciplines, as well as on particular knowledge of each child.

I-1.3   To recognize and respect the unique qualities, abilities, and potential of each child.

I-1.4   To appreciate the vulnerability of children and their dependence on adults.

I-1.5   To create and maintain safe and healthy settings that foster children's social, emotional, cognitive, and physical development and that respect their dignity and their contributions.

I-1.6   To use assessment instruments and strategies that are appropriate for the children to be assessed, that are used only for the purposes for which they were designed, and that have the potential to benefit children.

I-1.7   To use assessment information to understand and support children's development and learning, to support instruction, and to identify children who may need additional services.

I-1.8   To support the right of each child to play and learn in an inclusive environment that meets the needs of children with and without disabilities.

I-1.9   To advocate for and ensure that all children, including those with special needs, have access to the support services needed to be successful.

I-1.10   To ensure that each child's culture, language, ethnicity, and family structure are recognized and valued in the program.

I-1.11   To provide all children with experiences in a language that they know, as well as support children in maintaining the use of their home language and in learning English.

I-1.12   To work with families to provide a safe and smooth transition as children and families move from one program to the next.

Principles

P-1.1   **Above all, we shall not harm children. We shall not participate in practices that are emotionally damaging, physically harmful, disrespectful, degrading, dangerous, exploitative, or intimidating to children. This principle has precedence over all others in this Code.**

P-1.2   We shall care for and educate children in positive emotional and social environments that are cognitively stimulating and that support each child's culture, language, ethnicity, and family structure.

P-1.3   We shall not participate in practices that discriminate against children by denying benefits, giving special advantages, or excluding them from programs or activities on the basis of their sex, race, national origin, religious beliefs, medical condition, disability, or the marital status/family structure, sexual orientation, or religious beliefs or other affiliations of their families. (Aspects of this principle do not apply in programs that have a lawful mandate to provide services to a particular population of children.)

P-1.4   We shall involve all those with relevant knowledge (including families and staff) in decisions concerning a child, as appropriate, ensuring confidentiality of sensitive information.

P-1.5   We shall use appropriate assessment systems, which include multiple sources of information, to provide information on children's learning and development.

P-1.6   We shall strive to ensure that decisions such as those related to enrollment, retention, or assignment to special education services, will be based on multiple sources of information and will never be based on a single assessment, such as a test score or a single observation.

P-1.7   We shall strive to build individual relationships with each child; make individualized adaptations in teaching strategies, learning environments, and curricula; and consult with the family so that each child benefits from the program. If after such efforts have been exhausted, the current placement does not meet a child's needs, or the child is seriously jeopardizing the ability of other children to benefit from the program, we shall collaborate with the child's family and appropriate specialists to determine the additional services needed and/or the placement option(s) most likely to ensure the child's success. (Aspects of this principle may not apply in programs that have a lawful mandate to provide services to a particular population of children.)

P-1.8 We shall be familiar with the risk factors for and symptoms of child abuse and neglect, including physical, sexual, verbal, and emotional abuse and physical, emotional, educational, and medical neglect. We shall know and follow state laws and community procedures that protect children against abuse and neglect.

P-1.9 When we have reasonable cause to suspect child abuse or neglect, we shall report it to the appropriate community agency and follow up to ensure that appropriate action has been taken. When appropriate, parents or guardians will be informed that the referral will be or has been made.

P-1.10 When another person tells us of his or her suspicion that a child is being abused or neglected, we shall assist that person in taking appropriate action in order to protect the child.

P-1.11 When we become aware of a practice or situation that endangers the health, safety, or well-being of children, we have an ethical responsibility to protect children or inform parents and/or others who can.

SECTION II: ETHICAL RESPONSIBILITIES TO FAMILIES

Families[3] are of primary importance in children's development. Because the family and the early childhood practitioner have a common interest in the child's well-being, we acknowledge a primary responsibility to bring about communication, cooperation, and collaboration between the home and early childhood program in ways that enhance the child's development.

Ideals

I-2.1 To be familiar with the knowledge base related to working effectively with families and to stay informed through continuing education and training.

I-2.2 To develop relationships of mutual trust and create partnerships with the families we serve.

I-2.3 To welcome all family members and encourage them to participate in the program.

I-2.4 To listen to families, acknowledge and build upon their strengths and competencies, and learn from families as we support them in their task of nurturing children.

I-2.5 To respect the dignity and preferences of each family and to make an effort to learn about its structure, culture, language, customs, and beliefs.

I-2.6 To acknowledge families' childrearing values and their right to make decisions for their children.

I-2.7 To share information about each child's education and development with families and to help them understand and appreciate the current knowledge base of the early childhood profession.

I-2.8 To help family members enhance their understanding of their children and support the continuing development of their skills as parents.

I-2.9 To participate in building support networks for families by providing them with opportunities to interact with program staff, other families, community resources, and professional services.

Principles

P-2.1 We shall not deny family members access to their child's classroom or program setting unless access is denied by court order or other legal restriction.

P-2.2 We shall inform families of program philosophy, policies, curriculum, assessment system, and personnel qualifications, and explain why we teach as we do—which should be in accordance with our ethical responsibilities to children (see Section I).

P-2.3 We shall inform families of and, when appropriate, involve them in policy decisions.

P-2.4 We shall involve the family in significant decisions affecting their child.

P-2.5 We shall make every effort to communicate effectively with all families in a language that they understand. We shall use community resources for translation and interpretation when we do not have sufficient resources in our own programs.

P-2.6 As families share information with us about their children and families, we shall consider this information to plan and implement the program.

P-2-7 We shall inform families about the nature and purpose of the program's child assessments and how data about their child will be used.

P-2.8 We shall treat child assessment information confidentially and share this information only when there is a legitimate need for it.

P-2.9 We shall inform the family of injuries and incidents involving their child, of risks such as exposures to communicable diseases that might result in infection, and of occurrences that might result in emotional stress.

P-2.10 Families shall be fully informed of any proposed research projects involving their children and shall have the opportunity to give or withhold consent without penalty. We shall not permit or participate in research that could in any way hinder the education, development, or well-being of children.

[3]The term *family* may include those adults, besides parents, with the responsibility of being involved in educating, nurturing, and advocating for the child.

P-2.11   We shall not engage in or support exploitation of families. We shall not use our relationship with a family for private advantage or personal gain, or enter into relationships with family members that might impair our effectiveness working with their children.

P-2.12   We shall develop written policies for the protection of confidentiality and the disclosure of children's records. These policy documents shall be made available to all program personnel and families. Disclosure of children's records beyond family members, program personnel, and consultants having an obligation of confidentiality shall require familial consent (except in cases of abuse or neglect).

P-2.13   We shall maintain confidentiality and shall respect the family's right to privacy, refraining from disclosure of confidential information and intrusion into family life. However, when we have reason to believe that a child's welfare is at risk, it is permissible to share confidential information with agencies, as well as with individuals who have legal responsibility for intervening in the child's interest.

P-2.14   In cases where family members are in conflict with one another, we shall work openly, sharing our observations of the child, to help all parties involved make informed decisions. We shall refrain from becoming an advocate for one party.

P-2.15   We shall be familiar with and appropriately refer families to community resources and professional support services. After a referral has been made, we shall follow up to ensure that services have been appropriately provided.

SECTION III: ETHICAL RESPONSIBILITIES TO COLLEAGUES

In a caring, cooperative workplace, human dignity is respected, professional satisfaction is promoted, and positive relationships are developed and sustained. Based upon our core values, our primary responsibility to colleagues is to establish and maintain settings and relationships that support productive work and meet professional needs. The same ideals that apply to children also apply as we interact with adults in the workplace.

A. Responsibilities to Co-workers

Ideals

I-3A.1   To establish and maintain relationships of respect, trust, confidentiality, collaboration, and cooperation with co-workers.

I-3A.2   To share resources with co-workers, collaborating to ensure that the best possible early childhood care and education program is provided.

I-3A.3   To support co-workers in meeting their professional needs and in their professional development.

I-3A.4   To accord co-workers due recognition of professional achievement.

Principles

P-3A.1   We shall recognize the contributions of colleagues to our program and not participate in practices that diminish their reputations or impair their effectiveness in working with children and families.

P-3A.2   When we have concerns about the professional behavior of a co-worker, we shall first let that person know of our concern in a way that shows respect for personal dignity and for the diversity to be found among staff members, and then attempt to resolve the matter collegially and in a confidential manner.

P-3A.3   We shall exercise care in expressing views regarding the personal attributes or professional conduct of co-workers. Statements should be based on firsthand knowledge, not hearsay, and relevant to the interests of children and programs.

P-3A.4   We shall not participate in practices that discriminate against a co-worker because of sex, race, national origin, religious beliefs or other affiliations, age, marital status/family structure, disability, or sexual orientation.

B. Responsibilities to Employers

Ideals

I-3B.1   To assist the program in providing the highest quality of service.

I-3B.2   To do nothing that diminishes the reputation of the program in which we work unless it is violating laws and regulations designed to protect children or is violating the provisions of this Code.

Principles

P-3B.1   We shall follow all program policies. When we do not agree with program policies, we shall attempt to effect change through constructive action within the organization.

P-3B.2   We shall speak or act on behalf of an organization only when authorized. We shall take care to acknowledge when we are speaking for the organization and when we are expressing a personal judgment.

P-3B.3   We shall not violate laws or regulations designed to protect children and shall take appropriate action consistent with this Code when aware of such violations.

P-3B.4   If we have concerns about a colleague's behavior, and children's well-being is not at risk, we may address the concern with that individual. If children are at risk or the situation does not improve after it has been brought to the colleague's attention, we shall report the colleague's unethical or incompetent behavior to an appropriate authority.

P-3B.5   When we have a concern about circumstances or conditions that impact the quality of care and education within the program, we shall inform the program's administration or, when necessary, other appropriate authorities.

C. Responsibilities to Employees

Ideals

I-3C.1   To promote safe and healthy working conditions and policies that foster mutual respect, cooperation, collaboration, competence, well-being, confidentiality, and self-esteem in staff members.

I-3C.2   To create and maintain a climate of trust and candor that will enable staff to speak and act in the best interests of children, families, and the field of early childhood care and education.

I-3C.3   To strive to secure adequate and equitable compensation (salary and benefits) for those who work with or on behalf of young children.

I-3C.4   To encourage and support continual development of employees in becoming more skilled and knowledgeable practitioners.

Principles

P-3C.1   In decisions concerning children and programs, we shall draw upon the education, training, experience, and expertise of staff members.

P-3C.2   We shall provide staff members with safe and supportive working conditions that honor confidences and permit them to carry out their responsibilities through fair performance evaluation, written grievance procedures, constructive feedback, and opportunities for continuing professional development and advancement.

P-3C.3   We shall develop and maintain comprehensive written personnel policies that define program standards. These policies shall be given to new staff members and shall be available and easily accessible for review by all staff members.

P-3C.4   We shall inform employees whose performance does not meet program expectations of areas of concern and, when possible, assist in improving their performance.

P-3C.5   We shall conduct employee dismissals for just cause, in accordance with all applicable laws and regulations. We shall inform employees who are dismissed of the reasons for their termination. When a dismissal is for cause, justification must be based on evidence of inadequate or inappropriate behavior that is accurately documented, current, and available for the employee to review.

P-3C.6   In making evaluations and recommendations, we shall make judgments based on fact and relevant to the interests of children and programs.

P-3C.7   We shall make hiring, retention, termination, and promotion decisions based solely on a person's competence, record of accomplishment, ability to carry out the responsibilities of the position, and professional preparation specific to the developmental levels of children in his/her care.

P-3C.8   We shall not make hiring, retention, termination, and promotion decisions based on an individual's sex, race, national origin, religious beliefs or other affiliations, age, marital status/family structure, disability, or sexual orientation. We shall be familiar with and observe laws and regulations that pertain to employment discrimination. (Aspects of this principle do not apply to programs that have a lawful mandate to determine eligibility based on one or more of the criteria identified above.)

P-3C.9   We shall maintain confidentiality in dealing with issues related to an employee's job performance and shall respect an employee's right to privacy regarding personal issues.

SECTION IV: ETHICAL RESPONSIBILITIES TO COMMUNITY AND SOCIETY

Early childhood programs operate within the context of their immediate community made up of families and other institutions concerned with children's welfare. Our responsibilities to the community are to provide programs that meet the diverse needs of families, to cooperate with agencies and professions that share the responsibility for children, to assist families in gaining access to those agencies and allied professionals, and to assist in the development of community programs that are needed but not currently available.

As individuals, we acknowledge our responsibility to provide the best possible programs of care and education for children and to conduct ourselves with honesty and integrity. Because of our specialized expertise in early childhood development and education and because the larger society shares responsibility for the welfare and protection of young children, we acknowledge a collective obligation to advocate for the best interests of children within early childhood programs and in the larger community and to serve as a voice for young children everywhere.

The ideals and principles in this section are presented to distinguish between those that pertain to the work of the individual early childhood educator and those that more typically are engaged in collectively on behalf of the best interests of children—with the understanding that individual early childhood educators have a shared responsibility for addressing the ideals and principles that are identified as "collective."

Ideal (Individual)

I-4.1   To provide the community with high-quality early childhood care and education programs and services.

Ideals (Collective)

I-4.2   To promote cooperation among professionals and agencies and interdisciplinary collaboration among professions concerned with addressing issues in the health, education, and well-being of young children, their families, and their early childhood educators.

I-4.3   To work through education, research, and advocacy toward an environmentally safe world in which all children receive health care, food, and shelter; are nurtured; and live free from violence in their home and their communities.

I-4.4   To work through education, research, and advocacy toward a society in which all young children have access to high-quality early care and education programs.

I-4.5   To work to ensure that appropriate assessment systems, which include multiple sources of information, are used for purposes that benefit children.

I-4.6   To promote knowledge and understanding of young children and their needs. To work toward greater societal acknowledgment of children's rights and greater social acceptance of responsibility for the well-being of all children.

I-4.7   To support policies and laws that promote the well-being of children and families, and to work to change those that impair their well-being. To participate in developing policies and laws that are needed, and to cooperate with other individuals and groups in these efforts.

I-4.8   To further the professional development of the field of early childhood care and education and to strengthen its commitment to realizing its core values as reflected in this Code.

Principles (Individual)

P-4.1   We shall communicate openly and truthfully about the nature and extent of services that we provide.

P-4.2   We shall apply for, accept, and work in positions for which we are personally well-suited and professionally qualified. We shall not offer services that we do not have the competence, qualifications, or resources to provide.

P-4.3   We shall carefully check references and shall not hire or recommend for employment any person whose competence, qualifications, or character makes him or her unsuited for the position.

P-4.4   We shall be objective and accurate in reporting the knowledge upon which we base our program practices.

P-4.5   We shall be knowledgeable about the appropriate use of assessment strategies and instruments and interpret results accurately to families.

P-4.6   We shall be familiar with laws and regulations that serve to protect the children in our programs and be vigilant in ensuring that these laws and regulations are followed.

P-4.7   When we become aware of a practice or situation that endangers the health, safety, or well-being of children, we have an ethical responsibility to protect children or inform parents and/or others who can.

P-4.8   We shall not participate in practices that are in violation of laws and regulations that protect the children in our programs.

P-4.9   When we have evidence that an early childhood program is violating laws or regulations protecting children, we shall report the violation to appropriate authorities who can be expected to remedy the situation.

P-4.10   When a program violates or requires its employees to violate this Code, it is permissible, after fair assessment of the evidence, to disclose the identity of that program.

Principles (Collective)

P-4.11   When policies are enacted for purposes that do not benefit children, we have a collective responsibility to work to change these practices.

P-4.12   When we have evidence that an agency that provides services intended to ensure children's well-being is failing to meet its obligations, we acknowledge a collective ethical responsibility to report the problem to appropriate authorities or to the public. We shall be vigilant in our follow-up until the situation is resolved.

P-4.13   When a child protection agency fails to provide adequate protection for abused or neglected children, we acknowledge a collective ethical responsibility to work toward the improvement of these services.

GLOSSARY OF TERMS RELATED TO ETHICS

CODE OF ETHICS   Defines the core values of the field and provides guidance for what professionals should do when they encounter conflicting obligations or responsibilities in their work.

VALUES   Qualities or principles that individuals believe to be desirable or worthwhile and that they prize for themselves, for others, and for the world in which they live.

CORE VALUES   Commitments held by a profession that are consciously and knowingly embraced by its practitioners because they make a contribution to society. There is a difference between personal values and the core values of a profession.

MORALITY   People's views of what is good, right, and proper; their beliefs about their obligations; and their ideas about how they should behave.

ETHICS   The study of right and wrong, or duty and obligation, that involves critical reflection on morality and the ability to make choices between values and the examination of the moral dimensions of relationships.

PROFESSIONAL ETHICS   The moral commitments of a profession that involve moral reflection that extends and enhances the personal morality practitioners bring to their work, that concern actions of right and wrong in the workplace, and that help individuals resolve moral dilemmas they encounter in their work.

ETHICAL RESPONSIBILITIES   Behaviors that one must or must not engage in. Ethical responsibilities are clear-cut and are spelled out in the Code of Ethical Conduct (for example, early childhood educators should never share confidential information about a child or family with a person who has no legitimate need for knowing).

ETHICAL DILEMMA   A moral conflict that involves determining appropriate conduct when an individual faces conflicting professional values and responsibilities.

SOURCES FOR GLOSSARY TERMS AND DEFINITIONS

Feeney, S., & Freeman, N. (1999). *Ethics and the early childhood educator: Using the NAEYC code.* Washington, DC: NAEYC.

Kidder, R.M. (1995). *How good people make tough choices: Resolving the dilemmas of ethical living.* New York: Fireside.

Kipnis, K. (1987). How to discuss professional ethics. *Young Children 42*(4): 26–30.

STATEMENT OF COMMITMENT[4]

As an individual who works with young children, I commit myself to furthering the values of early childhood education as they are reflected in the ideals and principles of the NAEYC Code of Ethical Conduct. To the best of my ability I will

- Never harm children
- Ensure that programs for young children are based on current knowledge and research of child development and early childhood education.
- Respect and support families in their task of nurturing children.
- Respect colleagues in early childhood care and education and support them in maintaining the NAEYC Code of Ethical Conduct.
- Serve as an advocate for children, their families, and their teachers in community and society.
- Stay informed of and maintain high standards of professional conduct.
- Engage in an ongoing process of self-reflection, realizing that personal characteristics, biases, and beliefs have an impact on children and families.
- Be open to new ideas and be willing to learn from the suggestions of others.
- Continue to learn, grow, and contribute as a professional.
- Honor the ideals and principles of the NAEYC Code of Ethical Conduct

---

[4]This Statement of Commitment is not part of the Code but is a personal acknowledgement of the individual's willingness to embrace the distinctive values and moral obligations of the field of early childhood care and education. It is recognition of the moral obligations that lead to an individual becoming part of the profession.

REFERENCES

Aguillard, A., Pierce, S., Benedict, J., & Burts, D. (2005). Barriers to the implementation of continuity-of-care practices in child care centers. *Early Childhood Research Quarterly, 20*(3), 329–344.

Ainsworth, M.D.S., Blehar, M.C., Waters, E., & Wall, S. (1978). *Patterns of attachment: A psychological study of the strange situation*. Hillsdale, NJ: Erlbaum.

Alliance for Childhood (2004). *The importance of play*. Retrieved on May 31, 2006, from http://www.alliance-forchildhood.net/projects/play/index.htm

Alter, P., & Conroy, M. (n.d.). Preventing challenging behaviors in young children. *Recommended practices handout*. Retrieved on July 6, 2007 from http://challengingbehavior.fmhi.usf.edu/handouts_presentations/preventing_challenging_behavior.pdf

Altman, T. (2006). *The wonder years*. Elk Grove Village, IL: American Academy of Pediatrics.

Ambry, M., & Steinbrunner, R. (2007). Promises to practices: Learning a Proactive approach to ethical dilemmas. *Young Children, 62*(4), 90–96.

American Academy of Child and Adolescent Psychiatry (1997). Obsessive-compulsive disorders in children and adolescents. *Facts for Families, Number 60*, Author.

American Academy of Child and Adolescent Psychiatry (1999a). Children and TV violence. *Facts for Families, Number 13*, Author.

American Academy of Child and Adolescent Psychiatry (1999b). Posttraumatic stress disorder (PTSD). *Facts for Families, Number 70*, Author.

American Academy of Child and Adolescent Psychiatry (2000). The anxious child. *Facts for Families, Number 47*, Author.

American Academy of Child and Adolescent Psychiatry/AACAP (2004a). Bipolar disorder in children and teens. *Facts for Families, Number 38*. Washington, DC: Author.

American Academy of Child and Adolescent Psychiatry/AACAP (2004b). Children who can't pay attention. *Facts for Families, Number 6*. Washington, DC: Author.

American Academy of Pediatrics (2007). Consistent, frequent tv viewing causes behavior problems. *News Brief*, October 1. Retrieved on September 16, 2008 from http://www.aap.org/advocacy/releases/oct07studies.htm

American Academy of Pediatrics (2007). *Parenting corner Q & A: Developmental milestones*. Retrieved on June 10, 2008, from http://www.aap.org/parents.html

American Lung Association (2007). *Asthma and children fact sheet*. Web site. Retrieved on April 26, 2008 from http://www.lungusa.org/site/apps/nl/content3.asp?c=dvLUK9O0E&b=2058817&content_id={05C5FA0A-A953 4BB6-BB74-F07C2ECCABA9}&notoc=1

American Psychological Association. (1995, updated 2000). Learner- center psychological principles: A framework for school redesign and reform. Retrieved on June 8, 2008, from http://www.avln.org/olexpedition/apa.html

American Psychological Association (in consultation with NAEYC) (2003). *Teach carefully: How understanding child development can prevent violence*. Washington, DC: American Psychological Association.

American Psychological Association (2005). *Lesbian and gay parenting*. Retrieved on August 28, 2007, from http://www.apa.org/pi/lgbc/publications/lgparenting.pdf

American Speech-Language-Hearing Association. (2004). *Guidelines for the audiologic assessment of children from birth to 5 years of age*. Retrieved on July 6, 2008, from http://www.asha.org/docs/html/GL2004-00002.html#sec1.5

Anderson, C.A. (2004). An update on the effects of playing violent video games. *Journal of Adolescence, 27*, 113–122.

Angelsen, N.K., Vik, T., Jacobsen, G., & Bakketeig, L.S. (September, 2001). Breast feeding and cognitive development at age 1 and 5 years. *Archives of Disease in Childhood, 85*, 183–188.

Bakley, S. (1997). Love a little more, accept a little more. *Young Children, 52(1)*, 21.

Ball, M. (2002). Developmental coordination disorder: Hints and tips for the activities of daily living. London. Jessica Kingsley Publishers.

Bandura, A., Ross, D., & Ross, S. A. (1961). Transmission of aggressions through imitation of aggressive models. *Journal of Abnormal and Social Psychology, 63*(3), 575–582.

Bandura, A., Ross, D., & Ross, S. A. (1963). Imitation of film-mediated aggression. *Journal of Abnormal and Social Psychology, 66*(1), 3–11.

Bank Street (2005). Timeless values, timely actions: A strategic plan for Bank Street, Draft #2. *Report to the Bank Street Board of Trustees*, Friday, December 2.

Bank Street (n.d.). *Bank Street school for children curriculum guide*. Retrieved on January 3, 2008 from http://www.bankstreet.edu/sfc/curriculum.html

Baptiste, N. (1995). Professional development: Always growing and learning. *Day Care and Early Education, 22*(3), 38–39.

Baptiste, N., & Reyes, L. (2008). *Understanding ethics in early care and education*, 2nd ed. Upper Saddle River, NJ: Pearson, Merrill/Prentice Hall.

Barboza, D. (2007, September 11). Why lead in toy paint? It's cheaper. *New York Times*. Retrieved on September 16, 2008, from http://www.nytimes.com/2007/09/011/business/worldbusiness/11lead.html

Bardige, B. (2005). *At a loss for words*. Philadelphia: Temple University Press.

Barnes, J. (1995). *The Cambridge companion to Aristotle*. Cambridge, UK: Cambridge University Press.

Barnett, W.S. (2002). Early childhood education: Executive summary. In Alex Mohlnar (Ed.), *School reform proposals: Research evidence* (1–26). Greenwich, CT: Information Age Publishing, Inc.

Barnett, W.S., Hustedt, J., Hawkinson, L., & Robin, K. (2006). *The state of preschool 2006: State preschool yearbook*. Report from the National Institute for Early Education Research, funded by the PEW Charitable Trust. Retrieved on April 29, 2008 from http:// nieer.org/yearbook/pdf/yearbook.pdf

Bates, J.E., Viken, R.J., Alexander, D.B., Beyers, J., & Stockton, L. (2002). Sleep and adjustment in preschool children: Sleep diary reports by mothers relate to behavior reports by teachers. *Child Development, 73*, 62–74.

Baum, A., & King, M. (2006). Creating a climate of self-awareness in early childhood teacher preparation programs. *Early Childhood Education Journal, 33*(4), 217–222.

Baumeister, R. (1996). Should schools try to boost self-esteem? Beware the dark side. *American Educator, 20*(2), 14–19, 43.

Bauminger, N., Schoor-Edelsztein, H., & Morash, J. (2005). Social information processing and emotional understanding in children with learning disabilities. *Journal of Learning Disabilities, 38*, 45–61.

Baumrind, D. (1996). Parenting: The discipline controversy revisited. *Family Relations, 45*, 405–414.

Beaty, J. (2006). *Observing development of the young child*. Upper Saddle River, NJ: Merrill/Prentice Hall.

Bechtel, L., & Denton, P. (2004). Guided discovery in action. *Responsive Classroom Newsletter, 16*(3), 5 pages.

Bedrova, E., & Leong, D. (1996). *Play: A Vygotskian Approach*. San Luis Obispo, CA: Davidson Films.

Bedrova, E., & Leong, D. (2001). Pioneers in our field: Lev Vygotsky—playing to learn. *Early Childhood Today*. Retrieved on September 11, 2008 from http://www.scholastic.com/browse/article .jsp?id=3549

Belinda, C. (2005). Stop, look, listen, and write: Using observation with young children. *Better kid care newsletter*, Pennsylvania State University, December. Retrieved on June 18, 2008, from http:// betterkidcare.psu.edu/ENewsletters/ENews0512Dec.html

Bennett, T. (2001). Reactions to visiting the infant-toddler and preschool centers in Reggio Emilia, Italy. *Early Childhood Research and Practice, 3*(1). Retrieved on April 27, 2008, from http:// ecrp.uiuc.edu/v3n1/bennett.html

Bentzen, W. (2004). *Seeing young children*, 5th ed. Florence, KY: Delmar Cengage Learning.

Bergen, D. (2002). The role of pretend play in children's cognitive development. *Early Childhood Research & Practice, 4*(1), no page numbers. Retrieved on April 26, 2008, from http://ecrp.uiuc.edu/v4n1/bergen.html

Bergen, D., & Coscia, J. (2001). *Brain research and childhood education: Implications for educators*. Olney, MD: Association for Childhood Education International.

Berger, E.H. (2008). *Parents as partners in education*, 7th ed. Upper Saddle River, NJ: Merrill/Prentice Hall.

Berger, K. (2003). *The developing person through childhood*. New York: Worth.

Berk, L., & Winsler, A. (1995). *Scaffold children's learning: Vygotsky and early childhood education*. Washington, DC: NAEYC.

Bernard, B. (1995) *Fostering Resilience in Children*. ERIC/EECE Digest, EDO-PS-99.

Bialystok, E. (2006). Second language acquisition and bilingualism at an early age and the impact on early cognitive development. In Tremblay, R.E., Barr, R.G., & Peters, R.V. (Eds.), *Encyclopedia on early childhood development* (online) (pages 1–4). Montreal: Center for Excellence in Early Childhood Development. Retrieved on April 26, 2008, from http://www.excellence-earlychildhood.ca/documents/BialystokANGxp.pdf

Biber, B. (1973; updated 2005). *What is Bank Street?* Speech originally given at the Bank Street College of Education Convocation Luncheon, November 27. Retrieved on January 3, 2008, from http://streetcat.bankstreet.edu/essays/biber.html

Bickart, T., Jablon, J., & Dodge, D. (1999). *Building the primary classroom*. Washington, DC: Teaching Strategies.

Birch, S.H., & Ladd, G.W. (1997). The teacher-child relationship and children's early school adjustment. *Journal of School Psychology, 35*, 61–79.

Birmaher, B., Axelson, D., Strober, M., Gill, M.K., Valeri, S., Chiappetta, L., Ryan, N., Leonard, H., Hunt, J., Iyengar, S., & Keller, M. (2006). Clinical course of children and adolescents with bipolar spectrum disorders. *Archives of General Psychiatry, 63*(2), 175–83.

Birmingham, C. (2004). Phronesis: A model for pedagogical reflection. *Journal of Teacher Education, 55*(4), 313–324.

Bishop, S., & Rothbaum, F. (1992). Parents' acceptance of control needs and preschoolers' social behaviour: A longitudinal study. *Canadian Journal of Behavioural Science, 24*(2), 171–185.

Black, S. (2006). The power of caring. *American School Board Journal, 93*(10). Retrieved on April 27, 2008, from http://www.asbj.com/MainMenuCategory/Archive/2006/October.aspx

Blackwell, P.B. (2002). Screening young children for autism and other social-communication disorders. *Journal of the Kentucky Medical Association, 100*(9), 390–394.

Bodrova, E., & Leong, D. (1996). Scaffolding in the zone of proximal development. *Of Primary Interest, 3*(4). Retrieved on March 25, 2008, from http://naecs.crc.uiuc.edu/newsletter/volume3/number4.html

Bolger, K., Patterson, C., & Kupersmidt, J. (1998). Peer relationships and self-esteem among children who have been maltreated. *Child Development, 69*(4), 1171–1197.

Booher-Jennings (2007). Rationing education in an era of accountability. *Phi Delta Kappan, 87*(10), 756–761.

Bovey, T., & Strain, P. (n.d.). Using environmental strategies to promote positive social interactions. *What Works Briefs, 6.* Vanderbilt University: Center on the Social and Emotional Foundations for Early Learning. http://www.vanderbilt.edu/csefel/briefs/wwb6.html

Bowlby, J. (1979). *The making and breaking of affectional bonds.* London: Tavistock.

Bowlby, J. (1982). *Attachment.* New York: Basic Books.

Bowman, B., Donovan, M.S., & Burns, M.S. (Eds.). (2000). *Eager to learn: Educating our preschoolers.* Washington, DC: National Academies Press. A report to the committee on Early Childhood Pedagogy, National Research Council, chapter seven.

Brady, K., Forton, M.B., Porter, D., & Wood, C.(2003). *Rules in school.* Turner Falls, MA: Northeast Foundation for Children.

Brambring, M. (2006). Divergent development of gross motor skills of children who are blind or sighted. *Journal of Vision Impairment and Blindness, 100*(10), 620–634.

Brandt, R. (1995). Punished by rewards? A conversation with Alfie Kohn. *Educational Leadership, 53*(1), 6 pages. Retrieved on July 1, 2008, from http://www.alfiekohn.org/teaching/pdf/Punished%20by%20Rewards.pdf

Branscombe, A., Castle, K., Dorsey, A., Surbeck, E., & Taylor, J. (2003). *Early childhood curriculum: A constructivist perspective.* Boston: Houghton Mifflin.

Brassard, M., & Boehm, A. (2007). *Preschool assessment: Principles and practices.* New York, NY: Guilford Press.

Bredekamp, S. (2004). *Essentials textbook for CDAs: Summary of revisions.* Washington, D.C.: Council for Professional Recognition/National Association for the Education of Young Children (NAEYC). Retrieved on April 29, 2008 from http://www.cdacouncil.org/PDF/CDA%20Essentials%20articles%20sue1.pdf

Bredekamp, S., Copple, S. (Eds), (1997). *Developmentally appropriate practice in early childhood programs serving children from birth through age 8* (expanded edition). Washington, DC: NAEYC.

Bredekamp, S., & Copple, C. (1997). *Developmentally appropriate practice in early childhood programs* (revised ed.). Washington, DC: National Association for the Education of Young Children.

Bredekamp, S., & Rosegrant, T. (1995) *Reaching potentials: Appropriate curriculum and assessment for young children, Volume 1.* Washington, D.C.: NAEYC.

Brenner, E., & Salovey, P. (1997). Emotion regulation during childhood: Developmental, interpersonal, and individual considerations. In P. Salovey & D. Sluyter (Eds.) *Emotional literacy and emotional development* (pp. 169–192). New York: Basic Books.

Brett, C. (1998). *Understanding human nature* (paperback edition). Center City, MN: Hazelden Publishing.

Briggs, J. (1970). *Never in anger.* Cambridge, MA: Harvard University Press.

Broderick, P., Blewitt, P., & Weaver, J. (2002). *The life span: Human development for helping professionals.* Upper Saddle River, NJ: Merrill/Prentice Hall.

Brody, L.M., Nagin, D.S., Tremblay, R.E., Bates, J.E., Brame, B., Dodge, K.A., Fergusson, D., Horwood, J.L., Loeber, R., Laird, R., Lynam, D.R., Moffitt, T.E., Pettit, G.S., & Vitaro, F. (2003). Developmental trajectories of childhood disruptive behaviors and adolescent delinquency: A six-site, cross-national study. *Developmental Psychology, 39*, 222–245.

Bronfenbrenner, U. (1994). Ecological models of human development. In *International Encyclopedia of Education*, Vol. 3, 2nd ed. 1643–1647.

Brooks-Gunn, J., & Johnson, A. (2006). G. Stanley Hall's contribution to science, practice and policy: The child study, parent education, and child welfare movements. *History of Psychology, 9*(3), 247–258.

Brown, J.R., & Dunn, J. (1996). Continuities in emotion understanding from three to six years. *Child Development, 67*(3), 789–802.

Bruder, M.B. (2001). The individual family service plan (IFSP). *ERIC Digest.* Retrieved on November 10, 2007, from http://www.ericdigests.org/2001-4/ifsp.html

Bruner, J. (1960; 2006). *The process of education* (revised edition, 2006). Cambridge, MA: Harvard University Press.

Bruner, J. (1966). *Toward a theory of instruction.* Cambridge, MA: Harvard University Press.

Bruner, J. (1977). *The process of education*, 2nd ed. Cambridge, MA: Harvard University Press.

Bruner, J. (1990). *Acts of meaning: A cognitive view.* New York: Holt, Rinehart & Winston.

Buckner, J.C., & Bassuk, E.L. (1997). Mental disorders and service utilization among youth from homeless and low-income housed families. *Journal of the American Academy of Child and Adolescent Psychiatry. 36*(7), 890–900.

Buhs, E., & Ladd, G.W. (2001). Peer rejection in kindergarten: Relational processes mediating academic and emotional outcomes. *Developmental Psychology, 37*, 550–560.

Burts, D., Hart, C., Charlesworth, R., Fleege, P., Mosley, J., & Thomasson, R. (1992). Observed activities and stress behaviors of children in developmentally appropriate and inappropriate kindergarten classrooms. *Early Childhood Research Quarterly, 7*, 297–318.

Buss, K., & Kiel, E. (2004). Comparison of sadness, anger, and fear facial expressions when toddlers look at their mothers. *Child Development, 75*(6), 1761–1774.

California Department of Education (2006). *Prekindergarten Learning Guidelines.* Sacramento, CA: author. Retrieved on April 29, 2008 from http://www.cde.ca.gov/sp/cd/re/prekcontents.asp

Campbell, B. (2008). *Handbook of differentiated instruction using the multiple intelligences: Lesson plans and more.* Upper Saddle River, NJ: Allyn & Bacon.

Capezzuto, S., & Da Ros-Voseles, D. (2001). Using experts to enhance classroom projects. classroom projects. *Young Children, 56*(2), 84–85.

Carbonara, N.T. (1961). *Techniques for observing normal child behavior.* Pittsburgh, PA: University of Pittsburgh Press.

Carlson, F.M. (2006). *Essential touch.* Washington, D.C.: National Association for the Education of Young Children.

Carlson, G. (2008). *Bipolar disorder.* Speech on the AACAP web site. Retrieved on June 23, 2008, from http://www.aacap.org/cs/root/facts_for_families/bipolar_disorder_in_children_and_teens

Carlton, M. (2003). *Helping children at home and school.* Bethesda, MD: National Association of School Psychologists.

Carnes, R. (2005). *Verbs: Types and tenses.* Texas State University-San Marcos: Student Learning Assistance Center.

Carolina Abecedarian Project (n.d.). *The abecedarian project and major findings.* Retrieved on September 14, 2008 from http://www.fpg.unc.edu/~abc/#intervention

Cassidy, J., Parke, R., Butkovsky, L., & Braungart, J. (1992). Family-peer connections: The roles of emotional expressiveness within the family and children's understanding of emotions. *Child Development, 63*, 603–618.

Ceglowski, D., & Bacigalupa, C. (2002). Keeping current in child care research, annotated bibliography: An update. *Early childhood research and practice, 4*(1), Retrieved on June 25, 2008, from http://ecrp.uiuc.edu/v4n1/ceglowski.html#socialdev

Census Bureau News (2007). News release on single-parent households. Retrieved on December 10, 2007, from http://www.census.gov/Press-Release/www/releases/archives/families_households/009842.html

Center for Applied Special Technology (2007). UDL, *Universal Design for Learning Guidelines.* Retrieved on June 23, 2008 from http://www.cast.org/

Center for Disease Control and Prevention (2005). *Developmental screening.* Retrieved on July 7, 2008, from http://www.cdc.gov/ncbddd/child/devtool.htm

Center for Disease Control and Prevention (2005). *Child development.* Retrieved on June 10, 2008, from http://www.cdc.gov/ncbddd/child

Center for Evidence-Based Practice (2004). *Facts about young children with challenging behaviors.* Retrieved on April 9, 2008, from http://www.vanderbilt.edu/csefel/modules/module4/handout4.pdf

Center on Media and Child Health (2005). *The effects of electronic media on children ages zero to six: A history of research.* Report for the Henry J. Kaiser Family Foundation. Boston, MA. Retrieved on September 16, 2008 from http://www.kff.org

Center on the Social and Emotional Foundations for Early Learning (CSEFEL) (2003). *Inventory of practices for promoting children's social emotional competence.* Urbana-Champaign, IL: University of Illinois.

Chalmers, J.B., & Townsend, M. A. (1990). The effects of training in social perspective taking on socially maladjusted girls. *Child Development, 61*, 178–190.

Chen, K. (2006). Social skills intervention for students with emotional/behavioral disorders: A literature review from the American perspective. *Educational Research and Reviews, 1*(3), 143–149.

Child Care Bureau (2006). *Leading the way to quality early care and education.* Washington, D.C.: Administration for Children and Families. Retrieved on March 8, 2008, from http://www.acf.hhs.gov/programs/ccb/ta/pubs/cd/ltw_outline.htm

Child Welfare Information Gateway (2006). *Child maltreatment 2004: Summary of key findings.* Washington, DC: Children's Bureau, Administration for Children and Families, US Department of Health and Human Services.

Chilvers, D. (2005). Rethinking reflective practice in the early years. In K. Hirst & C. Nutbrown (Eds.), *Perspectives on early childhood education: Contemporary research.* Stoke on Trent, UK: Trentham Books, pages 163–180.

Christian, L.G. (2006). Applying family systems theory to early childhood practice. *Young Children Beyond the Journal, January.* Retrieved on April 2, 2008, from http://www.journal.naeyc.org/btj/200601/ChristianBTJ.asp

Clayton, M.K., & Forton, M.B. (2001). *Classroom spaces that work.* Turner Falls, MA: Northeast Foundation for Children.

Cohen, D., Stern, V., & Balaban, N. (1996). *Observing and recording the behavior of young children.* New York: Teachers College Press.

Cohen, L.B., & Cashon, C.H. (2002). Infant perception and cognition. In R. Lerner, M. Easterbrooks, & J. Mistry (Eds.), *Comprehensive handbook of psychology, Volume 6: Developmental Psychology* (pp 65–89). New York: Wiley.

Cohn, J.F., Campbell, S.B., Matias, R., & Hopkins, J. (1990). Face-to-face interactions of postpartum depressed and nondepressed mother-infant pairs at 2 months. *Developmental Psychology, 26,* 15–23.

Colombo, M.W. (2005). Reflections from teachers of culturally diverse children. *Young Children, Beyond the Journal.* Retrieved on August 26, 2007, from http://www.journal.naeyc.org/btj/200511/ ColomboBTJ1105.asp

Colorin Colorado (2007). *How to create a welcoming classroom environment.* Retrieved on April 13, 2008, from http://www.colorincolorado.org/educators/reachingout/welcoming

Columbus Magnet School (n.d.). Teaching and learning in a Bank Street classroom. Retrieved on September 22, 2008, from http://pages.cthome.net/columbusmgnt/bankst.html

Committee for Children (2007). *Second step overview.* Retrieved on June 26, 2008, from http://www.cfchildren.org/programs/ssp/overview

Community Empowerment (2001). Helping children cope with disaster. *Community Empowerment Newsletter–Iowa, 2*(5), 6.

Conroy, M. (2004). *Assessing challenging behaviors in early childhood: Strategies for teachers and trainers.* Presentation at the DEC Recommended Practices Training Series, Erlanger, KY: September 24.

Cookson, P. (2008). Poverty mars formation of infant brains. *Financial Times: Science & Environment Section.* Retrieved on February 16, 2008, from http://www.developingchild.net/pubs/persp/pdf/Policy_Framework.pdf

Coopersmith, S. (1967). *The antecedents of self-esteem.* San Francisco: W.H. Freeman.

Copple, C., & Bredekamp, S. (2005). *Basics of developmentally appropriate practice: An introduction to teachers of children 3 to 6.* Washington, DC: National Association for the Education of Young Children.

Copple, C., & Bredekamp, S. (2008). Developmentally appropriate practice in early childhood programs. Washington, D.C.: National Association for the Education of Young Children.

Corbin, C., & Pangrazi, R. (2003). Guidelines for appropriate physical activity for elementary school children. *A Position Statement for the Council for Physical Education of Elementary School Children (COPEC).* http://www.aahperd.org/naspe/pdf_files/input_activity.pdf

Council for Professional Recognition (2008). Definition of the Child Development Associate. Retrieved on February 26, 2008 from http://www.cdacouncil.org/cda_what.htm

Council on Sports Medicine and Fitness and Council on School Health (2006). Active healthy living: Prevention of childhood obesity through increased physical activity. *Pediatrics, 117*(5), 1834–1842.

Crick, N., & Dodge, K. (1994). A review and reformulation of social information processing mechanisms in children's social adjustment. *Psychological Bulletin, 115,* 74–101.

Crittenden, P.M. (1992). Children's strategies for coping with adverse home environments: An interpretation using attachment theory. *Child Abuse & Neglect, 16,* 329–343.

Cross, A.F., & Dixon, S.D. (2004) *Adapting curriculum and instruction in inclusive early childhood settings,* revised edition. Bloomington, IL: Indiana Institute on Disability and Community.

Crossen-Tower, C. (2002). *Understanding child abuse and neglect* (5th ed.). Boston: Allyn and Bacon.

Cruess, S., Johnston, S., & Cruess, R. (2004). "Profession": A working definition for medical educators. *Teaching and Learning in Medicine, 16*(1), 74–76.

Cryer, D., Hurwitz, S., & Wolery, M. (2001). *Continuity of caregiver for infants and toddlers in center-based child care:* Report on a survey of center practices. *Early Childhood Research Quarterly, 15*(4), 479–514.

Darling, N. (1999). Parenting style and its correlates. *Eric Digest,* ED 427896. Retrieved on September 18, 2008, from http://www.ericdigests.org/1999-4/parenting.htm

Davies, P., & Cummings, M. (1994). Marital conflict and child adjustment: An emotional security hypothesis. *Psychological Bulletin, 116,* 387–411.

Dawson, (2002). Normal growth and revised growth charts. *Pediatrics in Review, 23,* 255–256.

Day, C.B. (2004). *Essentials textbook for CDAs.* Washington, D.C.: NAEYC.

Day, T., & Kunz, J.T. (2001). *Guidance based on developmental theory* (unpublished manuscript). Ogden, Utah Weber State University.

de Waal, F. (2000). *Chimpanzee politics* (revised edition). Baltimore, MD: The Johns Hopkins University Press.

Dehghan, M., Akhtar-Danesh, & Merchant, A.T. (2005). Childhood obesity prevalence and prevention. *Nutrition Journal, 4*(9), 24–31.

DeNeve, P. (2006). Activity-based spelling practice. Observation in the DeNeve's classroom by the author of this textbook, February-April.

Denham, S., McKinley, M., Couchoud, E., & Hold, R. (1990). Emotional and behavioral predictors of preschool peer ratings. *Child Development, 61,* 1145–1152.

Denham, S.A. (2006). Social-emotional competence as support for school readiness: What is it and how do we assess it? *Early Education and Development, 17*(1), 57–89.

Deniz, C.B. (2004). Relationships between teacher beliefs and practices: A qualitative flowchart methodology. Paper presented in the paper session *Early Childhood Issues and Dilemmas* at the American Education Research Association Annual Meeting, April 12, Anaheim, CA.

Denton, P. (2005). *Learning through academic choice.* Turner Falls, MA: Northeast Foundation for Children.

Denton, P. & Kreete, P. (2000) *The first six weeks of school.* Turner Feills, MA: Northeast Foundation for children.

Derman-Sparks, L., & A.B.C. Task Force (1989). *Anti-bias curriculum: Tasks for empowering young children.* Washington, DC: National Association for the Education of Young Children.

Destafano, L., Shriner, J., & Lloyd, C. (2001). Teacher decision making in participation of students with special needs in large-scale assessment. *Exceptional Children, 68*(1), 7–22.

DeVries, R., Hildebrandt, C., & Zan, B. (2000). Constructivist education for moral development. *Early Education and Development, 11*(1), 9–35.

DeVries, R., Zan, B., Hildebrandt, C., Edmiaston, R., & Sales, C. (2002). *Developing constructivist early childhood curriculum: Practical principles and activities.* Williston, VT: Teachers College Press.

Dewey, J. (1897). My pedagogic creed. *The School Journal, 54*(3), 77–80. Read Dewey's Creed. Retrieved on September 11, 2008, from http://dewey.pragmatism.org/creed.htm

Dewey, J. (1902). *The child and the curriculum.* Chicago, IL: The University of Chicago Press.

Dewey, J. (1913). *Interest and effort in education.* Boston: Riverside.

Dewey, J. (1933) *How we think. A restatement of the relation of reflective thinking to the educative process* (revised ed.). Boston: D. C. Heath.

Dewey, J. (1933/1998). *How we think* (Revised ed.). Boston: Houghton Mifflin.

Dewey, J. (1938). *Experience and education.* New York: Macmillan.

Diamond, A. (2000). Close interrelation of motor development and cognitive development and of the cerebellum and prefrontal cortex. *Child Development, 71*(1), 44–56.

Dichtelmiller, M., & Ensler, L. (2004). Infant/toddler assessment: One program's experience. *Beyond the Journal: Young Children on the Web, January,* 7 pages.

DiTommaso, E., Brannen-McNulty, C., Ross, L., & Burgess, M. (2003). Attachment styles, social skills and loneliness in young adults. *Personality and Individual Differences, 35*(2), 303–312.

Division for Early Childhood (DEC) (2002). *Position statement: Code of Ethics.* Retrieved on September 10, 2007, from http://www.dec-sped.org/pdf/positionpapers/PositionStatement_CodeofEthics.pdf

Dixon, J.A., & Soto, C.F. (1990). The development of perspective taking: Understanding differences in information and weighting. *Child Development, 61*, 1502–1513.

Dodge, K., & Crick, N. (1990). Social information processing bases of aggressive behavior in children. *Personality and Social Psychology Bulletin, 16*(1), 8–22.

Dodge, K.A., Bates, J.E., & Petit, G.S. (1990). Mechanisms in the cycle of abuse. *Science, 250*, 1678–1683.

Donovan, F. (1997). Using the Reggio approach in a children's museum. In Joanne Hendrick (Ed.), *First steps toward teaching the Reggio way* (pp. 181–196). Upper Saddle River, NJ: Merrill/Prentice Hall.

Downs, J., Blagojevic, B., Labas, L. (2006). Daily Transitions—Time for a Change. The University of Maine Center for Community Inclusion and Disability Studies. Retrieved on June 29, 2007 from http://www.ccids.umaine.edu/ec/growingideas/transitionstip.htm

Dreikurs, R. (1958). *The challenge of parenthood* (rev. ed.). New York: Hawthorn.

Drucker, J. (1998). *Families of value: Gay and lesbian parents and their children speak out.* New York: HarperCollins.

Dubow, E. F., Huesmann, L. R., & Boxer, P. (2003). Theoretical and methodological considerations in cross-generational research on parenting and child aggressive behavior. *Journal of Abnormal Child Psychology, 31*(2), 185-192.

Dunn, J., & Brown, J. (1994). Affect expression in the family, children's understanding of emotions, and their interactions with others. *Merrill-Palmer Quarterly, 40*, 120–137.

Dunst, C.J., Trivett, C.M., & Cuspec, P.A. (2002). Toward an operational definition of evidence-based practice. *Centerscope, 1*(1), 1–10.

Dworkin, P., Bogin, J., Carey, M., & Honigfeld, L. (2006). *How to develop a statewide system to link families with community resources: A manual based on Connecticut's "Help Me Grow" Initiative.* New York, NY: Commonwealth Fund, 18 pages.

Eckstein, K., Mikhail, L., Ariza, A., Thomson, J., Millard, S., & Binns, H. (2006). Parents' perceptions of their child's weight and health. *Pediatrics, 117*(3), 681–690.

Economic Policy Institute (2005) *Losing ground in early childhood education: Declining workforce qualifications in an expanding industry, 1979–2004.* Retrieved on May 20, 2008 from http://www.epinet.org/studies/ece/losing_ground-full_text.pdf

Editors. (2003/2004). Good behavior needs to be taught. *American Educator,* Winter, 16–18.

Edwards, C., Gandini, L., & Forman, G. (1998). *The hundred languages of children: The Reggio Emilia approach advanced reflections.* Stamford, CT: Ablex.

Edwards, C.P. (2002). Three approaches from Europe: Waldorf, Montessori, and Reggio Emilia. *Early Childhood Research and Practice,4*(1). Retrieved on February 22, 2008, from http://ecrp.uiuc.edu/v4n1/edwards.html

Ehrich, J.F. (2006). Vygotskian inner speech and the reading process. *Australian Journal of Educational and Developmental Psychology, 6*, 12–25.

Eisenberg, N., Fabes, R., Schaller, M., Carlo, G., & Miller, P.A. (1991). The relations of parental characteristics and practices to children's vicarious emotional responding. *Child Development, 62*, 1393–1408.

Eisenberg, N., Fabes, R., Nyman, M., Bernzweig, J., & Pinuelas, A. (1994). The relations of emotionality and regulation to children's anger-related reactions. *Child Development, 65,* 109–128.

El-Sheikh, M. & Reiter, S. (1996). Children's responding to live interadult conflict: The role of form of anger expression. *Journal of Abnormal Child Psychology, 24*(4), 401–416.

Eleanor Roosevelt Papers (2003). *The great depression (1929–1939).* Retrieved on June 10, 2008 from http://www.nps.gov/archive/elro/glossary/great-depression.htm

Elkind, D. (2003). Thanks for the memory: The lasting value of true play. *Young Children, 58*(3), 46–50.

Elkind, D. (2005). Early childhood amnesia: Reaffirming children's need for developmentally appropriate programs. *Young Children, 60*(4), 38–40.

Elkind, D. (2006). The hidden power of play. *Boston Globe,* Monday October 9, Opinion Page. Retrieved on September 14, 2008 from http://www.boston.com/news/globe/editorial_opinionopinion/oped/articles/2006/10/09/the_hidden_power_of_play/

Elliott, E., & Dweck, C. (1998). Goals: An approach to motivation and achievement. *Journal of Personality and Social Psychology, 54(1),* 5–12.

Encyclopedia of Children's Health (2004). Retrieved on August 6, 2006 from http://health.enotes.com/childrens-health-encyclopedia/temperament

Engin, D., Erdal, H., & Ramazan, A. (2005). An investigation of social skills and loneliness levels of university students with respect to their attachment styles in a sample of Turkish students. *Social Behavior and Personality.* Retrieved on June 22, 2008, from http://findarticles.com/p/articles/mi_qa3852/is_200501/ai_n9520806?tag=artBody;col1

Epstein, A. (2003). How planning and reflection develop young children's thinking skills. *Beyond the Journal: Young Children on the Web,* September, 8 pages. Retrieved on October 3, 2007, from http://www.journal.naeyc.org/btj/200309/Planning&Reflection .pdf

Epstein, A.S. (2003). All about High/Scope. *ReSource.* Retrieved on January 4, 2008, from https://secure.highscope.org/Content .asp?ContentId=291

Epstein, A. S. (2007). *Essentials of active learning in preschool.* Ypsilanti, MI: High/Scope Educational Research Foundation.

Epstein, J.L. (1995). School-family-community partnerships: Caring for the children we share. *Phi Delta Kappan 76*(9), 701–712.

Epstein, J.L., Sanders, M.G., Simon, B.S., Salinas, K.C., Jansorn, N.R., & VanVoorhis (2002). *School, family, and community partnerships: Your handbook for action,* 2nd Edition. Thousand Oaks, CA: Corwin.

Erikson, E.H. (1950). *Childhood and Society.* New York: Norton.

Evans, M. K. (2003). *The effects of background television on very young children's play with toys (unpublished doctoral dissertation).* University of Massachusetts, Amherst.

Fabes, R. A., & Eisenberg, N. (1992). Young children's coping with interpersonal anger. *Child Development, 63,* 116–128.

Fabes, R., Eisenberg, N., Smith, M., & Murphy, B. (1996). Getting angry at peers: Associations with liking of the provocateur, *Child Development, 67*(3), 943–958.

FairTest (2007). *Reaction of Dr. Monty Neill to President Bush's State of the Union Proposals.* Retrieved on April 27, 2008, from http://www.fairtest.org/reaction-dr-monty-neill-executive-director-fairtes

Farah, M.J., Shera, D.M., Savage, D.H., Betancourt, L., Giannetta, J.M., Brodsky, N.L., Malmud, E.K., & Hurt, H. (2006). Childhood poverty: specific associations with neurocognitive development. *Brain Research, 1110*(1), 166–174.

Feeney, S. (2006). Which way should we go from here? Some thoughts on early childhood curriculum. *Beyond the Journal: Young Children on the Web,* 4 pages. Retrieved on April 29, 2008 from http://www.journal.naeyc.org/btj/200609/FeeneyBTJ.pdf

Feeney, S., & Freeman, N.K. (1999). *Ethics and the early childhood educator: Using the NAEYC code.* Washington, DC: NAEYC.

Fellmeth, R.C. (2003). Child poverty in the United States. *Human Rights Magazine, Summer.* Retrieved on August 10, 2007, from http://www.abanet.org/irr/hr/winter05/childpovertyinus.html

File, N. (1993). The teacher as guide of children's competence with peers. *Child and Youth Care Forum, 22,* 351–360.

Fite, K., Spencer, L., Toomey, M., & Tran, T. (2003). *Articulation and the child development associate credential: Understanding the complexities and efforts on behalf of students.* Retrieved on March 8, 2008 from http://nccic.acf.hhs.gov/pubs/goodstart/dpweavingelg-res.html

Florida Children's Forum (2005). *Birth to three leasrning and assessment resource guide.* Tallahassee, FL: Florida Partnership for School Readiness.

Forni, P.M. (2002). *Choosing civility.* New York: St. Martin's Press.

Forni, P.M. (2007). Workshops and speeches. Retrieved on August 21, 2007, from http://web.jhu.edu/civility/talksandworkshops.html

Fox, H. (2004). Involving parents in using the infant/toddler COR. *High/Scope ReSource, 23*(3), 14.

Fox, L., & Smith, B.J. (2007). *Promoting social, emotional and behavioral outcomes of young children served under IDEA: Policy brief.* Retrieved on April 10, 2008, from http://challengingbehavior.fmhi.usf.edu/policy%20brief_idea_outcomes.pdf

Frede, E. (2003). How teachers grow: Four stages. *High/Scope ReSource,* Spring 21–22.

Freedman, S.G. (2004, June 30). Beyond public health: Asthma, like poor housing, becomes an issue in the schools. *The New York Times*, p. A20.

Freeman, N., & Feeney, S. (2004). The NAEYC code is a living document. *Beyond the Journal: Young Children on the Web*, November. Retrieved on September 11, 2008, from http://journal.naeyc.org/btj/200411/freeman.asp

Freeman, N., Lacohee, H., & Coulton, S. (1995). Cued-recall approach to 3-year-olds' memory for an honest mistake. *Journal of Experimental Child Psychology*, 60(1), 102–116.

Friedman, M. J. (2006). Minority groups now one-third of U.S. population. *International Information Programs: Current Issues*. Retrieved on November 14, 2007, from http://usinfo.state.gov/ xarchives/display.html?p=washfile-english&y=2006&m=July&x=20060707160631jmnamdeirf0.2887079

Frost, J.L. (1998). *Neuroscience, play, and brain development*. Paper presented at IPA/USA Triennial National Conference, Longmont, CO, June 18–21.

Fu, V., Stremmel, A., & Hill, L. (2002). *Teaching and learning: Collaborative exploration of the Reggio Emilia approach*. Upper Saddle River, NJ: Merrill/Prentice Hall.

Gandini, L. (1994). *A message from Loris Malaguzzi. An interview by Lella Gandini with Loris Malaguzzi.* Performanetics Reggio Emilio, Italy (Distributed by Reggio Children USA).

Gandini, L. (1997). Foundations of the Reggio Emilia approach. In J. Hendrick (Ed.) *First steps toward teaching the Reggio way*. pp. 14–25. Upper Saddle River, NJ: Merrill/Prentice Hall.

Gandini, L. (2008). *Parents as partners in children's and teacher's learning.* Seminar in the Innovations in Early Education Series at Wayne State University, Detroit, Michigan, April 5.

Gandini, L., & Goldhaber, J. (2001). Two reflections about documentation. In L. Gandini & C. Edwards (Eds.), *Bambini: The Italian approach to infant-toddler care* (pp. 124–145). New York: Teachers College Press.

Gandis, B. (2005). Cognitive, language, and educational issues of children adopted from overseas orphanages. *Journal of Cognitive Education & Psychology*, 4(3), 273–289. Retrieved February 9, 2007, from http://www.coged.org/journal/V4I3/

Gardner, H. (1983). *Frames of Mind*. New York: Basic Books.

Gardner, H. (2003). *Multiple intelligences after twenty years*. Paper presented at the American Educational Research Association. Chicago, IL: April 21.

Geist, E. (2008). *Children are born mathematicians: Supporting mathematical development, birth to age 8*. Upper Saddle River, NJ: Merrill/Prentice Hall.

Geist, E., & Baum, A.C. (2005). Yeah, but is that what keeps teachers from embracing and active curriculum: Overcoming the resistance. *Young Children*, 60(4), 28–36.

General Information About Disabilities: Disabilities That Qualify Infants, Toddlers, Children, and Youth for Services under the IDEA.

Genishi, C. (1992). *Ways of assessing children and curriculum: Stories of early childhood practice*. New York: Teachers College Press.

Georgieff, M. (2007). Nutrition and the developing brain: nutrient priorities and measurement. *The American Journal of Clinical Nutrition*, 85(2), 614–620.

Gilliam, W., & Shahar, G. (2006). Preschool and child care expulsion and suspension. *Infants and young children*, 19(3), 228–245.

Ginsburg, H. (2005). Rethinking early childhood mathematics education: Children, curriculum, and pedagogy. Symposium presentation, Chicago, IL: Loyola Watertower Campus, October 28.

Ginsburg, H. P., Klein, A., & Starkey, P. (1998). The development of children's mathematical thinking: From research to practice. In W. Damon, I. Siegel, & A. Renninger (Eds.), *Handbook of Child Psychology*, Vol. 4, *Child Psychology in Practice*, 5th edition. New York: Wiley.

Ginsburg, K.R. (2006). The importance of play in promoting healthy child development and maintaining strong parent child bonds. *Pediatrics*, 119(1), 182–191.

Ginsburg, R., & Hermann-Ginsburg, L. (2005). *Research digest*. Accomplished teachers and their interactions with parents: A comparative analysis of strategies and techniques. Cambridge, MA: Harvard Family Research Project. Retrieved on September 12, 2007, from http://www.gse.harvard.edu/hfrp/projects/fine/resources/digest/accomplished.html

Goffin, S. (2001). The role of curriculum models in early childhood education. *Eric Digest*. Retrieved on April 29, 2008 from http://www.ericdigests.org/2001-2/curriculum.html

Golbeck, S.L. (2002). Instructional models for early childhood education. *Eric Digest* Retrieved on January 7, 2008, from http://ceep.crc.uiuc.edu/eecearchive/digests/2002/golbeck02.pdf

Goldhaber, J., & Smith, D. (2004). "You look at things differently." The role of documentation in the professional development of a campus child care staff. *Early Childhood Education Journal*, 25(1), 3–10.

Goleman, D. (1995). *Emotional development*. New York: Bantam Books.

Gonzalez-Mena, J. (2006). *The young child in the family and the community*, 4th ed. Upper Saddle River, NJ: Merrill/Prentice Hall.

Gonzalez-Mena, J. (2007). *50 early childhood strategies for working and communicating with diverse families*. Upper Saddle River, NJ: Merrill/Prentice Hall.

Gordon, S. (1989). The socialization of children's emotions: emotional culture, competence, and exposure. In C.

Saarni & P. Harris (Eds.), *Children's understanding of emotions* (pp. 319–349). New York: Cambridge University Press.

Gordon, S., & Maxey, S. (2000). *How to help beginning teachers succeed* (2nd ed.). Alexandria, VA: Association for Supervision and Curriculum Development.

Greenman, J. (2006). The importance of order. *Exchange*, July/August, 53–55.

Gronlund, G. (2001). Rigorous academics in preschool and kindergarten? Yes! Let me tell you how. *Young Children*, 56(2), 42–45. Reprinted in Gronlund, 2006.

Gronlund, G. (2006). *Make early learning standards come alive*. Minneapolis: Readleaf Press.

Gross, A.L., & Ballif, B. (1991). Children's understanding of emotion from facial expressions and situations: A review. *Developmental Review, 11*, 368–398.

Guddemi, M., & Case, B.J. (2005). Assessing young children. *Happenings: Assessment reports and articles. Harcourt Assessment Happenings, October*, 5–10. Retrieved on April 27, 2008, from http://harcourtassessment.com/hai/images/happenings/Happenings_Fall_2005.pdf

Guide to Urie Bronfenbrenner Papers (2004). Collection number 23-13-954, Division of Rare and Manuscript Collections. Ithaca, NY: Cornell University Library. Retrieved on April 1, 2008, from http://rmc.library.cornell.edu/EAD/htmldocs/RMA00954.html

Gullo, D.F. (2004). *Understanding assessment and evaluation* (2nd ed.). New York: Teachers College Press.

Guralnick, M.J., Connor, R., Hammond, M., Gottman, J.M., & Kinnish, K. (1996). Immediate effects of mainstreamed settings on the social interactions and social integration of preschool children. *American Journal of Mental Retardation, 100*, 359–377.

Guralnick, M.J., Paul-Brown, D., Groom, J.M., Booth, C.L., Hammond, M.A., Tupper, D.B., & Galenter, A. (1998). Conflict resolution patterns of preschool children with and without developmental delays in heterogeneous playgroups. *Early Education & Development, 9*, 40–77.

Hagele, D.M. (2005). The impact of maltreatment on the developing child. *NC Medical Journal, 66*(5), 356–359.

Hall, T. (2002). *Differentiated instruction*. Wakefield, MA: National Center on Accessing the General Curriculum. Retrieved on May 30, 2008, from http://www.cast.org/publications/ncac/ncac_diffinstruc.html

Hampl, S.E., Carroll, C.A., Simon, S., & Sharma, V. (2007). Resource utilization and expenditures for overweight and obese children. *Archives of Pediatric and Adolescent Medicine, 161*(1), 11–14.

Hamre, B.K., & Pianta, R. (2001). Early teacher-child relationships and the trajectory of children's school outcomes through eighth grade. *Child Development, 72*(2), 625–638.

Hannon, T.S., Rao, G., & Arslanian, S.A. (2005). Childhood obesity and type 2 diabetes mellitus. *Pediatrics Review, 116*(2), 473–480.

Hardy, D., Power, T., & Jaedicke, S. (1993). Examining the relation of parenting to children's coping with everyday stress. *Child Development, 64*, 1829–1841.

Harms, T., Clifford, R., & Cryer, D. (1998). *Early childhood environment rating scale* (revised ed.). New York: Teachers College Press.

Harms, T., Clifford, R., & Cryer, D. (2005). *Early childhood environmental rating scale (ECERS-R)*, revised edition. New York: Teachers College Press.

Hart, B., & Risley, T. (2003). The early catastrophe: The 30 million word gap by age 3. *American Educator*, Spring. Retrieved on September 18, 2007, http://www.census.gov/Press-Release/www/rclcases/archives/income_wealth/002484.html

Hart, C., Burts, D., Durland, M.A., Charlesworth, R., DeWolf, M., & Fleege, P. (1998). Stress behaviors and activity type participation of preschoolers in more and less developmentally appropriate classrooms: SES and sex differences. *Journal of Research in Childhood Education, 12*(2) 176–196.

Harter, S. (1993). Developmental perspectives on the self system. In P. Mussen (Ed.), *Handbook of child psychology* (Vol. 4). New York: Wiley.

Harter, S., & Whitesell, N.R. (1989). Developmental changes in children's understanding of single, multiple, and blended emotion concepts. In C. Saarni & P. Harris (Eds.), *Children's understanding of emotion* (pp. 81–116). Cambridge, England: Cambridge University Press.

Harvard Medical School (2004). Children's fears and anxieties. *Harvard Mental Health Letter, 21*(6). Retrieved on September 14, 2008 from http://www.health.harvard.edu/newsweek/Childrens_fears_and_anxieties.htm

Harvard University's Center for the Developing Child (2007). *A science-based framework for early childhood policy*. Cambridge, MA: Author. Retrieved on February 1, 2008, from http://www.developingchild.net/pubs/persp/pdf/Policy_Framework.pdf

Harvey, P. (2005). Motivating factors influencing teachers' engagement in postgraduate study: A study of five schools. Paper presented at the Australian Association for Research in Education Conference, Parramatter, June

Hashimoto, K., Shimizu, T., Shimoya, K., Kanzaki, T., Clapp, J.F., & Murata, Y. (2001). Fetal cerebellum: United States appearance with advancing gestational age. *Radiology, 221*(1), 70–74.

Head Start (2005). *Head Start child outcomes framework domain 5: Creative arts*. Washington, DC: Administration for Children and Families. Retrieved on April 26, 2008, from http://www.headstartinfo.org/leaders_guideeng/domain5.htm

Head Start Bureau (2001). Head Start child outcomes framework. *Head Start Bulletin 70*, 44–50.

Helm, J., & Beneke, S. (2003). The power of projects: Meeting contemporary challenges in early childhood classrooms. New York: Teachers College Press.

Helm, J., & Katz, L. (2001). *Young investigators: The Project Approach in the early years*. Published simultaneously by New York: Teachers College Press and Washington, DC: NAEYC.

Hemmeter, M.L., Maxwell, K., Ault, M., & Schuster, J. (2001). *Assessment of practices in early childhood classrooms*. New York: Teachers College Press.

Henderson, A.T., & Mapp, K.T. (2002). *A new wave of evidence: The impact of school, family, and community connections on student achievement*. Austin, TX: Southwest Educational Development Laboratory. Retrieved on August 24, 2007, from http://www.sedl.org/connections/resources/evidence.pdf

Henderson, B., Meier, D., & Perry, G. (2004). Teacher research in early childhood education. *Beyond the Journal, March*, three pages. Retrieved on February 24, 2008 from http://www.journal.naeyc.org/btj/vp/voicesintroduction.pdf

Hepburn, K. (2004). *Families as primary partners in their child's development and school readiness*. Washington, DC: Georgetown University, with funding from the Annie E. Casey Foundation. Retrieved on August 1, 2007, from http://www.aecf.org/upload/PublicationFiles/families.pdf

Hernandez, D. (2008). Age, not race, splits Latino Democratic vote. *This I Believe*, National Public Radio, January 31. Retrieved on February 4, 2008, from http://www.npr.org/templates/player/mediaPlayer.html?action=1&t=1&islist=false&id=18582325&m=18582299

Herzog, N. (2001). Reflections and impressions from Reggio Emilia: "It's not about art!" *Early Childhood Research & Practice, 3*(1) (online journal). Retrieved on September 13, 2008 from http://ecrp.uiuc.edu/v3n1/hertozog.html

High/Scope (2003). *Preschool child observation record (COR)*, 2nd ed. Ypsilanti, MI: High/Scope Press.

High/Scope (2008). *Social skills*. Retrieved on June 26, 2008, from http://www.highscope.org/Content.asp?ContentId=294

Hlebowitsh, P.S. (2006). John Dewey and the idea of experimentalism. *Education and Culture, 22*(1), 73–76.

Hopkins, G. (2007).The school day: It's not a race. *Education World*, interview with Chip Wood. Retrieved on July 4, 2007 from http://www.educationworld.com/a_issues/chat/chat009.shtml

Howe, M.L., & Courage, M.L. (1993). On resolving the enigma of infantile amnesia. *Psychological Bulletin, 113*, 305–326.

Howes, C. (1991). Caregiving environments and their consequences for children: The experience in the United States. In E. Melhuish & P. Moss (Eds.), *Day care for young children*. New York: Routledge.

Hudson, P. (2005). *Examining mentor's personal attributes*. Paper presented at the Australian Association for Research in Education (AARE), Parramatter, June 2005.

Huesmann, L.R., Moise-Titus, J., Podosky, C.L., & Eron, L.D. (2003). Longitudinal relations between children's exposure to TV violence and their aggressive and violent behavior in young adulthood: 1977–1992. *Developmental Psychology, 39*, 201–221.

Hughes, A.R., Farewell, K., Harris, D., & Reilly, J.J. (2007). Quality of life in a clinical sample of obese children. *International Journal of Obesity, 31*(1), 39–44.

Huling, L. (2001). Teacher mentoring as professional development. *ERIC Digest* 460125, Washington, DC: ERIC Clearinghouse on Teaching and Teacher Education. Retrieved on February 10, 2008, from http://www.ericdigests.org/2002-3/mentoring.htm

Hurtado, N. (2005). Code-switching as a communicative tool in the classroom discourse and peer interactions of bilingual students. Panel presentation for Symposium, Language Choice and Code-Switching in Multilingual Acquisition, Wednesday, July 27, 2005 Berlin, Germany.

Huston, A.C., & Wright, J.C. (1996). Television and socialization of young children. In T.M. MacBeth (Ed.), *Tuning in to young viewers: Social science perspectives on television* (pp. 37–60). Thousand Oaks, CA: Sage.

Huttenlocher, P.R. (2003). Basic neuroscience research has important implications for child development. *Nature Neuroscience, 6*, 541.

Hyson, M. (2000). *Teachers as thinkers*. NAEYC Early Childhood Summit, June 23.

Hyson, M. (2003). *Preparing early childhood professionals: NAEYC's standards for programs*. Washington, DC: National Association for the Education of Young Children.

Iidaka, T., Anderson, N., Kapur, S., Cabeza, R., & Craik, F. (2000). The effect of divided attention on encoding and retrieval in episodic memory revealed by positron emission tomography. *Journal of Cognitive Neuroscience, 12*(2), 267–280.

Illinois Early Care and Education Professional Development Network (2007). *Introduction to statewide credentials*. Retrieved on March 9, 2008 from http://www.ilgateways.com/credentials/index.aspx

Illinois State Board of Education (1997). *Illinois Learning Standards*. Retrieved on September 16, 2008 from http://www.isbe.net/ils/Default.htm

Illinois State Board of Education (2002). *Illinois birth to three program standards*. Springfield, IL: author Retrieved on April 29, 2008 from http://www.isbe.net/earlychi/pdf/birth_three_standards.pdf

Illinois State Board of Education (2004). *Illinois early learning standards*. Retrieved February 10, 2007, from http://www.isbe.state.il.us/earlychi/pdf/early_learning_standards.pdf

Illinois State Board of Education (2006). *Illinois learning standards kindergarten.* Springfield, IL: Author.

Illinois State Board of Education (ISBE) (2006). *Illinois early learning standards: kindergarten.* Springfield, IL: Author. Retrieved on April 26, 2008 from http://www.isbe.state.il.us/earlychi/pdf/iel_standards.pdf

International Food Information Council (2006). *Nutrition, health, and physical activity during childhood and adolescence.* November. Retrieved on April 23, 2008, from http://ific.org/nutrition/kids/index.cfm

International Play Association (2007). Purpose of IPA Retrieved September 15, 2008, from http://www.ipaworld.org/home.html

IRA/International Reading Association & NAEYC (1998). Learning to read and write: Developmentally appropriate practices for young children. A position statement. Retrieved on June 8, 2008, from http://www.naeyc.org/about/positions/pdf/PSREAD98.PDF#xml=http://naeychq.naeyc.org/texis/search/pdfhi.txt?query=ira+naeyc&pr=naeyc&prox=sentence&rorder=750&rprox=500&rdfreq=1000&rwfreq=1000&rlead=1000&sufs=2&order=r&cq=&id=4522568c8

Jablon, J., & Wilkinson, M. (2006). Using engagement strategies to facilitate children's learning and success. *Beyond the Journal: Young Children on the Web,* Washington, DC: NAEYC, 1–5. Retrieved September 16 from http://journal.naeyc.org/btj/200603/JablonBTJ.asp

Jacobson, J.L., & Jacobson, S.W. (2002). Effects of prenatal alcohol exposure on child development. *Alcohol Research and Health, 26*(4), 282–286.

James, A. (2005). *Fourth grade success: Everything you need to know to help your child learn.* Hoboken, NJ: Jossey-Bass.

Jenkins, J. (2000). Marital conflict and children's emotions: The development of an anger organization. *Journal of Marriage and the Family, 62*(3), 723–736.

Jerome, G. (2006). *Verse! Poetry for young children.* Tucson, AZ: University of Arizona Poetry Center.

Johnson, K. (2006). Learning to learn, Pre-kindergarten/kindergarten design implications. *A CEPPI Brief on Educational Facility Issues.* Scottsdale, AZ: The Council of Educational Facility Planners International.

Johnson, L.B. (1964). *Great society speech.* An address at the University of Michigan, May 22

Johnson, L.B. (1965). *Remarks on Project Head Start.* Speech given in the Rose Garden of the White House on May 18. Retrieved on June 5, 2008 from http://www.presidency.ucsb.edu/ws/?pid=26973

Jolonge, M.R. (2006). Social skills and young children: Working with teachers to develop social competence in the classroom. *Early Childhood Today (Scholastic), 20*(7), 8–9.

Jongmans, M. (2006). Seminar 2: Assessment. Assessment of atypical motor development trajectories: The challenges of identifying children with DCD at a young(er) age. *Leeds Consensus Statement 2006.* Retrieved on April 24, 2008, from http://www.dcd-uk.org/seminar2c.html

Kaczmarek, L.A. (2006). A team approach: Supporting families of children with disabilities in inclusive classrooms. *Beyond the Journal: Young Children on the Web,* January, 10 pages. Retrieved on February 1, 2008, from http://www.journal.naeyc.org/btj/200601/KaczmarekBTJ.asp

Kaland, M., & Salvatore, K. (2002). The psychology of hearing loss. *The ASHA Leader Online, January–March.* Retrieved on May 1, 2008, from http://www.asha.org/about/publications/leader-online/archives/2002/q1/020319d.htm

Kalliala, M. (2006). *Play culture in a changing world.* Maidenhead, England: Open University Press.

Kamii, C. (2000). *Young children reinvent arithmetic: Implications of Piaget's theory* (2nd ed.) New York: Teacher's College Press.

Karoly, L., Kilburn, M., & Cannon, J. (2005). *Early childhood interventions: Proven results, future promise.* Santa Monica, CA: Rand Corporation.

Kasari, C., Sigman, M., Baumgartner, P., & Stipek, D. (1993). Pride and mastery in children with autism. *Journal of Child Psychology & Psychiatry & Allied Disciplines, 34*(3), 353–363.

Kaser, C.H. (2007). The role of classroom schedules. *Series on Highly Effective Practices,* Darden College of Education, Old Dominion University. Retrieved on July 1, 2007 from http://education.odu.edu/esse/research/series/schedules.shtml

Katz, L. (1994). *The project approach.* ERIC Digest. Document EDO-PS-94-6. Retrieved on June 10, 2008 from http://ceep.crc.uiuc.edu/eecarchive/digests/1994/lk-pro94.html

Katz, L. (1997). A developmental approach to assessment of young children. *ERIC Digest,* ERIC Number EDO-PS-97-18, 2 pages. Retrieved on April 27, 2008, from http://ceep.crc.uiuc.edu/eecarchive/digests/1997/katz97.pdf

Katz, L. (1999). Curriculum disputes in early childhood education. *ERIC Digest.* ED436298.

Katz, L. (n.d.). The developmental stages of teachers. Clearinghouse on Early Education and Parenting, University of Illinois at Urbana–Champaign. Retrieved on February 1, 2008 from http://ceep.crc.uiuc.edu/pubs/katz-dev-stages.html#f1

Katz, L., & Chard, S. (1996). The contribution of documentation to the quality of early childhood education. *ERIC Digest.* Urbana, IL: ERIC Clearinghouse on Elementary and Early Childhood Education, ED 393 608.

Katz, L., & Chard, S. (2000). *Engaging children's minds: The project approach.* Second edition. New York, NY: Ablex.

Kernis, M., Brown, A., & Brody, G. (2000). Fragile self-esteem in children and its associations with perceived patterns of parent-child communication. *Journal of Personality, 68*(2), 225–252.

Kilbride, H., Thorstad, K., & Daily, D. (2004). Preschool outcome of less than 801-gram preterm infants compared with full-term siblings. *Pediatrics, 13*(4), 742–747.

Kim, Sook-Yi. (1999). The effects of storytelling and pretend play on cognitive processes, short-term and long-term narrative recall. *Child Study Journal, 29*(3), 175–191.

Klein, S. (2007). Personal communication with an art educator. June 3.

Knowles, M. (1998). The adult learner: The definitive classic in adult education and human resource development (5th ed.). Houston, TX: Gulf Publishing.

Kochanska, G. (2001). Emotional development in children with different attachment histories: The first three years. *Child Development, 72*(2), 474.

Kohn, A. (1996). *Beyond discipline.* Alexandria, VA: Association for Supervision and Curriculum Development.

Kohn, A. (2001). Five reasons to stop saying "good job." *Young Children 56(5),* 24–28.

Kokko, K., & Pulkkinen, L. (2000) Aggression in childhood and long-term unemployment in adulthood: A cycle of maladaption and some protective factors. *Developmental Psychology, 36*(4): 463–472.

Kovner Kline, K. & Maerlender, A. C. Jr. (2003). *Hardwired to connect: the new scientific case for authoritative communities.* New York: The Commission on Children at Risk/Institute for American Values.

Krafft, Kerry C., & Berk, Laura E. (1998). Private speech in two preschools: Significance of open-ended activities and make-believe play for verbal self-regulation. *Early Childhood Research Quarterly, 13*(4), 637–658.

Krapp, K., & Wilson, J. (2006). Developmental Delay. *Encyclopedia of Children's Health.* Kristine Krapp and Jeffrey Wilson (Eds.) Gale Group. *eNotes.com.* 2006. Retrieved on January 26, 2008, from http://www.enotes.com/childrens-health-encyclopedia/developmental-delay

Krashen, S.D. & Terrell, T.D. (1983). *The natural approach: Language acquisition in the classroom.* London: Prentice Hall Europe.

Krechevsky, M. (1998). *Project spectrum preschool assessment handbook.* New York: Teachers College Press.

Kriete, R. (2002). *The morning meeting book.* Turner Falls, MA: Northeast Foundation for Children.

Krugman, P. (2008). *Poverty is poison.* Op-Ed section, *New York Times,* February 18, page A19.

Ladd, G.W., & Profilet, S.M. (1996). The child behavior scale: A teacher-report measure of children's aggressive, withdrawn, and prosocial behaviors. *Developmental Psychology, 32*(6), 1008–1024.

Ladd, G.W., Birch, S.H., & Buhs, E. (1999). Children's social and scholastic lives in kindergarten: Related spheres of influence? *Child Development, 70,* 1373–1400.

Ladd, G.W., Kochenderfer, B.J., & Coleman, C.C. (1997). Classroom peer acceptance, friendship, and victimization: Distinct relational systems that contribute uniquely to children's school adjustment? *Child Development, 68,* 1181–1197.

Ladd, G.W., & Profilet, S.M. (1996). The Child behavior scale: A Teacher-report measure of children's aggressive, withdrawn, and prosocial behaviors. *Developmental Psychology, 32*(6), 1008–1024.

LaFramboise, T., Coleman, H.L.K., and Gerton, J. (1993). Psychological impact of biculturalism: Evidence and theory. *Psychological Bulletin, 114*(3), 395–412.

Laird, R.D., Pettit, G.S., Mize, J., Brown, E.G., & Lindsey, E. (1994). Parent-child conversations about peer relationships: Contributions to competence. *Family Relations, 43,* 425–432.

Larrivee, B. (2006). The convergence of reflective practice and effective classroom management. In C.M. Evertson & C. Weinstein (Eds.), *The handbook of classroom management: Research, practice, and contemporary issues* (pp. 983–999). Mahwah, NJ: Lawrence Erlbaum.

LeBlanc, L.A., & Matson, J.L. (1995). A social skills training program for preschoolers with developmental delays: Generalization and social validity. *Behavior Modification, 19,* 234–246.

LeBuffe, P., & Naglieri, J. (n.d.). *The Devereaux early childhood assessment clinical form information packet.* Retrieved on April 27, 2008, from http://www.devereux.org/site/DocServer/DECA-C-Booklet.pdf?docID=3262

Leeds Consensus Statement (2006). *Developmental coordination disorder as a specific learning difficulty.* Retrieved on April 21, 2008, from http://www.dcd-uk.org/index.html

Leonhardt, D. (2007). Bridging gaps early on in Oklahoma. *New York Times,* February 7. Retrieved on August 30, 2007, from http://www.nytimes.com/2007/02/07/education/07leonhardt.html?_r=1&fta=y&oref=slogin

Lepper, J. (2002). Frequently asked questions about Bing. An interview with Jean Lepper. Retrieved on June 1, 2008, from http:// www.stanford.edu/dept/bingschool/bingfaq.htm

Lerner, B. (1996). Self-esteem and excellence: The choice and the paradox. *American Educator, 20(2),* 41–42.

Levin, D. (1998). *Remote control childhood? Combating the hazards of media culture.* Washington, DC: NAEYC.

Lillard, A., & Else-Quest, N. (2006). Evaluating Montessori education. *Science, 313,* September, 19-893-1894. Retrieved on April 4, 2008, from http://www.montessori-ami.org/

LoCasale-Crouch, J., Mashburn, A., Downer, J., & Pianta, R. (2008). Pre-kindergarten teachers' use of transition practices and children's adjustment to kindergarten. *Early Childhood Research Quarterly, 23*(1), 124–139.

Locke, J. (1690; abridged version 1994). *Essay concerning human understanding.* Amherst, NY: Prometheus Books.

Loeb, S., Fuller, B., Kagan, S., Carrol, B., & Carroll, J. (2004). Child care in poor communities: Early learning effects of type, quality, and stability. *Child Development, 75*(1), 47–65.

Lopez, A.M. (2003). Mixed-race school-age children: A summary of Census 2000 data. *Educational Researcher, 32*(6), 25–37.

Lopez, M.L., Barrueco, S., Feinauer, E., & Miles, J.C. (2007). Research digest: Young Latino infants and families: Parent involvement implications from a recent national study. Cambridge, MA: Harvard Family Research Project. Retrieved on August 30, 2007, from http://www.gse.harvard.edu/hfrp/projects/fine/resources/digest/infants.html

Lowenthal, B. (1999, summer). Effects of maltreatment and ways to promote children's resiliency. *Childhood Education,* 204–209.

Main, M., & George, C. (1985). Response of abused and disadvantaged toddlers to distress in agemates: A study in the day care setting. *Developmental Psychology, 21*, 236–246, 407–412.

Marcon, R. (1993). Socioemotional versus academic emphasis: Impact on kindergartners' development and achievement. *Early Child Development and Care, 96*, 81–89.

Margellos-Anast, H., Whitman, S., Gutierrez, M., Seals, G., & Jajoo, D. (2006). *Use of lay health educators to improve asthma management among African American children.* Retrieved on April 25, 2008 from http://www.chicagoasthma.org/site/files/410/43477/171039/258655/2006_Data_Conference_1.pdf

Marion, M. (1997). Research in review: Guiding children's understanding and management of anger. *Young Children, 52*(7), 62–68.

Marion, M. (2004). *Using observation in early childhood education.* Upper Saddle River, NJ: Pearson Prentice Hall.

Marion, M. (2007). *Guidance of young children* (7th ed.). Upper Saddle River, NJ: Merrill/Prentice Hall.

Marois, R. (2005). Capacity limits of information processing in the brain. *Phi Kappa Phi Forum, 85*, 30–33.

Martin, J.H. (2003). *Neuroanatomy text and atlas* (3rd ed.). New York: McGraw-Hill.

Martin, M. (2005) Reflection in teacher education: How can it be supported? *Educational Action Research 13*(4), 525–542.

Maslow, A. (1954). *Motivation and Personality.* New York: Harper.

Maxwell, K., & Bryant, D. (2000). *The North Carolina school readiness assessment battery.* Chapel Hill, NC: Frank Porter Graham Child Development Center at the University of North Carolina at Chapel Hill. Retrieved on July 1, 2008, from http://www.fpg.unc.edu/~SchoolReadiness/battery.pdf

McCart, A., & Turnbull, A. (no date). A positive approach to problem behavior. *PBS Teacher,* Retrieved July 2, 2007 from http://www.pbs.org/teachers/earlychildhood/articles/concerns.html

McCaslin, J.M. (2004). *Developmentally appropriate practice: A case study for mentoring for teacher change.* Thesis: Louisiana State University, College of Human Ecology.

McClellan, D.E., & Kinsey, S.J. (1999). Children's social behavior in relation to participation in mixed-age or same-age classrooms. *Early Childhood Research and Practice* [online], *1*(1). Retrieved on August 29, 2006, from http://ecrp.uiuc.edu

McClellen, D.E., & Katz, L.G. (2001). Assessing children's social competence. *ERIC Digest* [Online]. Available: http://ericeece.org/pubs/digests/2001/mcclel01.html

McDevitt, T., & Ormrod, J. (2004). *Child development,* Upper Saddle River, NJ: Merrill/Prentice Hall.

McDevitt, T.M., Spivey, N. Sheehan, E.P., Lennon, R., & Story, R. (1990). Children's beliefs about listening: Is it enough to be still and quiet? *Child Development, 61*, 713–721.

McDevitt., T.M. (1990). Encouraging young children's listening skills. *Academic Therapy, 25*, 569–577.

McElroy, E.J. (2005). NCLB's unintended consequences. *Where We Stand,* May-June. Retrieved on Sept. 22, 2008 from http://www.aft.org/pubs-reports/american_teacher/mayjune05/stand.htm Retrieved July 8, 2007.

McEwen, B.S. (2003). Early life influences on life-long patterns of behavior and health. *Mental Retardation and Developmental Disabilities Research Review, 9*(3), 149–154.

McGuire, P. (1998). School-based prevention: One size does not fit all. *American Psychological Association Monitor, 29*(10). Retrieved August 28, 2006, from http://www.apa.org/monitor/oct98/size.html

McKenzie, M. (2005). *Stories of buoyancy and despondency: Five beginning teacher's experiences in their first year in the teaching profession* (master's thesis). School of Educational Leadership, Australian Catholic University.

McMullen, M., & Dixon, S. (2006a). Building on common ground: Unifying the practices of infant-toddler specialists through a mindful, relationship-based approach. Research in review. *Young Children, 61*(4), 46–52.

McMullen, M., & Dixon, S. (2006b). Building on common ground: Unifying the practices of infant-toddler specialists through a mindful, relationship-based approach. Poster Session at the National Association for the Education of Young Children's Annual Convention, Atlanta. Retrieved on April 29, 2008 from http://profile.educ.indiana.edu/Portals/15/Presentations/NAEYC% 202006%20Poster.ppt

McMullen, M., Elicker, J., Goetz, G., Huang, H., Lee, S., Mathers, C., Wen, X., & Yang, H. (2006). Using collaborative assessment to examine the relationship between self-reported beliefs and the documentable practices of preschool teachers. *Early Childhood Educational Journal, 34*(1), 81–91.

Medical News Today (2005). Children born with extremely low birth weight have considerable health and educational needs. *Medical News Today*, July 21. Retrieved on September 16, 2008, from http://www.medicalnewstoday.com/articles/27762.php

Meichenbaum, D.H., & Goodman, J. (1971). Training impulsive children to talk to themselves: A means of developing self-control. *Journal of Abnormal Psychology, 77*, 115–126.

Meisels, S.J. (1993). Remaking classroom assessment with the work sampling system. *Young Children, 45*(5), 34–40.

Meisels, S.J., (1995). Performance assessment in early childhood education: The work sampling system. *ERIC Digest*, ERIC Number ED382407, 3 pages.

Mindes, G. (2005). Social studies in today's early childhood curricula. *Beyond the Journal: Young Children on the Web*, 8 pages.

Minuchin, P., Biber, B., Shapiro, E., & Zimiles, H. (1969). *The psychological impact of school experience: A comparative study of nine-year-old children in contrasting schools*. New York: Basic Books.

Missiuna, C. (2006). Seminar 4—Intervention: New models for changing the environment, not the child. *Leed's Consensus Statement, 2006*. Retrieved on January 2, 2007, from www.dcd-uk.org

Mitchell, A. (2002). *Some thoughts on design factors to consider*. Retrieved on July 6, 2008, from http://www.naeyc.org/ece/pdf/ designfact

Mitchell, L. (2003). *Children, staff, and parents: Building respectful relationships in Australian and New Zealand early childhood contexts*. Keynote address, 8th Annual Early Childhood Convention, Palmerston North, September 22–25.

Mize, J. (1995). Coaching preschool children in social skills: A cognitive-social learning curriculum. In C. Carledge, & J.F. Milburn (Eds.). *Teaching social skills to children and youth: Innovative approaches* (3rd ed., pp. 237–261), Boston, MA: Allyn & Bacon.

Mize, J., & Abell, E. (1996). Encouraging social skills in children: Tips teachers can share with parents. *Dimensions of Early Childhood, 24*(3), 15–23.

Mize, J., & Pettit, G.S. (1994). From parent coaching to peer acceptance: Behavioral and social cognitive mediators. In J. Mize & M. Dekovic (Co-Chairs), *Mechanisms in the transmission of social competence*. Symposium presented at the International Society for the Study of Behavioral Development, Amsterdam. July.

Mize, M., Pettit, G.S., Lindsey, E., & Laird, R. (1993). Mothers' coaching of social skills and children's peer competence: Independent contributions of content and style. Paper presented as part of the symposium, *Lessons learned about peer relationships: How parents intentionally teach their children social skills*. Symposium presented at the biennial meeting of the Society of Research in Child Development, New Orleans, LA.

Moeini, H. (2008). Identifying needs: A missing part in teacher training programs. *International Journal of Media, Technology, and Lifelong Learning, 4*(1), 12 pages. Retrieved on June 8, 2008,from http://www.seminar.net/images/stories/vol4-issue1/moini-identifyingneeds.pdf

Mueller, C., & Dweck, C. (1998). Praise for intelligence can undermine children's motivation and performance. *Journal of Personality and Social Psychology, 75*(1), 33–52.

Murphy, K., DePasquale, R., & McNamara, E. (2003). Using technology in primary classrooms. *Beyond the Journal: Young Children on the Web,* November, 9 pages. Retrieved on June 8, 2008 from, http://www.journal.naeyc.org/btj/200311/techinprimaryclassrooms.pdf#xml=http://naeychq.naeyc.org/texis/search/pdfhi.txt?query=technology+as+an+issue&pr=naeyc&prox=sentence&rorder=750&rprox=500&rdfreq=1000&rwfreq=1000&rlead=1000&sufs=2&order=r&cq=&id=452255c4dd

Nader, P., O'Brien, M., Houts, R., Bradley, R., Belsky, J., Crosnoe, R., Friedman, S., Mei, Z., & Susman, E. (2006). Identifying risk for obesity in early childhood. *Pediatrics, 118*(3), 594–601.

National Archives (n.d.). *Guide to federal records*, records of the Works Projects Administration, Record group 69, 69.3.5 Records of the Emergency Education Program. Retrieved on June 8, 2008 from http://www.archives.gov/research/guide-fed-records/groups/069.html#69.3.5

National Association for Sport & Physical Education (2002). *Active start: A statement of physical activity guidelines for children birth to five years*. Reston, VA: author.

National Association for the Education of Young Children (1994). *Violence in the life of children*. Position Statement. Washington, DC: NAEYC.

National Association for the Education of Young Children (2003). Early childhood curriculum, assessment, and program evaluation. A position statement. Retrieved on April 27, 2008, from http://www.naeyc.org/about/positions/pdf/CAPEexpand.pdf

National Association for the Education of Young Children (revised 2005). *Code of ethical conduct and statement of commitment: A position statement of the National Association for the Education of Young Children*. Washington, DC: NAEYC.

National Association for the Education of Young Children (2005). Screening and assessment of young English language learners: A supplement to the NAEYC position statement on curriculum, assessment, and program evaluation. Retrieved on April 27, 2008, from http://www.naeyc.org/about/positions/ELL_Supplement.asp

National Association for the Education of Young Children (2006). *Guidance on NAEYC accreditation criteria*. Washington, DC: author.

National Association for the Education of Young Children (2006). *Principles of development and learning that inform developmentally appropriate practice. A position paper.* Washington, DC: Author. Retrieved on February 1, 2007, from http://www.naeyc.org/about/positions/dap3.asp

National Association for the Education of Young Children (1996). *Technology and young children—Ages 3 through 8. A position statement of NAEYC.* Washington, DC: Author.

National Association for the Education of Young Children (NAEYC) (1996 modified 2006). *The benefits of an inclusive education: Making it work.* Retrieved on April 28, 2008 from http:// www.naeyc.org/ece/1996/07.asp

National Association for the Education of Young Children (NAEYC) (2001). NAEYC *Standards for early childhood professional preparation initial licensure programs.* Washington, D.C.: Author. Retrieved on September 11, 2008, from http:// www.naeyc.org/faculty/pdf/2001.pdf

National Association for the Education of Young Children (NAEYC) (2001). NAEYTC *Standards for early childhood professional preparation initial licensure programs.* Washington, D.C.: Author. Retrieved on September 11, 2008 from http://www.naeyc.org/faculty/pdf/2001.pdf

National Association for the Education of Young Children (NAEYC) (2004). *NAEYC Advocacy Toolkit.* Washington, DC: Author.

National Association for the Education of Young Children (NAEYC) (2005). Code of ethical conduct and statement of commitment. *A Position Statement of NAEYC*, Washington, DC: Author.

National Association for the Education of Young Children, National Association for the Education of Young Children (2005). *Code of ethical conduct and statement of commitment. A Position Statement of NAEYC.* Washington, DC: Author.

National Association for the Education of Young Children (NAEYC) (2006a). *Building positive relationships through communication.* Retrieved on August 22, 2007, from http:// www.naeyc.org/ece/1998/14.asp

National Association for the Education of Young Children (NAEYC) (2006b). *Resources for supporting teachers, strengthening families.* Retrieved on August 29, 2007, from http://www.naeyc.org/ece/supporting/resources.asp

National Association for the Education of Young Children (2008). Technology and early childhood education. NAEYC's 17th National Institute for Professional Development. New Orleans, LA, June 8–11.

National Association for the Education of Young Children (NAEYC) (No date). *Using research in early childhood development and education.* Retrieved on September 13, 2008, from http://www.naeyc.org/resources/research/

National Association for the Education of Young Children (NAEYC) and The National Council of Teachers of Mathematics (NCTM) (2002). Early childhood mathematics: pro-moting good beginnings, *A joint position statement.* Washington, DC: NAEYC. Retrieved on September 11, 2008 from http://www.naeyc.org/about/positions/psmath.asp

National Association for the Education of Young Children (NAEYC)(2001). NAEYC Standards for Early Childhood Professional Preparation Initial Licensure Programs. Washington, D.C.: Author. Retrieved on September 11, 2008 from http://www.naeyc.org/faculty/pdf/2001.pdf

National Association for the Education of Young Children (No date). *Principles of child development and learning that inform developmentally appropriate practice.* Position Statement. Washington, DC: NAEYC.

National Association for the Education of Young Children (no date). Standard 4 NAEYC accreditation criteria for assessment of child progress. Washington, DC: Author. Retrieved on April 27 2008, from http://www.naeyc.org/academy/standards/standard4/standard4E.asp

National Association for the Education of Young Children/ NAEYC (2003). *Early childhood curriculum, assessment, and program evaluation, Position Statement,* Washington, D.C.: author. Retrieved on April 29, 2008 from http://www.naeyc.org/about/positions/pdf/CAPEexpand.pdf

National Association for the Education of Young Children/ NAEYC (2005). *Code of ethical conduct and statement of commitment.* Washington, D.C.: author. Retrieved on April 29, 2008 from http://www.naeyc.org/about/positions/PSETH05.asp

National Association for the Education of Young Children/ NAEYCC (2006). *Standard 2: NAEYC Accreditation Criteria for Curriculum.* Retrieved on September 22, 2008, from http://www.naeyc.org/academy/standards/standard2

National Association for the Education of Young Children/ NAEYC (2006). *Where we stand on standards to prepare early childhood professionals.* Washington, D.C.: Author. Retrieved on April 29, 2008 from http://www.naeyc.org/about/positions/pdf/programStandards.pdf#xml=http://naechq.naeyc.org/texis/search/pdfhi.txt?query=12+roles&pr=neyc&prox=sentence&rorder=750&rprox=500&rdfreq=1000&rwfreq=1000&rlead=1000&sufs=2&order=r&cq=&id=452256e737

National Association for the Education of Young Children/ NAEYC (2007). Intentionality in early childhood education. *NAEYC's 16th Institute for Early Childhood Professional Development*, Annual Meeting, Pittsburg, PA, June 10-June 13. Retrieved on May 13, 2007 from http:// www.naeyc.org/conferences/institute.asp

National Association for the Education of Young Children/ NAEYC (2007). Intentionality in early childhood education. *NAEYC's 16th Institute for Early Childhood Professional Development*, Annual Meeting, Pittsburg, PA, June 10–June 13.

National Association for the Education of Young Children & the National Council for Teachers of Mathematics/ NCTM

(2002). *Early childhood mathematics: Promoting good beginnings. A position statement.* Washington, DC: NAEYC.

National Association of Child care Resource and Referral Agencies. (2006). Helping Children Make Changes: Big and Small. *The Daily Parent, 34.* Retrieved on July 4, 2007 from http://www.childcareaware.org/en/dailyparent/volume.php?id=34

National Association of Music Education (1991). Position statement on early childhood education. Retrieved on September 16, 2008 from http://www.menc.org/about/view/early-childhood-education-position-statement

National Center for Health Statistics (2002). *2000 growth charts.* Hyattsville, MD. National Center for Chronic Disease Prevention and Health Promotion. Retrieved on April 26, 2008, from www.cdc.gov/growthcharts

National Center for Learning Disabilities (2007). *IDEA terms to know.* Retrieved on September 5, 2007, from http://www.ncld.org/content/view/921/456099/

National Conference of State Legislatures (2007). *Childhood obesity—2006 update and overview of policy options.* Retrieved on July 1, 2008, from http://www.ncsl.org/programs/health/ChildhoodObesity-2006.htm#nuted

National Dissemination Center for Children with Disabilities (2002). General information about disabilities. Retrieved September 20, 2007, from http://www.nichcy.org/pubs/genresc/gr3.htm (This information is copyright free.)

National Dissemination Center for Children with Disabilities (2002). General Information About Disabilities: Disabilities That Qualify Infants, Toddlers, Children, and Youth for Services under the IDEA. Retrieved April 13, 2008, from http://www.nichcy.org/pubs/genresc/gr3.pdf.

National Dissemination Center for Children with Disabilities (2004). *Emotional disturbance.* Disability Fact Sheet, Number 5, January. Retrieved on April 13, 2008 from http://www.nichcy.org/pubs/factshe/fs5.pdf

National Dissemination Center for Children with Disabilities (2008). Sub-Part A: General Provisions, Definitions. Retrieved September 20, 2008, from http://www.nichcy.org/Laws/IDEA/Pages/subpartA-PartBregs.aspx#34:2.1.1.1.1.1.36.7

National Education Association (2006). *NEA's positive agenda for the ESEA reauthorization, executive summary.* Retrieved on April 28, 2008, from http://www.nea.org/esea/posagendaexecsum.html

National Institute on Deafness and Other Communicative Disorders (2001). Speech and language developmental milestones. Retrieved on May 31, 2008 from http://www.nidcd.nih.gov/health/voice/speechandlanguage.asp#mychild

National Institute on Environmental Health Sciences (2005). *Lead and your health.* Retrieved on June 25, 2008, from http://www.niehs.nih.gov/health/docs/lead-fs.pdf

National Mental Health Association (2005). What every child needs for good mental health. *Children's Mental Health Matters.* Retrieved on August 12, 2005, from http://www.nmha.org

National Mental Health Association. (2004). Anxiety disorders in children. *Children's Mental Health Matters.* Retrieved on December 13, 2004, from http://www.nmha.org

National Research Council and Institute of Medicine, Board on Children, Youth, and Families. (2002). In J.P. Shonkoff, & D.A. Phillips (Eds.). *From neurons to neighborhoods: The science of early childhood development.* Washington, DC: National Academy Press.

National Television Violence Study Council (NTVS). (1997). Executive summary (vol. 2). J. Federman (Ed.). Santa Barbara, CA: Center for Communication and Social Policy, University of California, Santa Barbara.

National Television Violence Study Council (NTVSC). (1997). National television violence study (NTVS), executive summary, Volume 2. J. Federman (Ed.), Santa Barbara, CA: Center for communication and social policy, University of California, Santa Barbara.

National Association for the Education of Young Children (NAEYC) (2005). *Code of ethical conduct and statement of commitment.* A Position Statement of NAEYC, Washington, DC: Author.

National Association for the Education of Young Children (NAEYC) (2006). *Five early childhood associate degree programs earn NAEYC accreditation.* Washington, D.C.: Author. Retrieved on February 28, 2008, from http://www.naeyc.org/about/releases/20060803.asp

National Association for the Education of Young Children (NAEYC) (No date). *Using research in early childhood development and education.* Retrieved on July 27, 2007, from http://www.naeyc.org/resources/research/

National Council on the Accreditation of Teacher Education (2007). *The NCATE unit standards.* Retrieved on July 25, 2007, from http://216.139.214.92/documents/standards/UnitStandardsMay07.pdf

Navarro, M. (2008). Who are we? New dialogue on mixed race. *New York Times*, March 31. Retrieved on September 15, 2008 from http://www.nytimes.com/2008/03/31/us/politics/31race.html?_r=1&oref=slogin

Neihart, M. (2002). The social emotional health of gifted children: An interview with Maureen Neihar. *Center for Talent Development*, Northwestern University. Retrieved on April 8, 2008, from http://www.ctd.northwestern.edu/resources/socemoachieve/soc-emohealth.html

Nelson, D.A., Hart, C.H., Yang, C., Olsen, J.A., & Jin, S. (2006). Aversive parenting in China: Associations with physical and relational aggression. *Child Development, 77*(3), 554–572.

Neuman, B., & Roskos, K. (2005). Whatever happened to developmentally appropriate practice in early literacy? *Young Children, 60*(4), 22–26.

New Jersey Office of Early Childhood Education (2005). *Abbott preschool program implementation guidelines.* Trenton N. J., Author. Retrieved on September 17, 2008, from http://www.state.nj.us/education/ece/research/eoyr0506.pdf

New Teacher Center (2007). Intensive new teacher support pays off: A return on investment for educators and kids. Santa Cruz, CA: University of California. Retrieved on February 21, 2008, from http://www.newteachercenter.org/pdfs/hill-brief-release.pdf

New York State Department of Health (2002). *Assessment methods for young children with communication disorders.* Retrieved on April 27, 2008, from http://www.health.state.ny.us/community/infants_children/early_intervention/disorders/ch3_pt5.htm

New, R. (2000). *Reggio Emilia: Catalyst for change and conversation.* Champaign, IL: ERIC Clearinghouse on Early Education and Parenting. EDO-PS-00-15 Retrieved on March 15, 2008, from http://ceep.crc.uiuc.edu/eecearchive/digests/2000/new00.pdf

New York Times (1913). *Dr. Montessori talks of her mode of auto education.* Interview with Dr. Maria Montessori, December 7. Retrieved on May 30, 2008, from http://query.nytimes.com/mem/archive-free/pdf?res=9B03EFDF1F3BE633A25754C0A9649D946296D6CF

NICHD Early Child Care Research Network. (1996). Characteristics of infant child care: Factors contributing to positive caregiving. *Early Childhood Research Quarterly, 11*(3), 269–306.

Nieto, S. (2005). *Why we teach.* New York: Teachers College Press.

NIMH (National Institute of Mental Health) (2000). Child and adolescent bipolar disorder. Retrieved on June 18, 2000 from, http://www.nimh.nih.gov/health/publications/child-and-adolescent-bipolar-disorder/summary.shtml

North American Reggio Emilia Alliance (2008). Retrieved on March 11, 2008, from http://www.reggioalliance.org/index.php

North Central Regional Educational Laboratory (2007). *Reliability, validity, and fairness of classroom assessments.* Retrieved on April 27, 2008, from http://www.ncrel.org/sdrs/areas/issues/methods/assment/as5relia.htm

Northwestern University (2008, March 5). Children with autism may learn from 'virtual peers.' *ScienceDaily.* Retrieved April 23, 2008, from http://www.sciencedaily.com/releases/2008/02/080229115314.htm

Nowicka, P. (2005). Dietitians and exercise professionals in a childhood obesity treatment team. *Acta Paediatrica Supplement 448, 94*(6), 23–29.

Oesterrich, L. (2004). Language development. *Understanding children.* Ames, Iowa: Iowa State University, University Extension. Retrieved on Sept 22, 2008 from http://www.extension.iastate.edu/Publications/PM1529F.pdf.

Office of Head Start (2008). *About the office of Head Start.* Retrieved on June 6, 2008 from http://www.acf.hhs.gov/programs/ohs/about/index.html#factsheet

OFSTED (Office for Standards in Education) (2004). *Starting early: Food and nutrition education for young children.* United Kingdom: Food Standards Agency. Retrieved on April 26, 2008, from http://www.ofsted.gov.uk/assets/3672.pdf

Olbrich, S. (2002). *Children's mental health: current challenges and a future direction.* Washington, DC: The Center for Health and Health Care in Schools. Retrieved on August 12, 2005, from http://www.healthinschools.org

Olds, A.R. (1977). Why is environmental design important to young children? *Children in Contemporary Society, 11*(1), 58.

Oliner, S.P., & Oliner, P.M. (1988). *The altruistic personality: Rescuers of Jews in Nazi Europe.* New York: Free Press.

Olmsted, P. (2002). *Data collection and system monitoring in early childhood programs.* Paper prepared for the International Conference on Early Childhood Education and Care: International Policy Issues, Stockholm, Sweden, June 2001. Retrieved on July 2, 2008, from http://unesdoc.unesco.org/images/0012/001286/128636e.pdf

Olson, M. (2006). Strengthening families: Community strategies that work. *Young Children: Beyond the Journal,* Retrieved on August 22, 2007, from http://www.journal.naeyc.org/btj/200703/BTJOlson.asp

Ostrosky, M.M., & Jung, E.Y. (2003). Brief #12: Building positive teacher-child relationships. *What Works Briefs.* University of Illinois at Champaign-Urbana: Center on the Social and Emotional Foundations for Learning.

Ostrosky, M.M., Jung, E.Y., Hemmeter, M.L., & Thomas, (2003). *What works brief 3: Helping children understand classroom schedules and routines.* Champaign, IL: University of Illinois at Urbana-Champaign. Retrieved on Sept 22, 2008 from http://www.vanderbilt.edu/csefel/briefs/wwb3.pdf

Parkinson, P., & Humphreys, C. (1998). Children who witness domestic violence: The implications for child protection. *Child & Family Law Quarterly, 10,* 147–159.

Parlakian, R. (2001). *Look, listen, and learn: Reflective supervision and relationship-based work.* Washington, DC: Zero to Three.

Parlakian, R. (2003). *How culture shapes social-emotional development: Implications for practice in infant-family programs.* Cambridge, MA: Zero to Three.

PBS Parents (2002). *Child development.* Retrieved on June 10, 2008, from http://www.pbs.org/parents/childdevelopment

Peisner-Feinberg, E., Clifford, R., Yazejian, N., Culken, M., Howes, C., & Kagan, S. (1998). *The longitudinal effects of child care quality: Implications for kindergarten success.* Presentation at the American Educational Research Association Annual Meeting, San Diego, CA.

Pelander, J. (1997). My transition from conventional to more developmentally appropriate practices in the primary grades. *Young Children, 52*(7), 19–25.

Perry, B. (2000). Emotional development: Creating an emotionally safe classroom. *Early Childhood Today, August,* Retrieved on Sept 22, 2008, from http://content.scholastic .com/browse/article.jsp?id=3745868&FullBreadCrumb= %3Ca+href%3D%22%2Fbrowse%2Fsearch.jsp%3Fquery %3Dperry+safe+emotional%26c1%3DCONTENT30%26c2 %3Dfalse%22%3EAll+Results+%3C%2Fa%3E

Perry, B., & Szalavitz, M. (2007). *The boy who was raised by dogs.* New York: Basic Books.

Perry, B., Colwell, K., & Schick, S. (2002). Child neglect. In D. Levinson (Ed.), *Encyclopedia of crime and punishment, Vol. 1.* (pages 192–196). Thousand Oaks, CA: Sage.

Petrakos, H., & Howe, N. (1996). The influence of the physical design of the dramatic play center on children's play. *Early Childhood Research Quarterly, 11,* 63–77.

Piaget, J. (1932). *Moral judgment of the child.* London: Kegan Paul.

Piaget, J. (1972). *The psychology of the child.* New York: Basic Books.

Piaget, J. (1983). Piaget's theory. In Paul Mussen (Ed.), *Handbook of child psychology*, 4th Edition (103–128). Volume 1 History, theory, and methods, William Kessen (Ed.), New York: Wiley.

Piaget, J.P. (1952). *The origins of intelligence in children.* International Universities Press, New York.

Pianta, R. (1996). *Manual and scoring guide for the student-teacher relationship scale.* Charlottesville, VA: University of Virginia Press.

Pianta, R., & Stuhlman, M. (2004). Teacher-child relationships and children's success in the first years of school. *School Psychology Review, 33,* 444–458.

Pianta, R.C. (1992). Beyond the parent: The role of other adults in children's lives. *New directions in child development* (Vol. 57). San Francisco: Jossey-Bass.

Pianta, R.C., & Stuhlman, (2004). Teacher-child relationships and children's success in the first years of school. *School Psychology Review, 33,* 444–458.

Pollak, S., Cicchetti, D., Hornung, K., & Reed, A. (2000). Recognizing emotion in faces: Developmental effects of child abuse and neglect. *Developmental Psychology, 36*(5) 679–688.

Pollitt, E. (2000). Developmental Sequel from Early Nutritional Deficiencies: conclusive and Probability Judgments. Presented at the symposium entitled "Dietary Zinc and Iron—Recent Perspectives Regarding Growth and Cognitive Development" as part of the Experimental Biology 99 meeting held April 17–21 in Washington, DC.

Post, J., & Hohmann, M. (2000).*Tender care and early learning: Supporting infants and toddlers in child care settings.* Ypsilanti, MI: High/Scope Educational Research Foundation.

Primavera, L., Herron, W., & Javier, R. (1996). The effect of viewing television violence on aggression. *International Journal of Instructional Media 23*(2), 137–151.

Prior, M., Sanson, A., Smart, D., & Oberklaid, F. (2000). Pathways from infancy to adolescence: Australia's temperament project 1983–2000. *Research report No. 4.* Melbourne, Australia: Australian Institute of Family Studies. Retrieved on June 24, 2008, from http://www.aifs.gov.au/institute/pubs/ resreport4/aifsreport4.pdf

Program for Infant/Toddler Care (PITC), (2007). *PITC philosophy.* Retrieved on June 24, 2008 from http://www.pitc .org/pub/pitc_docs/about.html

Project Approach (n.d.). Five structural features, in the Project development part of the web site, http://www.projectap- proach.org/index.php?option=com_content&task =view&id=54&Itemid=67, retrieved July 11, 2007.

Project Construct (2001). Project Construct and developmentally appropriate practices: How children benefit. Retrieved on Sept 22, 2008 from http://www.projectconstruct .org/misc/pdf/articles/dipdap.pdf

Project Head Start (2000). *History of Head Start.* Retrieved on June 6, 2008 from http://www.gopb.org/History.htm

Project Zero and Reggio Children (2001). *Making learning visible: Children as individual and group learners.* Reggio Emilia, Italy: Reggio Children.

Purnell, L. (2004). Minority groups: An outdated concept? Guest editorial: *Journal of Advanced Nursing, 48*(5) page 429.

Rand, M.K. (1998). *The role of perspective taking in video case analysis in preservice teachers.* Paper presented at the Annual Meeting of the American Educational Research Association, San Diego, CA, April 13–17.

Rand. (2001). *Health Research Highlights: Mental health care for youth.* Retrieved on August 13, 2005, from http:// www.rand.org/

Rao, S.M., & Gagle, B. (2002). Learning through seeing and doing. *Teaching Exceptional Children, 38*(6), 26–33.

Raskind, M. (2005). *Research trends: Social information processing and emotional understanding in children with LD.* Retrieved January 31, 2007, from http://www .schwablearning.org/articles .aspx?r=974

Reading Rockets (2002) *Reading rockets: Family guide//Guia para la familia.* Washington, DC: Greater Washington Telecommunications Association. Retrieved August 25, 2007, from http://osepideasthatwork.org/parentkit/ family_guide.pdf

Reading Rockets (2007). *For families,* Retrieved August 25, 2007, from http://www.readingrockets.org/

Reed, B., & Railsback, J. (2003). *Strategies and resources for mainstream teachers of English language learners.* Portland, OR: Northwest Region Educational Laboratory. Retrieved on April 10, 2008, from http://www.nwrel.org/request/ 2003may/ell.pdf

Reese, E., & Fivush, R. (1993). Parental styles of talking about the past. *Developmental Psychology, 29*, 596–606.

Reggio Children (2008). *The hundred languages of children.* Retrieved on March 23, 2008, from http://zerosei.comune .re.it/inter/100exhibit.htm

Reggio Emilia Study Tour (2008). Five state study tour to Reggio Emilia, Italy to study the preschools of the municipality of Reggio Emilia. May 2–10, Reggio Emilia, Italy.

Reynolds, G, Wright, J., & Beale, B. (2003). The roles of grandparents in educating today's children. *Journal of Instructional Psychology,* December. Retrieved on October 12, 2007, from http:// findarticles.com/p/articles/mi_m0FCG/ is_4_30/ai_112686167

Richardson, V. (2003). *Global health care for children and the role of the pediatric nurse practitioner.* Annual Meeting of the National Association of Pediatric Nurse Practitioners, Orlando, Florida, April 9–12.

Rideout, V., Vandewater, E., & Wartella, A. (2003). *Zero to six: Electronic media in the lives of infants, toddlers, and preschoolers.* Menlo Park, CA: Kaiser Family Foundation.

Ridgeway, D., Waters, E., & Kuczaj, S.A. (1985). Acquisition of emotion-descriptive language: Receptive and productive vocabulary norms for ages 18 months to 6 years. *Developmental Psychology, 21*, 901–908.

Rike, C.J., & Sharp, K. (2006). *Early childhood education behaviors and dispositions checklist form.* College of Education, University of Memphis. Retrieved on March 8, 2008 from http://coe.memphis.edu/icl/pdf/FinalDispositionForm .pdf

Rimm-Kaufman, S. (2006). Social and academic learning study on the contribution of the *Responsive Classroom* approach. Available at and retrieved on January 1, 2008, from http://www.responsiveclassroom.org/pdf_files/sals_ booklet_rc.pdf

Rimm-Kaufman, S.E. (2006). *Summary of research on the Responsive Classroom approach.* Retrieved August 26, 2006, from http://www.responsiveclassroom.org/about/research .html

Rinaldi, C. (1996). Passages. *ReChild: Reggio Children Newsletter, April*, 1–3.

Rinaldi, C. (2001). The pedagogy of listening. *Innovations in Early Education: The International Reggio Exchange,* 8(4), 1–4.

Rinaldi, C. (2006). *In Dialogue with Reggio Emilia: Listening, Researching and Learning.* New York: Routledge.

Roberts, S. (2008). Rise in minorities is led by children, census finds. *New York Times,* May 1. Retrieved on May 30, 2008, from http://www.nytimes.com/2008/05/01/ washington/01census.html?_r=1&oref=slogin

Rodearmel, S., Wyatt, H., Barry, M., Dong, F., Pan, D., Israel, R., Cho, S., McBurney, M., & Hill, J. A family based approach to preventing excessive weight gain. *Obesity,* 14(8), 1392–1401.

Rogers, C. (1957). The necessary and sufficient conditions of therapeutic personality change. *Journal of Consulting Psychology, 21*, 95–103.

Rones, M., & Hoagwood, K. (2000). School-based mental health services: A research Review. *Clinical Child and Family Psychology Review, 3*(4), 223–241.

Rosberg, M.A. (2003). Work and play: Are they really opposites? Educational Resources Information Center, February, 1-16.

Royal College of Psychiatrists (2004). Child abuse and neglect, the emotional effects: For parents and teachers: Factsheet 19. Retrieved on April 12, 2008, from http://www .rcpsych.ac.uk/mentalhealthinformation/mentalhealthand growingup/19childabuseandneglect .aspx

Rubin, K.H., Bukowski, W., & Parker, J.G. (1998). Peer interactions, relationships, and groups. In W. Damon (series Ed.) and R.M. Lerner (Vol. Ed.). *Handbook of child psychology, Vol. 1. Theoretical models of human development,* 5th Ed. (pp. 619–700). New York: Wiley.

Ruffin, N. (2001). Human growth and development— A matter of principles. *Publication 350-053.* Blacksburg, VA: Virginia Cooperative Extension. Retrieved on September 11, 2008 from http:// www.ext.vt.edu/pubs/family/350-053- 350-053.pdf

Russell, K. (2004). Sitting down with Connie Kamii. *The Constructivist, 15*(1), 1–6.

Saarni, C. (1989). Children's beliefs about emotion. In M. Luszez & T. Nettelbeck (Eds.), *Psychological development: Perspectives across the life-span* (pp. 69–78). Amsterdam, The Netherlands: Elsevier.

Saarni, C., Mumme, D. L., & Campos, J.J. (1998). Emotional development: Action, communication, and understanding. In W. Damon & N. Eisenberg (Eds.) *Handbook of child psychology, 5th Edition, Volume III; Social, emotional, and personality development* (pp. 237–309). New York: John Wiley & Sons.

Saffold, F. (2005). Increasing self-efficacy through mentoring. *Academic Exchange Quarterly, 9*(4), 13–16.

Saltz, R. (1997). The Reggio Emilia influence at the University of Michigan–Dearborn child development center: Challenges and change. In Joanne Hendrick (Ed.), *First steps toward teaching the Reggio way* (pp. 167–180). Upper Saddle River, NJ: Merrill/Prentice Hall.

Saluja, G., Early, D.M., & Clifford, R.M. (2002). Demographic characteristics of early childhood teachers and structural elements of early care and education in the United States. *Early Childhood Research and Practice, 4*(1), Online. Retrieved on August 29, 2007, from http://ecrp.uiuc.edu/ v4n1/saluja.html

Sanson, A., Hemphill, S., & Smart, D. (2004). Connections between temperament and social development, a review. *Social Development, 13*(1), 142–170.

Schemo, D.J. (2007). Education column, *New York Times,* Wednesday, May 30, A23.

Schneider, W., & Pressley, M. (1989). *Memory development between 2 and 20*. New York: Springer-Verlag.

Schweinhart, L. J., Montie, J., Xiang, Z., Barnett, W. S., Belfield, C. R., & Nores, M. (2005). *Lifetime effects: The High/Scope Perry Preschool study through age 40*. (Monographs of the High/Scope Educational Research Foundation, 14). Ypsilanti, MI: High/ Scope Press.

Schweinhart, L.J. (2006) The High/Scope approach: Evidence that participatory learning in early childhood contributes to human development. In Watt, N.F., Ayoub, C., Bradley, R.H. et al. (Eds.) *The crisis in youth mental health; Critical issues and effective programs:* Vol. 4 *Early intervention programs*. Westport, CT, Praeger.

Schweinhart, L.J. (2006). The High/Scope Perry Preschool Study through age 40: Summary, conclusions, and frequently asked questions, 21 pages. Retrieved on June 6, 2008 from http://www.highscope.org/file/Research/PerryProject/3_specialsummary%20col%2006%2007.pdf

Schweinhart, L.J., Montie, J., Xiang, Z., Barnett, W.S., Belfield, C.R.I, & Nores, M. (2005). *Lifetime effects: The High/Scope Perry preschool project at 40*. Ypislanti, MI: High/Scope Educational Foundation.

Scott-Little, C., Kagan, S.L., & Frelow, V. (2003). Creating the conditions for success with early learning standards: Results of a study for state-level standards for children's learning prior to kindergarten. *Early Childhood Research & Practice, 5*(2), 157–173. Retrieved on Sept 22, 2008 from http://ecrp.uiuc.edu/v5n2/little.html

Seefeldt, C. (2005). *How to work with standards in the early childhood curriculum*. New York: Teachers College Press.

Seifert, K. (2004). Cognitive development and the education of young children. In B. Spodek & O. Saracho (Eds.), *Handbook of research on the education of young children* (2nd ed.). Mahwah, NJ: Erlbaum.

Selman, R.L. (1976). Social-cognitive understanding: A guide to educational and clinical practice. In T. Lickona (Ed.), *Moral development and behavior*. New York: Holt, Rinehart, & Winston.

Seplocha, H. (2004). Conferencing with families. *Young Children: Beyond the Journal*, September, Retrieved on September 11, 2007, from http://www.journal.naeyc.org/btj/200409/seplocha.asp

Shelov, S., & Hanneman, R. (2004). *Caring for your baby and young child: Birth to age 5*. New York: Bantam Books.

Shepard, L., Kagan, S.L., & Wurtz, E. (1998). *Principles and recommendations for early childhood assessments*. Washington, DC: National Education Goals Panel.

Sherwood, E., & Freshwater, A. (2006). Early learning standards in action. *Beyond the Journal: Young Children on the Web*, 13 pages, September. Retrieved on Sept 22, 2008 from http://www.journal.naeyc.org/btj/200609/SherwoodBTJ.pdf

Shoemaker, B.J. (1991). Education 2000 integrated curriculum. *Phi Delta Kappan, 72*(10), 793–797.

Shriver, T.P., & Weissberg, R.P. (2005). *No emotion left behind*. Column, *New York Times*, August 15.

Shulman, L. (1986). Those who understand: Knowledge growth in teaching. *Educational Researcher, 15*(2), 4–14.

Sigman, M. (2006). *Communication/social/emotional development: Response to NIH questions*. Washington, DC: National Institute of Child Health and Human Development. Retrieved on June 22, 2008, from http://www.nichd.nih.gov/publications/pubs/sos_autism/sub7.cfm

Skinner, E., & Wellborn, J. (1994). Coping during childhood and adolescence: A motivational perspective. In R. Lerner (Ed.), *Life-span development and behavior* (pp. 91–133). Hillsdale, NJ: Erlbaum.

Sleeter, C.E. (1995). White preservice teachers and multicultural education coursework. In J.M. Larking & C.E. Sleeter (Eds.). *Developing multicultural educational curricula* (17–29). Albany, NY: State University of New York Press.

Society for Neuroscience (2006). What is the cerebellum? *Brain Briefings*. Retrieved on September 16, 2008, from http://www.sfn.org/SiteObjects/published/0000BDF20016F63800FD712C30FA42DD/0000BDF200000625010ABE58E5899B1D/file/AutismMay06lyt2 .pdf

Soderman, A.K., & Farrell, P. (2008). *Creating literacy-rich preschools and kindergartens*. Boston, MA: Pearson/Allyn & Bacon.

Solit, G. (2002). Principles of early childhood learning from Reggio Emilia. *Odyssey: New Directions in Deaf Education, Spring/Summer*, 7 pages. Retrieved on March 18, 2008, from http://clerccenter.gallaudet.edu/odyssey/Spring-Summer2002/principles.pdf

Solley, B.A. (2007). *On standardized testing: An ACEI position paper*. Retrieved on June 6, 2008, from http://www.acei.org/testingpospap.pdf

Specker, B. (2004). Nutrition influences bone development from infancy through toddler years. *Journal of Nutrition, 34*(3), 691–695.

Spiegel, A. (2008). Old-fashioned play builds serious skills. *Morning Edition, National Public Radio*, Feb. 21.

Stahmer, A. & Mandell, D.S. (2007). State infant/toddler program policies for eligibility and services provision for young children with autism. *Administration and Policy in Mental Health, 34*(1), 29–37.

Stallings, J. (1975). Implementation and child effects of teaching practices in follow-through classrooms. *Monographs of the Society for Research in Child Development, 40*(78).

Stegelin, D.A. (2003). Application of the Reggio Emilia approach to early childhood science education. *Early Childhood Education Journal 30*, 163–169.

Stein, N., & Trabasso, T. (1989). Children's understanding of changing emotional states. In C. Saarni & P. Harris (Eds.), *Children's understanding of emotion* (pp. 50–80). Cambridge, England: Cambridge University Press.

Steinbeck, J. (1952). *East of Eden* (original edition). New York: Viking Press.

Steinhauer, J. (2005, May 22). Only 4 years old and expelled. Maybe preschool is the problem. *The New York Times, 154*, sec 4, p. 1, col. 1.

Stremmel, A. (2008). Supporting professional development through the processes of observation, documentation and interpretation. Seminar in the Innovations in Early Education Series at Wayne State University, Detroit, Michigan, February 2.

Sutherby, L. & Sauve, B. (2003). We all belong: Making early childhood programs more culturally sensitive. *Canadian Children, 28*(1), 4–8.

Swanson, E. (2007). *Patty Smith Hill*. Retrieved on June 9, 2008 from http://www.kdp.org/about/laureates/laureates/pattyhill.php

Tafarodi, R., & Swarm, W. (1995). Self-liking and self-competence as dimensions of global self-esteem: Initial validation of a measure. *Journal of Personality Assessment, 65*, 322–324.

Tanner, B. (2005). Keeping children safe is integral to their health. *Parents Together Primer*, Fall. Retrieved on Sept 22, 2008 from http://parentstogetherct.org/PTPrimerFall2005.pdf

Tarini, E. (1997). Reflections on a year in Reggio Emilia: Key concepts in rethinking and learning the Reggio way. In Joanne Hendrick (Ed.), *First steps toward teaching the Reggio way* (pp. 56–69). Upper Saddle River, NJ: Merrill/Prentice Hall.

Tarr, P. (2001). Aesthetic codes in early childhood classrooms. Retrieved on Sept 22, 2008 from http://www.designshare.com/Research/Tarr/Aesthetic_Codes_2.htm, retrieved July 10, 2007.

Tarr, P. (2001). Aesthetics codes in early childhood classrooms: What art educators can learn from Reggio Emilia. *Art Education 54*(3): 33–39. Retrieved on March 30, 2008, from http://www.designshare.com/Research/Tarr/Aesthetic_Codes_1.htm

Tarr, P. (2004). Consider the walls. *Young Children Beyond the Journal*. Retrieved on April 27, 2008, from http://www.journal.naeyc.org/btj/200405/walls.asp

Telluride Mountain School (2007). *First and second grade curriculum guide, 2006-2007*. Retrieved on Sept 22, 2008 from http:// www.telluridemtnschool.org/documents/1st2ndCurriculumguide.pdf

Termine, N.T., & Izard, C. E. (1988). Infants' responses to their mothers' expressions of joy and sadness. *Developmental Psychology, 24*, 223–229.

Thomas, R. (1992). *Comparing theories of child development* (3rd ed.). Belmont, CA: Wadsworth.

Toth, S.L., Cicchetti, D., MacFie, J., & Emde, R.N. (1997). Representations of self and others in the narratives of neglected, physically abused, and sexually abused preschoolers. *Development and Psychopathology, 9*(4), 781–796.

Tout, K., M. Zaslow, & D. Berry (2005). Quality and qualifications: Links between professional development and quality in early care and education settings. In *Critical issues in early childhood professional development*, M. Zaslow & I. Martinez-Beck (Eds.), (77–110). Baltimore: Brookes.

Troseth, G.L., Saylor, M.M., & Archer, A. H. (2006). Young children's use of video as a source of socially relevant information. *Child Development, 77*, 786–799.

Tsujimoto, S., Yamamoto T., Kawaguchi, H., Koizumi, H., & Sawaguchi, T. (2004). Prefrontal Cortical Activation Associated with Working Memory in Adults and Preschool Children: an Event-related Optical Topography Study. *Cerebral Cortex, 14*(July), 703–712. Retrieved on September 13, 2008, from http://cercor.oxfordjournals.org/cgi/content/abstract/14/7/703

Tur-Kaspa, H. (2004). Social-information processing skills of kindergarten children with developmental learning disabilities. *Disabilities Research and Practice, 19*(1), 3–11.

Tuttle, W.M. (2004). Part two: The American family on the home front. In M. Harper, et al., (eds.), *World War II and the American Home Front Theme Study*, Washington, DC: United States National Park Service, Retrieved on June 8, 2008 from http://www.nps.gov/nhl/themes/Homefront/Part2.pdf

U.S. Census Bureau (2007). Minority population tops 100 million. *U.S. Census Bureau News*, news release, May 17, 2007, updated August 9, 2007. Retrieved on August 11, 2007, http://www.census.gov/Press-Release/www/releases/archives/population/010048.html

U.S. Department of Education (n.d.). You and your preschool child. *Toolkit for Hispanic parents, My child's academic success*. Retrieved August 24, 2007, from http://www.ed.gov/parents/academic/involve/2006toolkit/preschool-en.html

U.S. Department of Health and Human Services (1999). *Mental health: A report of the surgeon general—executive summary*. Rockville, MD: National Institutes of Health, National Institute of Mental Health.

U.S. DHHS (2001). Executive Summary. *Mental Health: Culture, Race, and Ethnicity. A supplement to Mental Health: A Report of the Surgeon General*. Rockville, MD: U.S. Department of Health and Human Services, Substance Abuse and Mental Health Services Administration.

United Nations (1989). *Convention on the rights of the child*, Article 31. Retrieved February 2, 2007, from http://www.unhchr.ch/html/menu3/b/k2crc.htm

United States Department of Education (2004). Public Law 148-446, 108th Congress. Retrieved on April 27, 2008, from http:// idea.ed.gov/explore/view/p/%2Croot%2Cstatute%2C

United Way of Connecticut (2007). Retrieved August 24, 2007, from http://www.infoline.org/default.asp

University of Iowa (2007). *Effective people skills*. Human Resources Management, retrieved on October 2, 2007 from http://research.uiowa.edu/pimgr/?get=people

University of South Florida Health (2008). *Public health and education team up against childhood obesity*. Retrieved on April 26, 2008, from http://hscweb3.hsc.usf.edu/health/now/?p=329

University of Texas (2004). *Classroom environmental checklist 2005-2006*. Retrieved on Sept 22, 2008 from http://www.uth.tmc.edu/circle/pdfs/english_environ_checklist.pdf

Unten, A. (2003). Weaving the pieces together. In C. Copple (Ed.). *A world of difference* (185–186). Washington, DC: NAEYC.

Utah Education Network (2003). *Assessment in the early childhood classroom*. Retrieved on April 27, 2008, from http://www.uen.org/k-2educator/assessment.shtml

Utah Education Network (n.d.). *K-12 core curriculum, (visual arts standards)*, Retrieved on April 29, 2008 from http://www.uen.org/core/core.do?courseNum=1030

Vallance, R. (2000). Excellent teachers: Exploring self-constructs, role, and personal challenges. Paper presented at the Australian Association for Research in Education (AARE) Conference, Sydney, December 4–7.

Vernon-Feagans, L., Manlove, E.E., & Volling, B.L. (1996). Otitis media and the social behavior of day-care-attending children. *Child Development, 67*, 1528–1539.

Verschueren, K., Marcoen, A., & Buyck, P. (1998). Five-year-olds' behaviorally presented self-esteem: Relations to self-perceptions and stability across a 3-year period. *Journal of Genetic Psychology, 159*(9), 273–279.

Villegas-Reimers, E. (2003). *Teacher professional development: An international review of the literature*. Paris, France: Institute for Educational Planning. Retrieved on June 7, 2008, from http://unesdoc.unesco.org/images/0013/001330/133010e.pdf

Vukelich, C., Christie, J., & Enz, B. (2008) *Helping young children learn language and literacy: Birth through kindergarten*. 2nd ed. Boston. Allyn & Bacon (2008).

Vygotsky, L.S. (1978). *Mind in society: The development of higher psychological processes*. Cambridge, MA: Harvard University Press.

Vygotsky, L.S. (1933). *Play and its role in the mental development of the child*. Online version: Psychology and Marxism Archive. Retrieved on September 11, 2008 from http://www.marxists.org/archive/vygotsky/works/1933/play.htm

Warkenen, F., Chen, F., & Tomasello, M. (2006). Cooperative activities in young children and chimpanzees. *Child Development, 3*, 640–663.

Webster-Stratton, C. (2007). *Dina Dinosaur classroom curriculum*. Retrieved on April 9, 2008, from http://www.incredibleyears.com

Wheatley, C.F. (2002). Review of Branscombe, A., et al. (2003). Early childhood curriculum: A constructivist perspective. *Education Review: A Journal of Book Reviews*. Retrieved on April 29, 2008 from http://edrev.asu.edu/reviews/rev177.htm

Wheatley, C.F. (2003). Increasing computer use in early childhood teacher education: The case of the "computer muddler." *Contemporary Issues in Technology and Teacher Education 2*(4), online journal. Retrieved on April 29, 2008 from http://www.citejournal.org/vol2/iss4/general/article1.cfm

White House. *Biography of Lyndon B. Johnson*. Retrieved on June 7, 2008 from http://www.whitehouse.gov/history/presidents/lj36.html

WHO Multicentre Growth Reference Study Group (2006b). WHO motor development study: Windows of achievement for six gross motor development milestones. *Acta Paediatrica Supplement 450, 95*(4), 86–95.

WHO, World Health Organization (2006). *Challenges*. Retrieved on April 26, 2008 from http://www.who.int/nutrition/challenges/en/

Wien, C. (2006). Emergent curriculum. *Connections, 10*(1), 4 pages. Retrieved on Sept 22, 2008 from http://www.cccns.org/pdf/10.1.pdf

Wilcox-Herzog, A., & Ward, S. (2004). Measuring teachers' perceived interactions with children: A tool for assessing beliefs and intentions. *Early Childhood Research & Practice, 6*(2), online journal. Retrieved on April 29, 2008 from http://ecrp.uiuc.edu/v6n2/herzog.html

Wilson, B. (1999). Entry behavior and emotion regulation abilities of developmentally delayed boys. *Developmental Psychology, 35*, 214–222.

Winsler, A., Manfra, L., & Diaz, R. (2007). "Should I let them talk?": Private speech and task performance among preschool children with and without behavior problems. *Early Childhood Research Quarterly, 22*(2), 215–231.

Wittmer, D., & Petersen, S. (2006). *Infant and toddler development and responsive program planning: A relationship-based approach*. Upper Saddle River, NJ: Merrill/Prentice Hall.

Wong, P.T. (1992). Control is a double-edged sword. *Canadian Journal of Behavioral Science, 24*(2), 143–146.

Wood, C. (1999). Time to teach, time to learn: Changing the pace of school. *Responsive Classroom Newsletter 11*(3), 4 pages. Retrieved on Sept 22, 2008, from http://www.responsiveclassroom.org/PDF_files/11_3nl_1.pdf

Wood, C. (2007). *Yardsticks: Children in the classroom*, 3rd ed. Turner Falls, MA: Northeast Foundation for Children.

Wood, D., Bruner, J., & Ross, G. (1976). The role of tutoring in problem solving. *Journal of Child Psychology and Psychiatry, 17*, 89–100.

Work, B. (2002). *Learning through the eyes of a child: A guide to best teaching practices in early education*. ERIC #ED472193.

Wright, K., Stegelin, D.A., & Hartle, L. (2007). *Building family, school, and community partnerships* 3rd ed. Upper Saddle River, NJ: Merrill/Prentice Hall.

Young, D., & Behounek, L.M. (2006). Kindergarteners use PowerPoint to lead their own parent-teacher conferences. *Young Children, 61*(2), 24–26.

Zeren, A., & Makosky, V. (2000). *Teaching observational methods: Time sampling, event sampling, and trait rating technique*. In M. Ware & D. Johnson (Eds.) *Handbook of demonstrations and activities in the teaching of psychology, Vol. 1, 2nd Edition* (pp. 189–191). Mahwah, NJ: Lawerence Erlbaum.

Zero to Three (2000). What grown-ups understand about child development: A national benchmark survey. Retrieved August 6, 2007, from http://www.zerotothree.org/site/DocServer/surveyexecutivesummary.pdf?docID=821&AddInterest=1153

Zero to Three (2001). *Frequently asked questions about the brain*. Retrieved on April 26, 2008, from http://www.zerotothree.org/site/PageServer?pagename=key_brain

Zero to Three (2007). *Everyday ways to support your baby's and toddler's early learning*. Retrieved August 6, 2007, from http://www.zerotothree.org/site/DocServer/early_learning_handout.pdf?docID=3081

Zero to Three, & Hart, B. (1997). *Key findings from a nationwide survey among parents of zero-to-three-year-olds*. Retrieved August 6, 2007, from http://www.zerotothree.org

Zins, J., Bloodworth, M., Weissberg, R., & Walberg, H. (2004). The scientific base linking social emotional learning to school success. In J. Zins, R. Weissberg, M. Wang, & H.G. Walberg (Eds.), *Building academic success on social and emotional learning: What does the research say?* (pp. 1–22), New York: Teachers College Press, Columbia University.

AUTHOR INDEX

SUBJECT INDEX

PHOTO CREDITS